THE IMPACT OF THE ENGLISH CIVIL WAR ON THE ECONOMY OF LONDON, 1642–50

For Pam

The Impact of the English Civil War on the Economy of London, 1642–50

BEN COATES
The History of Parliament Trust, London, UK

ASHGATE

Published by
Ashgate Publishing Limited
Gower House
Croft Road
Aldershot
Hampshire GU11 3HR
England

Ashgate Publishing Company
Suite 420
101 Cherry Street
Burlington, VT 05401-4405
USA

Ashgate website: http://www.ashgate.com

British Library Cataloguing in Publication Data
Coates, Ben
   The impact of the Civil War on the economy of London, 1642-50
   1. London (England) – Economic conditions – 17th century
   2. London (England) – History – 17th century 3. Great Britain – History –
   Civil War, 1642-1649 – Economic aspects I. Title
   330.9'421'062

Library of Congress Cataloging-in-Publication Data
Coates, Ben
   The imapct of the English Civil War on the economy of London, 1642-50
   / Ben Coates
      p. cm.
   Originally presented as author's thesis (Ph.D.)–Leicester University.
   Includes bibliographical references (p.) and index.
   ISBN 0-7546-0104-8 (alk. paper)
    1. Great Britain–History–Civil War, 1642-1649. 2. Great Britain–History–
   Civil War, 1642-1649–Influence. 3. London (England)–History–17th
   century. 4. London (England)–Economic conditions. I. Title

   DA415.C58 2003
   330.9421'2062-dc22

                                                                              2003060080
ISBN 0 7546 0104 8

Printed and bound in Great Britain by MPG Books Ltd, Bodmin, Cornwall

Contents

List of Tables and Figures   *vii*
Preface   *ix*
Abbreviations and Conventions   *xi*

Introduction   1

1 London on the Eve of the English Civil War   4

2 Parliamentary Taxation and Levies   22

3 Parliamentarian Finance   53

4 Supplying Parliament's Armed Forces and Privateering   90

5 Economic Warfare   109

6 Domestic Trade and Consumer Spending   139

7 International Trade and Shipping   163

8 Manufacturing Industry   201

9 Economic Fluctuations 1642–50   219

Index   *233*

List of Tables and Figures

Tables

2.1	Receipts from parliamentary taxation	51
7.1	Customs' receipts in the port of London, 1641–50	167
7.2	The overseas trade of London, 1644	169
7.3	The overseas trade of London, 1648–49	176
7.4	The overseas trade of London, 1649–50	178

Figures

6.1	'Hallage' receipts, 1642–43	142
6.2	'Hallage' receipts, 1643–44	143
6.3	Receipts from the great beam and iron beam, 1635–47	150
6.4	The Vintners' Company, 1635–50	155
6.5	Pickage from the St. Bartholomew's Day fair, 1633–48	156
6.6	Receipts from the assize of brass weights, 1635–50	157
6.7	Blackwell Hall receipts, 1638–51	162
7.1	Broadcloth exports (pieces) from England to the Baltic, 1635–52	171
7.2	Receipts from the Vintners' tackle-house porters, 1635–50	173
7.3	English ships passing westward through the Sound, 1635–51	192
8.1	The Cordwainers' Company, 1635–50	203
8.2	Apprenticeship enrolments in the Brewers' and Bakers' Companies, 1635–50	204
8.3	Apprenticeship enrolments in the Clothworkers' and Pewterers' Companies, 1635–50	206
8.4	Quarterage receipts of the Weavers' Company, 1635–48	207
8.5	Daily averages of plate touched at Goldsmiths' Hall, troy ounces, 1636–50	208
8.6	Output of plumbers' solder, year to Michaelmas, 1635–50	210
8.7	Apprenticeship enrolments in the Blacksmiths' and Founders' Companies, 1635–50	212
9.1	Receipts from the enrolment of apprentices, 1633–50	223

Preface

This work began life as a PhD thesis at the Centre for Urban History, Leicester University under the supervision of Professor Peter Clark. I would like to thank him for his encouragement, patience and criticisms. I must also thank my examiners, Vanessa Harding and Paul Griffiths, for their unfailing encouragement and assistance beyond the call of duty. A great number of people who worked at the Centre for Urban History in the early 1990s provided me with help and support while I have been working there, especially Yoh Kawana and Phil Knowles. My thanks are also due to Ian Archer, Rosalind Collier, Richard Hoyle, Stephen Porter, Dinny Ravet and Ian Roy for reading all or part of this work and for their helpful suggestions. I would also like to thank Stephen Porter for generously sharing his own work on the economy of Civil War London with me, and Peter Edwards for providing me with a printout from his database.

I must also record my debt to the staff at the various record officers and libraries, especially the Guildhall Library, the Corporation of London Record Office, the Public Record Office and the British Library. I would also like to thank David Wickham, the former archivist of the Clothworkers' Company, David Beasley, librarian at the Goldsmiths' Company, and Ursula Carlyle, archivist at the Mercers' Company. Material from the Whitelocke Papers is included by permission of the Marquess of Bath, Longleat House, Warminster, Wiltshire. All the faults and omissions are entirely my own work.

Financially my thesis was supported by an Economic and Social Research Council research studentship from 1991 to 1994. Ian Archer, Professor Michael Hunter, and the History of Parliament Trust have subsequently kept me in gainful employment. Finally I would like to record my immense debt of gratitude to the unfailing generosity and support of my grandparents, Mrs Pam Cohen and the late Mr Leo Cohen.

Preface

Abbreviations and Conventions

Place of publication is London unless otherwise stated. Dates are given in the old style except that the year is taken to begin on 1 January. Monetary sums over £100 have been rounded to the nearest pound.

Barts.		St Bartholomew's Hospital, East Smithfield, Archives.
BL		British Library.
	Add. MS.	Additional manuscript.
	IOL	India Office Library.
	Harl. MS.	Harleian manuscript.
Bodl.		Bodleian Library.
CCAM		M.A.E. Green (ed.), *Calendar of the Proceedings of the Committee for Advance of Money, 1642–1654*, 3 vols (1888).
CCCD		M.A.E. Green (ed.), *Calendar of the Proceedings of the Committee for Compounding, 1643–1660*, 5 vols (1889–92).
CCMEIC		E.B. Sainsbury (ed.), *A Calendar of the Court Minutes etc. of the East India Company, 1635–71*, 11 vols (Oxford, 1909–38).
CH		Clothworkers' Hall Archives.
CJ		*Journal of the House of Commons.*
CLRO		Corporation of London Record Office.
	Jour.	Journals of the Court of Common Council.
	Rep.	Repertories of the Court of Aldermen.
CSPD		*Calendar of State Papers Domestic.*
CSPI		*Calendar of State Papers Ireland.*
CSPV		*Calendar of State Papers Venetian.*
EcHR		*Economic History Review.*
EHR		*English Historical Review.*
Firth & Rait		C.H. Firth and R.S. Rait (eds), *The Acts and Ordinances of the Interregnum, 1642–1660*, 3 vols, (1911).
GH		Goldsmiths' Hall Library.
GL		Guildhall Library.

HJ	*Historical Journal.*
HMC	*Historical Manuscripts Commission.*
JBS	*Journal of British Studies.*
Larkin	J.F Larkin (ed.) *Stuart Proclamations, Volume II, Royal Proclamations of Charles I, 1625–1646* (Oxford, 1983).
LJ	*Journal of the House of Lords.*
LMA	London Metropolitan Archives.
MJ/SBB	Middlesex session books.
MJ/SR	Middlesex session rolls.
MM	*The Mariner's Mirror.*
OED	J.A. Simpson and E.S.C. Weiner (eds), *The Oxford English Dictionary*, 2nd edn 20 vols (Oxford, 1989).
P&P	Past and Present.
Powell & Timings	J.R. Powell and E.K. Timings, *Documents Relating to the Civil War, 1642–1648* (Naval Record Society, 1963).
PRO	Public Record Office.
ADM	Admiralty.
AO	Audit Office.
C	Chancery.
E	Exchequer.
HCA	High Court of Admiralty.
PC	Privy Council.
PROB	Prerogative Court of Canterbury.
SP	State Papers.
Royalist Newsbooks	P. Thomas (ed.), *Oxford Royalist Newsbooks*, 4 vols (1971).
Rushworth *Collections*	J. Rushworth, *Historical Collections of Private Passages of State*, 2nd edn, 8 vols (1721–2).
TRHS	*Transactions of the Royal Historical Society.*
WAC	Westminster City Archive Centre.
WAM	Westminster Abbey Muniments.
Whitelocke, *Memorials*	B. Whitelocke, *Memorials of English Affairs*, 4 vols, (Oxford, 1853).

Introduction

It was the pioneering work of Ian Roy in the 1970s that made the study of the economic impact of the English Civil War the subject of serious historical research in its own right.[1] Previously the economic impact of the war had received little more attention than a few passing references in the standard textbooks of economic history.[2] The proliferation of county and regional studies has also deepened our knowledge of the impact of the war, including the economic disruption, but these works have tended to focus on the political implications of economic distress.[3]

Stephen Porter and Martyn Bennett, following on from the work of Ian Roy, have investigated the direct cost of the war. Porter has provided an extremely valuable study of property destruction in the Civil War, while the painstaking researches of Bennett in constables' account books have illuminated the enormous financial costs of the war.[4] However with the exception of a valuable survey published by Stephen Porter and two brief pages in Keith Lindley's recent study of popular politics in Civil War London the impact of the war on the capital has been neglected.[5]

The work of Porter and Bennett, like that of their predecessors, has focused on the direct cost of the fighting. In this regard the English historiography has followed on from the much more extensive work on the

---

[1] I. Roy, 'The English Civil War and English Society', in B. Bond and I. Roy (eds), *War and Society: A Yearbook of Military History* 1 (1975), 24–43; Idem, '"England turned Germany"? The aftermath of the Civil War in its European Context', *TRHS* 5th series, 28 (1978), 127–44.

[2] W. Cunningham, *the Growth of English Industry and Commerce in Modern Times, Part 1, The Mercantile System*, 6th edn (Cambridge, 1921) I, 191–2, 201–6; D.C. Coleman, *The Economy of England, 1450–1750* (Oxford, 1977), 106–110.

[3] A.M. Everitt, *The Local Community and the Great Rebellion* (1969), 24–6; J.S. Morrill, *Cheshire, 1630–60: County Government and Society during the 'English Revolution'* (Oxford, 1974), 91–2, 107, 134; Idem, *The Revolt of the Provinces: Conservatives and Radicals in the English Civil War, 1630–1650* (1976) 84–8; C. Holmes, *The Eastern Association in the English Civil War* (Cambridge, 1974), 137.

[4] S. Porter, *Destruction in the English Civil Wars* (Stroud, 1994); M. Bennett, *The Civil Wars in Britain & Ireland, 1638–1651* (Oxford, 1997), 169–202; Idem, *The Civil Wars Experienced: Britain and Ireland, 1638–1661* (2000), 24–43, 94–129.

[5] S. Porter, 'The Economic and Social Impact of the Civil War on London', in S. Porter (ed.), *London and the Civil War* (1996), 175–204; K. Lindley, *Popular Politics and Religion in Civil War London* (Aldershot, 1997), 333–5.

impact of the Thirty Years' War on Germany. The study of the impact of the Thirty Years' War on the small German principality of Lippe should warn against the assumption that money raised for war purposes was necessarily lost to the local economy. In Lemgo the contributions paid towards the Imperialist garrison were recycled back into the civilian economy through payments for supplies from local tradesmen.[6] The recently published research of Peter Edwards on the arms trade in the English Civil War has shown that a large proportion of the money taken out of the economy in taxation went back in again in contracts to supply the belligerents.[7] London was the main supplier of arms to Parliament and it was also Parliament's banker, advancing large sums of money at interest to finance the war. However the work of Jonathan Israel on the impact of the war with Spain on the Dutch economy in the seventeenth century has shown that war could have an immense impact on the economy far beyond the areas of fighting through the disruption of trade by embargoes, blockades and privateering. The royalists employed a similar strategy of economic warfare against London.[8]

The first chapter will analyse the London economy before the Civil War. The next three chapters will consider the direct impact of the war; chapter two is concerned with the impact of Parliament's exaction of resources for its war effort. Principally this took the form of money but the cost of service in the militia will also be considered. The following two chapters consider the extent to which the London economy profited from the war; in chapter three from financing the war effort, and in chapter four from contracting and parliamentary privateering. Chapter five analyses the use of economic disruption as a deliberate weapon of war by both sides, and in particular how the royalists sought to undermine the parliamentarian war effort by severing London's trade links with the rest of the country and abroad. The following three chapters deal with the impact of the war on the different sectors of the economy, overseas trade, domestic trade and manufacturing. The final chapter seeks to establish an overview of the London economy between 1642 and 1650, looking at fluctuations in the labour and property markets and other general indictors of general economic health.

Westminster has been omitted from this study. This is because the economy of Westminster was heavily influenced by the Royal Court and the central law courts located within it and increasing numbers of gentry and noble inhabitants. This differentiates its economy from that of other parts of London

---

[6]   G. Benecke, 'The Problem of Dearth and Destruction in Germany During the Thirty Years' War', *European Studies Review* 2 (1972), 240–53.
[7]   P. Edwards, *Dealing in Death: The Arms Trade and the British Civil Wars, 1638–52* (Stroud, 2000).
[8] J.I. Israel, *Dutch Primacy in World Trade, 1585–1740* (Oxford, 1989), 124–40; Idem, *The Dutch Republic. Its Rise, Greatness, and Fall 1477–1806* (Oxford, 1995), 312–15.

and raises quite separate issues about the impact of the war. Westminster however will be included in the discussion of the impact of taxation. The reason for this is that the excise accounts lump the whole of the metropolis together. This makes it necessary to include the 'West End' in the discussion of the other taxes if comparisons are to be made with the impact of the excise. In addition parliamentarian direct taxes are particularly well documented in Westminster.

Chapter 1

London on the Eve of the English Civil War

In the century or so before the outbreak of the English Civil War London underwent massive changes. This is mostly clearly evident in the rapid growth of the population. The population of the City of London and Southwark more than doubled between the mid-sixteenth century and the early 1630s, rising from less than 70,000 people to about 145,000. Moreover by the early seventeenth century London had expanded beyond the boundaries of the Corporation. Westminster, which in the Middle Ages had been a separate town, had grown to form a continuous urban area with the City, and new suburbs were growing up to the east in Tower Hamlets and to the north and north west in Holborn and Finsbury.[1] At the beginning of the seventeenth century the population of London was about 200,000, it doubled in the next half century: by which time at least half of all Londoners were living in the suburbs.[2]

The demographic growth was fuelled by the expansion of the London economy. In the 'West End' a substantial service economy grew up around a much-increased royal court and growing numbers of noble and gentry residents.[3] In the rest of the metropolis growth was fuelled by the expansion of trade, which stimulated the expansion of manufacturing. In the middle years of the sixteenth century London's overseas trade consisted predominantly of the export of undyed and unfinished cloth made in the provinces and the import of a wide range of manufactured goods. Neither exports nor imports required

---

[1] V. Harding, 'The Population of London, 1550–1700: a review of the published evidence', *London Journal* 15 (1990), 111–24. The figure for the population of the City and Southwark in the mid sixteenth century is taken from Dr Harding's estimate for the population of the 113 parishes derived from the Chantry certificates, while that for 1631 is taken from her estimates derived from 1631 population returns for the twenty five wards plus Jeremy Boulton's estimate of 25,718 for the population of Southwark at that date. (J.P. Boulton, *Neighbourhood and Society: a London suburb in the Seventeenth Century* (Cambridge, 1987), 19 table 2.3.)

[2] E.A. Wrigley, 'A Simple Model of London's Importance in Changing English Society and Economy, 1650–1750', in his *People, Cities and Wealth: The Transformation of Traditional Society* (Oxford, 1987), 133.

[3] J. Merritt, 'Religion and Society in Early Modern Westminster, c. 1525–1625', unpublished PhD thesis, University of London, 1992, 125, 268.

much processing in London. Moreover the geographical scope of London's foreign trade was small; it was largely confined to Antwerp, which meant that the shipping requirements were correspondingly limited. By 1642 the growth of the national economy led to increased foreign and domestic trade, mostly through London. There were also changes in the nature of London's trade that led to increased manufacturing in London. Foreign trade now spanned the globe, and therefore required more and bigger ships, which stimulated the shipping and ship building industries. Cloth was now generally exported dyed and fully finished, which led to the growth of the London dyeing industry. The increasing sophistication of English manufacturing meant more goods were made at home, this meant that by 1640 London imports consisted predominantly of raw materials, and London was the ideal place for the new sectors of manufacturing industry which used imported raw materials. The growth in manufacturing particularly led to a much greater level of employment in the London economy. Most of this new employment was poorly paid, which is why, as Ian Archer has observed, London society was 'filling out at the bottom', nevertheless this should not disguise the fact that this period saw a massive expansion in the economy of London.[4]

London's economy was extremely vulnerable to short-term fluctuations. Merchants were generally under-capitalized in the early stages of their careers. Even those of gentry origin had little start-up capital. Profits were low, and, because of primitive business accounting, merchants found it difficult to determine the rate of profit on their investments.[5] Credit was ubiquitous and tradesmen were reluctant to write off bad debts, and any chain of credit was only as strong as its weakest link. Fixed capital made up a small proportion of total investments, most of which consisted of circulating goods and money. This meant that disinvestment was easy in times of economic crisis. The result was that cash flow was very important in the early modern economy and every merchant's nightmare was a wave of bankruptcies, one triggering another. These factors must have made for a very unstable business community. Many livery company pensioners were formerly wealthy and senior members.[6]

Supple has argued that in this period economic activity was not rhythmical, instead economic crisis was the result of extraneous problems, including those arising from political upheavals such as war, currency manipulation and trade stoppages. The Cockayne project and the currency

---

[4]   I.W. Archer, *The Pursuit of Stability, Social Relations in Elizabethan London* (Cambridge, 1991), 13.

[5]   R. Grassby, 'The Rate of Profit in Seventeenth Century England', *EHR* 84 (1969), 731–8, 747–51; R.G. Lang, 'Social Origins and Social Aspirations of Jacobean London Merchants', *EcHR*, 2nd Series, 27 (1974), 40.

[6]   R. Grassby, *The Business Community of Seventeenth Century England* (Cambridge, 1995), 82–98; B. Supple, *Commercial Crisis and Change in England, 1600–42* (Cambridge, 1970), 8–10.

manipulations of the early years of the Thirty Years' War caused severe slumps in London's exports.[7] A further cause of economic instability was dearth in England, which depressed domestic markets.[8]

Foreign trade

The foundation of the economy of the City was its dominant position in England's internal and external trade. Unfortunately from 1604 syndicates of London financiers farmed the customs revenue for fixed annual rents. This had the advantage for the government of making the receipts from this vital source of revenue more dependable, but it had the disadvantage for the historian of making the customs accounts enrolled in the Exchequer virtually useless for measuring the level of trade. A great deal can be learnt from port books, which record foreign trade in vast detail, but they have survived only for certain years and must therefore be used cautiously for interpreting trends. An almost complete set of port books covering almost all aspects of imports and exports have survived for 1640 but this is unusual, there are none for exports by English merchants in the second half of the 1630s.[9]

Nevertheless, the major trends in London's overseas trade are evident. The seventeenth century saw a considerable expansion in England's overseas trade, which transformed the country into the greatest trading nation in Europe by the beginning of the eighteenth century. Not only did the range of imported and exported goods grow but also the geographical scope of English trade increased as merchants began to develop global commercial networks for the first time. These changes took place primarily in London and had a major impact on its economy. Many of them were already apparent by 1642, leading Fisher to argue that, 'The later years of the century saw little more than the intensification of trends already apparent before the Civil War'.[10]

In the sixteenth century the 'old draperies' dominated English exports, heavy woollen cloth which was generally sold in northern Europe. They were usually exported undressed to the Netherlands to be finished. In the early sixteenth century exports of the old draperies grew very rapidly until the boom reached its peak in 1550, when over 130,000 shortcloths were exported. This was followed by a major slump and what, at first glance, appears to be a longer

---

[7]   Supple, *Commercial Crisis*, 9.

[8]   Archer, *Pursuit of Stability*, 10.

[9]   F.J. Fisher, 'London's Export Trade in the Early Seventeenth Century', in his *London and the English Economy, 1500–1700*, P. Corfield and N. Harte (eds) (1990), 119, 121 table 1; A.M. Millard, 'Analysis of Port Books recording Merchandises Imported into the Port of London', PRO Library, Kew, table 1.

[10]   Fisher, 'London's Export Trade', 129.

period of stagnation in the second half of the sixteenth century. The triennial averages of shortcloth exports published by Fisher suggest that exports never rose above about 103,000 in the Elizabethan period, and were usually below 100,000.[11] However Fisher's figures are misleading, he fails to take into account the fact that after 1558 one cloth in ten was exported custom free, and was consequently unrecorded. Even taking into account the non-taxable cloths the numbers of shortcloths exported from 1559 onwards were still lower than the mid-century peak but the shortcloth was a notional measure devised for fiscal purposes and can be a misleading measure of trade. The custom of 6s 8d per shortcloth was designed to compensate the crown for the loss of the traditional duty on the export of raw wool because the wool was being exported as cloth. It was therefore designed to measure the amount of English wool in the cloth, rather than its value. Cloth was therefore taxed at the same rate whether it was dyed or dressed or not, although dyeing and dressing was estimated to add 50–100 per cent to the value of the cloth. This is important for the Elizabethan period because there was a significant expansion in exports to the Baltic in the second half of the sixteenth century. London exports to the Baltic consisted predominantly of expensive finished cloths, which nevertheless paid the same custom as the undressed cloths exported to the Netherlands. By 1598 exports to the Baltic accounted for about eleven per cent of shortcloths exported from London, in value the proportion was almost certainly significantly higher. Finally, the Elizabethan period saw the beginning of the export of new draperies, a range of worsted fabrics that were lighter and more colourful than the traditional woollens and were not recorded with the shortcloths in the customs records. Although, as yet, these exports were still small, at the end of the reign of Elizabeth exports from London other than shortcloths still totalled only about £130,000.[12]

Peace with Spain in 1604 led to a boom in London's overseas trade. Exports of old draperies increased from 114,000 shortcloths annually at the end of the 1590s to over 140,000 by 1614.[13] However the old draperies boom consisted mostly of exports of undressed shortcloths to the Dutch Republic. In the Baltic the English merchants were losing out to Dutch merchants exporting English cloth finished in Holland. In 1615 a cartel led by the governor of the Eastland Company, which controlled trade with the Baltic, persuaded the

---

[11] F.J. Fisher, 'Commercial Trends and Policy in Sixteenth Century England', *London and the English Economy*, 82–3.

[12] R. Davis, *English Overseas Trade 1500–1700* (1973), 17, 53 table II; R.W.K. Hinton, *The Eastland Trade and the Common Weal in the Seventeenth Century* (Cambridge, 1959), 2; H. Zin, *England and the Baltic in the Elizabethan Era* (Manchester, 1972), 162–3, 166 table 7.1, 174; C. Clay, *Economic Expansion and Social Change: England 1500–1700*, 2 vols (Cambridge, 1984), II, 117; L. Stone, 'Elizabethan Overseas Trade', *EcHR* 2nd series, 2 (1949), 45–6, 50; Fisher, 'London's Export Trade', 121 table 1.

[13] Davis, *English Overseas Trade*, 53 table II.

government to ban the export of unfinished cloth. The intention was to encourage dyeing and finishing in England. However the English dyeing industry was not large enough and the Dutch responded by forbidding the import of dyed English cloth. The project was soon abandoned but the interruption of English exports stimulated the textile industries of Germany and the Netherlands to expand to fill the gap. English exports lost further ground in the early years of the Thirty Years' War when currency devaluations in Germany and Poland drove up the price of English cloth, pricing them out of the market. Additionally the Dutch increased their taxes on English cloth to help pay for the renewed war with Spain in 1621. Barry Supple has argued that in the years leading up to the Civil War, the old drapery industry was clearly in decline, punctuated by severe depressions.[14]

In 1640 only about 87,000 taxable shortcloths were exported from London, although if the tax-free cloths are included the total was probably more like 96,000. This suggests that exports fell by about one-third between 1614 and 1640, but once again, shortcloths are a misleading measure of exports. The proportion of cloths exported undressed from London fell from nearly three-quarters in the early Jacobean period to about one-third by 1640. Consequently it is likely that the average value of the shortcloth was higher in 1640 than in 1614.[15] Moreover because the shortcloth duty was designed only to tax English wool cloth made partly from imported wool paid a lower rate. Exports of Spanish cloth, so called because it was made partly from Spanish wool, grew from nothing in the early 1620s to 13,517 cloths in 1640. Spanish cloth was a high quality fabric that cost nearly twice as much as traditional old draperies but was taxed at a lower rate. It is therefore perhaps more accurate to describe the course of old drapery exports after the Cockayne project as one not of decline but of adjustment. Native products in northern markets undercut the cheaper English cloths but more expensive fabrics, dyed and dressed in England, were finding a growing market. In part this was due to the expansion of cloth exports to the eastern Mediterranean, where English dyed broadcloths competed very successfully with the previously dominant Venetian textile industry, however Spanish cloths were almost entirely exported to the traditional export markets in northern Europe. In reality the value of exports of

---

[14] A. Friis, *Alderman Cockayne's Project and the Cloth Trade: The Commercial Policy of England in its Main Aspects 1603–25* (Copenhagen and London, 1927), 230–8; Fisher, 'London's Export Trade', 121, 123; J.D. Gould, 'The Trade Depression of the Early 1620s', *EcHR*, 2nd series, 7 (1954), 90; Clay, *Economic Expansion*, II, 119–121; Supple, *Commercial Crisis*, 124.

[15] Davis, *English Overseas Trade*, 53 table II; Supple, *Commercial Crisis*, 31, 257, 265; E. Kerridge, *Textile Manufactures in Early Modern England* (Manchester, 1985), 166.

old draperies probably did not fall nearly as much, if at all, as the decline in shortcloths would suggest.[16]

In the early seventeenth century new draperies were exported in ever increasing numbers to southern Europe and the western Mediterranean. Exports other than shortcloths from London, which consisted predominantly of new draperies, more than doubled between 1603 and 1619, by 1640 exports had risen to nearly £700,000. Fisher argued that by the eve of the Civil War, new drapery exports almost equalled the old. This is almost certainly an exaggeration. Valuing shortcloths at £8 each Stephens has suggested that at this time the old draperies amounted to 57.5 per cent of London's cloth exports, but this is probably an underestimate as Stephens fails to take into account the one cloth in ten which was exported custom free. If shortcloths were worth on average £8 each old draperies constituted sixty three per cent of cloth exports and fifty three per cent of all exports, including re-exports, consequently although the predominance of old draperies had been considerably eroded they still totalled more than all the other exports put together.[17]

The trend in the level of imports is superficially much clearer. The surviving port books have been analysed by A.M. Millard, who found that, valued according to the 1604 Book of Rates, imports rose from less than £1 million pounds a year in the 1590s to about £1.25 million after the conclusion of peace with Spain in 1604. They were still at this level in 1614 but by the early 1620s they exceeded £1.5 million. In the 1630s imports grew even faster, exceeding £2 million in 1633 and reaching over £3 million by 1638: there followed a decline of thirty nine per cent to £1.9 million in 1640.[18] At the beginning of the Elizabethan period manufactured goods made up half of all imports into London, by 1640 they formed one-quarter. Imports of raw materials and semi-manufactured goods rose at the same time from one-quarter of the total to slightly over half. Luxury goods became increasingly important. By the 1630s imports of wines, silks, sugar, raisins, currants, pepper and

---

[16] Supple, *Commercial Crisis*, 149–52; Clay, *Economic Expansion,* II, 147; Kerridge, *Textile Manufactures*, 33, 37–9; R. Davis, 'England and the Mediterranean, 1570–1670', in F.J. Fisher (ed.), *Essays in the Economic and Social History of Tudor and Stuart England in Honour of R.H. Tawney* (Cambridge, 1961), 120–3.

[17] Fisher, 'London's Export Trade', 121 table 1, 122, 126–7; W.B. Stephens, 'Further Observations on English Cloth Exports, 1600–1640', *EcHR* 2nd Series, 24 (1971), 254; Davis, *English Overseas Trade*, 17, 53 table II. Some new draperies were also exported custom free, but the totals seem to have been very small, see J. Thirsk and J.P. Cooper (eds), *Seventeenth-Century Economic Documents* (Oxford, 1972), 461.

[18] Millard, 'Analysis of Port', table 1.

tobacco accounted for forty three per cent of imports, twice the proportion of the 1560s.[19]

Millard's figures also suggest that the expansion in the geographical scope of London trade was much greater in imports than in exports. At the beginning of the century three-quarters of imports came from northern Europe, but by 1633 this had fallen to only thirty two per cent. Meanwhile imports from southern Europe and the Mediterranean grew from eighteen per cent in 1601–2 to thirty one per cent. Even more dramatic was the growth of the East Indies trade from virtually nothing in 1601–2, to one-third by 1633. In the early 1630s imports from America and the West Indies were still very small, only about three per cent of the total, but in the 1630s they rose substantially because of the growth of the tobacco trade. In 1638 nearly 3.8 million pounds of tobacco was imported compared with 423,226 lb. in 1633.[20] In the early seventeenth century exports outside Europe and the Mediterranean were minimal. Moreover Robert Brenner has argued that the growth of the Mediterranean trade was driven by demand for imports. Indeed Brenner argues that it was demand for imports that was the driving force behind the expansion of London's trade in the early seventeenth century.[21]

However once we look at the figures more closely the picture becomes more complicated. The patchy survival of the port books creates a danger that unrepresentative years, when the figures were affected by large imports of a particularly valuable commodity, can distort the overall picture. The high level of imports from the East Indies in 1633 seems to have been untypical. In 1630 imports by English merchants from the East Indies totalled £164,207, by 1633 they had risen to £762,639 but in the following year they had fallen to £205,061. As a result imports by English merchants other than wines fell from £1.8 million in 1633 to £1.3 million in 1633, and the proportion from the East Indies fell from forty one per cent to sixteen per cent. The principal reason for the rise in 1633 was a massive, but temporary, increase in imports of Persian raw silk, arising from the East India Company's Persian voyages. Imports of raw silk from the East Indies totalled only 11,638 pounds in 1630, but reached 484,354 pounds in 1633, in the same year an additional 125,743 pounds was imported from the Levant. Consequently raw silk, at Millard's valuation, was the most valuable import of that year, constituting almost one-quarter of the total. However in reality the price of raw silk was declining and as a result the company discontinued its Persian trade. Indeed the 1620s and 1630s were a

---

[19]   B. Dietz, 'Overseas Trade and Metropolitan Growth', in A.L. Beier and R. Finlay (eds), *London 1500–1700, The Making of the Metropolis* (1986), 126; Millard, 'Analysis of Port Books', table 5.

[20]   Ibid., table 28. For the imports of tobacco see tables 11 and 13.

[21]   R. Brenner, *Merchants and Revolution, Commercial Change, Political Conflict and London's Overseas Traders, 1550–1653* (Cambridge, 1993), 11.

period of increasing troubles for the East India Company. They had turned to trade with Persia because the Dutch squeezed them out of the trade with the Spice Islands in the 1620s; moreover trade with India was hit by a devastating famine, which hit the Gujarat in the 1630s. The company's imports of pepper that had reached nearly 3 million pounds in 1626 had fallen to only about 600,000 in 1640. The story of trade with the East Indies in the early seventeenth century was not one of linear growth.[22]

The import figures for 1638 are distorted by the great growth in the tobacco trade, which according to Millard's figures constituted twenty six per cent of all imports in that year. However the price of tobacco fell sharply in the early seventeenth century. The 1604 Book of Rates valued it at 6s 8d per pound, but by the late 1630s the price in London had fallen to less than 1s per pound. As a result of the collapse in tobacco prices cultivation was abandoned in the Caribbean plantations and restricted in Virginia. Consequently imports of tobacco fell by two-thirds between 1638 and 1640. This contributed significantly to total decline in imports recorded by Millard, imports including tobacco declined by thirty nine per cent between the two dates, while imports excluding tobacco declined by twenty eight per cent. Nevertheless at Millard's valuation tobacco still constituted twelve per cent of imports in 1640, however if we value tobacco at 1s per pound then tobacco only constitutes four per cent of imports in 1640 and seven per cent in 1638. This would reduce the figure for total imports to £2.5 million in 1638 and £1.8 million in 1640. On the eve of the Civil War the majority of London's import trade, like the export trade, was still with European and Mediterranean countries.[23]

Brenner is probably mistaken in emphasizing the importance of imports in the growth of London's trade; he never explains how the excess of imports he postulates was paid for abroad. It is possible a net outflow of precious metals bridged the adverse balance of payments, and indeed this was a recurrent fear of the Elizabethan and Jacobean authorities. But the evidence suggests that there was no shortage of precious metals in the early seventeenth century and that the money supply was expanding. The output of the mint grew in the early seventeenth century. Analysis of coin hoards from the Civil War suggests that there was about £10 million worth of coins then in circulation, compared with only £3.5 million at the beginning of the seventeenth century. Moreover the increased output of silver and gold goods by London also suggests that there was no shortage of precious metals in the early seventeenth

---

[22] Millard, 'Analysis of Port Books', table 3, table 4, table 33, table 34, table 35; K.N. Chaudhuri, *The English East India Company: The Study of an Early Joint-Stock Company 1600–1640* (1965), 67–4, 148, table 5, 205–4.

[23] Millard, 'Analysis of Port Books', table 1, table 3, table 4; R.R. Menard, 'The Tobacco Industry in the Chesapeake Colonies, 1617–1730: an Interpretation', *Research in Economic History* 5 (1980), 150.

century. Indeed the accumulation of specie indicates that England had a balance of payments surplus despite the increased imports.[24] The high value of sterling on the foreign exchanges in the 1630s also suggests that there was a trade surplus.[25]

The growth of London's trade with America and the East Indies was based not on imports but re-exports. The early success of the East India Company was dependent on the trade in pepper, but as demand for pepper in England seems to have been relatively static, the company depended on re-exports to the continent for its profits.[26] Kepler has shown that European markets for tobacco were a major factor in the early growth of the trade with Virginia. In the late 1620s the vast majority of the tobacco crop was shipped directly to European markets. Continental markets may have been even more important to the early Caribbean plantations. Tobacco from the Caribbean plantations was more heavily taxed than that from Virginia, giving the planters an extra incentive to send their produce directly to the continent. It was only during the late 1630s that, due to government regulation, the majority of tobacco was sent to London. It is likely that up until the late 1630s many London merchants who traded with the American and Caribbean colonies were operating a triangular trade: taking provisions from London to the plantations which they sold for tobacco, then taking the tobacco to the continent and selling it and purchasing imports for the English market.[27] By the late 1630s the declining price had substantially increased the market for tobacco in England, but about forty two per cent of Virginian tobacco imported into London was re-exported in 1640, indicating the continued importance of

---

[24] N.J. Mayhew, 'Population, money supply, and the velocity of circulation in England 1300–1700', *EcHR* 2nd Series, 48 (1995), 246–7; D. Mitchell, 'Innovation and the transfer of skill in the goldsmiths' trade in Restoration London', in D. Mitchell (ed.), *Goldsmiths, Silversmiths and Bankers: Innovation and the Transfer of Skill, 1550 to 1750* (1995), 11. Part of the increase in the output of the mint in the 1630s was due to the coining of Spanish silver but this would not have increased the money supply without a change in the balance of payments. C.E. Challis, *Currency and the Economy in Tudor and Early Stuart England* (1989), 15.

[25] J.J. McCusker and S. Hart, 'The Rate of Exchange on Amsterdam in London, 1590–1660', in J.J. McCusker, *Essays in the Economic History of the Atlantic World* (1997), 116 table 5.3; J. Battie, *The Merchants Remonstrance*, 2nd edn (1648), 12. The East India Company preferred to use the money from the sale of its pepper in Italy to purchase silk rather than use bills of exchange. *CCMEIC*, 1640–43, 293; *CCMEIC*, 1644–49, 39.

[26] Chaudhuri, *English East India Company*, 143–4.

[27] J.S. Kepler, 'Estimates of the Volume of Direct Shipments of Tobacco and Sugar from the Chief England Plantations to European Markets, 1620–1669', *Journal of European Economic History* 28 (1999), 122–4; R.C. Batie, 'Why Sugar? Cycles and the Changing of Staples on the English and French Antilles, 1624–54', *The Journal of Caribbean History* 8 (1976), 34. n. 34; PRO PROB11/178, ff. 425v–6. For government regulation of the tobacco trade, designed to increase customs revenue, see G.L. Beer, *The Origins of the British Colonial System 1578–1660* (Gloucester, Mass. 1959), 134–208.

continental markets. Additionally about eight per cent of tobacco exported from the Chesapeake was still being sent directly to the continent.[28]

The importance of imports to the growth of trade with the Mediterranean can also be questioned. Imports certainly were a major factor in the early development of trade with the eastern Mediterranean but by the 1630s the Levant Company merchants had become major exporters of English cloth, so much so that they were able to cease exporting bullion and occasionally complained that they lacked goods to import in return.[29] Harland Taylor has argued that merchants trading with Spain sold their new drapery exports at, or below cost price, and made profits on the goods they purchased in exchange. However a mid-seventeenth century tract he cites to support his argument states that before the Civil War England had a favourable balance of trade with Spain.[30] Moreover any assessment of trade with southern Europe must also take into account the export of fish. Fish was the most valuable commodity exported to the Canaries by the London merchant John Paige in the mid-seventeenth century; it was also an important export to Italy and Spain. Particularly important was the cod from the Newfoundland fisheries. Christopher Clay has argued that the shipment of Newfoundland fish played an important role in the growth of English trade with the western Mediterranean and the Iberian Peninsula. The West Country ports mostly exploited the fisheries but Londoners also played a major part. London merchants established a triangular trade, sending ships to Newfoundland for fish that they then shipped to southern Europe to be sold for imports for the English market, others purchased fish from West Country fishermen, which their ships took on board en route to southern Europe. In addition tin and lead was also loaded in the West Country, consequently London merchants were exporting considerably more goods to Southern Europe than was recorded in the London port books.[31] It is also possible that London participated in the illicit export of corn and hides that Evan Jones has discovered in sixteenth century Bristol. It is more likely that provincial ports had a trade surplus, boosted by the profits of

---

[28] Millard, 'Analysis of Port Books', table 1, table 3, Kepler, 'Estimates of the Volume of Direct Shipments', 119, 122–4; J.R. Pagan, 'Growth of the Tobacco Traade between London and Virginia, 1614–40', *Guildhall Studies in London History* 3 (1979), 235.

[29] Davis, 'England and the Mediterranean', 124; R. Davis, 'English Imports from the Middle East, 1580–1780', in M.A. Cook (ed.), *Studies in the Economic History of the Middle East* (1970), 194–5.

[30] H. Taylor, 'Trade, Neutrality and the "English Road", 1630–1648', *EcHR* 2nd Series, 25 (1972), 238; *A Brief Narration of the present Estate of the Bilbao Trade* (c. 1650), 3.

[31] G.F. Steckley (ed.), *The Letters of John Paige, London Merchant, 1648–58*, London Record Society (1984), xix; G. Pagano De Divitiis, *English Merchants in Seventeenth-Century Italy* (Cambridge, 1997), 156–66; G.T. Cell, *English Enterprise in Newfoundland 1577–1660* (Toronto, 1969), 5–6; Clay, *Economic Expansion*, II, 133; BL Add MS. 5489, Journal of the Voyage of the *Richard Bonadventure*, 1642, ff. 49–v.

the fisheries and the smuggling of grain and hides, while London, which was a better market for imports, may have had a trade deficit.[32]

During the 1630s London trade in the Mediterranean and the Iberian Peninsula was stimulated by the exclusion of their main rivals, the Dutch. Since the renewal of the war between Spain and the Dutch in 1621 the Spanish had adopted a deliberate policy of seeking to undermine Dutch trade. Spanish embargoes virtually excluded Dutch merchants from trading with Spain and Portugal. Spanish hostility also made it very risky, and consequently very expensive, for Dutch shipping to trade in the Mediterranean. This enabled the English to take over much of the trade within the Mediterranean and the coastal trade of Spain. They also took over the carriage of Spanish wool and colonial dyestuffs from Spain to Northern Europe. By the late 1630s eighty six per cent of the ships leaving Bilbao were English.[33] Nevertheless it is likely that the increased imports into London were being paid for by the still substantial cloth trade, supplemented by re-exports, triangular trade and earnings from shipping.

In a speech to the grand committee of the House of Commons for trade probably given in December 1640 the respected diplomat Sir Thomas Roe stated that 'It is a general opinion, that the trade of England was never greater'.[34] London merchants such as Lewis Roberts and Henry Robinson were becoming increasing self confident in demanding the restructuring of English commercial, legal and fiscal institutions to conform to their interests. In particular they saw an opportunity for London to become the dominant entrepôt of Europe. Nevertheless they were also aware that much of the recent success of English commerce was based on the exclusion of the Dutch. Roe argued that the future prosperity of English trade was dependent on the continuance of war in Europe. Were the war between Spain and the Netherlands to end the English would find it difficult to hold their position, and it is likely that a large part of the purpose of the reforms proposed by Roberts and Robinson was to strengthen English trade against that eventuality.[35]

---

[32] E.T. Jones, 'Illicit business: Accounting for Smuggling in Mid-Sixteenth-Century Bristol', *EcHR* 2nd Series, 54 (2001), 17–38.

[33] J.I. Israel, *Dutch Primacy in World Trade, 1585–1740* (Oxford, 1989), 136, 150, 154; Taylor, 'Trade, Neutrality and the "English Road"', 239, 253, 255, 258. In 1641 Henry Robinson argued that earnings from shipping compensated for England's deficit in visible trade. H. Robinson, *England's Safety in Trades Encrease* (1641), 50.

[34] T. Roe, *Sir Thomas Roe his Speech in Parliament* (1641), 1.

[35] L. Roberts, *The Merchants Mapp of Commerce* (1638), II, 257; Idem, *The Treasure of Traffike* (1641); Robinson, *England's Safety*, 2, 21–2; Roe, *Sir Thomas Roe*, 6–7; Clay, *Economic Expansion*, II, 185.

Internal trade

Internal trade was centred on London, not only because it was the main port but also because it was the centre of the transport network. There were major improvements in the internal communications in the Elizabethan and early Stuart period. Private coaches and the long four-wheeled goods wagons were introduced in the late sixteenth century. By the 1630s road carriers had built up a vast network for distributing goods to and from London. About two hundred towns had at least twice weekly services with the metropolis. River transport was improved with the introduction of the pound lock. Moreover the amount of shipping employed in the coasting trades increased three-fold between 1580 and 1700.[36]

From the fifteenth century there was a gradual increase in consumer spending in England. This continued through the sixteenth and early seventeenth centuries as the economy of England expanded and, as a result, internal trade grew.[37] Most of this growth was centred on London as the consumer goods were either imported through London or, increasingly from the late sixteenth century, made there. The landed elite purchased directly from London tradesmen while people lower down the social scale were supplied by shopkeepers, peddlers and chapmen who in turn purchased their goods from London wholesalers, either the latter's shops or at provincial fairs.[38]

The records of the coastal trade show that a high proportion of London imports were re-distributed to provincial markets. In 1628 over 1836 tons of grocery wares were shipped from London to provincial ports. Additionally more mundane items, such as ceramics, were imported into London before being shipped around the country. Londoners were also marketing new imports such as tobacco on a national scale. Falling prices in the 1630s meant that increasing numbers of English people could afford to buy tobacco, resulting in rapidly increasing domestic demand. Shammas has suggested that the mass consumption of tobacco in England began in the 1630s. By 1637 there were over two thousand licensed tobacco retailers, spread throughout England and

---

[36] P. Clark and P. Slack, *English Towns in Transition, 1500–1700* (Oxford, 1976), 66; D. Palliser, *The Age of Elizabeth, England under the later Tudors, 1547–1603*, 2nd edn (1992), 314–17; E. Kerridge, *Trade and Banking in Early Modern England* (Manchester, 1988), 9; J.A. Chartres, *Internal Trade in England, 1500–1700* (1977), 45.

[37] I.W. Archer, *The History of the Haberdashers' Company* (1991), 12–31; K. Wrightson, *Earthly Necessities: Economic Lives in Early Modern Britain* (New Haven, 2000), 160–81; C. Muldrew, *The Economy of Obligation: The Culture of Credit and Social Relations in Early Modern England* (Basingstoke, 1998), 15–36.

[38] M. Spufford, *The Great Reclothing of Rural England: Petty Chapmen and their Wares in the Seventeenth Century* (1984), 69–70, 72–4, 76, 79–80; Archer, *The History of the Haberdashers' Company*, 30–1; T.S. Willan, *The Inland Trade* (Manchester, 1976), 76, 122–6.

all but three of the counties of Wales, and there may well have been more who traded without a licence.[39]

Many sections of London's manufacturing industry, such as the pewterers, produced for nation-wide markets. They also benefited from rising demand; contemporaries noted the remarkable spread of pewter tableware in the sixteenth century.[40] Large quantities of soap were shipped from London to provincial ports, suggesting that London soap boilers produced for a national market. The coastal trade records also show that London shipped significant quantities of ironmongery, haberdasheries, paper and glass to provincial ports. Although many of these goods may have been imports, by the early seventeenth century they were increasingly likely to have been manufactured in London. For example in the early seventeenth century London tobacco pipes were in use in northeast England. The growth of the manufacturing sector ensured that the London economy was also reliant on internal trade for raw materials.[41]

As the national economy became more integrated in the early modern period, London became increasingly important as a centre of trade between regions.[42] Iron from the Weald was shipped from London to east coast ports.[43]London was the centre of the internal cloth trade; for example Bristol tradesmen purchased Norwich stuffs from London merchants. The domestic cloth trade may have been as important, if not more important, to the London economy as exports. One estimate from the early seventeenth century suggests that the home market accounted for sixty one per cent of total cloth production.[44] London was also the point of contact between the wool producing regions and the cloth producing regions.[45]

---

[39] T.S. Willan, *English Coasting Trade 1600–1750* (Manchester, 1938), 143; J. Allan, 'Some post-medieval documentary evidence for the trade in ceramics', in P. Davy and R. Hodges (eds), *Ceramics and Trade: The Production and Distribution of Later Medieval Pottery in North-West Europe* (Sheffield, 1983), 39; M.W. Beresford, 'The Beginning of Retail Tobacco Licences, 1632–41', in his *Time and Place: Collected Essays* (1984), 225–42; C. Shammas, *The Pre-industrial Consumer in England and America* (Oxford, 1990), 78–80.

[40] J. Hatcher and T.C. Barker, *A History of British Pewter* (1974), 262; G. Edelen (ed.), *The Description of England; The Classic Contemporary Account of Tudor Social Life by William Harrison* (New York, 1994), 201–3.

[41] Willan, *Inland Trade*, 30–1; Willan, *English Coasting Trade*, 97, 99, 143; D. Atkinson and A. Oswald, 'London Clay Tobacco Pipes', *The Journal of the British Archaeological Association* 3rd Series, 32 (1969), 203.

[42] Kerridge, *Trade and Banking*, 5–32.

[43] Willan, *Inland Trade*, 158.

[44] Kerridge, *Textile Manufactures*, 215–16; Chartres, *Internal Trade in England*, 10; G.D. Ramsay, *The English Woollen Industry, 1500–1700* (1982), 22–4; Willan, *Inland Trade*, 131.

[45] P.J. Bowden, *The Wool Trade in Tudor and Stuart England* (1962), 73–4, 92; Kerridge, *Textile Manufactures*, 149–50.

The health of England's internal trade was vital to the economy of London. The relative of importance domestic trade, as against overseas trade, to the London economy is difficult to judge but it is significant that in the Jacobean period perhaps half of London's aldermen were primarily concerned with domestic trade.[46] Internal trade was also crucial to overseas trade and manufacturing. Cloth exports needed to be brought from their place of manufacture to London, while imports and London manufacturers needed to be distributed to provincial shopkeepers. Any interference with London's domestic commercial networks would have significant implications for international trade. Large amounts of copper, lead, tin and iron were shipped to London from provincial ports. In 1600 ninety one per cent of coastal shipments of lead from Hull, the main port for the Derbyshire and Yorkshire lead miners, went to London. About forty to fifty per cent of England's lead production was exported and a large proportion of the remainder was used in London manufacturing.[47] Internal trade was also vital for more basic reasons; London's fast growing population needed ever growing quantities of food, fuel and other essentials. Grain was brought from Kent, East Anglia and the Thames Valley, but much of London's meat came from Wales or northern England. The geographical radius of London's food supplies was expanding; in the Elizabethan period most coastal shipments of butter to London had come from Suffolk, but by 1638 the largest source was the north east.[48] By 1638, coastal shipments of cereals totalled 95,714 quarters annually. Chartres has estimated that by the mid seventeenth century London consumed 61,000 cows every year.[49] Seventeenth-century London was also dependent on Newcastle coal for domestic and commercial heating. Shipments of coal to London grew from nearly fifty thousand tons a year in the 1580s to nearly three hundred thousand tons a year on the eve of the Civil War.[50]

---

[46] R.G. Lang, 'London's Aldermen in Business: 1600–1625', *Guildhall Miscellany* 3 (1969–71), 244.

[47] Willan, *Inland Trade*, 29; D. Kiernan, 'Lawrence Oxley's Accounts, 1672–81, in J.V. Beckett et al (eds), *A Seventeenth-Century Scarsdale Miscellany*, Derbyshire Record Society 20 (1993), 129; R. Burt, 'The Transformation of the non-ferrous metals industries in the Seventeenth and Eighteenth Centuries', *EcHR* 2nd Series, 48 (1995), 35.

[48] F.J. Fisher, 'The London Food Market, 1540–1640', in *London and the English Economy*, 62, 63, 66.

[49] Ibid., 62; J.A. Chartres, 'Food Consumption and Internal Trade', in Beier and Finlay, *London 1500–1700*, 183.

[50] J. Hatcher, *The History of the British Coal Industry, Vol. 1, Before 1700: Towards the Age of Coal* (Oxford, 1993), 40–1.

Manufacturing

Manufacturing played a crucial part in the economy of London, probably employing a majority of the working population even in the inner-city parishes.[51] Most of those employed in this occupational sector were involved in providing clothing, housing, food, and drink for the local population. Clothing was the largest single occupational sector in London. Tailors alone made up perhaps one-fifth of the work force. Nevertheless a significant and growing sector of London manufacturing was geared to the national market.[52] The London pewter industry expanded seven-fold from the early sixteenth to the mid-seventeenth century. As exports of pewter were stagnant throughout this period, the source of growth must have been the domestic market.[53]

London played a major part in the growth of English manufacturing in the Tudor and early Stuart period. This was stimulated by the government's policy of encouraging import substitution in the latter sixteenth century. New industries such as glass and paper manufacturing were a source of prosperity. Other industries were revived. In the first half of the sixteenth century the English pin making industry had been almost completely wiped out by Dutch competition but it revived in the Elizabethan period, until by 1608 it was said that the industry employed 2–3,000 in London and the suburbs. Tudor government had been particularly concerned to encourage domestic production of strategic items such as armaments. Although the Weald was the centre of the production of artillery, the eastern suburbs of London became centres for the production of small arms.[54]

The growing tendency of members of the landed elite to spend at least part of the year in Westminster encouraged the production of luxury goods in London. London particularly developed specializations in high-skilled crafts, such as the manufacturing of clocks, watches and spectacles.[55] One of the best examples of the importance of the demand for luxury goods is the growth of the silk industry. Although silk fabrics were produced in London in the Middle Ages, the industry seems to have only become firmly established in London in the Elizabethan period. In the 1620s the silk throwers alone were estimated to

---

[51]   A.L. Beier, 'Engine of Manufacture: the trades of London', in Beier and Finlay, *London 1500–1700*, 147, 150; Hatcher and Barker, *History of British Pewter*, 115, 262.

[52]   J.L. Archer, 'The Industrial History of London, 1603–40', unpublished MA thesis, University of London, 1934, 9, 12, 16, 19, 51.

[53]   Hatcher and Barker, *History of British Pewter*, 115–18, 138, 262.

[54]   J. Thirsk, *Economic Policy and Projects, The Development of a Consumer Society in Early Modern England* (Oxford, 1978), 16–17, 80; Dietz, 'Overseas Trade', 129; E.S. Godfrey, *The Development of English Glassmaking* (Oxford, 1975), 251–2; Clay, *Economic Expansion*, II, 214; Archer, 'Industrial History of London', 14.

[55]   F.J. Fisher, 'The Development of London as a Centre for Conspicuous Consumption in the Sixteenth and Seventeenth Centuries', *London and the English Economy*, 114; L. Stone, *The Crisis of the Aristocracy, 1558–1641* (Oxford, 1965), 388.

be employing eight thousand people, and in 1629 they were incorporated by Royal Charter. The rise of the industry is reflected in the growing imports of raw silk, from 9920 lb. in 1560 to 218,403 lb. in 1638. By the 1630s the growth of the domestic industry was causing a reduction in imports of silk fabrics.[56]

The growth of London's industrial sector was stimulated by the changing nature of her trade. In the sixteenth century the export of old draperies trade had had relatively little direct impact on industry in London as almost all cloth was manufactured in the provinces and finished in the Netherlands. By the eve of the Civil War cloth was more likely to be dyed at home, often in London. Moreover new industries emerged processing colonial imports, such as sugar refining and tobacco cutting.[57]

Surveys of English shipping in the 1580s and 1620s show that the nation's shipping increased from 67,000 tons to 115,000 tons. Ships over two hundred tons increased from eighteen to more than 145. London's shipping increased faster than the national average, by 163 per cent, her share of the nation's shipping increased from seventeen per cent to twenty seven per cent.[58] The rapid growth of shipping led to the development of hamlets to the east of the City where the industry was concentrated. Shadwell contained four docks and thirty two wharves, eight of which had timber yards attached, spread over 400 yards of river front. These hamlets became centres for ancillary industries such as rope making. According to the parish registers of Stepney in 1606, occupations in river and sea trades constituted roughly two-thirds of the population of Limehouse, seventy per cent of the population of Ratcliff and ninety per cent of the population of Shadwell.[59]

Industry in early modern London generally required little capital and was dominated by craftsmen with little or no surplus wealth. As a result, in the extra mural parishes of the City, Southwark, and the eastern and northern suburbs, wealth was not nearly as widely diffused as it was in the City. In Southwark about thirty one per cent of the householders were assessed for the poor rate, but a survey conducted in 1618 listed twenty six per cent of the

[56] W.M. Stern, 'The Trade, Art, Mystery of Silk Throwers of the City of London in the Seventeenth Century', *Guildhall Miscellany* 5 (1955), 25–8; Millard, 'Import Trade of London', 234–5, appendix table 3; Idem, 'Analysis of Port Books', table 13.

[57] Clay, *Economic Expansion*, II, 147; Dietz, 'Overseas Trade', 132.

[58] K.R. Andrews, *Ships, Money and Politics: Seafaring and Naval Enterprise in the Reign of Charles I* (Cambridge, 1991), 16–17; R. Davis, *The Rise of the English Shipping Industry in the Seventeenth and Eighteenth Centuries* (1962), 6, 10.

[59] Dietz, 'Overseas Trade', 129; M.J. Power, 'The Urban Development of East London, 1550–1700', unpublished PhD thesis, University of London, 1971, 181–2; Population Study Group of the East London History Group, 'The Population of Stepney in the Early Seventeenth Century', *East London Papers* 11 (1968), 84; Andrews, *Ships, Money and Politics*, 16–17; Davis, *Rise of the English Shipping Industry*, 224; M.J. Power, 'Shadwell: The Development of a London Suburban Community in the Seventeenth Century', *London Journal* 4 (1978), 38.

householders as poor.[60] Although Southwark, Tower Hamlets and the northern suburbs had distinct social and administrative structures, economically they were closely interrelated. The health of industrial and trading sectors was mutually interdependent. To a large extent the City, Southwark and the northern and eastern suburbs formed one economic structure and any general economic crisis in the City would also cause an economic crisis in those parts of the suburbs.

The growing crisis, 1640–42

In the summer of 1640 the Government seized first the merchants' bullion in the Mint, then pepper belonging to the East India Company. The seizures were both quickly converted into loans but the collapse in confidence sent panic through the English economy. In the spring of 1641 the clothiers complained that London merchants would neither buy their cloth nor pay their debts. In August 1641 the East India Company found that sales of their goods were very poor and the company decided that it would have to export its pepper to Italy.[61] In autumn 1641 the Irish rebellion sent another wave of alarm through London's merchant community. It was reported in February 1642 that London merchants had £120,000 of debts in Ireland. In the same month Essex and Suffolk clothiers complained that cloth exports had ceased because of the political crisis.[62] Nehemiah Wallington described May 1642 as, 'a dead time (of traiding)'.[63] On 4 June 1642 Giles Grene, the chairman of Parliament's customs committee, reported to the Commons that receipts from customs had fallen by more than one-quarter in the previous year.[64] In February 1642 George Warner, a Merchant Adventurer who also imported luxury fabrics from Italy, told his factors in Leghorn, that silk imports 'will come but to a dead market as hath beene this greate while'.[65] In the following month he complained that 'as the times now rules ... our returns must needs produce a certain losse besid the hazard of bad debts which hath in my time never beene the ½ of what its now', and that 'the times be very desperate'.[66] In May he wrote of the, 'still greate discontent betwixt the King and Parliament which

---

[60] Boulton, *Neighbourhood and Society*, 108, 115.
[61] Supple, *Commercial Crisis*, 125–9; *CCMEIC*, 1640–43, 185–6.
[62] *HMC Egmont MSS*, I, part 1, 164; Supple, *Commercial Crisis*, 130.
[63] BL Add. MS. 40883, Nehemiah Wallington's 'The Growth of a Christian', f. 29.
[64] V.F. Snow and A.S. Young (eds), *Private Journals of the Long Parliament, June to September 1642* (New Haven, 1992), 25.
[65] PRO SP46/85/1, f. 82.
[66] Ibid., ff. 83, 83v.

makes trade here very dead and the times such as we know not whome to give Creditt to'.[67]

However the economic crisis that preceded the war should not be exaggerated. Customs receipts from 1641–2 suggest that exports remained stable in the early 1640s. Receipt from the export of old draperies in the port of London by English merchants from 25 June 1641 to 24 June 1642 totalled nearly £28,691, indicating that about 86,000 taxable shortcloths were exported in that period, nearly the same as in 1640. Customs receipts from exports other than shortcloths by English merchants from the port of London totalled £26,993, suggesting that nearly £540,000 worth of goods, other than the old draperies and re-exports, were exported, which again is very close to the figure for 1640.[68] Receipts from the Hallage toll at the Blackwell Hall cloth market suggest that the cloth trade was basically stable in the late 1630s and early 1640s. Equally, although apprenticeship enrolments in the City of London fell in the year to Michaelmas 1639 and remained low in 1640, they rose in 1641.[69] However the worsening political crisis in the first half of 1642 deepened the problems of the London economy. The year to Michaelmas 1642 saw a substantial reduction in apprenticeship enrolments, while receipts of pickage from the St Bartholomew's Day Fair fell by about one-fifth.[70]

---

[67] Ibid., f. 89v.

[68] PRO E122/230/6, f. 7; PRO E122/230/9; Fisher, 'London's Export Trade', 120, 122 table 4. For 1640 export figures see ibid., 122 table 1.

[69] D.W. Jones, 'The "Hallage" Receipts of the London Cloth Markets, 1562–1720', *EcHR* 2nd Series, 25 (1972), 569; CLRO Cash Books, vols 1/2, 1/3 and 1/4. See Figure 5.7 and Figure 8.1 below.

[70] CLRO Cash Books, vols 1/2, 1/3, and 1/4. See Figure 5.5, and Figure 8.1 below. Pickage was a toll paid for setting up a stall at a fair, *OED*.

Chapter 2

Parliamentary Taxation and Levies

The seventeenth century is a pivotal period in the history of English taxation. England went from being, in European terms, a comparatively low taxed country to being a comparatively high taxed one and the Civil War played a crucial part in this transition. Crown and Parliament raised taxes to unprecedented heights to pay for their armies. Each introduced an excise, England's first general internal indirect tax, which subsequently became a permanent feature of state revenue. London was at the forefront of this transformation. Parliament imposed a bewildering variety of taxes on London's inhabitants during the Civil War. Morrill has argued that taxation from London was crucial to Parliament's finances; between one-quarter and one-third of the assessment, the major direct tax, came from the City. He also observed that Parliament's excise was only effective in London. Taxation was not the only way in which Parliament utilized the resources of the capital to fight the war. It also extracted manpower through the militia and raised further revenue through sequestration. What was the impact of this on the London economy? It might be expected that this heavy burden would depress the economy, but Ian Gentles has drawn attention to the high assessment arrears in London, taxes that are not paid can hardly be a burden. Moreover in his account of the rise of the English 'fiscal state' in the seventeenth century Braddick downplayed the economic importance of the increasing tax burden, arguing that complaints focused on the relative burden, especially perceived inequalities, not the absolute weight of taxation.[1]

The high level of wartime taxation became a focus for agitation in Civil War London, but taxation is rarely popular, and simple expressions of reluctance to pay are not necessarily evidence of real economic hardship. More importantly in this context the relative burden of taxation will increase when the economy is failing. The difficulties experienced by Londoners in the 1640s in paying their taxes may therefore be a consequence, rather than a cause, of problems in the economy. Taxation can become a scapegoat for wider economic problems and tax reductions can appear an easy way to boost the

---

[1] J.S. Morrill, 'Introduction', in J.S. Morrill (ed.), *Reactions to the English Civil War, 1642–1649* (1982), 19; I. Gentles, *The New Model Army in England, Ireland and Scotland, 1645–1653* (Oxford, 1992), 30; M.J. Braddick, *The Nerves of State: Taxation and the Financing of the English State, 1558–1714* (Manchester, 1995), 111–19.

economy. Agitation against taxation may be a symptom of economic problems whose causes lie elsewhere.

Direct taxes and forced loans

The first direct tax imposed by Parliament, the twentieth part, was initiated in November 1642. Anyone worth more than £100 who had not previously contributed to the cause, or had not contributed a twentieth of his or her estate, was liable to assessment. Those in the latter category had their previous contributions deducted from their assessment. This was not technically a tax but a forced loan as those who agreed to pay received the 'public faith' for repayment of their assessment, plus interest, but without security.[2] Subsequently Parliament introduced a weekly assessment in February 1643, which was followed by a jumble of further forced loans and levies. From 1644 Parliament increasingly settled on the monthly assessment as its primary form of direct taxation, a monthly levy based on a valuation of a householder's personal estate and the rental value of his or her house. Additionally Londoners also had to pay forced loans, weekly assessments and monthly assessments to pay for the British forces in Ireland and for the army of Parliament's Scottish allies, and there were additional levies for local defence.

In the City parliamentary direct taxation raised at least £490,728 in the 1640s. As this excludes receipts from the twentieth part after the middle of 1643, and other minor levies, the total was probably over half a million pounds. Estimating the amount received in the suburbs is more difficult, but it was almost certainly substantially less than receipts in the City. In Westminster receipts were at least £24,647 and probably more, as this excludes what was received from the twentieth part, and in Southwark about £13,078 was collected from the major assessments until 1648. In total, receipts from direct taxation in London from 1643–50 totalled at least £600,000 but probably not more than about three-quarters of a million pounds, which works out at little more than £100,000 per year.[3] Parliamentary taxation was undoubtedly much higher than pre-war levies. In the Act passed in early 1642 to raise £400,000 for the suppression of the Irish rebellion, the City's assessment had been £42,477, of which £27,337 was collected.[4]

---

[2] *Firth & Rait*, I, 38–41.

[3] For the receipts from Parliamentary taxation see B. Coates, 'The Impact of the English Civil War on the Economy of London, 1642–1650', unpublished PhD thesis, University of Leicester 1997, 51–62. For the total receipts from the various forms of parliamentary taxation see Table 2.1 below.

[4] *Statutes of the Realm* V (1819), 145, 147; PRO SP28/162, Account of the Treasurers of the Act for £400,000, ff. 1, 12.

Londoners were undoubtedly paying much more taxes in the 1640s, but raw totals tell us little about the economic impact. What proportion of the economy did taxation constitute? This is a very difficult question to answer because of the difficulty of establishing the size of the London economy. If Londoners were paying £100,000 per annum in direct taxes, and the total population of London was four hundred thousand then this suggests that per capita direct taxation came to 5s a year, less than four days' work for a building labourer.[5]

It would be natural to expect taxation receipts to be much higher in London than any other county; by the middle of the seventeenth century the capital constituted about seven per cent of the population of England. Londoners were generally richer than the rest of the population, wages were at least fifty per cent higher than in the rest of southern England and levels of consumer spending were significantly greater.[6] If the above totals for the receipts of direct taxes in London are correct, then they suggest that the burden of direct taxation may not have been as great as in other parts of the country controlled by Parliament. Alan Everitt estimated that in Kent £570,000 was raised from the assessment between 1644 and 1651, which as Kent was considerably less populous, suggests that per capita the burden of taxation in London may have been significantly lower. In the parts of the country where the fighting took place the receipts from parliamentary direct taxation were lower. Ann Hughes found that, in Warwickshire, receipts from the assessment between February 1643 and August 1646 were at most not much more than £150,000. This was probably counterbalanced by other burdens, especially the requisitioning of goods by soldiers known as free quarter. In Warwickshire the cost of free quarter was generally at least half as much again as taxation, and often much more. Additionally many parts of the county had to pay royalist taxes, which, like free quarter, were not inflicted on London.[7]

Londoners do not seem to have suffered particularly severely from parliamentary taxation; they may have got off rather lightly. However taxation may disrupt the economy without being a major fiscal burden. By 1646 the committee for the advance of money, the body that had taken over enforcing the twentieth part in London, had become deeply unpopular. It is unlikely that this was the result of the weight of the tax. It was largely confined to the wealthy; the assessments were not generally excessive and were frequently

---

[5]   J.P. Boulton, 'Wage Labour in Seventeenth-Century London', *EcHR* 2nd Series, 48 (1996), 279, table 1.

[6]   J.A. Chatres, 'Food Consumption and Internal Trade', in A.L. Beier and R. Finlay (eds), *London 1500–1700: the Making of the Metropolis* (1986), 170–6.

[7]   A.M. Everitt, *The Community of Kent and the Great Rebellion, 1640–1660* (Leicester, 1966), 159; A. Hughes, *Politics, Society and Civil War in Warwickshire, 1630–1660* (Cambridge, 1987), 188, 256.

substantially reduced on appeal. Consequently, assessment was more of an annoyance than an encumbrance.[8]

The principal objection against the twentieth part was that it disrupted links between London and other parts of the country rather than the weight of the tax. The City's remonstrance of May 1646 described it as 'One of the greatest Grievances of this City, and which, so long as it is continued, doth hinder the Concourse of People thereunto, and tendeth much to the Destruction of the Trade and Inhabitants thereof'.[9] Even people coming up to London for brief periods found themselves assessed. In 1644 £300 was demanded from Alexander Heatley, then staying in Covent Garden, despite the fact that he was a Scotsman in London on business, without any property in England, and had paid all his taxes and contribution in Scotland. He was only discharged after the intervention of the Scottish commissioners. A further grievance was that the committee assessed many who had voluntarily contributed to the cause under the mistaken impression that they were wealthier than they were, and that their contributions did not amount to the full twentieth part of their estate. The Remonstrance called for either the abolition of the committee, or restrictions on its powers. The latter request was granted in August 1646 when Parliament ordered the committee only to assess those who had not contributed to Parliament at all. Subsequently assessment was restricted exclusively to compounding royalists.[10]

The figures for the total receipts from Parliament's assessment ordinances give a misleading impression of their economic impact, far more was raised at some times than at others, consequently parliamentary taxation did have a significant impact at certain periods. The twentieth part was a one off payment; receipts were at first high but subsequently trailed off. Receipts from the assessment also varied widely. In the City precincts of Old Jewry and Lothbury in Coleman Street ward £700 had been collected from the weekly assessment by July 1643, but in 1645 the New Model Army assessment yielded only £338. In 1646 the total was slightly less, £331, while in 1647 the total fell to only £113. Thereafter the total increased, to about £559 in 1648, and in 1649 the total increased again to £819.[11]

In the early part of the war it was frequently reported that high taxes were driving people out of the City.[12] However when in January 1647 John Wall

[8]   Coates, 'Impact of the English Civil War', 48–50.
[9]   *LJ* VIII, 333.
[10]   *CCAM*, I, 35, 56; *A Vindication of the London Remonstrance Lately Presented to the High Court of Parliament* (1646), 9.
[11]   PRO SP28/170, Account of the Weekly Assessment in the Wards of London; PRO E101/67/11A, ff. 12, 39, 58, 74, 88, 106. The figure for 1649 includes only receipts from old assessments, not those introduced in that year.
[12]   *CSPV*, 1642–43, 216, 252; *CCAM*, I, 15; *CJ* III, 103; *LJ* VI, 198–9; CLRO Jour. 40, f. 73.

asked the parishioners of St Michael Cornhill for assurances that he would be exempted from taxation if he accepted the ministry of their parish the elders and churchwardens replied 'for the taxes they are so small here as not worth mentioning'.[13] It is noticeable that although the corporation complained vociferously that the City was over assessed when the weekly assessment was first established in 1643 these complaints were not repeated in subsequent years until the 1650s.[14] This indicates that the burden of direct taxation was high in 1643, subsequently fell, but reached a new peak at the end of the decade.

The changing burden of the assessment was partly a consequence of variations in the amount demanded by Parliament. When the weekly assessment was introduced in February 1643 the City was required to pay £10,000 a week. The Corporation claimed that this would mean that Londoners would have to pay four times as much as taxpayers in Surrey, but it only lasted for three months in the City, and a further two in the suburbs. Subsequent ordinances demanded much less money from London. When Parliament reorganized the monthly assessment to pay for the New Model Army in 1645 the combined assessment of London and Middlesex was only £8,060 per month .[15]

The impact of direct taxation also varied because the taxes were only rigorously collected at certain times, principally in 1643 and at the end of the decade. From 1644 the collection of the assessments became very slow and considerable arrears accumulated. An account of the City arrears for the New Model Army assessment prepared in August 1647 shows that about three-quarters of the first ten months of the tax had been paid. However nearly two-thirds of the assessment was still owed for the following six months and the final four months had not even been assessed.[16]

The high arrears derived primarily from the weakness of the economy, which made the collection of all taxation difficult. In June 1644 the Court of Aldermen found that, although the municipality was very short of money, this could not be remedied from the City's local tax, the fifteen, because many wealthy men had left the City, and those inhabitants who remained were increasingly impoverished.[17] The collection of tithes was also disrupted during

---

[13]   GL MS. 4072/1, St Michael Cornhill, Vestry Minutes, 1463–1697, ff. 179v, 181.

[14]   CLRO Jour. 41, ff. 46v. 89–v, 110.

[15]   *Firth & Rait*, I, 86, 615; C. Thompson (ed.), *Walter Yonge's Diary of Proceedings in the House of Commons, 1642–1645, Vol. 1, 19th September 1642–7th March 1643* (Wivenhoe, 1986), 320.

[16]   CLRO Jour. 40, f. 257v. According to the ordinances the six month assessment should have begun in December 1645 and the four month assessment from the beginning of the following June.

[17]   CLRO Rep. 57/1, f. 141.

the war, as were other local rates.[18] The economic problems afflicting London taxpayers made vigorous collection politically divisive.

In 1643 the political problems involved in raising taxation were over ridden by vigorous direction from Parliament. The committee for advance of money, a committee of both houses sitting at Haberdashers' Hall in the City, was the key instrument through which Parliament enforced its taxation ordinances in London in the early part of the war. The committee demanded regular accounts from the collectors and appointed special distaining collectors from different wards to collect arrears. Additionally Parliament ordered regular soldiers to help the collectors. The Commons also frequently ordered the imprisonment of individuals in the suburbs who abused the collectors and refused to pay.[19] In March the Venetian ambassador reported that parliamentary taxation was 'raised daily with the help of paid troops, who sack the houses and shops of everything without any reference to the amount due'.[20]

After 1643 the committee for advance of money mostly concerned itself with the twentieth part. A further factor probably contributing to the difficulties in executing the assessment ordinances may have been the lack of regular soldiers in London. Randal Manwaring's regiment was based in London during 1643, and soldiers from it were deployed to help collect taxes. It left London in January 1644, and was not replaced until 1645, when another regular regiment was raised, which was only used to man the fortifications, not enforce taxation. Elsewhere military force was very important in collecting taxes. In the Isle of Ely, troopers collected twenty one per cent of assessments for the Eastern Association. The Dorset county committee dealt with rising arrears by billeting soldiers on those who refused to pay. In November 1647 Fairfax sent Hewson's regiment to quarter in the City and help gather arrears but the Commons ordered that it be recalled.[21]

In December 1648 the army occupied the City, insisting that they would not leave until the arrears had been paid. This spurred the municipality into tackling the problem. Aldermen and common councillors from each ward bound themselves to the army treasurers for the payment of a new levy to pay the accumulated arrears. The Assessment Act passed in April 1649 appointed a new assessment committee for the City consisting of trusted political supporters rather than the senior aldermen who had previously dominated the

---

[18] M. Mahony, 'Presbyterianism in the City of London, 1645–1647', *HJ* 22 (1979), 96–8.

[19] *CCAM*, I, 2, 8, 12, 16–21; *Firth & Rait*, I, 77–9; PRO SP19/1, ff. 92 109, 113, 145; PRO SP19/79, ff. 87, 89; *CJ* III, 23, 26, 27, 31–2, 38, 43, 49.

[20] *CSPV*, 1642–43, 252.

[21] L.C. Nagel, 'The Militia of London 1641–1649', unpublished PhD thesis, University of London, 1982, 85–6, 231–2; C. Holmes, *The Eastern Association in the English Civil War* (1974), 139; C.H. Mayo (ed.), *The Minute Book of the Dorset Standing Committee, 23rd September 1646 to 8th May 1650* (Exeter, 1902), 352; Gentles, *New Model Army*, 226.

committee. The assessments were still made by the common councillors but in May 1649 the Common Council ordered that the names of those who refused to pay their assessments be returned to the agent for the army committee. He passed their names to officers of the army. In the 1650s soldiers seem to have been routinely used to assist collectors in levying arrears.[22]

Consequently except in 1643 and from 1649 onwards it is very unlikely that the economy was overburdened by the assessment. However this does not mean that all London taxpayers were paying what they could afford. There were repeated allegations that the assessment was unfair and that the less well off were overcharged. A petition presented to the Common Council in April 1645 stated that 'Assessments are made very unequal, whereby the Taxes laid upon the City, are made burthensome, and paid with much repining'.[23] There were also complaints about unequal assessment in some London newsbooks.[24] In April 1649, after the Common Council had been purged of moderates, the new common councillors for Walbrook ward argued that real estate had either not been assessed at all, or only at a very low level in previous assessments for the Army. They also alleged that the previous assessors had underrated both themselves, and the wealthy of the ward, while the less well off had been overrated. In the following July, the London assessment commissioners argued that the new assessments had not been made fairly.[25]

Jeremy Boulton has argued that the assessments imposed on Southwark in the Civil War reached a greater proportion of the population than previous taxes. He calculated that forty three per cent of Boroughside inhabitants were assessed towards the weekly assessment in 1643 compared with 30.7 per cent for the poor rate and only 15.5 per cent for the subsidy.[26]

The extent to which more Londoners were paying taxes in the 1640s can be examined in more detail if we take the example of Palace ward in St Margaret Westminster. A return from the 1641 poll tax indicates that there were 199 economically self-sufficient households in the ward. Of those, ninety two, or about forty six per cent, also paid the poor rate. In 1645 178 households

---

[22]   CLRO Rep. 59, f. 323; CLRO Jour. 40, ff. 310v–311, 319v; *Firth & Rait*, II, 38; PRO SP24/32, petition of Henry Bancks. For the London assessment committee see Coates, 'Impact of the English Civil War', 64.

[23]   J. Lilburne, *England's Birth-right Justified* (1645), 22.

[24]   *The Moderate Intelligencer*, 11, 8–15 May 1645, 85; *The Kingdomes Weekly Intelligencer*, 114, 19–26 August 1645, 916.

[25]   *A Declaration of the Well-Affected Common-Councel-Men of the City of London* (1649), 1–3; CLRO Jour. 41, ff. 3, 4v, 5.

[26]   J.P. Boulton, *Neighbourhood and Society: a London Suburb in the Seventeenth Century* (Cambridge, 1987), 108, 116. The assessments Boulton cites are for the Act for £400,000 rather than for Parliamentary assessments but assessments for the £400,000 were used as the basis for the Parliamentary assessments.

were assessed in the same ward.[27] At first glance this would appear to confirm Boulton's argument that more Londoners were paying taxes as a consequence of the Civil War, but such a conclusion is undermined when the assessments are examined in more detail.

The assessments for the suburbs were divided into two columns; the first was for the personal estate of the householder and the second part for the rental value of the house. The ordinances stated that assessments on rents were to be paid by the landlord if the property was let for its full market value. If the landlord failed to pay his share then it was to be paid by the tenant, who could deduct it from his or her rent. Most of those assessed in Westminster were rated only for their house; for example in an assessment made in 1648 in Palace ward, there were forty nine assessments for personal estate and 169 assessments for real estate. Someone assessed only for the house they lived in who paid the full market rent would either not have paid the assessment themselves or deducting what they paid from their rent. Consequently more people appear on the assessments than were paying the tax.[28]

For the assessment made in Westminster for three months from 29 September 1649 a different rate was set on the rents of 'outlandlords', the term used when the assessment was paid by an outside landlord, and 'inlandlords', who were householders who paid the rental part of the assessment themselves. Beside many of those rated for rents only, a small 'o' was written in the assessment book, which has been taken to signify that the assessment was placed on the 'outlandlord'. In Palace ward 177 were assessed in total, but of those, sixty, about one-third, were only assessed for their landlord's rents, therefore in practice only 117 were assessed, not many more than the total who were assessed on the poor rates in 1641. This suggests that the assessment did not penetrate as far down the social scale as the assessments initially suggest, and that it did not significantly widen the taxpaying section of the population.[29]

For much of the 1640s the impact of parliamentary direct taxation was mitigated by the fact that, as enforcement was left to the local elites, it was adapted to local conditions. It is, therefore, difficult to argue that direct taxation had a major impact on the London economy in the 1640s. Indeed economic difficulties may have been one of the causes of the problems with collection, as the municipality claimed. The economy affected the real levels of taxation rather than the other way round. This conclusion must be qualified in two

---

[27] PRO E179/253/10; WAC E155 St Margaret Westminster Overseers' Accounts, 1641; WAC E1580 St Margaret Westminster Weekly, Assessment for the Army in Ireland, 1645. Theoretically everyone except those in receipt of poor relief were liable to pay the 1641 poll tax, a one off levy which was not repeated. For the purposes of calculating the number of householders paying the assessment in the 1640s I have ignored the shops in Westminster Hall, who were included in the army rates but not in other taxes.

[28] WAC E1583 St Margaret Westminster, Monthly Assessment, 1648.

[29] WAC E1587 St Margaret Westminster, Monthly Assessment, 1649.

significant respects, direct taxation probably did have a major impact in 1643 and 1649, when the collection of taxation was backed up by intense pressure from the centre and military force, and although the proportion of the population taxed may not have increased significantly in the 1640s there is evidence to suggest that the less well off taxpayers may have shouldered a disproportionate share of the burden.[30]

The excise

In London indirect taxes, the customs and excise, accounted for the majority of Parliament's revenue. This was in sharp contrast to the rest of the country. The significance of indirect taxation to the London economy is reflected in a letter written by the London merchant Richard Best to his partner in Tenerife, John Turner, in July 1646. Best reported that hostilities were virtually over, nevertheless he complained 'many taxes are kept still on foote god putt an end unto them: besids the excyes which is no small mater allso the Plymoth deuty thowgh: the seeges be Removed yett still Contineu which is 8s uppon every pipe of wynne'.[31] It is noticeable that he does not mention the assessment.

The excise was the most important new form of taxation of the Civil War. It was the first general internal indirect tax; it survived the Interregnum becoming part of the crown's revenue in the Restoration settlement. The first excise ordinance was passed in July 1643 but it was never implemented, instead a new ordinance was passed in September with lower rates. The majority of the commodities taxed were imports; the exceptions were soap, beer, spirits and woollen cloth. The excise amounted to a five per cent tax on imported groceries, drugs, silks and other fine fabrics, linen textiles, haberdasheries, paper, glass and earthenware, leather and upholstered goods. Five per cent was the standard rate for the customs; the excise therefore amounted to a hundred per cent increase in the taxation of a range of consumer goods.[32]

Other imports were taxed according to volume. The rates on tobacco were originally set at 4d per pound for imports from English plantations and 2s per pound for tobacco from elsewhere. After agitation from the London tobacco traders a further ordinance was passed in December, in which Parliament acknowledged that the rates on tobacco from English plantations had 'something intermitted Trade in that Commoditie', but they only reduced the rates on tobacco already imported. What had already been brought into the country before the September ordinance was taxed at 1d per pound, and what

---

[30] CLRO Jour. 40, f. 255.
[31] PRO C110/151/2, Richard Best to John Turner, 17 July 1646.
[32] *Firth & Rait*, I, 202–14, 274–83.

had been imported between then and the December ordinance at 2d per pound. Nevertheless continued lobbying by the tobacco traders led to a further ordinance in March 1644 when the rate of 2d per pound for English tobacco was made permanent, while the rate on imports from foreign plantations was reduced to 1s per pound.[33]

The highest taxed commodity was wine, which was rated at £5 per tun, although this was a pound less than in the July ordinance. The Vintners' Company argued that the tax constituted one-quarter of the wholesale price of wine, while the existing customs accounted for a further quarter. A subsequent ordinance set the retail price on Spanish wines at 14d per quart, and French wines at 8d per quart. The excise therefore constituted 8.5 per cent of the retail price of Spanish wine and nearly fifteen per cent of the price of French wine.[34]

The excise on goods taxed according to their value was, like the customs, rated according to wholesale prices, but unlike the customs, the excise on imports was not levied from merchants when the goods first entered the country. Instead in theory the excise was to be paid by the first purchaser from either the importer or from a broker acting as intermediary between the merchant and retailer. Parliament seems to have intended the retailer to pay the excise. However the functions of domestic wholesaler and retailer were not clearly distinguished, as London shopkeepers also supplied goods to country retailers and chapmen. The London vintners paid the excise on the wine they supplied to their country colleagues, and it seems safe to suppose that most other London shopkeepers in similar circumstances did likewise.[35]

The excise was more than an additional import duty, a rate of 6d in the pound was put on all woollen cloth produced for the domestic market, and up to 10d a firkin on home produced soap. The excise on woollen cloth was to be paid by the first buyer but that on soap by the manufacturer. The most important domestic excise was that on beer and ale, which was taxed at the highest rate. Beer and ale, costing 8s a barrel or above, was taxed at 2s a barrel. Domestic brewed beer was assessed at half that rate, but most strong beer consumed in London at this time was probably commercially produced. Beer valued up to 6s a barrel was rated at 6d the barrel, whether brewed commercially or not.[36]

In April 1643 the metropolitan magistrates had set rates of 10s per barrel for strong beer, 8s per barrel for the second sort, 6s for the third sort and 4s a

---

[33] *Firth & Rait*, I, 275, 361–2, 394–5; HLRO, Main Papers, 23 December 1643, Petition of tobacco traders in and around London; PRO SP16/500/98; *CJ* III, 376–7.

[34] *Firth & Rait*, I, 208, 275, 305; GL MS. 15201/4, Vintners' Company, Court Minutes, 1638–58, ff. 132, 194.

[35] *Firth & Rait*, I, 278; GL MS. 15201/4, f. 131.

[36] *Firth & Rait*, I, 275–6, 277, 315–16; C.D. Chandman, *The English Public Revenue, 1660–1688* (Oxford, 1975), 51.

barrel for small beer and ale. The excise on beer was payable by the brewers, who were allowed to add the rates to their prices. Consequently the excise meant that the wholesale price of strong beer rose by twenty per cent, the second sort by twenty five per cent, the third sort by about eight per cent and small beer by 12.5 per cent.[37] The impact on the retail price of beer should, theoretically, not have been as great. Like the brewers, the retailers were allowed to add the excise to their prices, but they were expressly forbidden from raising their prices any further.[38]

Subsequently the excise was extended to other domestic goods. Meat and salt was added to pay for the navy, butchers had to pay five per cent of the value of all animals before they were slaughtered. In July 1644 all imports not formerly taxed, except foodstuffs, bullion and munitions, were rated at five per cent. More English goods were included: copperas, Monmouth caps, hats, saffron, starch and tin were rated at five per cent, alum, hops, wood, upholstery wares and silk goods not previously taxed, were assessed at 2.5 per cent. Subsequently herrings were added to pay for escorts for the fishing fleet. In November 1645, glass, gold, silver and copper wire and thread, and oil made in England were added, and the rates on lead, silk and soap were increased. The excise on meat and salt was repealed in 1647, but Parliament moved quickly to declare that all the other duties were to continue as before.[39]

Unfortunately there are no detailed accounts of the excise from the first Civil War, the first account covers the period from September 1647 to September 1650. A total of £853,345 was received during this period, of which £487,656; fifty seven per cent was collected in and around London. The average annual receipts in London would, therefore have been about £162,552. In comparison in the early 1660s, the annual rent of the farm of the excise in London, Middlesex and Surrey was £118,000 per year, which given that the Restoration excise covered a much more limited range of goods, suggests that the excise was not efficiently collected in the 1640s.[40]

In August 1647 Parliament declared that the net receipts on the excise had been £1,334,531, and that the cost of collection was only ten per cent of receipts. This suggests that the total gross receipts were about £1,467,986. Combined with the receipts mentioned above, up to September 1650, the excise may have come to £2,321,330 in total. If London's proportion of receipts was constant, i.e. fifty seven per cent, then about £1,323,158 was

---

[37] LMA MJ/SBB/31, f. 9; LMA MJ/SBB/56, f. 55; LMA MJ/SBB/58, f. 2; MJ/SBB/69, f. 2; LMA MJ/SBB/81, f. 92.

[38] *Firth & Rait*, I, 316.

[39] *Firth & Rait*, I, 364–6, 466–8, 496–7, 806–8, 1004–7; *LJ* IX, 253.

[40] PRO E351/1295, ff. 3–15; Chandman, *English Public Revenue*, 54.

collected from the introduction of the tax to September 1650, or around £189,023 per year.[41]

The predominance of London as a source of excise receipts was not because the tax was more effectively enforced there, rather it reflects London's role as the major port of the country. In the period from 1647–50 the majority of the receipts in London came from imported goods; receipts from the excise on imports of silk and linen textiles, grocery wares, drugs, wine, tobacco and saltery wares (the last included tar, pitch, hemp and tallow). Together these came to £273,062, more than half the total receipts in London and nearly one-third of all receipts. Ale, perry and cider account for only about one-quarter of the receipts, £128,214, in contrast to the rest of the country, where these items produced the majority of the revenue. The predominance of London as a source of excise receipts was a result of the fact that this was the place where the imports entered the country, and consequently where they were first traded.[42] To a lesser extent the disparity in the revenue also reflects London's dominance of the internal distribution of English manufactures. In 1647 over twice as much of the excise on woollen cloth was paid in London as in the rest of the country. This suggests that despite appearances the excise did not press more heavily on London than the rest of the country, most of the receipts were collected in London because that was where most of the trade in excisable goods took place. It is possible that the London tradesmen passed on much of the costs of the excise to their provincial customers.[43]

Complaints about the excise came from a very wide cross section of London's economy, petitions were presented to Parliament by brewers, merchant strangers, feltmakers, tobacco traders, tobacco-pipe makers, butchers, mercers, broad weavers, vintners, pewterers, poulterers, gold and silver wire makers and silkmen.[44] The agitation cannot be written off entirely as royalist inspired; the petition from the tobacco sellers was signed by a number of strong supporters of Parliament, including Alderman John Warner, who played a key role in parliamentary financial administration in the 1640s.[45] However all the agitation was concerned with specific rates on commodities of particular concern to the traders, not with the excise as a whole. Some of the complaints were against the way the excise was levied rather than the excise itself, the gold and silver wire makers were mostly concerned that it should be payable

---

[41] *Firth & Rait*, I, 1006.

[42] PRO E351/1295, f. 3; *CJ* VI, 380.

[43] PRO SP46/122B, f. 1.

[44] *HMC Fifth Report, House of Lords MSS*, 95, 104, 118, 119; PRO SP16/498/95; GL MS. 7086/3, Pewterers' Company, Wardens' Accounts, 1572–1663, f. 499; GL MS. 15201/4, f. 119; GL MS. 2150/1, Poulterers' Company, Wardens' Accounts, 1619–1705, unfoliated account for 1642–44; *CJ* III, 371; *CJ* IV, 95, 386–7, 389.

[45] HLRO, Main Papers, 23 December 1643, Petition of tobacco traders in and around London.

by the buyer rather than the manufacturer.[46] Moreover, Parliament showed itself willing to respond to pressure, the success of the tobacco traders has already been noted, and the excise on spirits was reduced in September 1644.[47]

A large amount of the criticism of the excise focused on the administrative burden that the tax placed on tradesmen, critics claimed that the need to be sending constantly for tickets from the excise office and so forth, obstructed internal trade. The vintners complained that, despite paying the excise when purchasing wine from the importers, when they sent deliveries to customers outside London their goods were seized by the officers of the excise, unless they obtained tickets from the excise office for each consignment first, which added to their expenses. It was also claimed that the excise discouraged people from stocking up, instead they only bought what they immediately needed.[48]

The strongest opponents of the excise were the vintners, brewers and butchers, however a close examination of their protests indicates how limited the opposition to the excise in London was. As early as 9 June 1643, before the first ordinance was passed, the Vintners' Company had set up a committee to oppose the excise. By the end of the month the company had prepared petitions for both the Lords and the Commons, claiming that their trade could not possibly support an excise of £6 per tun. On 19 July a general meeting of retailers of wine in London declared that they could not possibly consent to any levy. Following the implementation of the excise a further committee was established that drew up a remonstrance, which was presented to the commissioners for the new tax. Dissatisfied with the answer of the commissioners they drafted a petition to Parliament. This stated that, as a result of the excise, demand for wine had fallen so much they would soon have to abandon their trade. In the following April the Vintners' Company claimed that, since the introduction of the excise, demand for wine had fallen to less than one-quarter of what it had been before and they drew up yet another petition to Parliament.[49]

The Brewers' Company also began campaigning against the excise in June 1643. They renewed their protest in the summer of 1647, complaining that their margins were further reduced by the rising price of malt, resulting from the poor harvests. The brewers alleged that their customers were refusing to pay the excise and, consequently, the brewers, who had to pay the excise before delivering beer to their customers, were falling into arrears and were threatened with sequestration. Brewers who were in arrears were brought

---

[46] *HMC Sixth Report, House of Lords MSS*, 80.

[47] *Firth & Rait*, I, 511–12.

[48] *Severall Particulars Shewing the Many Great Conveniences of Receiving the Imposition or Excise at the Custome-House* (1650); GL MS. 15201/4, ff. 137, 145, 146, 229.

[49] GL MS. 15201/4, ff. 118, 119, 127, 130–2, 144, 156.

before the House of Commons, where they said that they would only pay what they owed when their customers paid them.[50]

The most violent protest against the excise in London in the 1640s came from the butchers. In Smithfield market on 15 February 1647 a crowd, led by butchers, burnt down the excise office and destroyed its records.[51] The butchers were not typical of other London traders in excise goods. Smithfield market brought the butchers of London together to an extent that was probably not the case with other occupations. This was strengthened by the workings of the excise; to avoid evasion Parliament ordered that all cattle brought to London had to be sold at Smithfield, and no animals could be removed until the tax was paid. This meant the butchers came into contact with the officials of the excise as a group rather than as separate individuals and gave the butchers the opportunity to engage in crowd activity specific to their occupation that other London trades did not possess. Also the excise riot was not the first time the butchers of Smithfield violently attacked Parliament's revenue officers. In July 1643 they had combined to assault and abuse the officers of the sequestration committee who had come to sequester oxen, raising the possibility that the riot was in part due to a high level of royalism among the butchers.[52]

It should also be stressed that butchers and brewers were in a different position to other London traders as they could argue that their products were necessities, and, as such, were not proper targets for taxation. Beer and beef were part of the diet of the very poorest in London society.[53] Opposition to the excise on these goods derived from the belief that goods bought by the poor should not be taxed, rather than the economic impact of the excise. It was the taxation of necessities that was the major focus of the critique of the excise expounded by the pro-parliamentary newsbook *The Moderate Intelligencer.*[54] The brewers placed considerable emphasis on the fact that beer was a key part of the diet of the poor, but this argument was not available to most traders in excised goods.[55]

---

[50] GL MS. 5445/17, Brewers' Company, Court Minutes, 1642–52, unfoliated, 21 June 1643, 26 September 1643, 9 January 1644, 23 January 1644, 17 August 1647; HLRO, Main Papers, 10 July 1643, Petition of the Brewers' Company; *CJ* III, 227; *LJ* IX, 402; R. Ashton, *Counter Revolution: The Second Civil War and its Origins, 1646–8* (New Haven, 1994), 72; *CJ* V, 276, 283.

[51] Braddick, 'Popular Politics and Public Policy', 597.

[52] Braddick, *Parliamentary Taxation*, 171. PRO SP20/6, ff. 27v–28; In February 1643 butchers' apprentices were reported to have attacked collectors of the assessment in the Shambles. K. Lindley, *Popular Politics and Religion in Civil War London* (Aldershot, 1997), 253.

[53] I.W. Archer, *The Pursuit of Stability: Social Relations in Elizabethan London* (Cambridge, 1991), 191, table 5.10.

[54] *The Moderate Intelligencer*, 59, 16–23 April 1646, 406.

[55] *LJ* IX, 402.

The opposition of the Brewers and Vintners to the excise should not be exaggerated. There is little mention of the excise in the records of the Brewers' Company between January 1644 and August 1647. The Vintners' complaints were concentrated on their own trade and quickly shifted from a general opposition to the tax to the level of the rates. By April 1644 their arguments had become particularly focused on the rate on French wine. Neither trade was typical because, as has already been noted, the excise rates were heavier on wine and beer than on other goods, and wine already paid a heavy import duty. The Vintners particularly stressed that wine was much more highly rated than other goods, and they argued that a reduction would increase receipts because it would increase demand. Administrative matters also became increasingly prominent in their complaints, issues such as the collection of tickets, the allowance of the full 252 gallons to the tun and the refusal of the excise officials to allow time for payment. Arguments about the rates only returned when they feared that increases were being contemplated.[56] Moreover, the agreement of the Brewers to enter negotiations for a farm of the excise on beer and ale in London in 1650 may be taken as an admission that their campaign against the excise had failed.[57]

It would therefore be unwise to interpret the opposition to the excise as a sign of the economic impact of the tax. In practice, most London tradesmen were able to pass on the costs of the excise to their customers. Although Parliament took steps to try to ensure that price rises were kept to a minimum, they do not seem to have been successful. It was widely alleged that the prices of excised goods rose more than was necessary to pay the duty, and, at the time, it was believed that retailers were benefiting from the excise. As early as January 1644 the Commons was alarmed by rises in the price of beer, ale and soap.[58]

The brewers and beer retailers were particularly successful in passing on more than the full cost of the excise to their consumers. The retail price of strong beer should not have risen by more than 18.75 per cent, but given the types of coin in circulation, the retailers could not add 18.75 per cent to the price of a quart of ale. Consequently they increased their prices by more than was strictly necessary to pay for the excise. In 1644 Parliament's committee for Irish affairs argued that, when the excise was first introduced, the 2s duty had amounted to two-thirds of a farthing on a quart of beer, so the retailers increased their prices by a farthing. But after the farthing was taken out of circulation in 1644 this became impossible so, according to the committee, beer, which had been retailed for six farthings, was now being retailed for 2d, a

---

[56] GL MS. 15201/4, ff. 130–1, 137, 144–6, 191, 229, 297, 300.

[57] GL MS. 5445/17, 15 and 24 October 1650.

[58] *CJ* III, 304, 365; *Firth & Rait*, I, 305, 316; E. Hughes, *Studies in Administration and Finance, 1558–1825* (Manchester, 1934), 124–5.

rise of one-quarter.[59] The claims of the committee are supported by a broadside published in March 1646 which stated that the brewers and the beer retailers had put up their prices by significantly more than was necessary to pay for the excise. The author claimed that brewers were selling ordinary beer and ale at 12s a barrel and strong beer at 16s the barrel, while retailers of beer were selling ordinary beer for the equivalent of over 21s per barrel, and strong beer for 30s per barrel.[60]

The protests of the brewers should, therefore, be taken with a large pinch of salt. The London brewing industry did not suffer particularly badly in the Civil War. Enrolment of apprentices in the Brewers' Company did not decline significantly, and, in the year to August 1647, rose to the highest total for more than a decade; but in subsequent years recruitment declined, indicating that this year marked downturn in their trade. The causes of the decline in their trade are not difficult to find. The run of bad harvests from 1646 onwards led to a substantial decline in real wages in London. Moreover London magistrates were seeking to restrict beer production to mitigate the rising price of grain. Declining consumption, together with the vigorous enforcement of price controls and crackdowns on unlicensed alehouse keepers, especially in the suburbs, may have been the real cause of the brewers' inability to recover the cost of the excise from their customers. The revival of the brewers' agitation against the excise may have been prompted by their changing economic fortunes, suggesting that agitation against the excise was more a reflection of general economic problems rather than evidence of the impact of the tax itself.[61]

The vintners and the butchers did not do so well during the Civil War as the brewers but in neither case does their opposition to the excise indicate that the new tax was the primary cause of their problems. The Butchers' Company's accounts suggests that their trade was recovering strongly in the immediate post-war period, in the year to October 1646 fifty two apprentices were enrolled, compared to thirty one in the year 1643–44. Additionally, in 1645–46 £7 5s 9d was collected for quarterage, only slightly less than in 1638–39. The 1647 riot came at a time when the butchers were experiencing a renewed prosperity, not when their trade was in decline.[62]

The vintners, unlike the brewers, found it difficult to get their customers to accept even the increases in prices authorized by Parliament and, in August

---

[59] *HMC Thirteenth Report, Portland MSS*, I, 199.

[60] T.A., *A Declaration of Severall Observations to the Reader Worthy of Perusall* (1646).

[61] See Figure 8.2 below; CLRO Rep. 58/2, f. 8; *Perfect Occurrences*, 66, 31 March–7 April, 1648, 469.

[62] GL MS. 6440/2, Butchers' Company, Wardens' Accounts, 1593–1646, part 2, ff. 587v, 607v, 611–12. In 1638–39 quarterage receipts totalled £7 9s 3d. Ibid., ff. 527v–529. Unfortunately the next volume of accounts is missing.

1644, they showed considerable concern in disciplining a member of their company who was found to be selling wine below the regulated price. However there is good reason to believe that the wine trade was untypical of the London economy as a whole, a combination of high customs and high excise rates made wine the most heavily taxed commodity. The vintners did not attribute their economic difficulties solely to the excise; heavy direct taxation and the general economic climate were also blamed. Indeed it is sometimes not clear whether they were arguing that the decline in their trade was the result of the excise or the cause of their inability to pay it. Moreover the evidence suggests that tavern keepers suffered a substantial decline in sales of food as well as wine.[63]

The difference between the brewers and the vintners was that the demand for beer remained buoyant during the war years, but the demand for wine did not, despite the fact that both commodities were heavily taxed. This suggests that the excise in itself did not significantly reduce demand, and where demand for a product remained strong, the cost of the excise could be absorbed. The opposition to the excise in London in the 1640s was a symptom of wider economic problems rather than a direct reaction to its cause. The higher price of beer undoubtedly worsened the plight of the London poor but there is little evidence that this led to a decline in consumption.

The excise was a major expansion of indirect taxation, extending its scope to include goods produced and consumed in England. It represented a shift in the burden of taxation to the less well off because indirect taxes are inherently regressive and because it included goods consumed by the poor, such as beer. Nevertheless the predominance of London in the receipts from the excise was a function of London's position within the national economy, rather than a sign that either tax weighed heavily on London. It is likely that much of the cost was passed on to the provinces in the form of higher prices. In terms of the prosperity of the economy as a whole, the excise had relatively little impact apart from exacerbating existing problems.

Customs

The first tax to be levied by an ordinance of Parliament alone was the customs. Since May 1641 Parliament had passed a series of short-term acts authorizing the collection of the customs while they overhauled the rates. In June 1642 the new Book of Rates was ready, and a new bill was passed by Parliament to implement it, but the King refused his assent, and the previous Act expired on

---

[63]   GL MS. 15201/4, ff. 131, 132, 145–6, 156, 194, 197; PRO C24/697/25.

1 July. In response, Parliament issued the new Book of Rates and started to levy the customs on its own authority.[64]

To encourage submission to taxation without the force of statute Parliament gave those willing to pay promptly a fifteen per cent reduction in their customs. Whether for this reason or because of support for Parliament Giles Grene, chairman of the Navy and Customs Committee, reported to the Commons that the merchants were willing to comply with the ordinance. The discount was retained until the Commonwealth abolished it to pay for convoys for the Mediterranean in 1650.[65] The 1642 Book of Rates increased the tax burden on some goods but decreased it on others.[66]

In November 1643 Parliament added a ten per cent surcharge on the customs for the defence of Plymouth, Poole and Lyme, which was doubled in the following September. The surcharged was levied on the basis of the full 1642 Book of Rates, without the fifteen per cent discount. From September 1644 until September 1646 merchants would have been paying, on balance, five per cent more than the 1642 rates. The duty was the focus of agitation among London merchants from 1645. In September 1646 the rate was reduced back to ten per cent, and it was finally abolished in January 1647.[67]

The only other modification in the customs rates made by Parliament was a reduction of the duties on tobacco imports. In March 1644 the custom on tobacco from English plantations was halved to 1d per pound. However in practice the rate was reduced only for tobacco for the home market. Under the 1642 Book of Rates fifty per cent of the duty paid on imports was rebated to the merchant when goods were re-exported, but the ordinance specified that this should no longer be paid for tobacco.[68]

A total of £1,414,726 was received by Parliament's customs' commissioners from 2 July 1642 to 24 June 1650 from the port of London, making the customs the largest source of taxation from London in the 1640s.[69] This does not include the Plymouth duty for which two accounts survive, one for the period up to the beginning of 1645 and the other from March 1646 until the tax was abolished in January 1647. These show that £58,321 was collected in the port of London, the receipts from the missing period can be estimated at £51,963, suggesting that total receipts from the Plymouth duty were £110,284, and that total customs' receipts were £1,525,010. The average annual receipts

---

[64] *CJ* II, 635, 642, 694, 695; V.F. Snow and A.S. Young (eds), *The Private Journals of the Long Parliament, 2nd June to 17th September* (New Haven, 1992), 216, 261; LJ V, 250.

[65] *Firth & Rait*, I, 16–20; II, 444; *CJ* II, 705.

[66] For the impact of the new Book of Rates see p. 165 below.

[67] *Firth & Rait*, I, 342, 505–6; PRO AO1/778/755; PRO SP105/143, ff. 113, 118; CLRO Jour. 40, f. 180v.

[68] *Firth & Rait*, I, 394–5; *The rates of merchandize* (1642), 56.

[69] PRO E122/226/17/4; PRO E351/643–650.

were £190,626.[70] In comparison Charles I received about £500,000 in 1640, but the decline was probably the result of a slump in trade rather than a fall in the rate of taxation.[71]

Sequestration

Although not a tax, the impact of parliamentary sequestration needs to be examined with that of taxation because it was also a device used by Parliament to extract money from the London economy to pay for the war effort. The sequestration ordinance of March 1643 declared that the estates of all 'delinquents', a category that encompassed all royalists and Catholics, were to be confiscated. Their land was to be leased out and personal estate sold off.

Parliament authorized the lord mayor, aldermen and common councillors to implement the ordinance in the City. In practice, the execution was delegated to a committee of common councillors who sat at Camden House.[72] The accounts of the central treasurers suggest that sequestration was more successful in London than most other parts of the country, receipts from the City totalled £33,268, only Suffolk paid more money.[73] However in most counties the majority of receipts from sequestration failed to reach the central treasury, but this was not the case in London. Everitt estimated that the total receipts in Kent were about £70,000 but only £22,618 was received by the central treasurers; an account from the London committee from 1643 shows that of the £21,548 received about £14,688, over two-thirds, was paid to the treasurers. The central treasury received £5,422 from Westminster, but there things resembled the rest of England, accounts to February 1644 indicate that less than half the receipts were paid to the central treasury. Nevertheless, despite its great wealth and large population, sequestration proved much less productive in London than other parts of the country.[74]

For those London tradesmen who were sequestered it could mean the destruction of their business. Sequestration was designed for a society where land was the main source of income. The estates of most of the royalist gentry and nobility were kept intact. Only the profits, the rents, were taken and most royalist landowners got their estates back after the Civil War by paying a

---

[70] PRO E122/236/14; PRO AO1/778/755. The estimate for the missing period is derived from the total receipts from the port of London in the customs accounts for the period 25 February–25 December 1645, this was then inflated to take into account the longer time period, 2 January 1645 to 23 February 1645, and the fifteen per cent discount, and then divided by five.

[71] F.C. Dietz, *English Public Finance, 1485–1641*, 2nd edn, 2 vols (1964), II, 376.

[72] *Firth & Rait*, I, 114; PRO SP20/1, f. 10v; PRO SP28/252/1, f. 46.

[73] PRO SP28/216, The Account of the Sequestrations Treasurers.

[74] Everitt, *Community of Kent*, 160–1; PRO SP20/6, ff. 72v–73; PRO SP46/104, f. 20.

composition fine. However the London merchants who were sequestered lost not just the profits on their estates but their capital as well. This was because although many London merchants owned housing in the City, and some owned land in the country, this was not the major source of their income. Indeed, for most merchants, fixed capital formed a very small part of their business. Instead, they had their current stock of goods and a network of credit. The continuance of their business was dependent on their own personal reputation and contacts. It would not be easy for the sequestrators to take over their business and operate it profitably. Moreover a merchant's stock and the money owed him were defined by Parliament as part of his personal estate, and therefore liable for sale. The 1643 accounts of the City sequestration committee show that only £849 was collected for sequestered rents while £19,296 had been received in money and goods from those sequestered.[75]

A number of members of the East India Company were sequestered. On 17 May 1643 the East India Company was ordered not to pay any money owing to Sir Peter Ricaut. His estate was sequestered in the following month and order was given to sell his 'adventure' in the company. This alarmed the company, which feared that Ricaut would seize their goods abroad in retaliation and also that if the order was enforced it would discourage men from investing. The first of the company's fears proved justified; by November 1646 the company had spent more than £600 protecting their goods from him in Venice, Leghorn and Goa.[76]

In early September 1643 a number of warrants were presented to the East India Company for the sequestration of the adventures of royalist investors. The company was ordered not to pay out any of the divisions due on the first general voyage until their representatives had appeared before the committee for advance of money. The company had no permanent stock at this time; the divisions represented not only the investors' profits, but also their principal.[77]

Sequestration had the greatest impact on trade with Africa. The sequestration of Sir Nicholas Crispe led to the virtual collapse of the Guinea Company. Crispe owned about half the stock of the company, and his agreement was required before any dividends could be paid or any fresh commercial ventures begun. Crispe was sequestered in 1643 for debts he owed as a customs' commissioner, and he subsequently fled to Oxford. In his absence the other members of the company decided to abandon their trade, their agents sold their remaining goods on the Gold Coast to the Dutch and shipped the proceeds home. By the end of 1644 the Dutch West India Company had come to the conclusion that the English had abandoned the Gold

---

[75] Grassby, *Business Community*, 243; B. Supple, *Commercial Crisis and Change in England, 1600–1642* (Cambridge, 1959), 8–9. PRO SP20/6, f. 67.
[76] *CJ* III, 90, 139, 140 143, 149, 151; *CCMEIC*, 1640–43, 330; ibid., 1644–49, 169.
[77] *CJ* III, 240; *CCMEIC*, 1640–43, 350, 351; *CCAM*, I, 25.

Coast entirely, but by this time interlopers were beginning to fill the gap. By the end of 1645 the company had been re-launched under Rowland Wilson, but Crispe was unable to recover his interest in the company when his sequestration was lifted in 1648 and by 1660 he was in prison for debt.[78]

Usually the result of sequestration was less drastic than the example of Sir Nicholas Crispe suggests. Merchants were able to recover at least part of their assets when their sequestration was lifted. Despite the order of Parliament Ricaut's shares in the East India Company do not seem to have been sold. In 1648 the company agreed to pay Ricaut the two divisions made in the previous year on the first general voyage, although he had to agree to discharge the company for what they had paid the sequestrators.[79] The number of merchants who were sequestrated was small. In the autumn of 1643 only six investors in the first general voyage, who between them owned less than eight per cent of the capital invested in the voyage, had been sequestered.[80] Nevertheless, when applied to mercantile estates, sequestration meant the appropriation not only of the revenue from the estate but the capital as well.

The impact of sequestration was not confined to those who actually suffered it. Sequestration proceedings were often begun but not carried through. The London sequestration committee's accounts for 1643 state that £71,285 had been seized upon all warrants issued by the committee but of that £50,089 was discharged by warrants from Parliament and orders of the committee. The issuing of a warrant for sequestration against a London tradesman would have rocked the tradesman's credit even if it were subsequently rescinded.[81]

All seventeenth-century English tradesmen were locked into intricate credit networks. Consequently debts formed a large proportion of the estates of sequestered Londoners, in 1643 a total of £27,953 in debts to delinquents were brought to light by the London committee. The attempts of the committee to collect these, and other debts which were subsequently discovered, ensured that sequestration had a knock on effect which went far beyond the delinquents it was designed for.[82]

Credit took a wide variety of forms, with formal bills obligatory the time of repayment was fixed and the demands of the sequestrators could be fended until the date specified. However debts on bonds and debts without formal

---

[78] PRO SP16/450/365–400; R. Porter, 'The Crispe Family and the African Trade in the Seventeenth Century', *Journal of African History* 9 (1968), 67–8; PRO SP23/206, ff. 203–4; *To the Right Honourable the Commons of England Assembled in Parliament. The Humble Petition of Sir Nicholas Crisp Knight* ([1660]).

[79] *CCMEIC*, 1644–49, 259–60, 261.

[80] PRO SP19/79, ff. 112–13; BL IOL/H/6, East India Company, Home Miscellaneous, ff. 116–83; *CCMEIC*, 1644–49, 293.

[81] PRO SP20/6, ff. 66v–67.

[82] Ibid.

paper security, the vast majority of debts in the seventeenth century, often had no date for repayment. The repayment was normally a matter of negotiation between the debtor and creditor; here the actions of the sequestrators could be very disruptive.[83] Among the goods seized by the London committee belonging to Timothy Wright was a bond for £115 owing by Nicholas Turbeville. The committee demanded payment of the bond from Turbeville but he refused, so Turbeville's estate was also seized.[84] In 1644 the Barber Surgeons' Company ran into trouble when it was discovered that they owed £1,000 to a sequestered royalist. The Company was threatened with sequestration unless the debt was paid. They were able to compound for the debt, paying £400 and promising a further £100 in two years' time, but this required the passage of a special ordinance of Parliament.[85]

By the mid-seventeenth century credit instruments were becoming increasingly used as currency, passing from hand to hand. This could make it difficult to establish which debts belonged to a delinquent. Among those sequestered in 1643 was Andrew King, a London wine merchant, who was owed £2,381 by twenty two Londoners, mostly vintners and coopers. The London committee proceeded to gather these debts but King's debtors were prosecuted by a number of individuals who claimed that the debts had been assigned to them. The Commons stepped in and ordered those prosecuting the debtors to desist, but this meant that the assignees, who may well have been King's creditors, would have lost the money King had assigned them.[86]

Further complications were created by business partnerships. Much of what was sequestered as the estate of Andrew King seems to have belonged in reality to King's partner, John Bland, then living in Seville. Bland feared that the King of Spain would seize his estate for his adherence to Parliament, so he made over his estate, worth £10,000, to King. When Bland returned to London, he found his estate had been disposed of, for Parliament. Bland was able to obtain an order for repayment of £2,719 but was only able to receive £150. He was forced to assign the order to one of his creditors, who was still trying to obtain payment in 1654.[87]

Many of those sequestered in the rest of the country were indebted to London tradesmen, who were generally obliged to give up to six months' credit to their customers. Sequestration made it difficult for them to obtain repayment

---

[83] C. Muldrew, *The Economy of Obligation: The Culture of Credit and Social Relations in Early Modern England* (Basingstoke, 1998), 95–119, 174–5. Goldsmiths' Hall, Court Book, 'W', 1642–45, ff. 248v, 251, 251v–2.

[84] PRO SP20/6, ff. 57v–8.

[85] GL MS. 5257/5, Barber Surgeons' Company, Court Minutes, 1621–51, ff. 328, 329, 330, 334, 335, 336–7; *LJ* VIII, 562. The Company had to pay for the passage of the Ordinance.

[86] E. Kerridge, *Trade and Banking in Early Modern England* (1988), 40–4; PRO SP20/6, ff. 56v–7; *CJ* III, 174.

[87] *CCCD*, V, 3285.

of their debts, which caused great economic difficulties to some London tradesmen. The London tailor William Perkins, who before the Civil War had many noble and gentry customers, was unable to collect his debts from his sequestered customers. He was unable to pay his own debts and, by April 1647, was imprisoned by his creditors. Repayment of debts owed by delinquents became a minor, but persistent, issue in London politics in the 1640s.[88]

On 8 May 1643 the Parliament's sequestration committee ordered that the charges of mortgages and judgements which had been executed on the lands of 'delinquents' should be paid by the sequestrators, but not debts on contracts, bonds, bills, specialities and judgements and statutes not executed. This was partly because they claimed this would frustrate the purpose of the ordinance, and partly because it would cause too many disputes. On the 13th of that month the committee ruled that personal debts on bonds, bills, contracts, judgements or statutes not executed were not to be allowed either out of the lands or goods of those sequestered except by special order of the committee.[89]

On 20 May 1643 the creditors of Marmaduke Royden, a prominent sequestered London merchant, petitioned the Commons for the payment of their debts. The Commons referred the petition to the sequestration committee and ordered that the creditors should be paid, but only after the debts to the state. The committee was clearly unsure what the Commons had intended and they decided to refer back to the House for further directions on the case, which do not seem to have been forthcoming.[90]

In February 1644 a petition was presented to the Court of Aldermen arguing that creditors should be able to reclaim their debts from sequestered estates and, in March, a similar petition was presented to the Common Council. A petition to Parliament was drawn up which was approved by the Common Council, and presented to the Commons on 3 August.[91] This issue was of particular importance in August 1644 because the Commons began to debate the sale of sequestered lands and it was feared that the delinquents' creditors would lose all rights to the money they were owed. It was claimed that about £2 million was owed Londoners and 'if just debts be not provided, men who ware estemed very able and so assesed will be worth Litle & so refuse to pay assesments as formerly'.[92] Meetings of creditors were organized by a group of scriveners; who agreed to advance money to Parliament. In return the creditors

---

[88] Grassby, *Business Community*, 82–3; *HMC Ormonde MSS, New Series*, I, 114–15. Although Perkins' finances were already shaky before the war, see A.B. Grossart (ed.), *The Lismore Papers* Second Series, 5 vols (1888), V, 118, 123.

[89] PRO SP20/1, ff. 15v, 24v.

[90] *CJ* III, 93; PRO SP20/1, f. 40v.

[91] *CJ* III, 577–8; CLRO Rep. 57/1, f. 47; CLRO Jour. 40, ff. 91, 103.

[92] PRO SP16/497/59. This undated document was assigned to March 1643 in *CSPD 1641–43*, 455, but internal evidence suggests 1644 is more likely.

wanted the estates of the delinquents made over to themselves in satisfaction for their debts. The propositions were presented to the Common Council. However Parliament decided against the immediate sale of delinquents' estates.[93]

As the sequestered estates were returned to their owners, after they compounded, the creditors could seek the usual forms of redress for repayment of their money. This would not have been true of those who had lent money to those who either were not permitted to compound, or refused to do so. Proposals to sell off sequestered estates created fresh alarms among creditors who feared that they would not receive their debts. In December 1647 fears that Lord Cottington's estate was going to be sold off to pay for the suppression of the Irish rebellion caused the East India Company to decide to sue for the money still owing for the pepper seized by the Crown in 1640, for which Cottington was one of the sureties, as soon as possible. This proved a false alarm, but in August 1649 fresh fears that the estate was going to be sold off led the company to resolve to petition the Rump for the repayment of their debt.[94]

In August 1650 a petition was presented to Parliament from the creditors of delinquents arguing that they should be repaid their debts before the estates were sold. As a result the trustees appointed by Parliament to sell the royalist estates were instructed to satisfy the creditors before the lands were put up for sale. Land was transferred to creditors in lieu of debts, where the creditors were London moneylenders they immediately resold the lands. The lands in the eastern suburbs of London belonging to the heavily indebted Earl of Cleveland, the owner of Stepney and Hackney manors, were parcelled out and sold to forty seven new owners.[95]

Sequestration produced considerable disruption in return for little yield for Parliament. For those London tradesmen who were sequestered, it was potentially much more catastrophic than for members of the gentry in a similar position, as they stood to lose their whole estate. The impact of sequestration went much wider as many Londoners were indebted to a sequestered royalist, and were threatened with sequestration unless they paid their debts promptly. Others found themselves unable to reclaim money that they had lent to men who had been sequestered. There were some positive benefits. It provided new areas of business for Londoners; some lent money to sequestered landowners to enable them to pay off their composition fines, others acted as agents

---

[93] *The Kingdomes Weekly Intelligencer*, 69, 20–27 August 1644, 555; *Mercurius Civicus*, 66, 22–29 August 1644, 623–6; CLRO Jour. 40, ff. 104v–5.

[94] *CCMEIC*, 1644–49, 249, 347. For the pepper debt see above p. 20.

[95] *To the Supreme Authority of this Common-Wealth* (1650); J. Thirsk, 'The Sales of Royalist Land During the Interregnum', in her *The Rural Economy of England. Collected Essays* (1984), 93–7.

helping royalists buy back their estates when they were sold off. In this respects sequestration contributed to the growth of the financial services sector in the London economy.[96] Moreover the disruption should not be exaggerated. The sequestrators often found it very difficult to collect delinquents' debts. In January 1649 the London committee delivered evidence of debts totalling £25,000, which had been sequestered but which they had been unable to collect, to the army committee.[97] Even in the case of Sir Nicholas Crispe and the Guinea Company, trade with Africa was only halted for a short period as other London merchants were soon willing to step into the breach. Whatever its impact on individuals sequestration had only a limited affect on the economy as a whole.

The militia

The militia formed another indirect financial burden on Londoners during the Civil War. From September 1642 the militia was deployed to defend London, each regiment serving for a week in turn, and in 1643 and 1644 London militia units were sent on active service to reinforce the armies of Waller and Essex. From the relief of Gloucester to the formation of the New Model Army trained band regiments served in every major campaign in southern England.[98]

During the Civil War the militia was substantially expanded; from September 1642 lodgers and those who traded in London, but did not reside there, could also be enlisted. How large the militia was in Civil War London is difficult to establish precisely. In 1642 the City agreed to raise forty companies, each with more than two hundred men, to be organized into six regiments, which would have meant a force of more than eight thousand. Emberton gives 5077 for the City Trained bands, but he seems to have missed out one of the regiments. He gives a figure of 4716 for the suburban regiments, while Pearl states that the trained bands of the whole metropolis totalled ten thousand men, which may be about right. This would suggest that there was one trained bandsman for every forty inhabitants or one for every eight households.[99]

---

[96] F.T. Melton, *Sir Robert Clayton and the Origins of English Deposit Banking, 1658–1685* (Cambridge, 1986), 46; Thirsk, 'Sales of Royalist Land', 90–2.

[97] *CSPD*, 1649–50, 486.

[98] CLRO Jour. 40, f. 37v; Nagel, 'Militia of London', 70, 89, 118, 135, 138, 156, 158, 168, 174, 183, 185, 192, 203, 204, 208, 215.

[99] Nagel, 'Militia of London', 46, 68; W. Emberton, *Skippon's Brave Boys: The Origins Development and Civil War Service of London's Trained Bands* (Buckingham, 1984), 33; V. Pearl, *London and the Outbreak of the Puritan Revolution. City Government and National Politics, 1625–43* (Oxford, 1961), 251.

Londoners could either serve in person, in which case they would be taken from their work, or they could send substitutes, which seems to have been most common. Wealthy inhabitants could be expected to provide up to three men. Either way they would incur financial loss. In October 1642 the Common Council fixed the allowance to be paid to substitutes at 12d per day and 12d per night, although in December 1643 this was reduced to 6d per day and per night. Those enrolled had to provide the arms and equipment for whoever actually served. The militia might therefore be seen, indirectly, as another form of wartime taxation. A petition from London tradesmen in February 1645 stated that service on the forts in the trained bands cost them more than £1,000 per week.[100]

A muster roll has survived for a company in the Blue trained band regiment from 1644. The roll is very similar to a taxation roll, it goes from house to house in Dowgate ward, assigning men to the householders specified, ranging from two men for one household to one-third of man, undoubtedly according to the wealth of the household. In one precinct, fifteen householders were responsible for supplying eleven men. Although relatively few substitutes are mentioned in the roll, this may underestimate the extent of the practice. Another muster roll has survived for the Tower Hamlets regiment, which covered the hamlet of Ratcliff. Here practically every man was supported by more than one householder, presumably because of the greater poverty of the eastern suburbs, but hired substitutes were uncommon, probably because the inhabitants of this poorer sector of London could not afford them. Of the 147 militia places to be filled only twenty were substitutes, fifty seven were not specified while seventy were filled by one or other of the assessed householders.[101]

In April 1644, the Haberdashers' Company was instructed to find two men for the trained bands for their Hall. Consequently, the company's accounts can be used to shed some light on the cost of the militia. Between 18 April and 22 November 1644 the company paid their two substitutes £6 6s. This indicates that the cost of a single man in this period was 9s a month. Comparison with other payments in the accounts suggests that the burden was a relatively minor one. The company's weekly assessment in 1643 had been £20 a week and the assessment for the New Model Army was £15 a month. The Dowgate muster roll suggests that two men was generally the highest rate in the City, few would have paid more than the Haberdashers. This indicates that for those able to afford substitutes the militia was not a major burden.[102]

---

[100] CLRO Jour 40, ff. 40v, 81v, 123; *Firth & Rait*, I, 452–4; Nagel, 'Militia of London', 61.

[101] Nagel, 'Militia of London', 60–1, 101.

[102] GL MS. 15866/1, Haberdashers' Company, Wardens' Accounts, 1633–53, ff. 442, 485, 524.

The impact of the militia on the London economy went further than the burden of paying for substitutes. In 1643 Hugh Fountaine served for Tobais Goodwyn in the Westminster trained band regiment at Basing house, but he fell ill and three days after his return he died, leaving a heavily pregnant wife in considerable poverty. Before the Westminster militia subcommittee, Goodwyn promised to pay 40s or 50s a year to Fountaine's widow as long as she remained unmarried, and 12d per week for the education of her child, although subsequently he tried to get out of his obligations and widow Fountaine had to take him to court.[103]

In addition to the regular trained bands, there were the auxiliary regiments recruited in 1643, which may have numbered about eight thousand, although many of the units were under strength. The City auxiliaries were recruited from the apprentices and other young men, and they, therefore, probably served in person. In the suburbs the auxiliaries were more likely to be established householders like the trained bands men. Many in the Southwark auxiliaries were watermen or had other trades, and many had families.[104]

Those serving on the expeditions should have been paid, as should the officers of the trained bands for their service at the fortifications, but this frequently was not the case, despite the fact that the officers' rates of pay were substantially reduced in December 1643. In 1643 the Ironmongers' Company sent two men on the campaign to relieve Gloucester, one of whom died at the battle of Newbury. This cost the company £6 8s, but they only got back £1.[105] In December 1644 the Common Council requested money to repay what was owed to those who had served Parliament, stating that 'with great clamours and ymportunities they [the men] are daily uncessant Complaynours'.[106] In the following January those who had served on the Lostwithiel campaign in the summer of 1644 were still owed over £6,500. In July 1645 officers of the trained bands petitioned the militia committee calling for the payment of their arrears.[107]

Many warrants for the payment of the trained bands had not been paid. On 22 March 1646 the militia committee issued a warrant for payment of £368 to Captain Thomas Juxon for service in the trained bands from 1 September 1643 to 3 September 1645, replacing an unpaid warrant previously issued for the period to September 1644. Juxon received £168 in cash on 9 April and was assigned the rest from the excise, but it is clear that many others still had arrears owing. In April 1648 a group of militia officers petitioned the Common

---

[103] PRO C24/702/43.

[104] Nagel, 'Militia of London', 80–4, 96–7; Emberton, *Skippon's Brave Boys*, 33.

[105] CLRO Jour. 40, f. 81v; GL MS. 16988/5, Ironmongers' Company, Wardens' Accounts, 1634–51, ff. 333, 342.

[106] CLRO Jour. 40, f. 118v.

[107] CLRO Jour. 40, ff. 120, 136.

Council in the name of five to six hundred citizens who had served in various expeditions for Parliament but were, they claimed, owed large arrears. In July 1649 the trained bandsmen petitioned the Commons, in response it was resolved that they could double their arrears on the estates of the Deans and Chapters. Men of the Westminster auxiliaries claimed that they had been defrauded of the money owed them by the commanders of their regiment.[108]

As the war dragged on there were growing complaints that service in the trained bands was damaging the economy by keeping men away from their trades. In May and June 1644 the Savoy militia sub committee paid out £35 for the relief of the families of the Westminster auxiliary regiment, then on active service with Waller around Farnham.[109] In October 1644 the *Parliament Scout* argued that the householders of the trained bands were the most unsuited for active service: 'whose absence puts all into a stand at home, and whose death is usually the beggering of wife and children'.[110]

There were calls for a professional garrison for London from December 1643. In October 1644 the City's fortifications committee began to consider raising a regiment solely to serve on the fortifications, and it was it was reported that the trained bands would rather pay for professional soldiers than continue serving themselves. In 1645 a new, full time, regiment was created to guard the metropolis, which began service in July. The Haberdashers' Company accounts illustrate the falling cost of the militia. Between 5 December 1644 and 9 September 1645 they paid their two substitutes £6 2s, less than 7s a month each and they were subsequently released from further service.[111]

The burden of the militia on the London economy as a whole was not great, probably less than direct taxation, but this disguises wide differences between different sections of society. The rich got off relatively lightly, as they were able to pay for substitutes. For the less well off, who had to serve in person, it was a real burden; they had to provide their own equipment and buy their own provisions while on campaign. Their absence from their work reduced their earnings and their pay came late if at all. If they died on campaign, it was an economic disaster for their families.

---

[108] PRO SP28/268, ff. 366–8; CLRO Jour. 40, f. 266v; *CJ* VI, 249; PRO SP28/265, f. 42. For doubling on the estates of the Deans and Chapters see below p. 67.

[109] PRO SP28/164/3 Account of John Honour for the Savoy Subcommittee.

[110] *The Parliament Scout*, 68, 3–10 October 1644, 543.

[111] CLRO Jour. 40, f. 80v; *The Parliament Scout*, 34, 9–16 February 1644, 290–1; *Mercurius Civicus*, 74, 17–24 October 1644, 690; Nagel, 'Militia of London', 227–32; *The Moderate Intelligencer*, 18, 26 June–3 July 1645, 143; GL MS. 15866/1, f. 524.

Conclusion

In total about £3,466,524 was collected in parliamentary taxation between 1642 and 1650, which was an average of about £433,316 a year. This was slightly over a pound a year for every inhabitant in the metropolis, at a time when the average daily wage of a craftsman in the building industry was 2s 6d.[112] Taxation was undoubtedly much greater than in the early Stuart period, but the size of the total is in some senses deceptive. The very high receipts from the customs and the excise, which between them make up over eighty per cent of the total, were the result of London's role in the economy. Because London was the major port of the country and the major centre for the distribution of consumer goods meant that indirect taxes were predominantly paid in London, where the taxed goods were traded. The goods were distributed throughout the kingdom and it is probable that at least part of the cost of these taxes was passed on to the provinces.

The total receipts also overestimate the drain of resources because a large proportion of the receipts were spent in London. Taxes were used to repay loans raised in London and buy munitions and equipment produced by metropolitan manufacturers, which will be the subjects of the following two chapters. In these cases, taxation represented redistribution, rather than loss, of wealth.

The damage done to the economy by wartime taxation cannot be counted solely in terms of the size of the receipts; fiscal devices such as the twentieth part, the excise and sequestration also disrupted London's economic networks, and in particular links with the provinces. The global totals for receipts also hide wide variations in the impact of taxation. Some sections of the population suffered more than others, the less well off were particularly affected by the extension of indirect taxation and the requirements of serving in the militia, and they probably paid a disproportionate total of the assessment. Among the wealthy, those that were unenthusiastic about the parliamentary cause suffered the twentieth part and the outright royalists ran the risk of sequestration. It is notable how much of the agitation against taxation centred on these concerns rather than the scale of the burden. The burden of taxation exacerbated an already difficult economic situation, rather than being the primary reason for the economic problems themselves.

---

[112] J.P. Boulton, 'Wage Labour in Seventeenth-Century London', *EcHR* 2nd Series, 48 (1996), 279, table 1.

Table 2.1 Receipts from parliamentary taxation

Tax	City	Middlesex Suburbs	Westminster	Southwark	Total
Twentieth Part[1]	£68,997			£3,009	£72,007[2]
First Weekly Assessment[3]	c. £89,000		£2,186	c. £1,920	c. £93,000[4]
Twentieth Part[5]					£109,875[6]
Second Weekly Assessment[7]	n.a.		£1,227		
Fifty Subsidies	£80,589	n.a.	n.a.	n.a.	£80,589
Magazine Money	n.a.	£2,526[8]		£2,191	
Monthly Assessment for Essex's Army[9]	£12,308	£3,013[10]		£704	£16,024
Weekly Meal		£14,069[11]			
Weekly Assessment for the Army in Ireland	c. £21,600		c. £1,183		c. £22,783[12]
Monthly Assessment for the New Model Army	£92,350	£24,048[13]	£7,265	£4,978	£128,640
Monthly Assessment for the Scottish Army	£5,952		c. £849		c. £6,801[14]

---

[1] First assessments, early 1643.
[2] City and Southwark only.
[3] To March 1644.
[4] City and Southwark only.
[5] Assessments made after the tax had been taken over by the Committee for Advance of Money, June 1643–July 1644.
[6] From within a twenty mile radius of London.
[7] To March 1644.
[8] Westminster and the Middlesex suburbs, excluding Tower Hamlets.
[9] To the end of August 1644.
[10] Westminster and the Middlesex suburbs.
[11] Westminster and the Middlesex suburbs, excluding Tower Hamlets.
[12] City and Westminster.
[13] Hundreds of Ossulston and Isleworth.
[14] City and Westminster.

Table 2.1 continued

Tax	City	Middlesex Suburbs	Westminster	Southwark	Total
£60,000 Monthly Assessment	£72,064		c. £3,170	£1,943	c. £77,177[15]
Reassessment for arrears	£23,139	n.a.	n.a.	n.a.	£23,139
Monthly Assessment for the Army in Ireland	£14,234		c. £1,030		c. 15,264[16]
£90,000 monthly assessment[17]	£33,634				
Total direct taxes	c. £490,728		c. £22,818		c. £618,356
Excise[18]					c. £1,323,158
Customs[19]					c. £1,525,010
Total Taxes					c. £3,466,524

The sources for this table are those referenced in B. Coates, 'The Impact of the English Civil War on the Economy of London, 1642–1650', unpublished PhD thesis, University of Leicester, 1997, pp. 47–90. Blanks indicate the data is missing, 'n.a.' (not applicable) indicates that the tax in question did not apply to that part of London.

---

[15]   City, Southwark and Westminster.
[16]   City and Westminster.
[17]   Receipts for the first six months.
[18]   To September 1650.
[19]   July 1642–June 1650.

Chapter 3

Parliamentarian Finance

The City of London was Parliament's major source of credit, and wealthy Londoners feature prominently among the treasurers and commissioners who administered Parliament's financial machinery. There are three aspects of the economic impact of parliamentary finance which need to be addressed: firstly the extent to which London profited or lost from these transactions, secondly whether parliamentary finance drew capital away from other sections of the economy, and thirdly did the war produce long term changes in the financial sector. There were a large number of minor loans raised in the City and Londoners often lent money for very short periods in times of crisis.[1] This makes it difficult to calculate the total amount of money lent towards Parliament's war effort, but by concentrating on the major loans raised by Parliament, it is possible to establish the broad outlines of the economic impact of parliamentary finance.

Loans to Parliament from London came from three sources: general subscriptions, the corporations of the City and Parliament's own treasurers. The interest on the loans, usually eight per cent per annum, and the earnings of the treasurers, brought money into the London economy in the war years, but these benefits were counteracted by Parliament's chronic financial problems. This meant that creditors frequently had major difficulties obtaining repayment. In the early part of the war a large proportion of the money lent to Parliament was on no security but the 'public faith', or the securities contingent on Parliament's victory in the war. As the war continued the loans were increasingly secured on the receipts of taxation, but at first Parliament frequently defaulted on these debts. This meant that a very large amount of money was owed to London creditors by the end of the war. Provisions were made to repay these debts from the sale of confiscated lands, but the way in which this was done, combined with the depressed state of the land market in the late 1640s, meant that it is unlikely that many were able to recover all they were owed.

The argument that the Civil War led to emergence of English private banking, first put forward in the 1670s, has now been largely discarded.

---

[1]   A. Hughes, *Politics, Society and Civil War in Warwickshire, 1620–1660* (Cambridge, 1987), 181; *CCAM*, I, 27.

Nevertheless, it remains a common assumption that the War led to a major expansion in public finances.[2] However this does not necessarily mean that the war saw a major increase in borrowing from the London money market. Public borrowing was already substantial before the war. From the beginning of the Long Parliament in November 1640 and the 1 June 1642 over half a million pounds had been borrowed to fund the settlement of the Bishops' Wars and to fight the Irish Rebellion.[3] Moreover most of the soldiers who fought in the war were part of garrisons and small local armies, who received little money from London, loans or otherwise. In Cheshire the parliamentarian forces only received £30,500 from London, compared to over £250,000 raised locally.[4]

General subscriptions

In June 1642 Parliament issued the 'propositions', calling for voluntary contributions to fight the King. This was the first and greatest general subscription. Those advancing money, plate, horses, horsemen and arms received the 'public faith', promised repayment with eight per cent interest, at some uncertain date in the future.[5] Subsequently there were three further major drives for fresh subscriptions on the propositions: in late August 1642, the middle of September 1642 and in January 1643. Exact figures are missing, but the impression given by the available sources is that these efforts, although initially well supported, proved increasingly unsuccessful.[6]

Anecdotal evidence suggests that in the summer of 1642 vast sums were enthusiastically pledged. On 15 June one correspondent reported 'the citizens are very forward in raising of men, arms, and money and horses…and they bring their plate in abundance to be coined for the raising of money — 'tis thought there will be a million raised that way'.[7] The churchwardens of St Swithin London Stone collected £298, which they made up to £300 and paid to the treasurers on 18 June.[8] On the same day the Commons was informed that large quantities of plate had been brought to the Guildhall. It was reported that

---

[2]   H. Roseveare, *The Financial Revolution, 1660–1760* (Harlow, 1991), 12; M.J. Braddick, *The Nerves of the State: Taxation and the Financing of the English State, 1558–1714* (Manchester, 1996), 37.

[3]   'A Declaration Concerning the Generall Accompts of the Kingdome' (1642), reprinted in *Lord Somers' Tracts*, 16 vols (1748–52), IV, 140–1.

[4]   J.S. Morrill, *Cheshire, 1630–60: County Government and Society during the 'English Revolution'* (Oxford, 1974), 106–7.

[5]   *Firth & Rait*, I, 6–9.

[6]   Ibid., 24–25; CLRO Jour. 39, f. 342v; CLRO Jour. 40, ff. 38–v; *LJ* V, 533–5.

[7]   W.C. and C.E. Treveleyan (eds), *Treveleyan Papers, part 3*, Camden Society 105 (1872), 227.

[8]   PRO SP16/491/24; GL MS. 559/1, St Swithin London Stone, Churchwardens' Accounts, 1602–1725, f. 44.

women contributed their wedding rings, thimbles and bodkins to the cause and that the Guildhall treasury was so overwhelmed with plate that it proved impossible at times to weigh it all.[9]

Returns in the state papers for subscriptions collected in the August drive show that very large sums were collected in the City. In Bishopsgate ward, £1,941 was received and a further £1,475 was subscribed. In comparison, the ward contributed £1,130 to the £50,000 loan to suppress the rebellion in Ireland raised in the autumn of 1641. In the Church and Old Bailey precincts of the ward of Farringdon Without £1,307 was subscribed, which was more than the three month's weekly assessment collected in 1643.[10] In September, in response to an appeal from the Earl of Essex, £100,000 was collected in just four days.[11] In the same month a newsbook reported that 'Plate and mony comes still very fast to Guild-hall, so that not withstanding the vast charge the Parliament is at, the great heaps of money and Plate do not decay'.[12]

In St Olave Southwark £4,151 was collected in money and plate in 1642–43 and £1,030 worth of horses and arms. A further £3,313 was raised in St Saviour Southwark and £575 in St Thomas Southwark. More money was raised in St Thomas' from the propositions than for all the major taxes levied by Parliament up to the autumn of 1644 combined.[13] Southwark was one of the more parliamentarian parts of the metropolis, but other areas also contributed large sums. More than £1,000 was raised in High Holborn.[14] The only accounts of collections covering the whole metropolis that survive concern the listing of horses and arms. These show that horses and arms worth at least £73,960 were subscribed from the summer of 1642 to the autumn of 1643, the vast majority by Londoners. This was only a fraction of total subscriptions on the propositions in London. In the accounts for St Olave Southwark, horses and arms represented only one-fifth of total subscriptions. If this was true of the

---

[9] *CJ* II, 632; K. Lindley, *Popular Politics and Religion in Civil War London* (Aldershot, 1997), 218; E. Hyde, Earl of Clarendon, *The History of the Rebellion and Civil Wars in England* (ed.) W.D. Macray, 6 vols (Oxford, 1888) II, 180; PRO SP28/253B, part 2, 'Interrogatories to be administered to [blank] concerning plate and money upon the Propositions'.

[10] PRO SP16/491/130; PRO SP28/198, part 1, f. 82; PRO SP28/170, account of the weekly assessment in the City of London.

[11] CLRO Jour. 39, f. 342v; CLRO Jour. 40, ff. 38–v; *The Earle of Essex his Letter to Master Speake* (Oxford, 1643), 5–6.

[12] *Speciall Passages*, 7, 20–27 September 1642, 55.

[13] PRO SP28/179, St Olave Southwark Parish Account; PRO SP28/180/260, St Saviour Southwark Parish Account Abbreviated; PRO SP28/179, St Thomas Southwark Parish Account, ff. 11, 43–51; PRO SP19/49, f. 79. There may be some overlap between these totals and early receipts on the 20th part, £34 14s of the Proposition money received in St Thomas Southwark was described as being on assessment.

[14] PRO SP28/167, Account of the collectors of the propositions in High Holborn.

metropolis as a whole, then the total raised on the propositions could amount to nearly £370,000.[15]

In August 1642 Captain Francis Vernon, deputy treasurer of Essex's army, received £100,000 from the proposition treasurers, the vast majority of which undoubtedly came from London.[16] In total the treasurers paid out £821,605 in the early part of the war and although this includes money received from the early loans secured on Parliament's assessment ordinances, the vast majority probably derived from the propositions.[17] It is possible that flow of money from the London economy to the war effort was no greater in the first half of 1643, after parliamentary taxation was introduced, than it had been in the summer and autumn of 1642.

In the earlier stages of the war various groups of Parliament's supporters came forward with schemes to raise forces, for which they were promised the 'public faith' for the money they collected. One of the most substantial of these schemes was approved by Parliament in mid November 1642. A group of Londoners promised to raise additional forces for Parliament to be paid for through a voluntary weekly subscription.[18] The parishioners of St Pancras Soper Lane agreed to support thirty eight men for three months, and those in Allhallows Honey Lane subscribed a further thirty four. By the end of November it was reported that £3,000 per week had been pledged and a month later that £6,659 had been collected. Despite this early success, the weekly subscriptions fizzled out in early 1643. In the parish of St Michael Queenhithe the churchwardens collected a total of £72 5s 6d in December, but the second payment was not made until 1 March, when only £58 12s 4d was raised, after which no further collections are recorded. The subscriptions were even less successful in the suburbs, in St Olave Southwark only £4 6s was collected.[19]

By the end of 1642 Londoners were increasingly weary of lending on the 'public faith'. The later subscription drives for the propositions were relatively unsuccessful. In November 1642 a petition from London complained that many had not paid their subscriptions. On 28 November it was reported that the arrears of subscriptions in Candlewick ward came to £785.[20] The January 1643 subscriptions proved particularly disappointing, only £40,000 had been

---

[15] PRO SP28/131, parts 3–5. There is also a fragment of another account in PRO SP28/237, consequently it is likely that this is a minimum figure.

[16] SP 28/143, f. 4. In the rest of the country receipts from the propositions were generally spent locally, A. Fletcher, *The Outbreak of the English Civil War* (1981), 337–8.

[17] SP 28/170, Payments by the treasurers of money and plate at Guildhall.

[18] *CJ* II, 847; *LJ* V, 445–6; *CCAM* I, 1–3.

[19] *CJ* II, 862; GL MS. 5019/1, St Pancras Soper Lane, Vestry Minutes, 1626–99, f. 83; GL MS. 5026/1, Allhallows Honey Lane, Churchwardens' Accounts, 1618–1743, unfoliated entry between the 1641 and 1642 accounts; *CCAM* I, 6; GL MS. 4825/1, St Michael Queenhithe, Churchwardens' Accounts, 1625–1706, ff. 61, 61v; PRO SP28/179, St Olave Southwark parish account.

[20] *CJ* II, 858; *LJ* V, 391; PRO SP16/492/103.

subscribed by the following month. Despite considerable pressure from the committee for advance of money, a substantial part of what was subscribed then had still not been paid at the end of March. The failure of the January subscriptions reflects the fact that Parliament could no longer hope to fund its war effort from loans without offering security for repayment. This was the last major general drive for subscriptions on the 'public faith' for the main army.[21]

After January 1643 taxation, and loans secured on taxation, were used to finance Essex's Army, but Parliament continued to use unsecured voluntary subscriptions to support the regional forces. In St Olave Southwark £247 was raised for Sir William Waller's West Country forces. The same parish raised £183 for Sir William Brereton's Cheshire forces, and £148 for Sir Thomas Middleton's Army in North Wales. Another £80 was raised for Lord Brooke's Midland forces and £150 for the Earl of Denbigh's.[22] General subscriptions were also used to help fund London's own forces. In May 1643 a subcommittee at Salters' Hall proposed that the inhabitants of London should pledge money equivalent to what they would normally spend on one meal a week to equip the auxiliary militia regiments. However only £1,647 was raised and the weekly meal had to be turned into a compulsory tax.[23]

In 1643 Parliament tried various expedients to give potential lenders at least the impression of greater security without tying up its immediate revenue. In May 1643 a loan of £50,000 was proposed to finance the capture of Newcastle, to be secured on the duties on the coal trade once the north east had been taken from the royalists. This proved unsuccessful, according to an account from November 1644, only a derisory £6,848 was collected in total.[24] More successfully in July 1643 about £11,810 was borrowed when, fearing the approach of the royalists, the City Government offered the security of the City's seal to those willing to lend £50 or more.[25] The largest voluntary subscription after the propositions, was initiated to finance the Scottish Army. In October 1643 an ordinance was passed to borrow £200,000. Creditors were promised repayment out of sequestered estates and, again, the rates on the Newcastle coal trade. In London the loan was highly successful. In St Bartholomew by the Exchange, £156 was rapidly collected, and a further £74 promised, in addition to £120 paid directly by parishioners to the treasurers.

---

[21] Bodl. Tanner MS. 64, reasons against the cessation, f. 131; *CCAM*, I, 11, 13, 17.

[22] PRO SP28/179, St Olave Southwark parish account.

[23] *A Declaration and Motive of the Persons Trusted* (1643); PRO SP 28/198, part 1, 2nd folder, ff. 4–5.

[24] CLRO Jour. 40, ff. 60, 117.

[25] CLRO Jour. 40, ff. 68–v; CLRO MS. 386A Money lent for the Support of City Forces, c. 1643–47/8, IV, f. 3v.

Nearly eighty five per cent of the £80,000 assigned to the City was collected voluntarily.[26]

In St Olave Southwark, over £6,500 was collected on voluntary subscriptions for Parliament in the first Civil War, which may well be more than the parishioners paid in parliamentary taxation. One contemporary estimated that £1.3 million was raised in total on the 'public faith' in the first Civil War.[27] A high proportion of economically self-sufficient inhabitants in the metropolis contributed to the unsecured loans. In 1642 the collectors for Church precinct, Farringdon Without, returned the names of sixty two people they thought capable of contributing to the propositions, of whom fifty were willing to subscribe.[28] In St Michael Queenhithe, a parish with about 130 householders, sixty seven people contributed to the first collection of the weekly subscription.[29] The individual sums given were relatively small; the inhabitants of Church precinct subscribed a total of £699, slightly under £14 each. Alderman Towse, one of the proposition treasurers, contributed only about £156, Alderman Atkin contributed in total £500, on the 'public faith', £300 in September 1642 and £200 in the following March. Both men were wealthy and strong supporters of Parliament, and had lent far larger sums before the war, £1,000 each on one loan in 1641.[30] Many may have contributed for fear of reprisals. From August 1642 the collectors of the propositions were ordered to return the names of those who refused to subscribe. At the end of October 1642 the committee for safety ordered the arrest of fifty six wealthy citizens and clergymen who had refused to contribute.[31] The propositions were beginning to be transformed into taxation, a process completed by the ordinances for the twentieth part.

The Independent minister, Hugh Peters, stated that many had lent more than they could afford. The economic impact was probably mitigated by the greater ability Londoners had to control the level of their contributions than they had with taxation, although this diminished as greater and greater pressure was brought to bear on the recalcitrant. Given the vagueness of the promises of

---

[26] *CCCD*, I, 1; *Firth & Rait*, I, 311–15, 322, 572; GL MS. 4384/2, St Bartholomew by the Exchange, Vestry Minutes, 1643–76, ff. 13–14; D. Laing (ed.), *Letters and Journals of Robert Baillie*, 3 vols (Edinburgh, 1841) II, 104; R. Bell (ed.), *Memorials of the Civil War*, 2 vols (1844), I, 109; PRO E351/1966.

[27] PRO SP28/179, St Olave Southwark Parish Account; M. Pope, *A Treatise of Magistracy* (1647), 121.

[28] PRO SP16/491/130.

[29] GL MS. 4825/1, f. 61; T.C. Dale (ed.), *The Inhabitants of London in 1638*, 2 vols (1931), II, 150–1.

[30] PRO SP16/491/130; *CCAM*, I, 567; BL Add. MS. 22620, Thomas Atkin to the mayor of Norwich, 10 September 1646, f. 80v; PRO SP28/162, Account of Treasurers for £95,900 loan, 1641.

[31] *Firth & Rait*, I, 24–25; *HMC Twelfth Report, II, Cowper MSS*, II, 324; *CJ* II, 819; *An Order of the Committee of the Lords and Commons at Guild-hall for the Defence of the Kingdom* (1642); *A Catalogue of Sundrie Knights, Aldermen, Doctors* (1642).

repayment the vast majority who contributed almost certainly did so, either to support a cause they believed in or to keep out of trouble. That these contributions were regarded as quasi-charitable is suggested by the example of Thomas Colwell of St Bartholomew by the Exchange, who pledged to give the £10 he lent towards the Scots Army in 1643 to the parish when it was repaid. Nevertheless large amounts of capital were being transferred from the civilian economy to the war effort from the summer of 1642.[32]

Underwriting assessments

After the introduction of parliamentary taxation towards the end of 1642, unsecured general subscriptions played a progressively smaller part in parliamentary finance. Loans were raised instead on the security of receipts from taxation. Not all the money advanced on Parliament's taxation ordinances was repaid as promised, and, in practice, a large proportion of these loans became part of the vast outstanding debt owed to Londoners by the end of the war. As a consequence popular enthusiasm for lending waned. In place of large numbers of small subscriptions, parliamentary finance came to be dominated by small numbers of large-scale lenders. The lenders were generally wealthy men closely associated with the parliamentary regime, or the City government, who could afford to wait a long time for repayment, and were sufficiently politically important to discourage Parliament from defaulting.

This transition did not happen at once. The first attempt to raise money on the credit of parliamentary taxation got an enthusiastic response. In November 1642 Parliament appealed to the City for a loan of £30,000 to be repaid out of their newly instituted tax, the twentieth part.[33] A large number of Londoners contributed to the loan. Over a thousand subscribers are recorded in returns from thirty City and Southwark parishes, four individuals contributed £200 each, the highest figure recorded, but most subscriptions were much lower, the average was less than £13.[34] There are many more returns from parishes and hamlets in and around London, at least 111 have survived, although most do not record the names of the individual contributors. These record subscriptions totalling £37,000, and there may be others which are now

---

[32] CLRO Jour. 40, f. 151; H. Peters, *Gods Doings, and Mans Duty* (1646), 45; Idem, *Mr. Peters Last Report of the English Wars* (1646), 11–12; GL MS. 4384/2, f. 13.

[33] *CJ* II, 847, 862; *LJ* V, 445.

[34] PRO SP16/492/66–100. The exact total is uncertain because there are double returns for three parishes. A number of parish returns are missing and some returns mention additional payments made directly to the Guildhall.

missing. This tends to substantiate contemporary newsbook reports that the loan was oversubscribed.[35]

Parliament broke faith with its creditors, and the receipts from the twentieth part were diverted to other uses. When, in the following February, Parliament tried to borrow £60,000 on the security of the weekly assessment, it proved impossible to collect more than about £23,000. In St Andrew Wardrobe only £55 was subscribed, compared with £109 on the £30,000 loan. In St James Garlickhithe no one was willing to subscribe to the loan. Even the radical parliamentarian William Walwyn refused. Parliament turned to the Court of Aldermen, who were asked for £40,000, but some prominent aldermen were reluctant to lend. To reassure Londoners Parliament ordered that the receipts of the weekly assessment from London be paid to the proposition treasurers, who were City aldermen, instead of the treasurer of the army. Furthermore the treasurers were ordered to repay the loans before making any other payments.[36]

Despite these promises, in early May Parliament sent the first £23,000 received from the weekly assessment in London to the Army. The first lenders were now told that they would have to wait until the £40,000 borrowed from the aldermen had been paid off, although they received the additional security of the receipts from the weekly assessment in Westminster, Southwark, Middlesex, Hertfordshire, Essex and Suffolk, and also the twentieth part. A further attempt was made to raise £17,000 from the common councillors on the credit of the weekly assessment, but they only subscribed £7,261.[37] Londoners lent about £70,000 on the security of the first weekly assessment, all, or most, of which was still owed at the end of the war.[38]

It is hardly surprising that when Parliament was looking for a new loan on the credit of the second weekly assessment ordinance, it had to be raised as a forced loan from the livery companies.[39] An attempt to raise £20,000 in April 1644 on the security of the excise to pay the trained bands then serving with Waller was a failure. On 2 May 1644 it was reported that only £6,000 had been subscribed, and the rest of the money had to be raised from funds that had been assigned to repay loans from the livery companies.[40] It is a sign of the growing

---

[35]   PRO SP16/492/65–101; PRO SP19/78, ff. 1–2, 5, 8, 7, 11, 27, 29, 91–105. *Speciall Passages*, 16, 22–29 November 1642, 138; *Speciall Passages*, 17, 29 November–6 December 1642, 139, 143; *A Continuation of Certain Speciall and Remarkable Passages*, 21, 24 November–1 December 1642, 5.

[36]   *CJ* II, 971, 983, 999; GL MS. 2088/1, St Andrew Wardrobe, Churchwardens' Accounts, unfoliated entries between the 1641–2 and 1642–3 accounts; PRO SP19/79, ff. 37, 86; V. Pearl, *London and the Outbreak of the Puritan Revolution. City Government and National Politics, 1625–43* (Oxford, 1961), 260, 267; *Firth & Rait*, I, 98, 128–9.

[37]   *Firth & Rait*, I, 143–4; PRO SP19/79, f. 86.

[38]   PRO SP28/256, Notes of bills doubled at Goldsmith Hall.

[39]   CLRO Jour. 40, ff. 71v, 72v.

[40]   CLRO Jour 40, ff. 91v, 93Bv, 94v.

stability of parliamentary finance that the money was repaid but lenders continued to lack confidence in Parliament. Consequently when in October 1644 Parliament borrowed £22,000 on the security of the excise provision was made to compel wealthy Londoners to pay an assessed proportion if the full sum could not be raised voluntarily. Those who paid willingly profited from the loan. Those who lent in Westminster were repaid their principal, with interest at eight per cent within a year as the ordinance had specified.[41]

When Parliament decided to create the New Model Army in early 1645 they realized that a substantial loan from the City would be needed to finance the reorganization. Consequently they approached the City to raise £80,000 on the security of the new monthly assessment ordinance. In order to reassure subscribers Parliament agreed to allow the lenders to nominate the treasurers who were to receive the receipts from the assessments and repay the loan.[42] Only seventy eight lenders were willing to trust Parliament with their money but the subscriptions were much larger than those for the £30,000 loan in 1642, about two-thirds were for £500 or above. The most common sum lent was £1,000, the largest £5,350. The most substantial subscribers were the eight treasurers who, between them, contributed £36,250, or about forty five per cent of the total.[43] The vast majority of the lenders were Londoners; over ninety per cent of the money came from freemen of the City. All but three aldermen subscribed, and their subscriptions came to £40,000, half the total. At least twenty six of the remainder were common councillors in 1645, who lent a further £24,316, consequently more than eighty per cent of the money came from members of the City government.[44]

The economic interests of those who subscribed were diverse. Seven of the subscribers were members of the committee of the East India Company, and various other subscribers had strong connections with the company, twenty one were investors in the first particular voyage.[45] On the other hand, four subscribers were members of the Courteen association, or Assada adventurers, which competed with the company for the East Indies' trade. Several

---

[41] GL MS. 2596/2, St Mary Magdalene Milk Street, Churchwardens' Accounts, 1806–67, f. 91v; *Firth & Rait*, I, 526–28; PRO SP28/162, Account of the Treasurer at Savoy, Account of Money lent for the City Guard.

[42] *CJ* IV, 74; *Firth & Rait*, I, 656–660; CLRO Jour. 40, f. 125.

[43] PRO SP28/350/5, part 2; *Firth & Rait*, I, 656.

[44] The Aldermen were identified from A. Beavan, *The Aldermen of the City of London*, 2 vols (1908–13); there is no complete list of common councillors for this period, the 26 were identified either from journal of the Common Council or from parish and ward records. A handful of subscribers, notably Sir John Maynard and Richard Newdigate, were not connected with the government of the City. Nevertheless the connection with the corporation is almost certainly underestimated. Other subscribers, such as Stephen Estwicke, are highly likely to have been common councillors in 1645.

[45] *CCMEIC*, 1644–49, 32; BL IOL/H/6, East India Company, Home Miscellaneous, ff. 113–179.

prominent Merchant Adventurers advanced money, including John Kendrick and Christopher Pack. There were also a number of internal traders and manufacturers among the lenders, including drapers such as James Bunce and Robert Tichborne, the distiller Edward Hooker and the cutler Lawrence Bromfield.[46] A number of the subscribers had conservative political backgrounds, including Sir John Cordell, who had been imprisoned in 1642 for refusing to subscribe to the propositions. A further six had subscribed to the Benyon petition in February 1642 calling for control of the London militia to be returned to the royalist lord mayor, Sir Richard Gurney. Only one of the lenders was a woman, Katherine Highlord, who was the widow of an alderman.[47]

Repayment of the loan was delayed by problems in collecting the assessment, but the creditors did receive their entire principal back, plus interest. The last repayment was made on 13 January 1646. In total £83,610 had been paid out in principal and interest, suggesting that the lenders cleared a profit of 4.5 per cent. This was low because some of the money was not received until July 1645, and the lenders received the first third of their capital back again in late September and early October. Only three repayments were collected by assignees of the subscribers rather than by, or for, the original investors. If this was typical then it suggests that there was little trading in parliamentary securities during the Civil War, probably because of an underlying lack of confidence in Parliament's credit.[48]

The ordinances that established the weekly assessment to pay for the forces in Ireland also contained provisions to borrow money on the security of the receipts, but the only substantial sum raised in this way was a loan of £40,000 raised from the assessment treasurers in May 1646.[49] Greater sums were raised for the Scottish army. Unlike the £200,000 loan initiated when the Scots entered the war in 1643, the subsequent borrowing was secured on immediate receipts from sequestration and compositions. Parliament borrowed over £40,000 in Spanish dollars and rials for the Scottish army from Merchant Adventurers and London Goldsmiths, mostly in 1644. The introduction of the monthly assessment to pay for the Scottish army in 1645 provided further security for borrowing. In June Parliament borrowed £31,000 on the security of the first assessment ordinance and a further £30,000 was requested in October.

---

[46] R. Brenner, *Merchants and Revolution, Commercial Change, Political Conflict and London's Overseas Traders, 1550–1653* (Cambridge, 1993), 192–3, 489.

[47] Pearl, *London and the Outbreak of the Puritan Revolution*, 292–308; HLRO House of Lords Main Papers, 24 February 1642, Petition of the Citizens of London.

[48] PRO SP28/350/5, part 2; *Firth & Rait*, I, 818.

[49] H. Hazlett, 'The Financing of the British Armies in Ireland, 1641–9', *Irish Historical Studies* 1 (1936–9), 33; *Firth & Rait*, I, 851.

In total the £115,180 was repaid, with £1,998 interest, on loans for the Scottish army.[50]

The Long Parliament continued to use the excise to fund substantial loans; in 1645 they raised £60,000 for the New Model Army in this way. In February 1646 a further £32,000 was raised on the excise to fund London's fortifications and guards. However by September 1645 the London press was reporting that fears that the excise was becoming overburdened with loans made lenders reluctant to advance more money on its security. Consequently Parliament continued to make provisions to compel lenders if necessary. The City authorities charged with raising these loans seem to have found it necessary to search further and further afield to raise the loans. In January 1646 Sir Cheny Culpeper, a Kentish parliamentarian, was ordered to lend money although he claimed he could not afford to. The City had great difficulties raising the £32,000 for the fortifications. In June 1646 the Common Council had to authorize the committee for arrears to borrow £5,000 on the security of the future receipts of the loan. In August it was reported that the whole £32,000 had been raised, however in many cases the City's creditors were given assignments to receive what they were owed out of the excise office. Rather than trying to borrow fresh money the City had transferred its debts to the excise.[51]

In July 1646 Parliament tried to raise a further £50,000 on the security of the excise to fund its forces in Ireland. Unlike the previous excise loans this was to be voluntary. Consequently it proved very difficult to raise the money, even after lenders were offered a substantial premium over and above the legal maximum rate of eight per cent interest. The parliamentarians were reluctant to openly break the law so lenders were sold assignments on the excise at a discount. For example the churchwardens of St Olave Jewry purchased an assignment for £110, payable out of the excise with eight per cent per annum payable every six months, for £100. In total only £46,491 was received, for which Parliament was committed to pay 8.6 per cent interest plus £3,509 when the loan was due to be repaid. Despite the inducements only £12,700 was received by 23 September; the whole sum was not raised until 16 February 1646.[52]

---

[50] *CCCD*, I, 2, 3, 4, 5, 9, 17, 21 22; *CJ* IV, 173, 186, 188, 298, 305–6, 362, 369; *Firth & Rait*, I, 702–3; PRO E351/1966.

[51] *Firth & Rait*, I, 526–28, 723–5, 786–9; *CJ* IV, 413, 426; PRO E351/302; *The Moderate Intelligencer*, 27, 28 August–4 September 1645, [216]; M.J. Braddick and M. Greengrass (eds), 'The Letters of Sir Cheney Culpeper (1641–1657)', in *Seventeenth-Century Political and Financial Papers*, Camden Society, Fifth Series, 7 (1996), 257; CLRO Jour 40, ff. 167v, 173v, 186v, 189v.

[52] *LJ VIII*, 440–1; *CSPI, 1633–47*, 497, 518; PRO SP28/139/13; GL MS. 4415/1, St Olave Old Jewry, Vestry Minutes, 1574–1680, ff. 133v, 134; GL MS. 4409/2, St Olave Old Jewry, Churchwardens' Accounts, 1643–1705, unfoliated.

Lending on the security of the excise was becoming increasingly unpopular in London. This is despite the fact that lenders received their principal and interest in full. The unpopularity was almost certainly in part a continued legacy of Parliament's failure to repay the loans it first raised on the security of its taxation ordinances. It also reflected uncertainties about when the loans would be repaid. The ordinances for the excise loans did not give a specific date for repayment, stating merely that they would be repaid 'in course', when the money became available after previous commitments had been repaid. The £50,000 loan raised to fund the war in Ireland in 1646 was not repaid until three years later; in a period when loans were rarely made for longer than twelve months.[53]

Nevertheless Parliament's financial administration improved considerably in the latter stages of the war, and her creditors began to make a profit on their loans. It is a sign that some confidence was returning to parliamentary finance that those entrusted with public and charitable funds were beginning to be willing to lend money to Parliament. The churchwardens of St Mary Magdalene Milk Street advanced £50 for the Scottish Army in October 1645. Loans on the security of the excise may not have been popular but they were trusted. The governors of Christ's Hospital advanced £100 from a legacy in late 1645 on the security of the excise, and added a further £100 in the following year.[54]

The still shaky confidence in Parliament's finances was rocked by the political crisis of the summer of 1647. In the following October the governors of Christ's decided that it was to dangerous to keep money at the excise office, instead the money was transferred to private hands, although the interest on offer was only six per cent.[55] The loss of confidence is exemplified by the difficulties experienced trying to raise £80,000 in the autumn of 1647 for the army, on the security of the £60,000 monthly assessment. The army treasurers advanced £30,000, but there were difficulties in raising the rest of the money. Some Londoners offered to re-lend sums that they were due to be repaid from the excise on the fortifications loan of February 1646, and it was reported that others were willing to lend fresh sums to make up a total of £32,000. In October 1647 Parliament passed an ordinance securing the £32,000 on the monthly assessment. Only £11,800 was raised, but those who did lend received their money and interest promptly.[56]

Towards the end of the decade Londoners were increasingly unwilling to advance money to Parliament. In 1649 the Commonwealth failed to persuade

---

[53]   GL MS. 4415/1, f. 143.
[54]   GL MS. 2596/2, f. 91v; M. Pope, *A Treatise of Magistracy* (1647), 117; GL MS. 12819/7, Christ's Hospital, Treasurers' Accounts, 1645–52, accounts for 1645–6, and 1646–7.
[55]   GL MS. 12806/4, Christ's Hospital, Court Minutes, 1632–49, f. 522.
[56]   *Firth & Rait*, I, 1019–21; *LJ* IX, 472–3; PRO E351/302; PRO SP28/350/5, part 2.

the City to lend £120,000 on the security of the monthly assessment. Moreover the excise became overburdened with debts and as result payments to lenders were becoming even slower than before. By July 1649 the churchwardens of St Olave Old Jewry had not received interest on the money they had advanced on the £50,000 loan for the forces in Ireland for over a year, although previously they had been paid every six months. In April 1649 a large number of debts were transferred from the security of the excise. Although many of the debts were assigned to the receipts from the sale of the estates of the Deans and Chapters, creditors could not be sure that this would yield enough money to pay them. When the City was approached to lend £150,000 on the security of the excise in July less than one-third of that sum was forthcoming, even though lenders were promised prompt repayment and that their debts would not be transferred to another branch of the revenue. Even this limited success may only have been achieved because the £50,000 loan raised to fund the war in Ireland on the security of the excise in 1646 was now about to be repaid. The lenders were allowed to transfer their capital to the new loan at the nominal value they had been given to disguise the higher interest rates Parliament had been forced to offer. Indeed those who did re-lend their money may have done so out of a fear that if they did not their debts would be transferred to a more doubtful security, or not repaid at all.[57]

Doubling

By the end of the first Civil War very large numbers of Londoners were owed money by Parliament, not only for loans on the 'public faith', but also for loans raised on the early taxation ordinances, and the City began to press Parliament for repayment. Consequently, when in September 1646, Parliament approached the City about raising £200,000 to pay off the Scottish Army, the Common Council suggested the procedure that became known as 'doubling'. Those who had previously lent money on the 'public faith' were encouraged to double their loan: to lend as much again as Parliament already owed them in principal and interest, in return for which they were promised repayment of the combined debt out of the receipts of the sale of the Bishops' lands. In addition they would receive interest at eight per cent for the combined debt, every six months, from the excise.[58]

---

[57] H.J. Habakkuk, 'Public Finance and the Sale of Confiscated Property during the Interregnum', *EcHR* 2nd Series, 15 (1962–63), 83; *CJ* VI, 183, 191–2, 249, 258; *Firth & Rait*, II, 99–101, 102, 158–60; PRO E351/1295, f. 18; GL MS. 4415/1, ff. 143, 146v; GL MS. 4409/2, unfoliated.
[58] BL Add. MS. 15903, Thomas Atkin to the mayor of Norwich, 23 November 1646, f. 61; CLRO Jour. 40, f. 191v; *Firth & Rait*, I, 884.

Doubling at first proved spectacularly successful. The £200,000 was raised in eight days. When Parliament wanted to raise another £200,000 in May 1647 the same procedure was followed and the money was raised in only seven days. Such was the popularity of doubling that it even attracted the generally conservative City corporations. The governors of Bridewell Hospital doubled £100 in May 1647 and the Apothecaries' Company debated whether to double money they had lent Parliament in 1642 towards suppressing the Irish rebellion. A third ordinance raised a further £42,000 in June, but by this time the enthusiasm was beginning to fade.[59] Subscriptions were still open in November 1648 when the Fishmongers' Company decided to double money they were owed for arms they had contributed to Parliament. It is a sign of the declining confidence in the subscriptions that in the same month the parishioners of St Swithin London Stone decided not to double the money they had contributed on the propositions in June 1642 but instead to petition Parliament for repayment.[60]

The bills brought to the treasurers for doubling on the first ordinance included not only the propositions, but also those loans raised on the security of parliamentary taxation that had not been repaid, such as the £30,000 loan of December 1642 and other outstanding loans including the £200,000 raised for the Scottish Army in October 1643. Londoners were also able to double on some of the taxes they had paid. Those who had paid their twentieth part promptly had been given 'public faith', and they were even able to double on their bills for the weekly assessment from 1643, having been promised repayment of sixty per cent of the assessment on the 'public faith'. There is no evidence that bills from the forced loan of fifty subsidies, for which the City seal rather than the 'public faith' had been given, or debts owed by Parliament from before the Civil War, were used to double on the first ordinance. These debts were explicitly included in the second ordinance, which may explain the continued enthusiasm for doubling. Doubling, therefore, probably covered the majority of the taxes and loans raised by Parliament from London in the early part of the Civil War.[61]

As the ordinances permitted doubling on assigned bills, those who could not afford to double could sell their bills. On the eve of the opening of subscriptions for the first ordinance, it was reported that 'public faith' bills were circulating at almost their full value in London, this is confirmed by the requests from some subscribers to lend more than double their 'public faith'

---

[59] *Firth & Rait*, I, 928–35, 948–953; PRO SP28/350/2; GL MS. 33063/1, Bridewell Hospital, Treasurers' Accounts, 1643–48, unfoliated; GL MS. 8200/1, Apothecaries' Company, Court Minutes, 1617–51, f. 459v.

[60] GL MS. 5570/4, Fishmongers' Company, Court Minutes, 1646–64, f. 102; GL MS. 560/1, St Swithin London Stone, Vestry Minutes, 1647–1729, unfoliated.

[61] PRO SP28/256, Notes of bills doubled at Goldsmiths' Hall; *Firth & Rait*, I, 928–35.

bills. Had bills been available at a discount it would have been cheaper to buy the bills and double, than subscribe the whole amount in new money.[62] However demand never again reached the same levels, and the value of bills suffered accordingly. Shortly after the closing of subscriptions on the first ordinance public faith bills were sold in London at fourteen to fifteen shillings in the pound, and four days before the opening of subscriptions on the second ordinance they were still valued at only three-quarters of their face value.[63] Prices subsequently fell to nine to twelve shillings in the pound as confidence in doubling declined.[64]

Habakkuk has argued that during the Commonwealth doubling on other confiscated properties was increasingly less successful, but the evidence suggests that the ability of the new regime to raise money varied according to perceptions of its political and financial stability. In the early days of the Commonwealth, the perception was clearly not good. In April 1649 the Rump attempted to raise £300,000 by doubling on the capitular estates, but the money came in slowly. In June the number of debts that could be doubled was extended, and the interest on the 'public faith' bills that were not doubled was reduced to six per cent. According to a report to the Council of State in the following October, only £170,833 had been received. The growing military strength of the Commonwealth then inspired a renewal of confidence, by October 1650 the £300,000 loan had been oversubscribed, and a subsequent £120,000 loan on the remaining estates of the Deans and Chapters was successful; in total £455,621 was raised from doubling on capitular lands. In February 1651 a £250,000 doubling loan on the fee farm rents also proved successful. The first doubling loan on the sale of royalist confiscated estates, initiated in July 1651 for £250,000, proved so successful that an additional £14,446 was deposited with the treasurers in expectation of a further loan. However receipts on further doubling loans on the fee farm rents and royalist estates, initiated during the First Dutch War, fell short of expectations. An attempt to raise £600,000 on a third batch of royalist land sales in November 1652 raised only £114,644, and the attempt to raise £400,000 by doubling on the royal forests in 1653 brought in no money at all. This suggests that creditors took fright at the deterioration of public finances resulting from the Dutch War. In total over £1.75 million of debts were secured on the various doubling loans.[65]

---

[62] D. Gardiner (ed.), *Oxinden and Peyton Letters, 1642–1670* (1937), 92; BL Add. MS. 15903, f. 61; *CJ* II, 726.

[63] BL Add. MS. 28001, Oxinden Correspondence, f. 178v; CLRO Rep. 58/2, f. 103.

[64] PRO E101/699/20; PRO C8/140/40; *The Second Centurie* (1648); A.H. Johnson, *The History of the Worshipful Company of Drapers of London*, 5 vols (Oxford, 1914–22), III, 219; P. Chamberlen, *The Poore Mans Advocate* (1649), 16.

[65] Habakkuk, 'Public Finance', 73, 74, 83–4; *Firth & Rait*, II, 91, 140–2, 154, 498, 531, 582, 615, 947; *CJ* VI, 223, 249, 253 475; *CJ* VII, 210; *CSPD*, 1649–50, 359; W.A. Shaw,

For those Londoners who doubled, the profitability of their investment depended on the sales of confiscated lands. The doubled bills could be redeemed from the receipts of the sales of the confiscated lands, or could be used to purchase them. The latter was favoured, and only a very small amount of cash was realized from the sales. Ian Gentles argued that the episcopal lands were sold at a considerable discount and that those who used their doubled bills to purchase lands made high profits. The lands were sold after only hasty surveys, which undervalued their rental value. Moreover the sales were generally at eleven to twelve years' purchase, much lower than the eighteen to twenty years which was usual in the seventeenth century.[66]

Rents fell substantially during the 1640s, and the surveys may well have accurately reported current values. Moreover in the late 1640s the land market was depressed. In 1648–49, when most of the episcopal lands were sold, fifteen to sixteen years' purchase was common for other sales. This still suggests that the lands were sold at a discount but this is not surprising. Up until Charles II's defeat at Worcester in 1651 the survival of the new regime looked doubtful. Potential purchasers would have been well aware that the restoration of the monarchy would immediately throw the legality of the land sales into question. The return of prosperity in the 1650s, and growing confidence in the survival of the Protectorate meant that the value of the former episcopal lands rose substantially. As a consequence those who had purchased lands and later resold them could make a substantial profit, often forty per cent.[67]

Most Londoners had no intention of buying confiscated lands; instead they sold their doubled bills. Only about one-third of the episcopal lands were sold to London merchants and tradesmen, although contemporaries complained that Londoners monopolized the doubling subscriptions, and probably at first held the majority of the bills. All doubled bills were heavily discounted. Bills on the episcopal estates were sold at fifteen to thirty per cent less than their face value in the late 1640s, rising to thirty five per cent in early 1652. Habakkuk says that bills on the capitulator estates were generally traded at a twenty five to thirty per cent discount, but this may be an underestimate as the churchwardens of St Margaret Westminster were able to buy them at a forty

---

A History of the English Church during the Civil War and under the Commonwealth, 2 vols (1900), II, 515; PRO E351/438.

[66] Habakkuk, 'Public Finance', 72–5, 86 & n. 1; I. Gentles, 'The Sales of Bishops' Lands in the English Revolution, 1646–1660', *EHR* 95 (1980), 582, 585.

[67] J. Broad, 'Gentry Finances and the Civil War: The Case of the Buckinghamshire Verneys', *EcHR* 2nd series, 32 (1979), 186–8, 193; Gentles, 'Sales of Bishops' Lands', 585, 587; G.B. Tatham, 'The Sale of Episcopal Lands During the Civil War and Commonwealth', *EHR* 23 (1908), 108.

per cent discount. The discount on bills for royalist lands was even greater, probably nearly forty five per cent.[68]

The first three doubling ordinances produced £884,000 worth of doubled bills, but the sales of episcopal lands came to only £676,387. The bills from the first ordinance, called Goldsmiths' Hall bills, were given priority in purchasing episcopal lands. Bills from the two latter ordinances, called Weavers' Hall bills, could not be used to buy lands until most of the Goldsmiths' Hall bills had been liquidated. By the end of 1652 Weavers' Hall bills totalling £256,574 were still outstanding, although virtually all the Bishops' lands had been sold. The subscribers had also been promised the estates of royalists as additional security, but after consultation with the creditors, the Rump decided to transfer the debt to the excise. In December 1653 the Protectorate Council of State stopped repayment of the principal, consequently £222,082 worth of bills were still in circulation at the Restoration. The payment of interest out of the excise continued throughout the intervening period, but the holders of the bills never recovered their principal.[69]

Most of Parliament's creditors suffered losses in the way the Long Parliament settled its debts. A few who purchased episcopal estates profited, and those who sold their 'public faith' bills in November 1646 probably recovered nearly all the money they had lent. Those who sold their public faith bills after November 1646, or who doubled and then sold their bills lost at least part of what they had lent to Parliament. Moreover many Londoners failed to double. The money contributed by the parishioners of St Swithin London Stone in June 1642 on the propositions was still recorded as owing in the parish accounts in the late 1660s.[70] Over £90,000 was borrowed on the security City seal from the summer of 1643 to fight the royalists, either as voluntary subscriptions or as the forced loan of fifty subsidies. Of this money less than forty per cent was doubled, £58,215 was still outstanding at the Restoration.[71]

Nonetheless many of the securities doubled, especially those from the weekly assessment and fifty subsidies had probably been long written off as taxes. Indeed many Londoners may have had little expectation of receiving any part of what they had paid towards the propositions, regarding the money as

---

[68]   BL Add. MS. 28001, ff. 178–v; Gentles, 'Sales of Bishops' Lands', 583, 588–9; CLRO Rep. 62, f. 93v; Habakkuk, 'Public Finance', 81 & n. 2; WAC E30, St Margaret Westminster, Churchwardens' Accounts, 1650–1.

[69]   Habakkuk, 'Public Finance', 79; Gentles, 'Sales of Bishops' Lands', 592–593; CSPD, 1653–54, 448; CJ VIII, 238–241. The payment of interest on Weavers' Hall Bills from 1653 to 1659 is recorded in the excise accounts, PRO E351/1297, f. 15; PRO AO1/889/3, f. 4v; PRO AO1/890/5 unfoliated; PRO AO1/891/7, f. 5; PRO AO1/891/9, f. 7; PRO E351/1298, f. 4v; PRO E351/1299, f. 4v.

[70]   GL MS. 559/1, f. 72.

[71]   CLRO, Alchin Papers, Q/CV, Bonds (Extracts from Reporteries) for which the City's Seal was given in the Troubles and alphabetical lists of Persons lending money, 1643–80; CLRO MS. 386A.

political contributions rather than investments. It is therefore possible that any returns from these sums were regarded as a bonus. In this way doubling mitigated the financial cost of the Civil War to the inhabitants of London.[72]

Corporate lending

Two groups of potential lenders existed over whom Parliament was able to exert a greater degree of pressure to lend money; firstly, the corporations of the City, the livery and merchant companies, and, secondly, Parliament's own revenue officers. Although the City corporations were only a relatively small source of finance for Parliament their lending had a significant impact on the companies themselves. While the livery companies struggled to receive repayment of even a small proportion of what they lent the merchant companies not only got back most of what they lent, with interest, they also frequently derived significant non-financial benefits.

In October 1640 £50,000 was borrowed from the livery companies to provide funds until the Long Parliament could meet, followed in June 1642 by a loan of £100,000 to suppress the rebellion in Ireland. On 11 August 1643 the Common Council agreed to borrow a further £50,000 from the livery companies for the army, on the security of the second weekly assessment ordinance. The companies were expected to provide a set quota for each loan. This was assessed in accordance with the amount of corn the company had to keep in store, to be sold in times of bad harvest.[73]

Some companies, such as the Cordwainers, paid their proportions promptly. Others proved more obdurate. The Clothworkers protested that they could not pay their existing debts. On 17 August 1643 the Assistants of the Pewterers' Company claimed that their debts were greater than their assets, and their members could not raise the money because of the decline in trade, and their own heavy taxes. A meeting with the 'better sort' of the yeomanry also produced no results. At a court held on 28 September 'with divers of the generality' about the loan, only one member was willing to advance £5 towards the loan.[74] At the end of September it was reported to the Commons that about £20,000 was still in arrears. In October £1,000 had to be borrowed from the prominent London parliamentarian, Stephen Estwicke, because of delays in the collection of the loan. He was promised repayment out of the receipts from

---

[72]   Habakkuk, 'Public Finance', 86; *CJ* VI 608.

[73]   CLRO Jour. 40, f. 70v; CLRO Minutes of Common Hall, I, f. 79v; *LJ* VI, 195; Ashton, *Crown and the Money Market*, 135–6.

[74]   GL MS. 7353/1, Cordwainers' Company, Court Minutes, 1622–53, f. 262; CH, Orders of Court, 1639–49, f. 83v; GL MS. 7090/4, Pewterers' Company, Court Minutes, 1611–43, ff. 352, 353–v, 354.

the loan, but was still waiting for his money in January 1645.[75] Parliament threatened to sequester the lands of those companies in arrears, but this was not carried through. Nevertheless there was a protracted struggle until 1645 between the committee for advance of money and the more recalcitrant companies.[76]

Most of the livery companies were unable to raise the loan from their own resources. Their wealth came from legacies from deceased members and consequently their expenditure was tied to charitable projects of various kinds. They were generally compelled to borrow to pay the loan. This need not have been a problem if the loan was repaid promptly. Even a craft based company like the Cordwainers was able to borrow the necessary money at seven per cent interest, one per cent less than the companies had been promised by Parliament.[77]

In May 1644 the receipts that had been assigned to repay the livery companies were diverted to pay the trained bands on active service. Instead the companies were promised repayment out of the excise. In April and May 1645 the companies that had paid promptly received one-third of their principal back, plus the interest due on that third. The City tried to persuade the companies to re-lend the major part of their repayments for the Cheshire forces, but only three were willing to do so, contributing £1,500.[78] No further repayments were forthcoming and this was the last time the livery companies lent substantial sums of money to the Long Parliament. The Rump tried to persuade the companies to double the money they had lent on the £100,000 loan on the capitular estates in 1649, but by this time confidence in parliamentary finance had collapsed. The Drapers' Company preferred to try to sell their part of the debt, even if it meant accepting ten shillings in the pound.[79]

Lending to Parliament left the livery companies heavily indebted. In November 1652 the Grocers' Company claimed that the total amount they had lent the state, together with the accumulated interest, came to £30,180, of which they had received only £1,237, which left £28,943 still outstanding, while the company's own debts totalled £13,725. In that year the company spent £7,417, of which £4,250 was debt repayments, and a further £1,335 interest. In 1651, in an effort to increase its immediate receipts, even at

---

[75] *CCAM*, I, 337; *CJ* IV, 12–13.

[76] W.P. Harper, 'Public Borrowing, 1640–1650', unpublished MSc thesis University of London, 1927, 67; *CCAM*, I, 114–16.

[77] Harper, 'Public Borrowing', 67; GL MS. 7353/1, f. 262; *LJ* VI, 195.

[78] CLRO Jour. 40, f. 94; CLRO Rep. 57/1, ff. 167v–168v; GH, Court Book, W, 1642–5, ff. 225–v, 291–v, 293v–4; PRO SP28/168, f. 157; GL MS. 7351/2, Cordwainers' Company, Wardens' Accounts, 1636–78, 1644–45 accounts.

[79] *Firth & Rait*, II, 140; GL MS. 8200/1, f. 459v; Johnson, *History of the Worshipful Company of Drapers*, III, 219.

the expense of its long-term revenue, the Court of Assistants ordered all the company's existing and new leases be made up to ninety nine years. At the same time the Court also cut back expenditure, ordering that all the company's pensions and exhibitions to scholars not founded by specific benefactors should cease.[80] Lending to Parliament was a major blow to the finances of the livery companies, which diminished the role they played in London society and contributed to their declining importance in the second half of the seventeenth century.

The Long Parliament also borrowed substantial sums from the merchant companies, generally in return for the confirmation of their privileges. In December 1641 the Merchant Adventurers offered to lend £50,000 towards the costs of suppressing the Irish rebellion; this was soon made up to £70,000 and in return in May 1642 a bill was introduced in the Commons to confirm the company's charter. It was read twice and committed but got no further. Nevertheless the Merchant Adventurers did get their money back, plus interest.[81] In December 1642 the company offered to lend £20,000, presumably to encourage Parliament to pass a draft ordinance which they had presented ten days earlier to confirm their charter. Parliament failed to take up the loan, but in the following August they opened negotiations with the Merchant Adventurers to advance £60,000 for the navy. The company was offered the security of the customs from March 1644, the right to nominate the customs' commissioners, and confirmation of their privileges. The company agreed to lend the money, but when they insisted on receiving the customs from Michaelmas 1643 (which contradicted Parliament's commitment to the existing commissioners) the loan was rejected.[82] Finally in the following October the Merchant Adventurers lent £30,000 for the navy on the security of the excise, and in return Parliament confirmed their charter. The company was promised repayment of one-third of their principal every three months, but in the following January they were persuaded to lend £10,000, presumably the first instalment of their principal, for six months for Waller's forces in the west. The repayment of the final £10,000 due in July was repeatedly deferred, but the loan was probably eventually repaid.[83]

---

[80] GL MS. 11571/13, Grocers' Company, Wardens' Accounts, 1642–52, 1651–2 accounts; GL MS. 11588/4, Grocers' Company, Court Minutes, 1640–68, ff. 266, 267, 271; In 1650 the Cordwainers' Company sold lands totalling £790 to repay their debts, GL MS. 7353/1, ff. 340, 351, 353.

[81] Coates, *D'Ewes*, 348; *CJ* II, 357, 588, 591; PRO SP28/162, Accounts' of the Treasurers of the Act for raising £400,000, ff. 19–20; PRO SP28/237, The Merchant Adventurers Account of Money Issued forth for the use of the Parliament.

[82] C. Thompson (ed.), *Walter Yonge's Diary of Proceedings in the House of Commons 1642–1645, Vol. 1, 19th September 1642–7th March 1643* (Wivenhoe, 1986), 211; *CJ* II, 893; *CJ* III, 222, 235, 236, 237, 239, 243; BL Harl. MS. 165, Parliamentary Journal of Sir Simonds D'Ewes, 1641–43, f. 194v.

[83] *CJ* III, 255, 265, 274, 364, 405–6, 417, 582, 722; *CJ* IV 104; *CJ* VI, 15.

Parliament borrowed further sums from the Merchant Adventurers in the latter part of the decade. In November 1647 the company lent £15,000 in return for a promise that Parliament would repay £8,804 which the company had paid to the King of Denmark for a shipment of arms he had sent to the royalists in 1643, which had been intercepted by the parliamentarians. The combined debt was secured on the excise. A year later £10,000 was borrowed for the navy, which was repaid out of the customs. By April 1649 £10,000 plus interest had been repaid out of the excise, the remaining £13,804 owed to the company was transferred to the capitular lands. This debt could not be used for the purchase of lands, and, as only a very small amount of money was raised in cash for the land sales in September 1650, the debt was removed from this security.[84]

The Merchant Adventurers' Company was by far the largest single lender to Parliament. In November 1643 the navy committee was authorized to negotiate with any company of merchants for loans on the security of the excise on meat and salt. The committee negotiated a loan for £8,000 from the Levant Company and another for £6,000 from the East India Company. In return the Commons passed ordinances for the confirmation of the charters of both companies, although that for the East India Company was blocked in the Lords. The records of the Levant Company show that their loan was repaid, although they did not receive the interest until March 1646, and it seems probable that the East India Company was also repaid. Once the Levant Company had received confirmation of their privileges they did not lend any more money to Parliament in the 1640s, but in July 1648 the navy committee persuaded the East India Company to advance £10,000 on the customs of goods they had recently imported.[85]

The merchant companies, unlike the livery companies, usually profited from their loans to Parliament. Although the repayments of their loans were frequently delayed the £13,804 owed to the Merchant Adventurers in 1650 is the only clear case of Parliament defaulting on its debts to a merchant company. The Long Parliament's willingness to repay debts to the merchant companies even extended to the Guinea Company, despite the fact that half the stock of the company was owned by Sir Nicholas Crispe, one of the most notorious London royalists. At the end of that year the company's ship, the *Star*, returned to London laden with £11,000 of gold. With the whole cargo in Parliament's hands, the rest of the investors were induced to advance £5,000 worth of the gold for the navy until Crispe's share had been determined. They were promised repayment of whatever proportion was found not to be owing to

---

[84] *CJ* V, 362, 369, 373 458; *CJ* VI, 56 462; *LJ* IX, 552; PRO E351/1295, ff. 16, 22, 23; *Firth & Rait*, II, 99–102. For the seizure of the King of Denmark's arms shipment see p. 120 below.

[85] *CJ* III, 312, 313, 395, 412; *CCMEIC*, 1640–43, 365–6; *CCMEIC*, 1644–49, 196, 278; *LJ* VI, 393; PRO SP105/143, ff. 101, 102v, 103v, 104, 105, 113; PRO SP105/159, f. 126.

Crispe with eight per cent interest in the following March. Crispe's brother Samuel was doubtful whether Parliament could repay them, but, after the company claimed that all the money was due to their creditors, they were paid £3,039 in December 1644.[86]

The merchant companies also received the less tangible, but important, asset of the goodwill of the Long Parliament. This was important to the merchant companies because of the widespread opposition to their privileges. The confirmation of the Merchant Adventurers' monopoly of cloth exports to Germany and the Netherlands aroused particularly strong protests, but the company's opponents made little headway. In June 1644 the House of Commons voted down a proposal to exempt the new draperies from the Merchant Adventurers' monopoly. In May 1645 a petition against the company's monopoly received widespread favourable press coverage, but when it was presented to the Commons it was referred to Giles Grene. As chairman of the navy committee he had played a key role in negotiating the loans from the merchant companies, and there were no further proceedings.[87] The privileges of the Levant Company aroused less controversy than those of the Merchant Adventurers, but it relied on the support of the navy committee, which also supervised the customs, to ensure that the company's monopoly of trade with the eastern Mediterranean was upheld, and especially that Levant goods were not imported indirectly by non-company merchants.[88]

The companies lent relatively small amounts of money in the 1640s, compared to Parliament's total borrowing, however the loans had substantial repercussions for London society. The failure of Parliament to honour the loans from the livery companies created major financial problems that diminished the role that those institutions played in London society, most obviously in the relief of poverty. In contrast the lending of the merchant companies ensured the ratification of their charters and meant that, despite considerable opposition, they survived the Civil War with their privileges intact.

Borrowing from revenue officers

From 1643 borrowing from Parliament's own treasurers and revenue commissioners in anticipation of their revenues became an increasingly

---

[86] *CJ* VI, 15; *LJ* VI, 321–2; PRO SP16/540/365–400; Bodl. Tanner MS. 62, Samuel Crispe to Sir George Strode, 12 December 1643, f. 438; PRO E351/644.

[87] *CJ* III, 486, 487, 518; *CJ* IV, 152; *The True Informer*, 5, week ending 24 May 1645, 37–8; *Mercurius Britanicus*, 84, 19–26 May 1645, 767; *Mercurius Civicus*, 104, 15–22 May 1645, 934. It is probably also relevant that the navy committee had recently negotiated a substantial loan from a new group of customs' commissioners, all of whom were prominent Merchant Adventurers, see below p. 77.

[88] PRO SP105/143, f. 102v; PRO SP105/109, f. 215.

important part of Parliament's credit. The officers in question were generally wealthy London merchants and financiers who were appointed because of their willingness and ability to advance substantial sums. Almost all treasurers advanced money to Parliament and these men were the only Londoners to profit consistently from Parliament's finances, receiving not only interest on their loans, but also fees or salaries for their posts. The largest lenders were the customs' commissioners, the excise commissioners and, after 1645, the treasurers of the New Model Army, the latter advancing £125,891 up to the end of 1650.[89]

It is possible that the revenue officers brokered loans to Parliament from the wider London financial community, as treasurers and customs' farmers had done for Charles I. One instance where something like this can be documented concerns the £10,000 advanced by the treasurers of the weekly assessment for the forces in Ireland in 1646. They in turn borrowed £100 from Richard Chambers. Chambers was a City Alderman who contributed to other loans for Parliament, and had been a customs' commissioner between 1642 and 1645. Moreover he received the full eight per cent for his loan. Consequently this does not suggest that the borrowing by the treasurers broadened the basis of Parliamentary finance, not did it provide the treasurers with an opportunity to profit by borrowing at lower rates of interest than the rates they received for their loans.[90]

The first revenue officers to lend to Parliament were the customs' commissioners appointed in May 1641. By December 1642 they had advanced at least £50,000 for the navy as well as smaller sums for miscellaneous purposes, such as transporting the contents of the Hull magazine to London in August 1642. They also contributed £4,000 towards the propositions. On 24 December 1642 Parliament approached them to borrow a further £20,000 for the army on the 'public faith'. The commissioners claimed that this would be difficult because they were already engaged to lend £20,000 for the navy, but offered to negotiate if Parliament would appoint a committee to meet them. Presumably, they were seeking better security. However on receiving the King's belated proclamation threatening to punish anyone who collected the customs without the authority of statute, the commissioners abandoned their posts.[91] On 21 January 1643 a new group of customs' commissioners were appointed in their place. Parliament tried to persuade the new commissioners to

---

[89] PRO E351/302.

[90] Ashton, *Crown and the Money Market*, 25–6; PRO SP28/57, f. 839.

[91] *CJ* II, 710, 900–1; PRO SP19/78, f. 81; Thompson, *Walter Yonge's Diary*, 164, 204; *England's Memorable Accidents*, 9–16 January 1643, 148; *CSPV*, 1642–43, 223; *Royalist Newsbooks*, I, 52; *Larkin*, 830–3.

lend £30,000 on entering office but they were only able to obtain £20,000, secured on the receipts of the customs.[92]

Robert Brenner has argued that the new customs' commissioners were drawn from the leaders of the 'new merchants', the opponents of the merchant companies who had arisen from the American trades, and their political allies. Certainly Maurice Thompson, Thomas Andrewes, and Francis Berkeley all had strong interests in the trade with the American colonies, and Francis Allein was an investor in the Bermuda Company. Also Thompson, Andrewes, Stephen Estwicke, and James Russell were all involved in the Courteen association that traded with the East Indies in contravention of the East India Company's monopoly. However, the economic interests of the new commissioners were more diverse than Brenner suggests. Berkeley's main interest was in trade with France, James Russell was a member of the Merchant Adventurers' Company, and John Fowke and Richard Chambers were members of the Levant Company. Thomas Andrewes was a wholesale linen draper and had previously been an undersharer in the customs farm. Estwicke was generally described as a 'haberdasher of small wares', while Francis Allein was a jeweller.[93]

Parliament had problems obtaining further finance from the new commissioners. Proposals for fresh loans in March and August 1643 were rejected by the commissioners, which led Parliament to approach the Merchant Adventurers to take over the customs. As has already been noted, the negotiations with the company proved fruitless, but this induced the commissioners to lend £20,000 in September. In March of the following year the commissioners agreed to lend a further £22,000, but by 23 May only £15,000 had been received. More money was advanced in the second half of 1644 but Parliament's patience eventually ran out and the commissioners were replaced in February 1645. During their time in office they advanced about £111,000 for the navy. When compared with the Caroline customs' farmers, who advanced over £104,000 to Charles I in 1640 alone, their record was disappointing. It probably reflects the poor state of the customs revenue at this time, and the reluctance of the commissioners to over commit themselves.[94] The commissioners received £16,450 in interest on their loans, but their salary was their principal source of profit, in twenty five months they paid themselves £20,833. Their accounts also show separate payments for the customs officers

---

[92] *CJ* II, 902, 919, 927–8, 937, 1001–4; Thompson, *Walter Yonge's Diary*, 206, 253–4, 261, 341. The royalist press reported that the new commissioners found it difficult to raise even £20,000, *Royalist Newsbooks*, I, 71.

[93] Brenner, *Merchants and Revolution*, 175, 432; Pearl, *London and the Outbreak of the Puritan Revolution*, 309, 314, 315, 317; *CJ* VI, 320.

[94] *CJ* III, 2, 19, 243, 245; Bodl. Rawlinson MS. A221, Journal of the Committee for the Navy, 1643–44, ff. 6v, 50; PRO E351/643–5; BL Harl. MS. 164, Parliamentary Journal of Sir Simonds D'Ewes, 1642–43, f. 354; BL Harl. MS. 165, f. 154v; Ashton, *Crown and the Money Market*, 110–11.

and expenses, so most of this must have been clear profit. In total they made £37,282 from their office.[95]

Senior members of the Merchant Adventurers' Company dominated the new customs' commission appointed in February 1645. They accepted a much smaller salary, £1,000 per quarter instead of £2,500, and they advanced £50,000 on entering office. Subsequently they lent a further £80,000 for the navy before the Commonwealth removed them from office in July 1649. They paid themselves £20,348 in interest and £16,667 for their salary. In total the various customs' commissioners received £74,296 in salaries and interest payments from the beginning of 1643 to July 1649.[96]

The money advanced on the customs went to the navy, but the introduction of the excise in 1643 provided an opportunity to borrow money for other purposes. Like the customs, the excise was put in the hands of a group of London merchants, almost certainly to facilitate raising loans on future receipts.[97] In the first year of its existence the excise commissioners were ordered to pay over £249,000 by Parliament, a large part of which must have been advanced, especially in the early days before the revenue was firmly established. However the excise commissioners were significant lenders to Parliament for a relatively short time. By September 1644 the commissioners were complaining that they could not raise all the sums charged on the excise. In March 1646 they refused to advance money to Lord Inchiquin, who had recently been voted £6,000 from the excise. By the time of the commissioners' first surviving account, which covers the period 1647–50, the commissioners themselves seem to have been only very minor creditors. The only sums which can be said with certainty to have been advanced by the commissioners during the time of this account were £10,000 advanced in November 1647 to the treasurers of the New Model Army, followed by a further £2,775 a month later.[98]

The lack of any accounts for the excise before 1647 makes it difficult to establish to what extent the commissioners profited from their office. They protested that they were being asked to advance more money than the revenue could afford but, like the customs' commissioners, they seem to have managed to avoid becoming over extended. Moreover they received six pence in the pound as salary as well as the interests on their loans. The private accounts of one of the commissioners, Thomas Cullum, show he earned around £1,300 per

---

[95] PRO E351/643–5.

[96] Brenner, *Merchants and Revolution*, 434 n. 81; *LJ* VII, 265; *CJ* V, 122, 168, 331, 468, 514, 537, 647, 652, 678; PRO E351/645–9.

[97] *CJ* III, 239, 240, 243.

[98] J.S. Wheeler, *The Making of a World Power: War and the Military Revolution in Seventeenth Century England* (Stroud, 1999), 153; *HMC Thirteenth Report, Portland MSS*, I, 184; *HMC Egmont MSS*, I, part 1, 283; PRO E351/1295, f. 22; *LJ* IX, 533, 553.

year from his post between 1644 and 1650 which was probably typical of the other commissioners.[99]

Salaries and interest payments were not the only way the customs and excise commissioners made money in the 1640s. The excise commissioners claimed that their posts would take up almost all of their time. John Fowke told the Commons that the most of the customs' commissioners had abandoned their businesses to concentrate on the administration of the customs. But, although Fowke did stop trading (at least with the Levant), this is not true of his colleague Richard Chambers or the excise commissioners, John Langham and Simon Edmonds, who were also members of Levant Company. Moreover Thomas Cullum continued his drapery business while he was an excise commissioner. It is possible that, like the Caroline customs' farmers, they used the receipts in their hands for private financial transactions before the money fell due. When Alderman John Towse died in 1645 it became apparent that he had appropriated some of the money that he received as a proposition treasurer for his own purposes.[100]

It is also possible that other Londoners who held office in Parliament's financial machinery were profiting illicitly from their offices by embezzlement and corruption. There were certainly plenty of allegations of this kind at the time. Francis Allein, customs' commissioner from 1643 to 1645 and subsequently one of the treasurers of the New Model Army, was said to have made £70,000 in this way. However many of these allegations came from royalist or other politically biased sources and are clearly unreliable. One tract claimed that Alderman Thomas Atkin profited from his position as treasurer of the army, a post he never held. Blair Worden and Gerald Aylmer have tended to discount these allegations, and there is no reason to believe that the parliamentarian regime was any more corrupt than its predecessors, although this is not saying very much. It is suggestive that Cromwell, at least, believed the allegations against Francis Allein.[101]

Possibly the greatest opportunities for enrichment came in the aftermath of the Civil War with the large-scale sales of confiscated lands. As has already been noted those able and willing to make substantial purchases of episcopal property with doubled bills probably made large profits and many of the revenue officers fit this description. Those appointed to administer the land sales were generally Londoners who were already prominent in Parliament's

---

[99] A. Simpson, 'Thomas Cullum, Draper, 1587–1664', *EcHR* 2nd series, 11 (1958), 26–7.

[100] BL Harl. MS. 165, f. 154v; PRO SP105/159, ff. 40, 84, 99; Simpson, 'Thomas Cullum', 26–7, 34; Ashton, *Crown and the Money Market*, 14; *CCAM*, II, 567.

[101] B. Worden, *The Rump Parliament, 1648–1653* (Cambridge, 1974), 95; *Second Centurie*; G.E. Aylmer, *The States Servants: The Servants of the English Republic, 1649–1660* (1973), 328; I. Gentles, *The New Model Army in England, Ireland and Scotland, 1645–1653* (Oxford, 1992), 433.

financial machinery, and this put them in a good position to find the best bargains. Moreover, because most purchases were made with doubled bills rather than cash, there was often not enough money to pay the officers' salaries; they were instead paid in confiscated lands. Parliament's revenue officers were also generally owed large sums on the public faith, which they were able to double and use to purchase lands. In early November 1646, on the eve of the opening of subscriptions for the first doubling ordinance, Parliament voted the three surviving proposition treasurers £5,000 on the 'public faith' for their services. One of the three, Alderman John Warner, died in 1648 in financial difficulties, as did the fourth proposition treasurer, John Towse. This may well be because they died too early to take advantage of the land sales. In contrast the two proposition treasurers who survived into the 1650s, Sir John Wollaston and Alderman Thomas Andrewes, invested in Bishops' lands and prospered.[102]

The various revenue commissioners made considerable sums of money lending money to Parliament, which is almost certainly more than can be said for most of Parliament's creditors, but few made their fortunes this way. Their ability to advance large sums suggests they were wealthy men before the war. Sir John Wollaston, perhaps the most important of Parliament's revenue officers, made his fortune before the war running the mint for Charles I. William Berkeley died bankrupt despite being a customs' commissioner from 1643 to 1645.[103] The success of the customs and excise commissioners in profiting from their offices may, in part, be due to their ability to restrict the amounts they lent. This reduced their potential profits, but it also made it less likely that Parliament would default on their debts.

Parliamentary borrowing and the London money market

W.R. Scott argued that the massive growth in public borrowing during the Civil War led to a shortage of capital in the rest of the economy. In 1643 Robert Campion withdrew the £1,000 he had on loan to the East India Company, at low interest, and instead advanced it towards the parliamentary war effort, where the interest rates were higher.[104] However the East India Company was still able to borrow large sums of money below the legal

---

[102] Pearl, *London and the Outbreak of the Puritan Revolution*, 310–11, 325, 327, 328–331; *CJ* IV, 715; Habakkuk, 'Public Finance', 73 n. 3.

[103] C.E. Challis, 'Lord Hastings to the Great Silver Recoinage, 1464–1699', in C.E. Challis (ed.), *A New History of the Royal Mint* (Cambridge, 1992), 294–5; G.F. Steckley (ed.), *The Letters of John Paige, London Merchant, 1648–58*, London Record Society (1984), 106.

[104] W.R. Scott, *The Constitution and Finance of English Joint Stock Companies to 1720*, 3 vols (Cambridge, 1910–1912), I, 232; 238; CLRO, Alchin Papers, Q/CV, Papers touching Mr Campion's debt.

maximum rate of interest, so that by August 1645 the net debts of the fourth joint stock in England totalled £120,000, and, unlike the late 1620s, the company was not forced to borrow abroad.[105] Moreover the City of London and the livery companies borrowed large sums below the legal rate of interest during the Civil War.

In 1624 the legal maximum rate of interest was reduced to eight per cent but by the 1630s borrowers able to offer good securities paid well below this. In 1635 the treasurer of the East India Company reported that he had converted virtually the whole of the company's debt to between 6.5 and seven per cent. In the 1630s the livery companies were generally able to borrow at around six to seven per cent. In 1639 the Goldsmith's Company was even able borrow money at only five per cent.[106] It was not only institutions which could borrow below the legal maximum: Sir William Russell, the treasurer of the navy, borrowed money at seven per cent to lend to the crown at eight per cent, and this was probably also true of the custom farmers.[107] Charitable and public funds were usually lent at six per cent, presumably because it was believed that this was as much as could be obtained from borrowers whose credit was good.[108]

The successive loans imposed upon the livery companies from 1640 onwards forced them to borrow large sums. There was also a major expansion in borrowing by the corporation to pay for London's defences. The more prominent companies included the wealthiest merchants of the City, but they did not borrow at preferential rates from their own members. Often the lenders were apparently unconnected with the company, and they were frequently procured through brokers and financial scrivener, indicating that they were paying the market rates for secure borrowers. The interest they paid was undoubtedly lower than all but perhaps the wealthiest Londoners could obtain, but it would reflect the prevailing market conditions. If capital was in short supply we would expect the interest rates paid by the livery companies to start to rise towards the legal maximum.

On the eve of the Civil War there are signs that capital was becoming more expensive. Initially some livery companies borrowed money at eight per cent when they raised money for the £50,000 loan in 1640, but this was

---

[105] CCMEIC, 1644–49, 163; K.N. Chaudhuri, The East India Company: The Study of an Early Joint-Stock Company, 1600–1640 (1965), 220.

[106] L. Stone, The Crisis of the Aristocracy, 1558–1641 (Oxford, 1965), 530–1; GH, Wardens' Accounts and Court Minutes, S/2, 1635–7, ff. 324, 367, 410, 411, 412, 431, 433, 446, 447, 455, 436, 457, 458, 460, 469, 481, 494, 507; GH, Court Book, U, 1637–42, ff. 4, 11; GL MS. 5255/1, Barber Surgeons' Company, Wardens Accounts' and Audit Books, 1603–59; CCMEIC, 1635–39, 24.

[107] Ashton, Crown and the Money Market, 25; For an example of a prominent Merchant Adventurer borrowing at seven per cent see CSPD, 1635–36, 354.

[108] GL MS. 16967/4, Ironmongers' Company, Court Minutes, 1629–46, ff. 272, 273.

probably because they believed that the money would be promptly repaid, and many of their creditors at this stage were their own senior members.[109] The real cost of borrowing was probably not as great as this suggests. Companies borrowed at lower rates in 1641 and in that year a balance of account prepared by the East India Company puts the interest on the debts of the third joint stock at seven per cent.[110] Nevertheless the evidence for corporation borrowing suggests there was a modest increase. In the three years to Michaelmas 1641 the City borrowed £12,700 on bonds for repayment in 6 months and paid an average of 6.9 per cent in interest. In the following year the corporation borrowed almost as much again, paying slightly over seven per cent.[111]

By the summer of 1642, when the companies considered how to raise their proportions of the £100,000 loan to suppress the rebellion in Ireland, they were much more wary of Parliament's promises of repayment. The Grocers agreed that if any part of the loan were not repaid then the members would make good the loss and other companies made similar agreements. This may be why the Merchant Tailors preferred to borrow from their own members rather than outsiders, even if that meant borrowing at the legal maximum rate, and the Grocers also raised their proportion from among their own members at eight per cent.[112] In these cases the interest rates paid by the companies did not reflect the conditions of the financial market in London. However there is also evidence from those companies who were willing to look outside their own membership for finance that it was becoming much more difficult to raise money below the legal rate. The Fishmongers raised £1,500 at 7.5 per cent but had difficulty finding any more money at this rate. The Ironmongers offered eight per cent to lenders but still had difficulty raising their quota, £1,000 was outstanding in September 1642.[113]

The evidence suggests that borrowing got more expensive in the early part of the war. In 1643 the Scottish traveller William Lithgow wrote that

---

[109] GH, Court Book, U, 1637–42, f. 83v; GL MS. 15842/1, Haberdashers' Company, Court Minutes, 1583–1652, f. 304v.

[110] GL MS. 15866/1, Haberdashers' Company, Wardens' Accounts, 1633–53, f. 337 (7%); GL MS. 5255/1, unfoliated, accounts for 1641–2 (6%); GL MS. 11571/12, Grocers' Company, Wardens' Accounts, 1632–42, f. 382; BL IOL/H/39, East India Company, Home Miscellaneous, f. 161.

[111] CLRO Cash books, 1/3, ff. 34–v, 125; 1/4, 30v. Six month bonds were the most common form of borrowing used by the corporation and have been singled out for comparability.

[112] GL MS. 11588/4, ff. 51–2; GL MS. Merchant Tailors' Company, Court Minutes, vol. 9, 1636–54, f. 149v; GL MS. 11571/12, ff. 427v–9v; GL MS. Merchant Tailors' Company, Wardens' Accounts, vol. 18, 1641–44, unfoliated accounts for 1641–42.

[113] GL MS. 5570/3, Fishmongers' Company, Court Minutes, 1631–46, ff. 607–9; GL MS. 16967/4, ff. 373, 374, 377–8, 382.

'there is a general muttering that money is hard to come by'.[114] In November 1643 the East India Company complained to their representatives in India about the 'scarsity of monyes'.[115] In the following March they wrote 'for monies the life of trade they are so difficull in their procuring both from forraigne parts & here at home that wee are come much short of what wee desired you should have bin supplied withall'.[116] The average interest paid by the Chamber of the City of London on six month bonds rose to nearly 7.25 per cent in the year to Michaelmas 1643.[117] The accounts of the Merchant Tailors' Company for the year 1643–44 show that it was paying an average of 7.33 per cent in interest on its loans, while in the same period the Grocers' Company paid 7.11 per cent.[118]

The difficulties experienced by potential lenders in finding money were not necessarily caused by the expansion of public borrowing. Lithgow says it was due to the decay of trade, which made those with capital reluctant to invest.[119] This was reinforced by the difficulties creditors were experiencing obtaining repayment of what they had lent. In February 1643 Joseph Bynns, a London surgeon, wrote to his cousin, Joseph Colston, then in Italy, that he could not receive payment of a bond due Colston 'for monye was never worse to come by'.[120] The prevailing attitude was epitomized by Sir John Leake, who wrote to the Earl of Cork 'itt is noe time to pay mony now'.[121]

The shortage of capital in the Civil War should not be exaggerated. Despite its complaints, the East India Company was able to borrow very large sums of money during the war. Moreover there is no evidence that they had to pay higher interest rates. An account of the fourth joint stock drawn up in 1644 records the interest on the debts as seven per cent, just as the account for the third joint stock had done in 1641.[122] The livery companies were increasingly successful in finding sources of finance substantially below the legal rate. In November 1642 the Goldsmiths' Company was able to borrow money at seven per cent to repay debts originally taken up at eight per cent. In January 1643 they borrowed £1,200 from Mrs Ann Humble at six per cent, and in May one of the company's creditors agreed to re-lend the company at six per cent money originally lent at eight per cent.[123] In March 1643 the Fishmongers'

---

[114] W. Lithgow, 'The Present Surveigh of London and Englands State' (1643), reprinted in Lord Somers' Tracts, 16 vols (1748–52), IV, 536.

[115] BL IOL/G/40/12, East India Company, Factory Miscellaneous, f. 53v.

[116] BL IOL/G/40/12, f. 65.

[117] CLRO City Cash Books, 1/4, ff. 200v–202; 1/5, ff. 33v–4.

[118] GL MS. Merchant Tailors' Company, Wardens' Accounts, vol. 18, 1641–4, unfoliated accounts for 1643–4; GL MS. 11571/13, accounts for 1643–4.

[119] Lithgow, 'Present Surveigh', 536.

[120] BL Sloane MS. 118, f. 77.

[121] A.B. Grossart (ed.) The Lismore Papers, 2nd Series, 5 vols (1888) V, 124.

[122] BL IOL/H/39, ff. 161, 169A.

[123] GH, Court Book, W, 1642–5, ff. 31, 33, 38v–9, 56.

Company was offered £500 at six per cent. In the following June one of the company's creditors, from whom it had borrowed £1,000 the year before at 7.5 per cent, agreed to accept seven per cent for the following year rather than receive his money back again. In the same month the Ironmongers transferred their debts to seven per cent.[124]

The livery companies continued to reduce the interest on their debts in 1644. In August the wardens of the Goldsmiths' Company were given a general warrant to borrow money at interest not exceeding seven per cent. In the following November the company agreed to pay off all its debts at seven per cent, unless the creditors would accept six or 6.5 per cent, as the company believed that it could borrow what it needed at those rates.[125] In the first half of 1645, when Parliament was raising the £80,000 loan to finance the New Model Army, the average rate of interest on the loans raised by the Goldsmiths' Company was about 6.25 per cent. The other major livery companies were also able to borrow substantially below the legal interest rate; the Grocers paid an average of 6.75 per cent, the Merchant Tailors 6.66 per cent and the Haberdashers 6.4 per cent.[126] It was not just the major companies that could borrow at these rates, in April 1645 the Barber Surgeons borrowed £1,000 at 6.5 per cent, and the Carpenters borrowed £200 at six per cent.[127] The interest rates paid by the Chamber of the City of London was also declining, although more gradually, from 7.25 per cent in 1642–43 to 7.1 per cent in 1644–45.[128]

Interest rates continued to fall in the second half of the decade. The average interest rates paid by the Grocers' Company was less than 6.2 per cent from 1645–46, and only slightly over six per cent in 1647–48 and 1648–49. The rates paid by the Merchant Tailors fell even further, as by 1647–48 the company was paying an average of only 5.66 per cent on the money it had borrowed.[129] In March 1646 the Fishmongers' Company raised over £3,000 at six per cent to repay those of its members who had subscribed in 1642 to the £100,000 loan to suppress the rebellion in Ireland. In January 1647 the Ironmongers reduced the interest rate they were paying on their debts from seven per cent to six per cent.[130] The average interest paid by the Chamber also

[124] GL MS. 5570/3, ff. 652, 674; GL MS. 16967/4, f. 391.

[125] GH, Court Book, W, 1642–5ᵗ ff. 254, 264v.

[126] Ibid., ff. 288, 299; GL MS. 15866/1, f. 512; GL MS. Merchant Tailors' Company, Wardens' Accounts, vol. 19, 1644–8, unfoliated accounts for 1644–5; GL MS. 11571/13, accounts for 1644–5.

[127] GL MS. 5257/5, f. 338; GL MS. 4329/5, Carpenters' Company, Court Minutes, 1635–56, unfoliated.

[128] CLRO City Cash Books, 1/5, ff. 137v–8.

[129] GL MS. Merchant Tailors' Company, Wardens' Accounts, vol. 19, 1644–8; GL MS. 11571/13.

[130] GL MS. 5570/3, ff. 901–2, 938; GL MS. 16967/5, Ironmongers' Company, Court Minutes, 1646–60, f. 10.

fell, reaching 6.33 per cent in 1646–47, and although it rose in the following year it remained below seven per cent for the rest of the decade.[131]

Other evidence indicates that borrowing was cheap in the second half of the 1640s for those who could offer good security. In 1645 the City money scrivener Robert Abbott arranged a loan for John Prettyman, secured on jewellery, for £120 at 6.66 per cent.[132] In 1647 Lord Dacre was able to borrow at six per cent and in the same year one tract alleged that brokers borrowed money at four to five per cent interest, six at most, to re-lend at usurious rates. In January 1648 the fact that the lord mayor, John Warner, had borrowed £1,000 at seven per cent was cited as evidence of his precarious finances. In the same year David Papillon believed that his son Thomas, then a young merchant in London, would be able to borrow £100 at six or seven per cent.[133]

The cost of borrowing did therefore rise in the early part of the Civil War, however it is doubtful whether this can be attributed to the expansion of state finance. Parliament continued to borrow substantial amounts in the rest of the decade, and became better at repaying its debts, but interest rates fell steadily. Credit was probably no more expensive in the latter 1640s than it had been in the 1630s. It is more likely that interest rates rose because potential investors were reluctant to lend during the early war years. As the war started to turn in Parliament's favour the perceived dangers of investing in London diminished, and credit became cheaper. Moreover there is little sign, even when credit did become more expensive, that this had a major impact on the London economy. Most major livery companies had substantial stocks of money entrusted to them by wealthy benefactors to lend to young tradesmen at easy rates, but during the war they often had difficulties finding recipients for the loans, suggesting that demand for capital had declined.[134]

There were undoubtedly large amounts of capital in the London economy looking for safe investment opportunities, especially the portions of widows and orphans. This money was available to potential lenders well below the legal maximum rate of interest but only if they could offer sound security. In the 1630s the crown could tap into this source of funds via intermediaries such as Sir William Russell, and the customs' farmers. However the failure of Parliament to repay the early loans secured on taxation receipts ensured that it could not borrow from those sources. Instead this money was directed to the livery companies and the Corporation. It was not until the 1650s that a new

---

[131] CLRO City Cash Books, 1/6, ff. 30v–33v, 132v–6v; CLRO Chamber Accounts, 16/63, Loans Journal, 1649–74, ff. 1–3v, 15–17v.

[132] GL MS. 2931, Robert Abbott's account book, 1646–52, f. 4.

[133] Stone, *Crisis of the Aristocracy*, 531; *Two Knaves for a Penny* (1647), 6; *A Case for the City-Spectacles* (1648), 5; Centre for Kentish Studies, U1015/C10/2, Papillon Papers.

[134] Johnson, *History of the Worshipful Company of Drapers*, III, 174; GL MS. 11588/4, f. 104.

group of intermediaries, principally the Goldsmith bankers, emerged who could channel these funds towards the government.[135]

The middle years of the seventeenth century saw the origins of the earliest English private banks, started by goldsmiths and financial scriveners. One famous account of the origin of the goldsmith banks entitled *The Mystery of the new Fashioned Goldsmiths*, published in 1676, argued that as a result of the enlistment of so many apprentices in the army, many London merchants, who previously had entrusted their cash to one of their apprentices, started instead to deposit their cash with goldsmiths. Subsequently, the author argued the goldsmiths began to pay interest on their deposits and lend out the money they received to merchants and the Cromwellian regime.[136] However it has been argued that this pamphlet was a government inspired attempt to justify the 1672 stop on the Exchequer, which had ruined many of the goldsmith bankers. The origins of English banking were probably much less dramatic than this suggests, and the Civil War may not have had much to do with it.[137]

Before the Civil War many goldsmiths were involved in a variety of financial services, mostly in the field of foreign exchange, but some also lent money on pawned plate and jewellery, discounted bills of exchange and traded in bullion. They also received deposits and it has been suggested that the goldsmith banker was a reality by at least the reign of James I, if not before. Thomas Vyner, one of the first goldsmith bankers, was a working silversmith before the war but he also changed bullion and foreign coin for English currency. One merchant, Andrew King, sold him plate and foreign coins but kept the proceeds on deposit with Vyner, who then made payments on King's orders.[138] The goldsmiths were not the only providers of financial services in this period. From at least the Jacobean period some scriveners who specialized in drawing up financial instruments had become loan brokers. One account book from the 1630s records the deposit of over £30,000 in the space of eighteen months in one London scrivener's shop. Many London tradesmen acted as agents and factors for provincial merchants and landowners who had dealings with the metropolis, they received and paid out money for their clients

[135] Ashton, *Crown and the Money Market*, 25.

[136] Reprinted in J.B. Martin, *The Grasshopper in Lombard Street* (1892), 285–292.

[137] H. Roseveare, *The Financial Revolution, 1660–1760* (1991), 12, 83.

[138] A.V. Judges, 'The Origins of English Banking', *History* 16 (1931), 142–3; D.K. Clark, 'A Restoration Goldsmith-Banking House: The Vine on Lombard Street', in *Essays in Modern English History in Honor of Wilbur Cortez Abbott* (Cambridge, Mass., 1941), 3–4, 7; WAM, Sir Andrew King Papers, 10076–7, 10085, 11423; E. Kerridge, *Trade and Banking in Early Modern England* (Manchester, 1988), 67.

and lent out surpluses to London merchants, they even allowed their clients overdrafts.[139]

The first clear evidence of Londoners specializing in banking comes from the mid-seventeenth century. Robert Abbott's scrivener bank was operating by the end of the war. By the late 1650s a few of the goldsmiths had established 'running cashes', they received deposits and lent the money they received to merchants and to the Protectorate regime, but at what stage this practice began is difficult to establish. There does not seem to be any contemporary evidence to tie the beginning of goldsmith banking to the Civil War. The most recent study of goldsmith bankers has dated their origins to the 1650s rather than the Civil War period.[140]

The origins of the banks had little connection with Parliamentary borrowing in the Civil War. Abbott was a royalist who consequently is unlikely to have been involved in lending to Parliament. Vyner is known to have lent only £100 to Parliament during the Civil War, although he did lend money immediately before and after the war. His major financial transactions in the wartime seem to have been confined to the private sector, and he did not become prominent in public finance until the 1650s.[141] The same seems to have been also true of the scrivener Martin Noel who, like Vyner, emerged as a major financier in the Protectorate but seems to have had little involvement in lending to Parliament in the 1640s. During the Civil War Noel acted as a financial scrivener, lending money for clients to, among others, the Haberdashers' Company.[142]

---

[139] R.D. Richards, *The Early History of Banking in England* (1929), 15–16; F.T. Melton, *Sir Robert Clayton and the Origins of English Deposit Banking, 1658–1685* (Cambridge, 1986), 20–30, 44; Kerridge, *Trade and Banking*, 46–7.

[140] Melton, *Sir Robert Clayton*, 46; Richards, *Early History of Banking*, 37; S. Quinn, 'Balances and Goldsmith Bankers: the co-ordination and control of inter-banker debt clearing in Seventeenth-Century London', in D. Mitchell (ed.), *Goldsmiths, Silversmiths and Bankers: Innovation and the Transfer of Skill, 1550–1750* (1995), 61; Kerridge, *Trade and Banking*, 76–7.

[141] Roseveare, *Financial Revolution*, 12; Melton, *Sir Robert Clayton*, 46; PRO SP28/162, Account of Treasurers for £95,900 loan, 1641, f. 2; *CCAM*, I, 27; PRO SP28/350/5, part 1, f. 8; PRO C107/17, account book of Grace Ashe, 1644–48; V.B. Redstone, 'The Diary of Sir Thomas Dawes, 1644', *Surrey Archæological Collections* 37 (1927), 10.

[142] GL MS. 15866/1, f. 525. The best account of the career of Martin Noel is still E. Hughes, *Studies in Administration and Finance, 1558–1835* (Manchester, 1934), 132–5. However the sources he cites for Noel's loans to Parliament in the 1640s in fact concern his financial dealings with sequestered royalists. *CCAM*, I, 525; *CCCD*, IV, 2426.

Conclusion

Parliamentary loans can be divided into two types, those which were raised on the 'public faith' alone, and those raised on specific securities, either taxation or land sales. Contributing to the former can best be regarded as a political act, while the latter were more like economic investments. It is the loans raised on security which belong properly to the history of English public finance, but during the war itself it was probably unsecured borrowing which raised the most money.

The funded loans raised by Parliament in London during the Civil War were surprisingly small. The largest single loan, the £80,000 for the New Model Army, is significantly less than the loan provided by the customs' farmers for Charles I in 1640. As far back as 1607 the customs' farmers had lent £120,000, and a similar sum had been advanced by the Corporation in the late 1620s as part of the Great Contract. Sir Paul Pindar alone lent Charles I £85,000 in 1638–39.[143]

In total between 1645 and 1651 the New Model Army treasurers borrowed less than £250,000 at interest on the credit of their receipts, of which they supplied £125,891 themselves. They also borrowed £81,733 without interest from various parliamentarian treasuries and officials, and they received sums borrowed on the security of other revenues, such as the excise. All these sums are dwarfed by the £5,228,873 they received from the assessment, which constituted sixty nine per cent of their total receipts. London credit played only a minor role in financing the New Model Army.[144] Credit plays a larger part in the accounts of the excise commissioners, between 1647 and 1650 they paid £193,016 interest and repaid £261,905 in principal, which together make up fifty five per cent of the total payments from the excise. However the excise constituted a much small proportion of Parliament's finances than the assessment, the total receipts being only £853,344 in 1647–50.[145] Moreover not all the debts charged on the excise were loans from Londoners. For example in May 1647 Parliament ordered the excise commissioners to pay £17,138, plus interest, to former officers of Lord Fairfax's army for their arrears.[146]

A very large proportion of Parliament's forces, those in local garrisons and the provincial armies, were financed directly from the area in which they were located. The highly decentralized nature of the war effort made metropolitan finance less important to Parliament than it might otherwise have been. In Warwickshire money from London initially played an important role

---

[143] Ashton, *Crown and the Money Market*, 24, 84, 110–11, 132–3.
[144] PRO E351/302. The second largest source of receipts was delinquency compositions.
[145] PRO E351/1295, ff. 15–26.
[146] *LJ IX*, 203–4.

in financing the local parliamentary forces but this proved inadequate and instead a system was established for paying the soldiers directly out of the taxes raised in the parishes where they were quartered.[147] Even the army of the Eastern Association, the largest of the provincial armies, was largely financed from taxes raised from its constituent counties. The only substantial loan raised in London was the £5,000 raised in October 1644. In contrast the treasurers for the weekly assessment for the Eastern Association received over £250,000 in 1644 alone.[148] As has been noted, there is little evidence that the capital became short in Civil War London because of government borrowing. Other than taxation Parliament financed the war through free quarter, the propositions and the accumulation of arrears rather than large scale borrowing in the London money market.

Consequently the amount of money accruing to the London economy from interest payments was relatively small. The Goldsmiths' Hall treasurers paid less than £2,000 in interest on loans. The various groups of customs' commissioners paid £24,928 between 1643 and 1650. The New Model Army treasurers paid £251,599 in repaying loans but it is unlikely that interest payments made up a large proportion of this sum. The interest payments on the £80,000 came to only £3,610, the £11,800 loan raised in late 1647 was repaid three months later, and consequently the creditors received only £236 in interest. The only treasurers who paid substantial sums in interest were the excise commissioners, who paid £193,016 in interest between 1647 and 1650, or about £64,339 a year. This compares with annual receipts from London of £162,552, consequently even if all the interest payments had gone into the London economy, which is unlikely, this would only have been a fraction of the money taken out in taxation receipts.[149]

Except for the propositions and other unsecured subscriptions, the methods used by Parliament appear to have been broadly similar to those employed by the early Stuart monarchs. Both borrowed large sums from those appointed to receive their revenues, whether commissioners, treasurers or farmers.[150] Both the Crown and Parliament used the City government as an intermediary in their dealings with wealthy London citizens, which often meant that senior members, especially the aldermen, formed a large proportion of lenders. Under both the Crown and Parliament, when the credit of the state began to wear thin, large-scale land sales were used to secure future loans and repay creditors.[151]

---

[147] Hughes, *Politics, Society and Civil War in Warwickshire*, 181, 186–7, 194, 214.

[148] PRO SP28/20, f. 223; PRO SP28/144/3, f. 5.

[149] PRO E351/1966; PRO E351/643–50; PRO E351/302; PRO SP28/350/5; PRO E351/1295.

[150] Ashton, *Crown and the Money Market*, 18, 23, 24–5, 99.

[151] Ibid. 119–20, 122, 127, 132–3.

From 1645 Parliament's financial administration began to improve, but lingering doubts about Parliament's good faith meant that many were unwilling to lend. This meant that few profited from this improvement. Doubling generated much greater enthusiasm, but it is probable that most Londoners who doubled did not make a profit. Those who lent money in the early years of the war, unless they had the money to double, found it very difficult to receive more than a small fraction of their money back. Those who did double, but were not able or willing to invest in the Bishops' lands, were able to get a larger part of their money back but only by selling their bills at a substantial discount.

The Civil War did not result in a major change in the London money market, at least as far as public finance was concerned. The loans were generally raised as before, the difference being the absence of major financiers of the stature of Sir Paul Pindar in the 1630s, or Vyner and Noel in the 1650s and 1660s. The failure of the war to make a significant impact may have been due to the failure of the Long Parliament to establish a reputation for trustworthiness in the early part of the war. The success of the £30,000 loan of December 1642 shows that at this stage a very large proportion of Londoners were willing to trust Parliament with their money. Had their trust been fulfilled Parliament could easily have raised very large sums from subsequent subscriptions. Lending to the state might have come to play an important part in the London economy not only for the very wealthy but also for a high proportion of London's economically active citizens. The only time that Londoners would again develop enthusiasm for lending to the Long Parliament was with the first two doubling ordinances, when they had the chance to recover at least a fraction of what they had lent in the early part of the war. The consequence of Parliament's reneging on its creditors was that parliamentary finance was handicapped during the 1640s and 1650s. Parliament's debts were never in themselves so large as to be unmanageable, they were only a small fraction of those accumulated by the British state in the early eighteenth century. What made Parliament's finances problematic was not their scale but the lack of any belief among London's moneyed men that they would be discharged faithfully.[152]

---

[152] Habakkuk, 'Public Finance', 83.

Chapter 4

Supplying Parliament's Armed Forces and Privateering

The vast majority of Parliament's military expenditure went on paying the wages of the soldiers. Between 1645 and 1651 the treasurers of the New Model Army spent about £250,000 on arming and equipping the army in England but over £4.25 million on pay. Nevertheless Parliament spent large sums of money on arming and equipping its forces and a high proportion of the contracts went to Londoners. Parliamentary privateering also needs to be considered in this context. To supplement their blockade of royalist and Irish ports Parliament authorized private individuals to send out warships in return for a share of the captured prizes. The privateers were therefore an auxiliary navy. Because they were mostly supplied by Londoners they, like the contracts for the conventional forces, provided opportunities for Londoners to profit, which compensated, at least in part, for the wartime taxes.[1]

Establishing the scale of expenditure on arms and equipment in the Civil War is complicated by the fact that purchases were made by a very large number of people and institutions. The major customers were the main armies and the navy, but Londoners also supplied the provincial forces and garrisons, which together may well have provided at least as much demand for arms and equipment as the main armies.[2] Moreover the way Parliament supplied its main field armies changed as the war continued. Consequently the evidence for contracting was scattered across a large number of sources many of which have not survived. However thanks to the heroic researches of Peter Edwards an overview of this subject is emerging. At least £450,000 was spent in London on purchasing arms, clothing and equipment for the armies between 1638 and 1652.[3] However this must be seen as a minimum figure, not only is

---

[1]   I. Gentles, 'The Arrears of Pay of the Parliamentary Army at the end of the first Civil War', *Bulletin of the Institute of Historical Research* 48 (1975), 63.

[2]   See for example PRO SP28/5, f. 362; A.M. Everitt (ed.), *Suffolk and the Great Rebellion, 1640–60*, Suffolk Records Society 3 (1960), 89–91.

[3]   P. Edwards, *Dealing in Death: The Arms Trade and the British Civil Wars, 1638–52* (Stroud, 2000). The figure is taken from a printout generously supplied by Dr Edwards from his database of military contracts. Only those contracts paid in full have been included. All mistakes are my own.

much of the evidence lost, but there are also other forms of expenditure, such as the navy, which also need to be included. The war also stimulated private demand for arms, for example at the outbreak of hostilities Edmund Heaman, a clothier from Devon, employed his brother, then living in London to purchase arms for himself and his servants.[4]

Large sums were also spent by the City on its own defences, and in particular on constructing the fortifications around the City, the eleven mile long 'lines of communication'. Although volunteers did much of the work, skilled craftsmen were also employed and large amounts of materials, especially timber, were purchased. However the contractors found it difficult to obtain payment. On 1 December 1643 the Common Council received a petition from various carpenters, bricklayers, smiths and other craftsmen who had worked on the fortifications, claiming £7,434 arrears for materials they had supplied. In the following April a further petition, probably from the same group of craftsmen, claimed roughly £7,500 for work and materials. A year later another petition was delivered to the Common Council for the payment of the arrears due for building the fortifications, and in the following December the craftsmen employed on the fortifications delivered yet another petition. In response to this last petition the Common Council successfully lobbied Parliament to obtain a grant of £32,000 from the excise to pay the arrears due to the contractors and also the guards who served on the fortifications.[5]

Recently published research by Aryeh Nusbacher on the victualling of the New Model Army has suggested that London may have also played an important role in feeding the armies. Soldiers in the Civil War were not usually supplied with rations by their army's administration unless they were involved in a siege. Instead they bought their own food with their pay, or, if they were not paid, their food was bought by those on whom they were quartered who received free quarter bills which, in theory, were paid at a later date. Aryeh Nusbacher has shown that the food was purchased from a travelling market, which followed the army on campaign, and he has argued that the food sold at the market came from London. If this was the case it would mean that a high proportion of the £4.25 million spent on the pay of the soldiers of the New Model Army went into the London economy, probably dwarfing the total spent in London on arming, equipping and clothing the army. However there is no direct evidence to show that the market was supplied from London and every reason for supposing that it was not. It was not economic to move foodstuffs other than livestock long distance by land and for most of the army's life it would not have been possible to supply it by water. The cost of transporting

4   PRO HCA13/60, examination of Richard Heaman, 8 May 1645.
5   V. Smith and P. Kelsey, 'The Lines of Communication: The Civil War Defences of London', in S. Porter (ed.), *London and the Civil War* (Basingstoke, 1996), 117–45; CLRO Jour. 40, ff. 80v, 91–2, 136, 156, 160, 162v–3.

food from London to the army would therefore have been prohibitively expensive. When the New Model Army was on active service its soldiers were paid promptly, they were therefore able to pay for their food with ready cash, and the high command made sure that the market was protected. Given these favourable circumstances it is likely that the farmers in the regions through which the army passed flocked to supply the market.[6]

London was not the sole source of supplies for Parliament's armed forces. In the early years of the war a large proportion of the arms bought by Parliament were imported. Most of the artillery was made in the Weald, although some of the smaller pieces were made in London. Parliament's regional and local forces were generally supplied with clothing and some of their arms from local sources. However London was the major source for personal weapons for all Parliament's forces and was also the principal supplier of clothing for the main field armies. Londoners also sometimes benefited from contracts placed outside the metropolis. Gunpowder was generally made in mills in Surrey and the Lea Valley, many of which were owned by Londoners.[7]

The impact of military contracting was not always entirely beneficial. Privateering proved a risky business and never became such a major enterprise as it had been during the Elizabethan Spanish wars. In the early part of the war Parliament's suppliers generally found it very difficult to get payment for their contracts, consequently military contracting may have had a deflationary impact on the London economy. By 1645 Parliament's wartime administration had improved substantially, and ready payment became the norm. Prices were low, but in the latter part of the war the resources that contracting brought in to the London economy must have been considerable. In the long term the war brought about a major expansion in the London armament industry. However it is difficult to ascribe any major structural changes to the war. The livery companies played a significant role in military contracting, providing a point of contact between Parliament and the craftsmen and helping with quality control. There is little evidence that the war lead to shift towards more 'capitalistic' modes of production.

---

[6]   A.J.S. Nusbacher, 'Civil Supply in the Civil War: Supply of Victuals to the New Model Army on the Naseby Campaign, 1–14 June 1645', *EHR* 115 (2000), 145–60; M. Overton, *Agricultural Revolution in England: The Transformation of the Agrarian Economy 1500–1850* (Cambridge, 1996), 137–40; P. Musgrave, *The Early Modern European Economy* (Basingstoke, 1999), 76. Also in the summer of 1645 the New Model Army marched from 136 miles in fifteen days. Unless the suppliers of the market knew where the army was going they would have found it very difficult to know where to direct their wagons. I. Gentles, *The New Model Army in England, Ireland and Scotland, 1645–1653* (Oxford, 1992), 66. I owe this point to Dr Ian Archer.

[7]   Edwards, *Dealing in Death*, 92–7,108–12.

The main armies

When the Earl of Essex's army was raised in the summer of 1642 the job of keeping it supplied with arms and equipment was divided between three bodies. The provision of clothing was placed under the control of Stephen Estwicke, a prominent London supporter of Parliament, together with two partners, Francis Peck and Thomas Player. The supply of munitions was divided between a new store established under two more London supporters of Parliament, Owen Rowe and John Bradley, and the existing Ordnance department in the Tower. Moreover money was often paid directly to Essex's officers to buy equipment for their units. The system was dogged by financial difficulties, primarily because sufficient money was not available, although the administrative fragmentation must also have played a part.

In August 1642 Stephen Estwicke was commissioned to purchase clothing for the Earl of Essex's army. It was agreed that he would be paid by the treasurer of the army, Sir Gilbert Gerrard, 15s 4d for every man clothed. Not long after the clothing previously purchased for the forces in Ireland was transferred to Estwicke's keeping to be issued for the use of Essex's soldiers, but this provided only a small part of what was needed. In the first eight months of the war, Estwicke issued over £23,000 worth of clothing, of which less than £2,000 came from the Irish stores. Unfortunately the surviving records do not tell us where the additional clothing was purchased from, but, as Estwicke was a London haberdasher, it seems likely that much of it came from London.[8]

At first Estwicke was paid promptly but his accounts soon fell into arrears. When Essex issued a warrant to pay Estwicke £1,500 on 13 August 1642, he received the first £60 on the same day and the balance three days later. When a further warrant to pay him £1,500 was issued on 1 September it was not fully paid until 10 October. On 4 October Gerrard was ordered to pay Estwicke £600 per week for twelve weeks, but by 10 December he had only received six such payments. On 7 November Gerrard was ordered to pay Estwicke £400 per week for twelve weeks but this time only three payments were made, while when a new order was issued to pay him £400 per week for twelve weeks on 4 December no payments were made at all.[9]

An audit of Estwicke's accounts made on 28 April 1643; showed a deficit of £12,164 and revealed that he had not received any money since 3 December 1642. In the following month another warrant was issued to pay him

---

[8] PRO SP16/491/103, 124; PRO SP28/146, ff. 123–9. V. Pearl, *London and the Outbreak of the Puritan Revolution: City Government and National Politics 1625–1643* (Oxford, 1961), 315.

[9] PRO SP28/1A, ff. 85–v; PRO SP28/2A, f. 38; PRO SP28/146, ff. 123–9; PRO SP28/261, ff. 430–3; PRO SP28/262, f. 317.

£1,000 a week for twelve weeks, but nothing had been paid to him by August when Parliament ordered Estwicke to provide a further £8,000 worth of clothing for the soldiers. At the same time Parliament assigned £10,000 from the receipts of the twentieth part in London, Westminster and Middlesex to pay Estwicke's debts. The order to satisfy Estwicke's arrears was probably made to enable him to make fresh purchases, as it would have given Estwicke's suppliers hope that their bills would be paid. The £8,000 for the new order was not fully paid until 12 April 1644. Evidence for the payment of Estwicke's arrears is sketchy, the last reference to a payment is in April 1644, at which date the balance was still owing. It is possible that the full sum was never paid. It is likely that the contractors who supplied Estwicke and his colleagues had to wait a very long time for the payment of their bills.[10]

Other suppliers suffered similarly in the early years of the war. In 1642 Parliament gained control of a large magazine of arms at Hull. In the summer they were shipped to London and placed in the keeping of Rowe and Bradley who were ordered to issue them to the army. Subsequently they were authorized to buy additional weaponry. By the summer of 1644 they had purchased over £34,000 of arms. A large proportion of this went into the London economy. In September 1642 alone they contracted for 16,127 swords, 15,620 sword belts and carbine girdles and 7720 bandoleers from various London craftsmen.[11]

The craftsmen who supplied Rowe and Bradley found it difficult to obtain payments of their bills. On 14 April 1643 Sir Gilbert Gerrard wrote on a bill for £77 5s due to Marmaduke Saunders for 1030 sword belts delivered in the previous November: 'I am informed this man is very poore there is owing unto him three bills besides this, and if this bee not paied he is like to be arres[t]ed'.[12] In October 1643 the Gunmakers' Company petitioned Parliament complaining that large sums were owed to them for arms they had supplied. On 13 March 1644 the Commons was petitioned by a group of girdlers, saddlers, cutlers and other craftsmen, almost certainly concerning the money owed them for equipment they had supplied. In July 1644 and December 1645 the excise was extended to new commodities to help pay Parliament's debts for arms and equipment. But in October 1646 various craftsmen again petitioned the Commons for the payment of their debts. At the Restoration, Parliament still had debts of £17,012 to various London gunsmiths dating from the 1640s.[13]

---

[10]   PRO SP28/146, ff. 123–9; PRO SP28/264, f. 362; PRO SP16/497/142; *LJ* VI, 175; *CCAM*, I, 29, 337; III, 1490, 1491.

[11]   PRO SP28/147, ff. 562–97; PRO SP28/261, ff. 426, 428.

[12]   PRO SP28/264, f. 90.

[13]   HLRO House of Lords Main Papers, 26 October 1643, Petition of the Gunmaker's Company; *CJ* IV, 76, 250, 681; *Firth & Rait*, I, 466, 806–9; *CJ* VIII, 242.

In the early months of the war the ordnance office only provided artillery and shot for Essex's army and the parliamentarian garrisons. Initially the office was poorly funded, however in 1644 it began to receive substantial subventions from the excise. The office took over the role of Rowe and Bradley's stores, becoming the main purchaser of armaments for Essex's army. With the creation of the New Model Army in the beginning of 1645 the Ordnance Office took control over the whole work of supplying the army.[14]

Parliament imported the majority of its arms. Imports of firearms were particularly important because the pre-war gunmaking industry had been relatively small and was almost entirely occupied refurbishing existing stocks in the early months of the war. In September 1642 Parliament employed Alderman Thomas Andrewes and Stephen Estwicke to purchase £15,000 worth of arms in Holland and France. Moreover initially a large proportion of the arms purchased by Rowe and Bradley were imports. However the increased demand of the war years led to an expansion of production. By the spring of 1643 significant quantities of small arms were coming from London producers. By October 1643 the London Gunsmith's Company were arguing that they could supply all of Parliament's needs. Nevertheless in the early months of the war a large proportion of spending on supplying the armies was going abroad.[15]

Essex's army was not the only army raised by Parliament during the early part of the Civil War. The arrangement for supplying the army of the Eastern Association was separate from that of Essex's army, but it relied on similar sources for the purchase of armaments. Initially there were large purchases of arms from the Low Countries; one merchant from King's Lynn imported nearly £8,000 of munitions in early 1644. However London was also a major source of arms. Between February and mid April 1644 the Association's representative in the capital purchased £6,665 worth of arms. From May the Association stopped buying imported arms and London became the main source of supply. However London provided only a small proportion of the army's clothing. Except for important purchases in December 1644, the main sources of clothing were East Anglian craftsmen. It is likely that the Eastern Association was typical of Parliament's regional and local forces in purchasing its clothing locally but its arms first abroad and later from London.[16]

---

[14] Edwards, *Dealing in Death*, 31, 32, 46–7; PRO SP28/17, ff. 11, 13, 35, 37, 43, 45, 47, 49.

[15] Edwards, *Dealing in Death*, 71–2; 199; PRO SP28/2B, f. 540; PRO SP28/261, f. 284; PRO SP28/5, ff. 377, 378; HLRO House of Lords Main Papers, 26 October 1643, Petition of the Gunmakers' Company.

[16] C. Holmes, *The Eastern Association in the English Civil War* (1974), 151–2.

By the time the New Model Army was established in early 1645 the London armaments industry had grown sufficiently to supply the army with most of what it needed, which meant that the London economy at last began to benefit from supplying the war. The accounts of the treasurers of the New Model Army show that they spent about £257,000 on supplies for the Army in England. The majority of this expenditure took place in the early part of the army's existence; £116,823 was contracted for in its first year. There were about 200 suppliers and, where the addresses are given, they seem always to have been Londoners. Only a few of the contracts for powder and match were specifically for imported goods. Moreover most of the contracts were made directly with craftsmen rather than merchants. The level of imports may have been higher than this suggests. Many of the contractors may have been assembling components imported from abroad. During the Civil War large numbers of sword blades and gunlocks were imported from the Netherlands. Moreover low prices left little scope for war profiteering. Nevertheless the contracts for the New Model Army were paid promptly. It is evident that a very substantial proportion of what was raised in the metropolis from the monthly assessment for the New Model Army returned to the London economy through contracting. Indeed it is likely that, in the first year of its existence, supplying the New Model Army resulted in a net inflow of resources into London. This did not last as expenditure on equipment declined after the end of the first Civil War, although further sums were expended on equipment for the army's campaigns in Ireland and Scotland.[17]

The navy and privateering

The navy did not expand significantly during the Civil War. Parliament built no new ships in the state dockyards until 1646. Eight ships were bought for the navy between 1642 and 1645, but none of them were very large vessels, and the largest, the frigate the *Warwick*, was probably one of the two frigates purchased in Holland in early 1643. Nevertheless the Civil War may well have stimulated the shipping and maritime industries in the metropolis. The navy itself may not have been augmented, but large numbers of merchant ships were employed in Parliament's navy: 124 were hired in the years 1643–45, at a cost of £250,184, mostly from London ship owners. Moreover in the immediate

---

[17] Gentles, *New Model Army*, 41–2; Idem, 'Arrears of Pay', 62; Edwards, *Dealing in Death*, 178, 201, 211.

post-war period Parliament did start to build new ships, and the Commonwealth period saw a major expansion of the navy.[18]

The navy did not escape the financial problems that beset Parliament in the early part of the war. The owners of merchant ships often had difficulties in receiving prompt payment for the freight of their ships; in December 1643 William Cockayne, the deputy governor of the East India Company, petitioned the navy committee complaining that he was still owed £444 from the previous year. In the summer of 1643 the navy suffered a major financial crisis when the customs' commissioners refused to lend money to pay off the summer fleet. Parliament was unable to pay the freight for the merchant ships hired for the summer fleet in that year, and they were kept on for several months after they had returned to port, while the seamen came to the doors of Parliament clamouring for wages. In 1645–46 £41,007 was paid to the owners of hired ships, but £92,124 remained due. At the Restoration £26,000 was still owed for ships employed by Parliament in the first Civil War.[19]

The London economy may well have been more stimulated by parliamentarian privateering. In November 1642 Parliament authorized privateers to prey on merchant ships trading with ports controlled by the royalists. This effectively extended provisions which had been made the month before to authorize privateering against the Irish Rebellion. Parliamentary privateers attacked royalist and Irish shipping indiscriminately. The Venetian ambassador reported that this was generally welcomed because of the lack of alternative employment for shipping. Moreover new ships were built in London for privateering, such as the *Constant Warwick*.[20]

Privateering vessels were very expensive, one ship cost between £1,500 and £1,600 to purchase and fit out. They therefore needed to take a large number of prizes to become profitable. In February 1644 a group consisting predominantly of London merchants sent out a squadron of five ships, four prizes were taken, but the costs exceeded the returns, and the ships were recalled in the following November. In January 1644 Maurice Thompson, one of the most active promoters of parliamentarian privateering, sent out the *Hopeful Mary* as a privateer. It took four vessels, two of which were sold for £1,300, but the other two were not adjudged good prizes and were returned to

---

[18] R.C. Anderson, *List of English Men of War, 1509–1649* (1959), 305–366; K.R. Andrews, *Ships, Money and Politics, Seafaring and Naval Enterprise in the Reign of Charles I* (Cambridge, 1991), 191.

[19] G. Grene, *A Declaration in Vindication of the Honour of the Parliament* (1647), 11–12; BL Harl. MS. 165, Parliamentary Journal of Sir Simonds D'Ewes, 1641–43, f. 159v; J.R. Tanner (ed.), *Two Discourses of the Navy, 1638 and 1659, by John Hollond*, Naval Record Society (1896), 138–40; Bodl. Rawlinson MS. A221, Journal of the Committee for the Navy, 1643–44, f. 302; PRO E351/2285; *CJ* VIII, 244.

[20] *Firth & Rait*, I, 33–6, 42–4; A.W. Johns, 'The Constant Warwick', *MM* 18 (1932), 254; *CSPV*, 1642–43, 220.

their owners. Consequently the proceeds from the prizes failed to compensate for the costs that Thompson and his partners incurred.[21] Thompson was a part owner of the *Discovery*, one of most successful of the privateers, capturing as many as twenty seven prizes in the Irish Sea. But the owners claimed that their captain had been obliged to deliver £7,447 worth of the goods he had captured to Lord Inchiquin, the commander of the pro-parliamentarian forces in Munster. In April 1645 Thompson and his colleagues petitioned Parliament claiming that they could not pay off their sailors without reimbursement, nevertheless they did not obtain an order for payment until August 1647. Moreover they were only voted £4,642, of which over £2,000 was still outstanding in April 1651.[22] The largest single private naval enterprise in this period was the 'sea adventure' initiated in 1642 against the Irish rebels. Investors were promised reimbursement of their capital in land confiscated from the Irish rebels when Ireland was re-conquered in addition to any prizes taken by their ships. A total of £43,000 was subscribed and the forces raised by the 'sea adventure' soon became engaged against the royalists as well as the Irish. Nevertheless it proved a disappointment, in October 1642 the investors demanded a guarantee that they would be repaid their expenses within a year, and, by June 1643, it had run out of money.[23]

K.R. Andrews found that the most profitable Elizabethan privateering ventures were those that combined trade with privateering. There were similar ventures in the 1640s, it seems to have been relatively common for commanders of ships setting out to trade with the plantations in America and the Caribbean to take letters of marque with them. Consequently there were a number of clashes between ships from London and ships from royalist ports in the waters off Newfoundland, New England, Virginia, Nevis and Barbados. In 1645 the *Samuel* sailed from London on a fishing voyage to Newfoundland, the fish was then carried to Spain where it was sold and a range of Spanish goods were purchased for import into England. Additionally while the *Samson* was in Newfoundland she took three ships from royalist ports in the West Country. The advantage of privateering like this for London merchants was that if the voyage was successful as a trading venture then any prizes were pure profit. However privateering of this kind risked enraging the colonial authorities. After two London ships attacked a Bristol ship in Virginia in 1644

[21] PRO C24/699/67; S. Groenveld, 'The English Civil Wars as a Cause of the First Anglo-Dutch War, 1640–52', *HJ* 30 (1987), 51 & n. 37; E.J. Courthorpe (ed.), *The Journal of Thomas Cuningham of Campvere, 1640–1654* (Edinburgh, 1928), 73–4, 101; PRO C24/699/46; PRO C24/704/52.

[22] Andrews, *Ships, Money and Politics*, 194; PRO SP28/265, ff. 1, 9–10; *LJ* IX, 389–90; PRO E351/2514.

[23] Andrews, *Ships, Money and Politics*, 195–7; K.S. Bottigheimer, *English Money and Irish Land: The 'Adventurers' in the Cromwellian Settlement of Ireland* (Oxford, 1971), 81–2; PRO SP28/7, f. 486.

they were forced to leave the colony without a cargo. Moreover most privateers were warships sent out solely to attack the royalists, which operated in conjunction with Parliament's navy in the Irish Sea or the Channel.[24]

Parliamentarian privateering during the Civil War was limited compared with previous conflicts. A list of prize judgements passed by the High Court of Admiralty between December 1643 and October 1646 contains 268 sentences, more were passed before this date but they are relatively few. In contrast between 1626 and 1630, when England was at war with Spain and France, at least 737 prizes were taken. Moreover a substantial proportion of the prizes taken during the Civil War were captured by the regular navy. In June 1646 Parliament's navy commissioners claimed that 149 vessels had been taken by the navy, suggesting that it was responsible for about fifty per cent of the prizes. The collectors appointed by Parliament in early 1644 to sell prizes taken by navy ships received £76,188 between February 1644 and the end of July 1646. It is likely that the receipts of the privateers were not much more, and certainly substantially less than the £100–200,000 a year taken by the Elizabethan privateers.[25]

The majority of the privateers were supplied merchants such as Maurice Thompson, who were active supporters of Parliament. The fact that privateering failed to attract a broad range of investors suggests that it was not profitable.[26] Indeed the low profits from privateering was recognized by Parliament, which subsidized their victualling costs from December 1643, although only those ships sent out solely as privateers were eligible. Nevertheless privateering did provide employment for a significant number of ships and seamen during the war. In the summer of 1644 twenty five vessels were listed as privateers receiving the subsidy and in total Parliament paid for forty eight privateering vessels during the first Civil War. It is likely that the fundamental problem for the privateers was that the parliamentarians controlled the major ports; consequently there were simply not enough

---

[24] K.R. Andrews, *Elizabethan Privateering: English Privateering during the Spanish War, 1585–1603* (Cambridge, 1964), 135; PRO HCA24/106/276, 332; PRO HCA24/108/20; PRO HCA13/60, Examinations of James Small 10 May 1645, Aron Ruddock 5 May 1645, Nicholas Browne 13 November 1645, John Skinner 10 November 1645, John Smith, 28 September 1646; R.S. Dunn et al (eds), *The Journal of John Winthrop 1630–44* (Cambridge Mass., 1966), 606; D.P. de Vries, 'Voyages from Holland to America, 1632–1644', *New York Historical Society Collections* 2nd Series, 3 (1857), 126; Andrews, *Ships, Money and Politics*, 197–8.
[25] PRO HCA34/1; Groenveld, 'English Civil Wars', 550, n. 33; R.G. Marsden (ed.), *Documents Relating to Law and Custom of the Sea*, Naval Record Society, 2 vols (1915–1916), I, 525–7; N.A.M. Rodger, *The Safeguard of the Sea: A Naval History of Britain, Volume One, 660–1649* (1997), 361; *The Answer of the Commissioners of the Navie* (1646), 10; PRO E351/2513; Andrews, *Elizabethan Privateering*, 128.
[26] Groenveld, 'English Civil Wars', 548.

merchant ships which traded with the royalist ports to make privateering worthwhile.[27]

Contracting and the structure of the London economy

The war led to a major expansion in London's armaments industry. Over 30,000 pikes, 102,000 swords, and 111,000 firearms were produced between August 1642 and September 1651. Munitions constituted more than half the money spent on contracting for the armies between 1638–51, during which time over £200,000 was spent on muskets and pistols alone.[28] However there is little evidence that military contracting qualitatively changed the structure of the economy. Most manufacturing industry continued to be workshop based and there is little sign of a move towards larger, more capital intensive, modes of production. Where large contracts were placed with small numbers of suppliers they were usually acting as representatives of larger groups of manufactures. The conservatism in the methods of production is exemplified by the continuity of personnel. Many of the men who supplied Parliament, such as the gunfounder John Browne, had also been involved supplying the Caroline regime with arms. Contracts for swords were shared between members of the London Cutlers' Company and outsiders like Benjamin Stone, as they had been during the Bishops' Wars.[29]

Firearms continued to be produced with the traditional workshop based methods. Large numbers of gunmakers supplied Parliament, mostly producing small quantities. Matchlock muskets, which made up the vast majority of muskets in the Civil War, could be made by ordinary blacksmiths. Consequently higher levels of production were achieved by the influx of more craftsmen into gunmaking rather than an increase in the scale of production. Some suppliers of swords operated on a larger scale. Benjamin Stone had established a blademill at Hounslow Heath in 1629 which enabled him to produce swords in large numbers. However it is not clear what happened to Stone's mill after his death in early 1643. It is possible that Lawrence Bromfield, who supplied Parliament with 24,000 swords, may have had a similar plant but large numbers of swords were also made by cutlers in small workshops. Even a large producer like Stone needed partners such as Abraham Ivory who in December 1642 supplied him with swords to fulfil a contract, which they had agreed should be made in Stone's name only. Stone agreed to

---

[27] *Firth & Rait*, I, 347–51; *Powell & Timings*, 139–40; Andrews, *Ships, Money and Politics*, 192 n. 20.

[28] Edwards, *Dealing in Death*, 71. Figures for expenditure from data supplied by Dr Edwards.

[29] M.C. Fissel, *The Bishops' Wars, Charles I's Campaigns against Scotland, 1638–1640* (Cambridge, 1994), 100, 103–6; Gentles, *New Model Army*, 42; PRO SP28/261, f. 428.

pay him £31 for his costs plus half the profits if the contract was paid within three days, or the full profits if they were kept waiting any longer. Ivory's subordinate position is explained by his own admission that he was a beginner. It is highly likely that many other contracts were farmed out to junior craftsmen. Increased specialization and division of labour also expanded production. Contractors would have been able to assemble large numbers of arms in a short space of time by buying components from others. This would have enabled the more highly skilled craftsmen to concentrate on those components, such as gunlocks, which were difficult to produce. Components were also frequently imported even when the finished product was assembled in London.[30]

The production of armaments was only a small part of London's manufacturing industry before the war but received the majority of contracts to supply the military. Consequently the impact of contracting on the armaments sector is likely to have been more far reaching than that on other sectors of manufacturing. The effect of army contracting on other sectors of manufacturing industry can be illustrated by studying the provision of shoes. The London Cordwainers' Company was still closely connected with the craft in this period, which means that the trade is relatively well documented. Alan Everitt has argued that Northampton was the main source for shoes for Parliament's armies, but this seems to be incorrect.[31] Shoes were purchased in the town to supply the forces sent to Ireland in early 1642 but there is no evidence that Northampton supplied shoes on a regular basis to the main parliamentarian armies during the Civil War. It has not been possible to establish who made the shoes for Parliament's armies in the early part of the war because they were purchased by Stephen Estwicke, and none of his contracts have survived. It is possible that Estwicke was purchasing shoes in Northampton, but the contract book for the New Model Army shows that in 1645 all the shoes were purchased in London. They may have sub-contracted some of the work to Northampton shoemakers, but this is unlikely because the contracts had to be fulfilled quickly. In February 1645 the army committee placed a contract for eight thousand pairs of shoes stipulating that they were to be delivered to the Tower of London within a fortnight.[32]

---

[30] Edwards, *Dealing in Death*, 2, 68–7, 72–3; PRO SP28/263, ff. 96–v.

[31] A.M. Everitt, *The Local Community and the Great Rebellion* (1969), 14.

[32] V.F. Snow and A.S. Young (eds), *The Private Journals of the Long Parliament, Vol. 3: 2nd June to 17th September 1642* (New Haven, 1992), 422; *CJ* III, 493; PRO SP28/305, unfoliated; *CSPD*, 1648–9, 227, 230; Mungeam, 'Contracts for the Supply of the "New Model" Army', 75–6. Edwards, *Dealing in Death*, 136. Dr Edwards argues that the production of shoes was sub-contracted to Northampton shoemakers because in 1648 contracts were paid out of the Northamptonshire monthly assessment, however the London shoemakers went to Northampton to collect their money, if they had purchased the shoes there it would surely have been more efficient for them to have assigned the money to their suppliers.

Part of the reason why the Northampton industry did not play a larger part in supply shoes in the 1640s was because it was disrupted by labour shortages during the war. A further reason may have been prices. The shoes purchased in Northampton in 1642 were only slightly cheaper than those provided by the Londoners, at most the difference was 2d a pair, and this excluded the cost of transport. The contacts with the Northampton shoemakers specified delivery at Northampton and, given that the main depot for the New Model Army was at Reading, when transport costs were included London shoes may well have been cheaper.[33]

The Cordwainers' Company was not usually directly involved in contracting, although the company officers were employed to check the quality of deliveries for the army. An exception was a contract for £1,575 to provide boots for Parliament's Scottish allies which seems to have been made with the Cordwainers' Company.[34] There is no record of contracts being made with the company for the supply of English forces but contracts for other items were sometimes placed with livery companies. In April 1645 contracts were made with the Cutlers' Company to provide 3200 swords, and with the Saddlers' Company to provide 600 saddles for the New Model Army. The companies provided a useful point of contact between the parliamentarian authorities and the London craftsmen, and this may have enhanced the role of the livery companies in the London economy.[35]

The most important contractor for shoes for the New Model Army was Jenkin Ellis. Sometimes the contracts are in his name only, but generally there are others named with him. The recurrence of the same names and phrases like 'Jenkin Ellis and his Company' suggests a reasonably stable partnership, although in early 1646 they appear to have combined with seven other contractors to fulfil an exceptionally large contract for seven thousand pairs of shoes. It is likely that where only his name occurs he was acting as representative for the partnership. They provided 19,500 of the 32,000 pairs of shoes purchased in the first year of the New Model Army's existence. They were not new to army contracting, Jenkin Ellis and one of his regular partners,

---

[33] V.F. Snow and A.S. Young (eds), *The Private Journals of the Long Parliament, Vol. 2: 7th March to 1st June 1642* (New Haven, 1987), 462; Snow and Young, *Private Journals of the Long Parliament, Vol. 3*, 388, 422; PRO SP28/1B, f. 672; PRO SP28/1C, f. 194; PRO SP28/1D, f. 451; Gentles, *New Model Army*, 40.

[34] GL MS. 7351/2, Cordwainers' Company, Wardens' Accounts, 1636–78, accounts 1645–46; *CSPD*, 1649–50, 412, 561; PRO E351/1966.

[35] Mungeam, 'Contracts for the Supply of the "New Model" Army', 114. There is no record of the contracts made directly with the companies in their own records, probably they were informally distributed among the membership.

John Mings, supplied shoes for Sir William Waller's Army. Ellis and his partners also provided shoes for Parliament's Scottish allies in 1644.[36]

Jenkin Ellis and John Mings were both members of the livery of the Cordwainers' Company when the war started. This meant they were part of the elite of the company chosen by the court of assistants and from whom the ruling wardens were drawn, and Ellis became one of the company's wardens in 1647. Another frequently mentioned member of the partnership, Francis Marriot, was not as senior in the company hierarchy, but he was nominated by the court of assistants to be one of the company's searchers of leather in 1642 and 1643. In 1645 he was chosen to be one of the stewards of the company's dinner on Lord Mayor's Day, an office which brought with it automatic elevation to the livery at the end of the year. Men like Ellis and his partners were not at the top of the company's hierarchy when they started supplying shoes for the army but they do not appear to have been disaffected from the company's government, they appear to have been rising men who had the support of the company's rulers.[37]

Ellis and his partners were not the only members of the Cordwainers' Company to supply shoes to Parliament. Contracts to provide shoes for the New Model Army also went to Laurence Stanley who, like Ellis and Mings, had joined the livery in 1641, and Robert Botley, who became a liveryman in April 1645. Botley worked with two junior members of the company, Jeffrey Badger who became a freeman in July 1641, and John Jones who had only been admitted in August 1642. Jones was probably not as young as his recent entry into the company suggests. He became a freeman by redemption, which means he bought his way in, and his subsequent rise through the company hierarchy was comparatively rapid. He became a liveryman in November 1645 and was elected a warden of the company in 1650, although he preferred to pay a fine rather than serve. Stanley, Jones, Botley and Badger had all provided shoes for the Scottish Army in 1644. Moreover Stanley, Jones and Badger supplied shoes for the army raised to suppress the Irish rebellion in 1642. Another Cordwainer who provided shoe for the soldiers sent to fight the Irish was Edward Poole who also supplied the army of the Eastern Association in 1644.[38]

---

[36] Mungeam, 'Contracts for the Supply of the "New Model" Army', 75, 78, 83, 89, 109, 115; PRO SP28/37 f. 356; PRO SP46/106, ff. 3, 4, 29, 35, 49; *LJ* VII, 192.

[37] PRO E179/251/22; GL MS. 7351/1, Cordwainers' Company, Wardens' Accounts, 1595–1636, unfoliated; GL MS. 7351/2, unfoliated; GL MS. 7353/1, Cordwainers' Company, Court Minutes, 1622–53, ff. 2, 65, 225v, 247v, 262v, 287, 300.

[38] Mungeam, 'Contracts for the Supply of the "New Model" Army', 109, 105; GL MS. 7353/1; PRO SP46/106, ff. 3, 29, 49; Snow and Young, *Private Journals of the Long Parliament, Vol. 2*, 462; Snow and Young, *Private Journals of the Long Parliament, Vol. 3*, 388; Edwards, *Dealing in Death*, 137.

Several of the contractors were subsequently elected wardens of the Cordwainers' Company, including Botley, Marriott and Stanley, but they had usually started their rise through the company's hierarchy before the war and army contractors certainly never dominated the company, as most of the wardens elected in the 1650s had not previously been contractors. Moreover it is unlikely that the contractors became very wealthy as a result of supplying the armies. The prices of shoes, like other goods supplied to the army, fell as the war progressed. Parliament paid 2s 3d a pair for the shoes for the New Model Army in 1645, in contrast to 2s 5d or 2s 6d a pair paid for shoes for the army in Ireland in 1642 and 2s 10d a pair paid by the Clothworkers' Company for shoes purchased as part of a charitable foundation in 1640–41. Contracting does not seem to have stimulated social mobility in London.[39]

The majority of the shoes provided for the New Model Army came from members of the Cordwainers' Company, but contracts also went to shoemakers who were not freemen of the City. Some of them were suburban craftsmen such as Thomas Taylor, who lived in Covent Garden, and Edward Chipperfield who lived in Holborn. The Cordwainers' Company would not necessarily have been hostile to them. Suburban shoemakers did not need to be members of the company and sometimes bound their apprentices at Cordwainers' Hall even though they were not members. Indeed Taylor undertook one contract for the New Model Army in partnership with Lawrence Stanley. Other non-free shoemakers worked within the City; the Edward Johnson who contracted for shoes for the New Model Army in 1645 was probably the same Edward Johnson who was listed as an unfree shoemaker living in Martins le Grand in 1641. This was one of the ancient ecclesiastical liberties which had only been brought within the jurisdiction of the City in 1608 and which still contained many craftsmen who were not free of the City. Legally the Cordwainers' Company could have prosecuted Johnson for not being a freeman but in practice the company may have been willing to tolerate him. He was part of partnerships with members of the company which supplied shoes for the army raised to fight the Irish rebellion in 1642 and which supplied the Scottish Army in 1644. However at least the Cordwainers' Company regarded one of the non-free shoemakers who provided shoes for the New Model Army, Richard Crafter of Blackfriars, with hostility; they prosecuted him in 1645–46.[40]

There are other examples of contracts being placed with people who were outside the traditional structures of the London economy and in conflict with the livery companies. The New Model Army was supplied with saddles

---

[39] Snow and Young, *Private Journals of the Long Parliament, Vol. 3*, 388; CH, Wardens' Accounts, 1639–49, Quarter Wardens' accounts, 1640–1.

[40] Mungeam, 'Contracts for the Supply of the "New Model" Army', 75, 89, 99, 109; PRO E179/252/1; Snow and Young, *Private Journals of the Long Parliament, Vol. 3*, 388; PRO SP46/106, f. 3; GL MS. 7351/2.

by Elizabeth Betts who was prosecuted by the Saddlers' Company because she was the widow of a non-freeman. However disputes between livery companies and non-freemen were endemic in seventeenth-century London, consequently cases such as that of Betts and Crafter do not indicate that contracting encouraged production by non-freemen. An exception to this was the production of arms. During the war there were complaints from gunmakers and armourers that large numbers of non-freemen were entering their craft. It is likely that in these crafts, where the war saw a massive increase in demand there was a large infusion of new workers, many of whom were not freemen, but that in the production of goods such as shoes and saddles, which were much in demand in the peacetime economy, the war probably made less difference and consequently there was more continuity.[41]

Many of the Cordwainers involved in supplying the army were craftsmen, Jeffrey Badger, Robert Botley, John Mings, Francis Marriott, and Edward Poole all became free of the company on submission of examples of their work. Nevertheless given the size of the contracts it is likely that a large part of the work was sub-contracted to other craftsmen. However there was nothing new in poorer shoemakers working for their wealthier colleagues. Most shoemakers in seventeenth-century London were masters rather than wage earners, but by the 1630s there were large numbers who had no shops, referred to in the Cordwainers' records as 'chamber workers'. The most successful shopkeepers could not produce enough shoes to supply their customers so they purchased additional stocks, which led to the increase in the numbers of the 'chamber workers'. This provided a ready pool of labour, which the army contractors could utilize in the 1640s. Moreover some wealthier Cordwainers were also dealers in leather, buying up stocks from tanners, having it cured, and then selling it to the 'chamber workers'.[42] It is possible that the army contractors were drawn predominantly from the dealers in leather. They would have had the necessary contacts with the craftsmen, and they would have been able to supply them with the leather they needed. James Graves purchased £42 of leather seized by the Cordwainers' Company in 1639–40. He provided shoes for the forces sent to Ireland in 1642 and the Scottish Army in 1644. He is regularly mentioned as a partner with Jenkin Ellis in contracts placed during the Commonwealth and it is possible that he was an unnamed member of the Ellis' partnership which supplied the New

---

[41] Mungeam, 'Contracts for the Supply of the "New Model" Army', 66, 80, 81, 114; GL MS. 5385, Saddlers Company, Court Minutes, 1605–65, ff. 247, 255 260v, 262v; CLRO Rep. 57/2, f. 81; GL MS. 12071/3, Armourers' Company, Court Minutes, 1621–75, f. 144v.

[42] T.R. Forbes, 'Weaver And Cordwainer: Occupation in the Parish of St Giles Cripplegate, London in 1654–1693 and 1729–1743', *Guildhall Studies in London History* 4 (1980), 123; GL MS. 7353/1, f. 100; L.A. Clarkson, 'The Organisation of the English Leather Industry in the Late Sixteenth and Seventeenth Centuries', *EcHR* 2nd Series, 13 (1960), 251.

Model Army. Also Edward Poole was among the owners of a consignment of 165 Irish hides seized in December 1640 because they were poorly tanned.[43]

The production of clothing was probably organized on a similar basis to that of footwear, with the contractors, who were almost always drapers, providing the textiles to tailors and seamstresses who made the clothes. The difference was that distinction between the contractors and the craftsmen was more clear cut. The failure of tailors to contract for the supply of clothing reflects changes which had taken place in the organization of the clothing industry in London since the Elizabethan period. The sale of clothing had become increasingly divorced from its production. A group of intermediaries, called 'salesmen' had emerged who retailed, but did not produce, clothing. By the middle of the seventeenth century the demand for clothing from the London population, which numbered 400,000, was enormous. Consequently there was a large pool of craftsmen and women employed making ready-made clothing for others who could be utilized by the military contractors.[44]

The very limited impact on contracting for the army on sectors other than the production of arms is also shown by Peter Edwards's study of the supply of horses. He has emphasized the importance of a small group of Smithfield market dealers in providing horses for the Parliament's armies. Between 3 April and 26 August 1645 they sold 6708 horses for the New Model Army. He has argued that those who were most involved in supplying the armies were not particularly committed to the cause, but prominent, long established, traders who needed some means of maintaining their businesses in the war years. On the other hand he has also argued that the contractors tended to operate outside the existing markets and fairs, and suggested that the war encouraged the growth of private trading in horses. Nevertheless this only accelerated existing changes in economic practices and structures.[45]

It was the pre-existing structure of the London economy that determined the way in which supplies were produced for the army, and there is little evidence of any changes in economic organization. Although the production of small arms expanded enormously it mainly continued in the same, workshop based, manner as before. The production of clothes and shoes was also craft based but long-term changes in the London economy had eroded the independence of craftsmen in these sectors. Production was becoming increasingly divorced from retailing. This created a large pool of poor craftsmen who could be mobilized to meet the demands of the army. Moreover

---

[43] GL MS. 7351/2, accounts 1636–37, accounts 1639–40; CLRO Rep. 55, ff. 29, 31v–2. Jenkin Ellis may also have been a dealer in leather, he sold leather to the Navy in the 1650s, see BL Add. MS. 22546, Papers relating to naval affairs, 1643–77, f. 158.

[44] Edwards, *Dealing in Death*, 128, 133–5.

[45] P. Edwards, 'The Supply of Horses to the Parliamentarian and Royalist Armies in the English Civil War', *Historical Research* 68 (1995), 61–5.

the war made much fewer demands on the London clothing industry than on the armaments industry, the amount of money spent on clothing contracts was much smaller. Londoners only clothed the main armies which even at their largest were much smaller than the population of London, the New Model Army numbered only 24–25,000, consequently the contracts were probably relatively small compared with pre-war civilian output. Moreover it is likely that civilian demand fell substantially during the war because of the economic disruption, which would have freed up productive resources to supply the armies. Meeting the needs of the army would not, therefore have required any significant expansion of the production or any structural changes, as a consequence the long term impact was probably negligible. However production does not seem to have been organized by the retailers, instead tradesmen who could supply the necessary materials undertook it. Wartime contracting reveals a highly flexible economic structure, in which production could be quickly switched from supplying the retail market to supplying the military and then back to the retailers once the war was over.[46]

Conclusion

In the early years of the war demand for war materials had relatively little impact on the London economy because a high proportion of the arms purchased by Parliament were imported. Those contracts which were placed with Londoners were paid slowly or not at all. Moreover there is not much evidence to suggest that London merchants made large profits from parliamentary privateering. It never reached the same scale as in the Elizabethan period, or the late 1620s, and in some cases the privateers lost money. However from 1644, and especially from 1645, contracting did start to bring significant resources into the London economy. This was the result of two factors; firstly the expansion of the London armaments' industry, which meant that it could now supply most of Parliament's needs. And secondly Parliament's improved financial administration, which meant that contractors were paid promptly. However the benefits of this change were very unevenly spread in the London economy, mostly accruing to those who could adapt their skills to making muskets and pistols. There is little sign of any structural changes to the economy as a result of wartime contracting, the role of the livery companies was not eroded, and production continued to be small scale and craft based. Where changes were taking place they were the result of long term trends rather than the impact of the war.

---

[46] Gentles, *New Model Army*, 36.

The history of parliamentary contracting can be fitted together with that of taxation and finance to establish an overview of the flow of resources into and out of the London economy as a result of the war. The early part of the war probably saw a significant net outflow of resources from the London economy. Large sums of money were raised by Parliament in 1642–43 first from the propositions and later in taxation. Little of this money went back into the local economy from contracts or the repayment of loans. However from 1644 there may have been a net inflow of resources. The burden of taxation was diminished from 1644 and did not rise again until 1649. Very large amounts of arms and other materials were purchased in London for the army and improvements in parliamentary financial administration meant that creditors and contractors were paid what was due them. This meant that some Londoners made money from the war in its latter stages, but only if they had the skills to make arms or the capital to lend. Many were deterred by Parliament's previously poor record of payments, which certainly continued to prove a problem when it came to raising loans. Moreover the demands of the state for goods and capital was only one aspect of the impact of the war and needs to be seen in conjunction with disruption of trade to assess the impact of the war on the London economy.

Chapter 5

Economic Warfare

This chapter will examine the disruption of London's trade networks caused by the war. As the war developed the belligerents began to realize that economic blockades would undermine the financial resources of their opponents, thereby contributing to their defeat. The parliamentarians acted first and began to restrict trade with royalist controlled territories in January 1643.[1] The royalists initially believed that cutting off trade with London would do more damage to those parts of the country under their own control than to the parliamentarians. Nevertheless they were well aware that London's wealth was fuelling Parliament's war effort. This led to a reversal of policy. In the summer of 1643 the royalists tried to sever London's internal trade networks by forbidding all commerce with the capital. The King also attacked London's overseas trade by authorizing royalist privateers, and trying to prevail on foreign powers to take action against London merchants.[2]

Royalist economic warfare was never totally effective but it did cause great damage to the London economy. In the early part of the first Civil War the most effective part of the strategy was the blockade of domestic trade, but it was unpopular in the royalist parts of the country. The re-opening of trade with London brought with it the prospect of raising much needed revenues from excise duties and other levies. Consequently the blockade was largely abandoned in the latter part of the war. The attempt to stop London's external trade was not very effective in the first Civil War, although there is evidence that royalist privateering was becoming increasingly effective from 1645. In contrast in the late 1640s a number of factors brought London's overseas trade to crisis point: privateering became increasingly effective, the 1648 naval mutiny delivered a fleet into the hands of the royalists and the increasingly radical turn of events in England led to growing hostility from foreign monarchs. All this took place at a time when Dutch international trade and merchant shipping was recovering from the impact of the Thirty Years' War, and was, therefore becoming an increasing threat to London's trade and shipping.

---

[1]   *CJ* II 930, 931.
[2]   *Larkin*, 826 n. 2; E. Hyde, Earl of Clarendon, *The History of the Rebellion and Civil Wars in England*, (ed.) W.D. Macray, 6 vols (Oxford, 1888), III, 29; PRO SP16/507/14.

The blockading of internal trade

Local parliamentary commanders, like their royalist counterparts, were obstructing London's domestic trade before economic blockades became official policy. In late 1642 parliamentary forces at Hull seized goods belonging to London merchants in transit to royalist controlled York. When the owners appealed to Parliament their goods were restored but on the understanding that they would not be sent to York. Parliament's hostility to trade with the royalists was encouraged by the decision of the Earl of Newcastle, the King's principal commander in the north, to levy heavy taxes on the coal sent from the northeast to London to help finance his army. In response Parliament made the first substantial step towards halting internal trade when on 14 January 1643 an ordinance was passed banning the coal trade. This policy was quickly extended, trade between London and all areas occupied by the King's army was prohibited to stop money and munitions being sent to the royalists. The clothiers of royalist occupied Reading were prevented from sending their cloth to London, although cloth from the still parliamentarian West Country sent through Reading was exempted from the prohibition. Finally at the end of October Parliament forbade all communication with those parts of the country controlled by the royalists.[3]

In contrast in June 1642 Charles I issued a proclamation ordering that all persons and goods should have free passage throughout the Kingdom. Despite this many local royalist commanders ignored the King's commands. In the summer of 1642 a journeyman sent by Francis Rowe, a Cheapside mercer, to collect debts in Worcester had the goods he had distrained taken from him by the royalist garrison commander. In November 1642, in York, another royalist commander, Francis Neville, seized bonds for debts owed to a London grocer, George Hadley, from Hadley's apprentice, Adam Bland. Neville then collected the money due on the bonds from Hadley's creditors. Incidents like these created a climate of fear and uncertainty, which had a major impact on London's domestic trade.[4]

When the royalists advanced on London, after the battle of Edgehill on 23 October 1642, the King's soldiers intercepted carriers, particularly those carrying cloth from the West Country to London. This initially had the tacit support of the royalist high command, for instance on 29 November Sir Arthur Aston, the royalist governor of Reading, was ordered to prevent provisions

---

[3]   *CJ* II 912, 930, 931; J. Hatcher, *The History of the British Coal Industry, Vol. 1, Before 1700: Towards the Age of Coal* (Oxford, 1993), 85–6; *Firth & Rait*, I, 63, 327–8; J.M. Guilding (ed.), *Reading Records. Diary of the Corporation; Volume IV, Charles I and the Commonwealth (1641–1654)* (1896), 75, 79.

[4]   *Larkin*, 755–7; PRO C24/696/56, f. 17; PRO C2/CHASI/N9/25; PRO C24/709/29; PRO C24/710/92.

passing down the Thames to London. Nevertheless in a proclamation issued on 8 December, the King again ordered his forces not to obstruct trade and promised all those who had lost goods, compensation. However the enforcement of the proclamation was haphazard. In January a petition from the inhabitants of Berkshire to the King complained that London dealers were denied access to the Reading grain market. Complaints of attacks on carriers were particularly common in March. The King himself wrote to the governor of Reading ordering him to prevent the passage of supplies to London. In the same month Prince Rupert plundered wagons taking goods worth £2,500 from London to Bristol.[5] Western clothiers whose carriers were attacked in early 1643 sometimes recovered their goods on payment of a fee, although this privilege was denied known parliamentarians, and in June it was reported that Oxford shopkeepers were growing rich dealing in plundered cloth.[6]

In other regions the trade was entirely cut off. In the north the Earl of Newcastle tried to maintain the Newcastle coal trade with London to help finance his forces, but otherwise he ignored the King's orders concerning free trade. In February 1643 he rejected a petition from the Derbyshire lead miners for free trade with London via Hull. The royalist garrison at Wakefield prevented all trade between London and the West Riding cloth towns. Trade was reopened when the Yorkshire parliamentarians cleared the royalists out of the West Riding at the end of January, but their defeat at Atherton Moor in the following June brought the clothing towns under royalist control, and the trade with London was again brought to a halt.[7]

In the first half of 1643 London newsbooks frequently reported royalist attacks on carriers in the Midlands. Here royalist and parliamentarian garrisons were interspersed, which made communications particularly vulnerable to attack. Lord Henry Hastings, the royalist commander of Ashby de la Zouch, became notorious, earning himself the nickname 'rob-carrier' in the London press.[8] In some cases 'tit for tat' cycles of seizures arose with damaging

---

[5]   BL Harl. MS. 6851, Papers of the Royalist Council of War, f. 234v; *Larkin*, 825–6; *The Humble Petition of Divers of the Knights, Gentry, and other Inhabitants of the County of Berkes* (1643), 5; I.G. Philip (ed.), *The Journal of Sir Samuel Luke, Scoutmaster General to the Earl of Essex, 1643–44*, Oxfordshire Records Society, 4 vols (1947–1953), I, 20; *HMC Eleventh Report, VII, Reading MSS*, 215.

[6]   *England's Memorable Accidents*, 2–9 January 1643, 144; *Certaine Informations*, 10, 20–27 March 1643, 79; *LJ* V, 670; *Mercurius Civicus*, 5, 1–8 June 1643, 34.

[7]   *Certaine Informations*, 5, 13–20 February 1643, 35–6; H. Heaton, *The Yorkshire Woollen and Worsted Industries from the Earliest Times to the Industrial Revolution* (Oxford, 1965), 208–11.

[8]   *Speciall Passages*, 24, 17–24 January 1643, 198; *Certaine Informations*, 4, 6–13 February 1643, 26; *A Continuation of Certain Speciall and Remarkable Passages*, 40, 6–13 April 1643, unpag; *Certaine Informations*, 16, 1–8 May 1643, 121. For evidence of the disruption of internal trade from the royalist side see W. Phillips (ed.), *Ottley Papers Relating*

consequences for London trade. On 5 July 1643 the parliamentarian committee at Coventry informed Speaker Lenthall that the royalists had taken carriers from Coventry. In retaliation the committee seized goods from royalist Shrewsbury, which they thought would halt the trade of that town, 'which we knowe not howe prejudiciall it may be to London'.[9] Nevertheless sometimes goods could still be recovered, at least from the royalists. For example in April 1643 Isaak Knipe got back cloth he had sent to London which had been seized by the royalist garrison at Newark. Moreover Parliament's ban on trade from London to royalist controlled areas does not seem to have been effectively enforced, so much so that in June 1643 one newsbook reported that illicit trade had led to a substantial increase in activity on some routes.[10]

On 8 July 1643 the royalist council of war received a petition from a group of Gloucestershire carriers whose goods, carts and cattle had been seized on their way to London. However instead of returning the goods to the petitioners a committee was appointed to re-examine the free trade policy. On 17 July Charles I issued a new proclamation forbidding all trade from the provinces to London, and in October trade from London to royalist territories was also forbidden. In November the royalist council of war established a committee to hear appeals against seizures and judge whether or not goods had been confiscated in accordance with the proclamations. In December the King forbade the paying of debts to Londoners, instead the money was to be paid to the royalist Exchequer.[11] This only served to legitimize what was already common practice among local commanders. After the fall of Bristol in July 1643 the inhabitants were forced to pay the debts they owed Londoners to the royalist authorities, and parliamentarian scouts received similar reports from Reading in the following November.[12] In November 1644 it was reported that the royalists in Bristol searched for goods belonging to Londoners which were seized and sold.[13]

Clarendon subsequently claimed that the royalist blockade was fatally undermined by the corruption of local garrison commanders who levied tolls for safe conducts and made seizures for their own profits.[14] In the 1690s Jonathan Priestley remembered that his brother Thomas, a West Riding

---

to the Civil War, Shropshire Archæological Society Transactions 2nd Series, 6 (1894), 66–7, 68.

[9]   Bodl. Tanner MS. 62, f. 147.

[10]   PRO HCA13/59, ff. 161v–164; Mercurius Civicus, 6, 8–16 June 1643, 41.

[11]   BL Harl. MS. 6852, Papers of the Royalist Council of War, ff. 117, 149, 203; Larkin, 932–4, 961–4, 986–7.

[12]   Certaine Informations, 29, 31 July–7 August 1643, 223; H.E. Nott (ed.), The Deposition Books of Bristol: Vol. I. 1643–1647, Bristol Record Society, 6 (1935), 51–2; Philip, Journal of Sir Samuel Luke, III, 198.

[13]   Mercurius Civicus, 78, 14–21 November 1644, 721.

[14]   Clarendon, History of the Rebellion, III, 292.

clothier: 'bought cloth; travelled to London with 8 or 9 horses all the time of the Civil Wars; sometimes he and others that was with him hired convoys, and sometimes they went without, and were never taken, he or his horses or goods, all that dangerous time'.[15] There is contemporary evidence that the blockade was never totally effective. In December 1643 the King found that special licences issued to supply his household were being used to continue trade from London to Oxford, and he revoked all the licences. Yet in February 1644 the Privy Council set up a committee to investigate allegations that trade with London continued with the connivance of the royalist garrisons, or through the corruption of officers of the King's army.[16] The reports received by the scoutmaster general, Sir Samuel Luke, show that considerable trade continued between London and Oxford during 1643.[17]

The royalist blockade was never completely watertight, but it did initially make a major difference to London's communications with areas controlled by royalists. Early in August 1643 London newsbooks reported that it had become very difficult to get any news from the West Country because, since the issuing of the proclamation, all post and carriers had stopped. At the end of the month the assistants of the Carpenters' Company even considered it too dangerous to travel to Godalming. It is striking that in the second half of 1643 stories about attacks on carriers become scarce in the London newsbooks, in contrast with the previous six months, suggesting that very few carriers dared to break the blockade.[18] The impact of the embargo was compounded by the attitude of Parliament. On 7 August 1643 the clothiers of Gloucestershire complained to the King that they could not sell their goods and all their capital was tied up in debts owed them by London merchants. The King gave them permission to go to London to collect their money but Parliament responded by banning merchants from paying debts to clothiers from royalist control areas.[19] In December 1643 parliamentarian scouts reported that new royalist garrisons on the Thames were stopping the movement of goods down the river to London.

---

[15] J. Priestley, 'Some memoirs concerning the family of the Priestleys', in C. Jackson (ed.) *Yorkshire Diaries and Autobiographies in the Seventeenth and Eighteenth Centuries,* Surtees Society Publications 77 (1883), 23.

[16] *By the King. His Majesties Declaration Whereby to Repeale and Make Voyd, all Licenses, by Himselfe Granted for Bringing any Goods or Commodities, From the Cities of London and Westminster* (Oxford, 1643); *Privy Council Registers, Volume XII, 1640–45,* facsimile edn (1968), 224.

[17] Philip, *Journal of Sir Samuel Luke,* I, 45; II, 158; III, 206, 207.

[18] *Mercurius Civicus,* 11, 3–11 August 1643, 87; *Certaine Informations,* 30, 7–14 August 1643, 227; GL MS. 4329/5, Carpenters' Company, Court Minutes, 1635–56, unfoliated, 31 August 1643, 5 September 1643.

[19] F. Madan, *Oxford Books: A Bibliography of Printed Works Relating to the University and City of Oxford or Printed or Published There; With Appendixes, Annals, and Illustrations,* 3 vols (Oxford, 1895–1931), II, 287; *CJ* III, 214; 241.

For the duration of the war normal traffic on the Thanes was suspended, what there was consisted largely of military transportation.[20]

Counteracting the embargo became an important military objective for the parliamentarians. When Parliament wanted to persuade the Common Council to approve the use of London militia regiments to reinforce the army in October 1643 they argued that their immediate objective, the retaking of Reading, would reopen trade routes to the West Country.[21] In May 1644 the Earl of Denbigh, Parliament's commander in the West Midlands, justified his decision to attack Rushall Hall in Staffordshire by arguing that it was 'a place much considerable (if gaynd) for trade from Cheshire, Staffordshire, and other parts'.[22] When the London newsbooks reported the taking of Greenland House on the Thames in July 1644, they told their readers that this would enable barges to pass down the river to the capital which previously the garrison had prevented.[23]

Evidence from around England and Wales shows a major decline in internal trade. In August 1643 Lord Herbert of Cherbury, probably writing from Montgomery Castle on the Welsh borders, lamented 'Wee are here almost in as great straits as if the warre were amongst us. Shrewsbury, which is our ordinary magazine, being exhausted of wine, vinegar, hops, paper; and pepper at four shillings the pound; and shortly, a want of all commodities that are not natives with us, will follow, the intercourse betweene us and London being interdicted'.[24] In September 1643 the mayor of Reading wrote that his town could not repay its loans or pay new taxes, in large part because of the destruction of their trade, and a royalist investigation reported that the town had become impoverished by the blockade. In the following April the town petitioned the King requesting that merchants from London be allowed to come to Reading to make purchases. In May clothiers from Worcester, Reading and elsewhere, argued before the Privy Council for the re-opening of trade with London, or at least that London merchants should be allowed access to Reading to buy their cloth. In North Wales the justices of the peace complained that their region was becoming impoverished because the cattle trade with London had ceased. In October 1643 a petition from the inhabitants of Oxfordshire stated that they were unable to pay their taxes unless the royalists would accept payment in corn, or allow them access to the London market. In

---

[20] Philip, *Journal of Sir Samuel Luke*, III, 218; Idem, 'River Navigation at Oxford during the Civil War and Commonwealth', *Oxoniensia* 2 (1937), 155, 158.

[21] CLRO Jour 40, f. 78v.

[22] PRO SP16/501/145.

[23] *The Kingdomes Weekly Intelligencer*, 63, 9–16 July 1644, 509; *A Continuation of Certain Speciall and Remarkable Passages*, 2, 10–17 July 1644, 3.

[24] R. Warner (ed.), *Epistolary Curiosities* (1818), 32.

December 1643 the inhabitants of Henley complained to the Privy Council that their malt trade with London was dead.[25]

In the Midlands the scattered pattern of royalist garrisons meant that they could attack trade between parliamentarian towns. In September 1644 it was reported that no carrier would risk the roads of the East Midlands without military protection, but this added to their costs. In March 1644 one group of carriers from Manchester was offered a convoy south by the Stafford garrison, at a cost of 10s a pack. The carriers refused, only to lose eighty packs of goods to the royalists.[26] Often trade with London was only possible when the local parliamentarians were doing well. In February 1644 the defeat of local royalists enabled Melton Mowbray carriers to reach London for the first time for many months.[27]

In June 1644 the newsbook *Mercurius Civicus* reported that 'The Cavaliers have plundred most of the Carriers which have gone out from *London*'.[28] However this report coincided with the first signs that the royalists were abandoning their blockade of London. In the same month it was reported in the London newsbooks that the Worcester clothiers had obtained permission from the King to trade with London.[29] In August Charles I permitted trade to resume between Oxford and London.[30] However the royalists taxed internal trade heavily; the Worcester clothiers paid a levy of over 10s a cloth. Soon a regular system of 'licence money' was established to tax the trade with the enemy, this was levied over and above customs and excise. Initially the additional duty amounted to fifteen per cent of the value of the goods, although it was later reduced to ten per cent.[31]

Permission to trade with the enemy did not guarantee protection from royalist garrisons, and from the summer of 1644 the newsbooks again provide many accounts of attacks by royalists. The Worcester clothiers who had received the King's permission to trade with London in June 1644 were nonetheless plundered. In July a report, confirmed by the royalist press, stated that the Winchester garrison took sixteen wagons from western carriers at Andover with goods valued at £6,000. In November it was reported that a

[25] *HMC Eleventh Report, Part VII, Reading MSS*, 216; BL Harl. MS. 6804, Papers of the Royalist Council of War, f. 182; Philip, *Journal of Sir Samuel Luke*, III, 198; *Privy Council Register, Vol. XII*, 219, 226; R. Hutton, *The Royalist War Effort, 1642–6* (1982), 136, 164.

[26] *A Perfect Diurnall* 60, 16–23 September 1644, 479–80; *The Military Scribe*, 4, 12–19 March 1644, 29; *HMC Thirteenth Report, Portland MSS*, I, 130.

[27] *Mercurius Anglicus*, 1, 31 January–7 February 1644, 4.

[28] *Mercurius Civicus*, 57, 20–27 June 1644, 555.

[29] *Perfect Occurrences*, 27, 21–28 June 1644, unpaginated.; *The Weekly Account*, 44, 26 June–3 July 1644, unpaginated.

[30] O. Ogle et al (eds), *Calendar of the Clarendon State Papers*, 5 vols (Oxford, 1869–1970), I, 251.

[31] *Perfect Occurrences*, 27, 21–28 June 1644, unpaginated; Ogle, *Calendar of Clarendon State Papers*, I, 294; *HMC Sixth Report, House of Lords MSS*, 56.

Bristol carrier was plundered taking goods to London, although he had a pass for his journey and many of the goods he carried belonged to Bristol royalists.[32] In January 1645 a couple of Bristol tradesmen travelling from London to Bristol were plundered of all their goods by a party of royalist cavalry and only regained them on payment of a fine.[33] In May 1645 it was reported in the London press that a group of Wiltshire clothiers had obtained a licence to take their wares to London from the governor of Devizes in return for agreeing to pay £400 excise on their return. However they were subsequently forced to pay the £400 up front to the governor of Donnington Castle, only to lose their cloth, carts and horses to royalist cavalry from Wallingford.[34]

Evidence of the impact of royalist attacks on carriers is not confined to the press; in December 1644 there were complaints in the Common Council that the royalist garrisons in Hampshire and Berkshire were preventing cloth from reaching London. The Common Council was also becoming concerned that cloth was being shipped from Exeter and Dartmouth to the Netherlands 'whereby the trade is much carried away from this Citie to the impoverishment thereof'.[35] In January 1645 a petition was prepared for Parliament stating that the Dutch had recently sent ships to Dartmouth, that they had returned to Holland and Zealand with four ships laden with western cloth, and that they were preparing another fleet.[36] In August 1645 the royalist garrisons in Oxfordshire, Buckinghamshire, Berkshire and Hampshire were described in the Common Council as 'a great hindrance unto the trade of the Citie'.[37] The carriers were often able to avoid the royalist garrisons by taking devious and circuitous routes, but this made their journeys longer and consequently added to their costs.[38]

Internal trade was also hampered by the damage done by the war to the transport infrastructure; strategic bridges were destroyed and highways deteriorated due to abnormally heavy use. The upkeep of roads and bridges was neglected because of the general decline in traditional administrative activity in the war years; surveyors of the highways were not appointed and communal obligations lapsed. In January 1645 the Commons ordered the committee of the associated counties of Oxfordshire, Buckinghamshire and

---

[32] *The Weekly Account*, 44, 26 June–3 July, unpaginated; *Mercurius Civicus*, 60, 11–17 July 1644, 576; *Royalist Newsbooks*, III, 155–6; *Mercurius Civicus*, 78, 14–21 November 1644, 721; *Perfect Passages*, 6, 20–27 November 1644, 42.

[33] Nott, *Deposition Books of Bristol*, 152–3.

[34] *Mercurius Veridicus*, 5, 10–16 May 1645, 35; I. Roy, '"England turned Germany"? The aftermath of the Civil War in its European Context', *TRHS* 5th series, 28 (1978), 139–40.

[35] CLRO Jour. 40, f. 119.

[36] Ibid., ff. 121v–122; I. Roy (ed.), *The Royalist Ordnance Papers, 1642–46*, Oxfordshire Record Society, 2 parts (1963–1973), II, 42; CLRO Jour. 40, f. 122.

[37] Ibid., f. 140v.

[38] J. De Le Mann, *The Cloth Industry in the West of England from 1640 to 1680* (Oxford, 1971), 3.

Berkshire to repair the locks on the Thames that had been broken, preventing barges carrying foodstuffs reaching London.[39]

Despite the successes of the New Model Army in 1645, the London newsbooks were still reporting attacks on carriers at the end of the year.[40] A letter written by Robert Boyle describing his journey from London to his estates in Dorset in February 1646, illustrates the continued dangers of travel even at this late stage in the war. As late as May 1646 there were reports that royalist soldiers from Wallingford had plundered two men travelling to London near Reading.[41] But gradually the remaining royalist garrisons fell, and internal trade routes began to re-open, which became a theme of thanksgiving sermons in 1646. In April Hugh Peters celebrated 'the blessed change we see, that can travell now from *Edenburgh*, to the lands end in *Cornwal*, who not long since were blockt up at our doors! To see the highwayes occupied again; to heare the Carter whistling to his toiling team; to see the weekly Carrier attend his constant mart; to see the hills rejoycing, the vallies laughing!'[42]

The impact of the second Civil War on the London economy was felt principally through the naval mutiny. The land fighting in 1648 was probably over too quickly to have much impact on internal trade, although the Court of Aldermen were concerned that the food supplies from Essex and Kent would be blocked. The exception to this was the siege of Colchester, one of the principal centres of the new draperies. In June 1648 the bay and say makers of the town petitioned the royalist commanders for free passage to London, stating that for the previous three weeks passage had been blocked. Their request was supported by the royalists but rejected by Fairfax, who, however, did allow a weekly market on Lexden Heath, outside the town.[43]

Foreign states and London's overseas trade

In January 1643 the King threatened that, if London continued to support Parliament, he would withdraw his protection from London merchants overseas, and instruct his representatives abroad to treat them as his enemies, so that '*all foreign Princes shall know, That as such Person hath parted with*

---

[39] J.S. Morrill, *Cheshire, 1630–1660: County Government and Society during the 'English Revolution'* (Oxford, 1974), 91–2; P. Tennant, *Edgehill and Beyond, The People's War in the Southern Midlands, 1642–45* (Stroud, 1992), 151, 152; *CJ* IV, 7; *LJ* IX, 55, 65.

[40] *Mercurius Civicus*, 135, 18–24 December 1645, 1182.

[41] M. Hunter et al (eds), *The Correspondence of Robert Boyle 1636–91*, 6 vols (2001), I, 31–4; *Perfect Occurrences*, week ending 8 May 1646, unpaginated.

[42] H. Peters, *Gods Doings, and Mans Duty* (1646), 24.

[43] CLRO Rep. 59, f. 235; Rushworth *Collections*, VII, 1152; *HMC Fourteenth Report, IX, Round MSS*, 285.

his Loyalty to us, so he must not hope for any Security by us'.[44] One royalist correspondent wrote: 'either the last clause of denying his protection to the merchants will work, or inevitable prove the ruin of all trade. It is a high strain and of dangerous consequence, but no course must be left unattempted; if this work not with the merchants nothing will'.[45]

In February 1643 the King approached the Merchant Adventurers for a loan of £20,000, to be paid in Holland. The company informed the Commons, which naturally forbade payment. In order to allay the company's fears of reprisals the Commons ordered their navy committee to consider how to protect their property in Holland and provide escorts for the company's ships. Nevertheless the Merchant Adventurers were sufficiently alarmed to petition Charles I for some assurance of his continued protection abroad, to which the King replied that if they remained loyal then they had nothing to fear.[46]

The parts of London's overseas trade over which the King had the most direct influence were those with Ireland and the American colonies. In the autumn of 1644 the royalists established a commission to seize goods and debts belonging to Londoners in Dublin but after nearly three years of rebellion London's Irish trade was probably small, especially as Parliament had already prohibited trade with those parts of Ireland under the King's control. Nevertheless there were some agents working for London merchants collecting debts in Dublin and the interior, and the commissioners imprisoned a number.[47]

A potentially more fruitful area for the royalists were the new colonies of the Chesapeake Bay, the source of London's rapidly growing tobacco imports before the war. In February 1644 the King issued a commission to Leonard Calvert, the governor of Maryland then visiting Oxford, to seize the goods, debts and ships of Londoners under his own jurisdiction and in Virginia. Moreover relations between London and the Chesapeake colonies were clearly deteriorating before Calvert had time to return to America. In April two London vessels attacked a ship from royalist Bristol in the James River, Virginia. Afterwards the two London ships were unable to land and were forced to leave the colony without taking on tobacco. In Maryland the captain of one London merchant ships, Richard Ingle, was arrested for treason, although he was subsequently allowed to leave the colony. In June 1644 the Commons ordered the committee for the navy to consider the best way to bring Virginia under its control. However in 1644 war broke out between the Virginians and the Native American Powhatan confederation. This probably deterred the colonist from severing links with London and relations with Parliament were patched up. In August 1644 a

---

[44] *Rushworth*, V, 121.

[45] *HMC Thirteenth Report, Portland MSS*, I, 85.

[46] *CJ* II, 982; *To the Kings most Excellent Maiesty* (1643); *Certaine Informations*, 7, 27 February–6 March 1643, 55; *Certaine Informations*, 12, 3–10 April 1643, 9.

[47] *HMC Egmont MSS*, 1, part 1, 240; PRO C2/CHASI/H19/53; PRO C24/700/45.

group of London merchants received permission from Parliament to ship munitions and other supplies to the colony. Moreover Parliament agreed to release the estates of those planters which had been sequestered for royalism. Consequently when Calvert tried to execute his commission in Virginia he was unsuccessful. He even faced opposition in Maryland, where he was forced to admit was not covered by the commission. Moreover in early 1645 Richard Ingle returned to Maryland with a military force and he seized control for more than a year. Nevertheless London merchants were deterred from trading in Virginia, and the colony had to pass a special act in February 1645 confirming the legality of their trade.[48]

In February 1644 a Dutch translation of the King's proclamation prohibiting trade with London was sent to the Netherlands, together with a letter calling for an embargo on the Merchant Adventurers, but the King's efforts to sever trade between London and the Netherlands failed. The Prince of Orange, whose heir had recently married Charles I's eldest daughter, wanted to do all he could to help the royalists, but the States of Holland, supported by the Calvinist church opposed him. The Regent class was politically sympathetic to Parliament and did not wish to disrupt trade, whilst the Dutch Calvinist Church supported Parliament's religious reforms.[49]

The only country that took action against London merchants in the early part of the Civil War was Denmark. This had serious implications for London's merchants because Christian IV controlled their access to the Baltic and Hamburg. The latter was particularly important because Hamburg was the German staple of the Merchant Adventurers' Company, which in 1640 accounted for nearly one-quarter of London's old drapery exports. The King of Denmark controlled access to Hamburg from the North Sea thanks to his fortress at Gluckstadt on the mouth of the Elbe. Earlier in 1643 he had used his naval power to force Hamburg to acknowledge his sovereignty over the river. In August the King of Denmark, Christian IV, ordered that all ships belonging to parliamentarian ports be seized in the Sound, in Norway and at Gluckstadt; he also banned the import of goods from London.[50]

---

[48] PRO SP16/508, ff. 55–70; R.J. Brugger, *Maryland, A Middle Temperament, 1634–1980* (Baltimore, 1988), 19–20; B.C. Steiner, 'Maryland During the English Civil Wars', *John Hopkins University Studies in Historical and Political Science*, 2 parts, Series 25 4–5 (1907) II, 23, 33, 37, 42–3; G.L. Beer, *The Origins of the British Colonial System 1578–1660* (Gloucester, Mass., 1959), 354; PRO HCA13/60, Examinations of Robert Popelye, 26 June 1645, and John Lewger, 6 August 1645; *CJ* III, 525, 607; P.C. Mancall, 'Native Americans and Europeans in English America, 1500–1700', in N. Canny (ed.), *The Origins of Empire: British Overseas Enterprise to the Close of the Seventeenth Century* (Oxford, 1998), 338; *HMC Sixth Report, House of Lords MSS*, 158.

[49] *Larkin*, 973 n.1; P. Geyl, *Orange and Stuart, 1641–72* (1969), 12–13.

[50] R.C. Anderson, *Naval Wars in the Baltic: During the Sailing-ship Epoch*, 2nd edn (1969), 45; B. Supple, *Commercial Crisis and Change in England, 1600–42* (Cambridge, 1970), table 3, 259; *CJ* III, 226, 230; S.W. Murdoch, 'Scotland, Denmark-Norway and the House of

Christian IV claimed that his actions were merely retaliation for the seizure of one of his own ships, which had been captured by Parliament's navy carrying arms for the royalists in August. The ship had been returned to Denmark but the arms were confiscated. This is also the explanation given in royalist sources but the parliamentarian newsbook *Certaine Informations* argued that the dispatch of the Danish ship to Newcastle was intended to give the Danish King an excuse to seize English merchant shipping. Also a member of the Merchant Adventurers at Hamburg attributed the seizures to Charles I's proclamation that all who traded with London were rebels.[51] There are good reasons for believing this last explanation is the correct one. Since 1642 rumours had been circulating that Christian IV would intervene militarily on behalf of his cousin Charles I, but in March 1643 it was reported from Amsterdam that 'As for his [Christian IV's] designs for England, it is believed that underhand he will endeavour to do what he can to assist the King, but will never engage himself very far in any open way against Parliament except he may do it with the consent of his Kingdom'.[52]

On 10 October a petition from the Eastland Company to the House of Lords stated that the King of Denmark had seized five of their ships at the Sound, one outward bound and four returning. It also said that they had other vessels in the Baltic ready to return, which were prevented from passing the Sound. In early November the London newsbooks reported that the King of Denmark was continuing to refuse English ships passage through the Sound. Their plight was compounded by the decision of the King of Poland to refuse English ships permission to winter in his ports unless they had a pass from Charles I. In the following March there were still two English ships stuck in the Baltic.[53]

At Gluckstadt the King of Denmark's officers seized the Merchant Adventurers' cloth ship and its cargo. According to one London newsbook the cloth was worth £30,000. This seems to have been an exaggeration, possibly due to the editor confusing it with an estimate of the total losses at the Sound and the Elbe. Avery wrote that the Merchant Adventurers had to buy back their ship and the cloth for 15,000 Imperial thalers (about £3,125), which he says was almost as much as they were worth, and added that some of the goods

---

Stuart 1603–1660: A Diplomatic and Military Analysis', unpublished PhD thesis, Aberdeen University, 1998, 157–8; P.D. Lockhart, *Denmark in the Thirty Years' War, 1618–1648: King Christian IV and the decline of the Oldenburg State* (1996), 255.

[51] Ibid., 157–8; PRO SP75/16, ff. 168–v; *CSPD*, 1660–61, 296; *Royalist Newsbooks*, II, 52; *Certaine Informations*, 36, 18–25 September 1643, 291–2; *CSPD*, 1644, 195.

[52] *HMC Lord Montagu of Beaulieu MSS*, 159.

[53] HLRO House of Lords Main Papers, 10 October 1643, Petition of the Eastland Company; *Certaine Informations*, 42, 30 October–6 November 1643, 330; *Certaine Informations*, 43, 6–13 November 1643, 338; *Mercurius Civicus*, 24, 2–9 November 1643, 188; F.K. Fedorowicz, *England's Baltic Trade in the Early Seventeenth Century: A Study in Anglo–Polish Commercial Diplomacy* (Cambridge, 1980), 252; BL Add. MS. 72435, Dispatches from The Hague to the Committee for Both Kingdoms, 1643–48, f. 13v.

were retained by the King.[54] The Danes sold at least part of the goods they seized from English merchants at Gluckstadt and the Sound, and they subsequently scuttled some of the captured English ships at the entrance to Gothenburg harbour. Christian IV permitted English merchants to resume their trade but only until the following February, moreover he greatly increased the Sound tolls. Consequently few London merchants were willing to resume their trade. At the end of March he issued an order to allow English merchants to trade freely again and agreed to discuss compensation for their losses.[55]

Christian IV's change of policy can be attributed to the outbreak of hostilities with Sweden in December 1643, and the Swedish army rapidly inflicted a crushing defeat on the Danes. Early in 1644 it was reported in the London press that intercepted letters from royalist agents said that their efforts to advance the King's cause had been stymied by Sweden's recent victory.[56] In April 1645 a settlement was finally reached with the King of Denmark. The English merchants were promised 174,000 Imperial thalers (about £36,350) in compensation for their losses, and by June 1647 the treaty had been confirmed.[57]

The only other occasion when the royalists caused significant disruption to London's foreign trade in the first Civil War took place in the Ottoman Empire. In 1646 the ambassador, Sir Sackville Crowe, tried to extort money from the merchants of the Levant Company to finance Charles I's dwindling war effort. At the beginning of that year he persuaded the Ottoman authorities to prevent the loading of English ships in Izmir and Istanbul, the two principal ports of the Levant Company's trade. In May 1646 Crowe seized the goods of members of the company in those ports, imprisoned their factors and prevented the departure of their ships. He justified his actions by claiming that he was seeking compensation for the sequestration of his estate in England by Parliament; and by asserting that that the Levant Company had detained money

---

[54] *Certaine Informations*, 36, 18–25 September 1643, 292; PRO SP75/16, ff. 168–v, 170v. The exchange rate, 4.8 thalers to the pound sterling, is taken from G. Parker (ed.), *The Thirty Years' War* (1984), xii. Other reports state that the merchants had been forced to buy back their goods at, or above, their full value in cash. BL Add. MS. 72436, Documents relating to special embassies from England to Denmark etc., 1643–46, ff. 61, 118v.

[55] PRO SP75/16, ff. 170v, 202v, 205; BL Add. MS. 72436, ff. 128, 131, 135; Murdoch, 'Scotland, Denmark-Norway and the House of Stuart', 158–9.

[56] Anderson, *Naval Wars in the Baltic*, 47, 62; *The Kingdomes Weekly Intelligencer*, 42, 30 January–7 February 1644, 322.

[57] M. Sellers (ed.), *The Acts and Ordinances of the Eastland Company*, Camden Society (1906), 159–166; *47th Annual Report of the Deputy Keeper of the Public Records* (1886), 75. None of the compensation money promised by Christian IV to the merchants was paid, and the debt had to be written off by Charles II in 1667. Murdoch, 'Scotland, Denmark-Norway and the House of Stuart', 163 n. 136, 168.

which was rightfully due to him.[58] However the factors refused to pay what Crowe demanded and were able to outbid him for the support of the Turkish officials and obtain their own release. They then recovered their principals' goods and resumed their trade. Nevertheless some of the goods seized were not recovered until the following July and many of the ships were held for several months. Although Crowe failed to raise any money for his monarch he had paralysed one of the most profitable branches of London's overseas trade for about half a year. The company put the total cost of the whole affair, including the diminution of their trade, at £100,000.[59]

In the aftermath of the execution of Charles I in January 1649 the threat to London merchants abroad heightened as a consequence of the general European revulsion against the regicide and in some places it was not safe for them to walk the streets. This problem was compounded by the determination of exiled royalists to exact revenge against those they believed to be collaborators with the new regime; and Charles II's need to raise money from the English merchant communities abroad to fund his cause. In Hamburg the head of the Merchant Adventurers and other leading members of the company were kidnapped by a royalist agent who demanded a £30,000 ransom for their release, although they were quickly rescued by musketeers hired by the company. In Poland the King, Jan Kazimierz, enthusiastically supported Charles II's request for funds from the English merchants. He demanded that all English merchants contribute a tenth of their goods to the royalist cause, those who refused were charged before the courts. The parliamentarian authorities protested and were supported by the City of Danzig, which was fearful of reprisals against their trade in England. Charles II sent an envoy to insist that the contribution should be voluntary, but voluntary or not it was reported that £10,000 was raised.[60]

The most serious reaction to the execution of Charles I came from the Russian Tsar and the French authorities. In Russia the Muscovy Company enjoyed considerable privileges before the Civil War, including exemption from paying customs. In 1645 Tsar Aleksei sent an envoy, Dokhturov, to Charles I. However Parliament refused to allow Dokhturov to travel from London to Oxford to fulfil his mission. On his return to Russia Dokhturov submitted a critical report on the political situation in England, moreover he informed his superiors that the members of the Muscovy Company supported Parliament against their sovereign. In 1646 the Tsar rescinded the exemption of

[58] PRO SP105/150, f. 112v; D. Goffman, *Britons in the Ottoman Empire, 1642–1660* (Seattle, 1998), 68–87; BL Egerton MS. 2533, Nicholas Papers, ff. 429–432, 438–9v.

[59] PRO SP105/150, ff. 121–3, 134; PRO SP105/143, ff. 117, 143–145, 217–v, 219; A.C. Wood, *A History of the Levant Company* (Oxford, 1935), 91.

[60] J.T. Peacy, 'Order and Disorder in Europe: Parliamentary Agents and Royalist Thugs 1649–1650', *HJ* 40 (1997), 961, 962; Fedorowicz, *England's Baltic Trade in the Early Seventeenth Century*, 252–3.

the Muscovy Company from Russian customs. Although the decision was taken too early to have been influenced by Dokhturov's report, the Russian authorities would have already received a letter from Parliament informing them that they had prevented Dokhturov from delivering Aleksei's message to Charles I. In response the factors of the Muscovy Company refused to sell their goods, which the company subsequently claimed cost them over £50,000. In 1649, when news reached Russia of the execution of Charles I, the Tsar responded by expelling the London merchants from all parts of the country except the port of Archangel, they lost their houses and were prevented from collecting their debts, which the company estimated cost them over £30,000. In 1652 the London merchant John Langley informed the Council of State that the English were burdened with unprecedented customs while the Dutch were given wide privileges, effectively excluding the English from trade with Russia. The expulsion of the Muscovy Company was not simply the result of the Tsar's horror at events in England; Russian merchants had long criticized the company's privileges. Aleksei, facing internal problems of his own in the late 1640s, probably welcomed the opportunity to appease internal criticism. Nevertheless the regicide played a major part in prompting Aleksei's decision, indeed Russia's own internal troubles made it more important for the Tsar to be seen to take firm action against the English.[61]

The Russian trade played a relatively small part in the London economy, however French hostility was a much more serious matter. During the trial of Charles I the French government issued a proclamation calling for a European coalition to wage a crusade against the new regime.[62] However French hostility to the parliamentarians went back to the first Civil War. London merchants often faced legal harassment in France during the 1640s under a number of pretexts. An early sign of French hostility was the refusal of the French admiralty to release the *Mercury*, a London merchant ship captured in 1644, despite a ruling by the French courts in favour of her owners. In October 1648 the import of English woollen and silk textiles was prohibited.[63] This was done largely for protectionist reasons, but towards the end of that year French warships were sent out to attack English shipping in the Mediterranean, beginning an unofficial naval war which continued until the middle of the next decade. In December a French man-of-war took the *Greyhound* off Sardinia.

---

[61] G.M. Phipps, 'The Russian Embassy to London of 1645–6 and the Abrogation of the Muscovy Company's Charter', *Slavonic and East European Review* 68 (1990), 257–76; PRO SP18/42/149; PRO SP91/3, ff. 72, 81.

[62] T. Carte (ed.), *A Collection of Original Letters and Papers*, 2 vols (1739), I, 195–7.

[63] P.A. Knachel, *England and the Fronde: The Impact of the English Civil War and Revolution on France* (Ithaca, New York, 1967), 122–3, 127–8; CJ *IV*, 376; *Firth & Rait*, I, 1224–6; PRO HCA24/109/137.

Not long after, the *Talent* was destroyed by another French warship.[64] Other losses rapidly followed, until by February 1649 the company was claiming that its members had lost eight ships to the French, which, with their cargo, were worth £300,000. They claimed that their whole trade was threatened.[65] English shipping in French ports was also seized. By April 1650 the Levant Company and other Mediterranean merchants estimated that their losses from the attacks by the French and royalist privateers totalled nearly £1 million.[66] In retaliation the Commonwealth authorized privateers and forbade the import of French wines, wool and silk in August 1649, though they stopped short of banning imports of linen cloth.[67] In December 1649 the Vintners' Company stated that the price of wine was rising rapidly as a consequence of the prohibition of trade with France.[68] Moreover the naval attacks in the Mediterranean meant the consequences of the conflict went beyond trade with France. In May 1650 a London merchant wrote 'this year few or none goes for the Straits as formerly because the French take many of our ships'. Merchants instead preferred to go to Bilbao and purchase Mediterranean goods indirectly.[69]

In September 1650 the Levant Company decided to petition the Council of State for escorts for their departing ships. To pay for this they proposed a twenty per cent surcharge on the customs.[70] Having received confirmation from the Council of Trade that the Mediterranean trade had been virtually abandoned the Rump agreed to provide a naval squadron to escort their ships. To pay for it they abolished the fifteen per cent discount on the customs, which merchants had received since the summer of 1642. The escorts enabled London's Mediterranean trade to survive, at least until they were withdrawn in the first Dutch War. Moreover a large contraband trade meant that England was never totally deprived of supplies of French wine. But the French reaction to the execution of Charles I had substantially reduced London's trade and added considerably to the costs of her merchants and a final settlement of the conflict with France was not concluded until 1655.[71]

Despite the efforts of royalist agents there was no general European embargo of trade with London. Only a few states took action against London merchants and the impact was weakened by their failure to act simultaneously.

---

[64]   PRO HCA13/61, ff. 359v–362, 393; PRO HCA13/62, examinations of Edward Crasse and Richard Binge, 3 July 1649.

[65]   *CSPD*, 1649–50, 11–12, 16.

[66]   Ibid., 274, 460, 564; *CSPD*, 1650, 106–7.

[67]   *CSPD*, 1649–50, 274; *CJ* VI, 258; Whitelocke, *Memorials*, III, 92.

[68]   GL MS. 15201/4, Vintners' Company, Court Minutes, 1638–58, f. 300.

[69]   G.F. Steckley (ed.), *The Letters of John Paige, London Merchant, 1648–58*, London Record Society (1984), 19.

[70]   PRO SP105/151, ff. 40, 40v; *CJ* VI, 489.

[71]   *CSPD*, 1650, 379, 417; *CJ* VI, 490; *Firth & Rait*, II, 444; B. Capp, *Cromwell's Navy, the Fleet and the English Revolution, 1648–1660* (Oxford 1989), 71, 93; *CSVP* 1647–52, 240.

By the time they came under attack from the French and Russians London merchants had regained access to those parts of their trade that had been threatened by the dispute with Denmark. However for those who traded in the affected areas the impact of foreign opposition was potentially catastrophic. Consequently although the impact was limited the actions of the pro-royalist states undoubtedly caused considerable disruption to specific aspects of London's trade.

Privateering

In the 1640s London's trade was disrupted by large losses of merchant shipping to the royalists, initially because ships were forced by bad weather into ports controlled by the King, and later as a result of attacks by royalist and Irish privateers. By the end of the decade increasing privateering, together with the unofficial war with France, and the mutiny in Parliament's navy, led to a general crisis in London's shipping.

In December 1642 London merchant ships returning from Spain were forced by storms into royalist held Falmouth, where the King's forces seized them. This was before the royalists decided on a full-scale embargo on trade with London, consequently the owners of the goods on board the *Elias and Elizabeth* obtained a letter from Charles I ordering the release of half their goods, and they were to be given a bond for payment for the remainder, although it is not clear if any of this was carried through.[72] Nevertheless the London merchant community was alarmed, especially as at least £200,000 in silver was imminently expected from Spain. The merchants put pressure on Parliament to blockade Falmouth but on 17 January forty ships were driven into the control of Pendennis Castle in Cornwall. This was probably the expected shipment of silver as its capture enabled the local royalist commanders to pay their soldiers' arrears, and give them a fortnight's pay in advance.[73]

As the royalists took further ports in 1643 more London ships were captured. It was reported that forty ships belonging to Londoners fell into royalist hands when Dartmouth was taken in October 1643.[74] As late as August

---

[72] *England's Memorable Accidents*, 19–26 December 1642, 124–5; CLRO MCD1/83; PRO HCA13/58, ff. 631v–632v.

[73] PRO SP16/497/4; *CJ* II 932; *Powell & Timings*, 58; M. Coate, *Cornwall in the Great Civil War and Interregnum, 1642–60*, 2nd edn (Truro, 1963), 39, 41, 117; J.R. Powell, *The Navy in the English Civil War* (1962), 33.

[74] *CSPV*, 1643–47, 34.

1648 the *Rose*, returning from Montserrat to London, carrying sugar and tobacco, was forced to take refuge in the royalist controlled Scilly Isles.[75] A few London merchant ships were lost when their masters defected to the royalists, the most spectacular example being in 1644 when the East India Company ship, the *John*, was converted into a royalist privateer.[76]

The greatest threat to London shipping in the 1640s came from privateering, however the evidence of its impact is very fragmentary. Most of the records generated by the Irish and royalist admiralties have been lost. Consequently there is no complete list of prizes from which the total London shipping losses can be established. One list of prizes that does survive from the royalist admiralty in Ostend records fifty four vessels, and goods from three others. Ostend was never a major royalist base and the list only covers the period from March 1649 to August 1650, and therefore this can only be a small fragment of the total.[77] The records of the Spanish Admiralty in Flanders record sixty nine English ships condemned as prizes between 1642 and 1650, but the vast majority of the prizes would have been dealt with by the Irish or royalist authorities.[78] Historians have been forced to fall back on qualitative sources, which give some idea of the scale of privateering. Ohlmeyer found evidence of 250 vessels taken by the Irish privateers from March 1642 to July 1650 and Appleby calculated that privateers operating from the Channel Islands captured between 118 and 121 ships. It is probable that these totals are underestimates, and there were many more privateering bases.[79] It is impossible to calculate the total London shipping lost to privateering, but the economic damage that it caused is clear from the anxiety it engendered in London.

In 1642 the Irish rebels began to recruit privateers from the Spanish Netherlands where a large privateering industry had grown up during the long war with the Dutch, and the main port, Dunkirk, had become synonymous with piracy. As early as May 1642 an Irish frigate took the *Marigold*, an English merchant ship en route to Bilbao. From the end of 1642 royalist privateering began to develop from bases in Cornwall and the north east.[80] By early 1643 the East India Company was alarmed by the privateers, they ordered their

---

[75]   PRO HCA24/109/56.

[76]   *CCMEIC*, 1644–49, vii, 71; PRO HCA13/60, examinations of Christopher Lansdale, John Potts and Simon Beer, 16 August 1645.

[77]   S. Groenveld, 'The English Civil Wars as a cause of the First Anglo-Dutch War, 1640–52', *HJ* 30 (1987), 558 n. 67.

[78]   R. Baetens, 'The Organisation and Effects of Flemish Privateering in the Seventeenth Century', *Acta Historiae Neerlandicae, Studies on the History of the Netherlands* (The Hague, 1976), 68–9.

[79]   J.H. Ohlmeyer, 'Irish Privateers During the English Civil War, 1642–50', *MM* 76 (1990), 127; J.C. Appleby, 'Neutrality, Trade and Privateering, 1500–1689', in A.G. Jamieson (ed.), *A People of the Sea: The Maritime History of the Channel Islands* (1986), 102.

[80]   Ohlmeyer, 'Irish Privateers', 120–2; *The Kingdomes Weekly Intelligencer*, 27 December 1642–3 January 1643, 2–3; *Certaine Informations*, 10, 20–27 March 1643, 79.

vessels to stick together and made elaborate preparations to enable their homeward bound ships to avoid the royalists.[81] Another sign of increasing concern about privateers in London in 1643 was the coverage they were beginning to get in the London press. From early February the attacks of the Cornish privateers were receiving considerable coverage.[82] In the following month the Channel was said to be infested with Irish and royalist privateers, and Falmouth was described as a 'new Algiers', a reference to the notorious corsairs of North Africa.[83] By May the London press was reporting that the privateers were causing increasing complaints among the merchant community.[84]

In the course of 1643 the capture of ports such as Bristol, Dartmouth and Scarborough strengthened the royalist naval resources. By December Parliament was so worried that they sought Dutch naval assistance. In the following year the Earl of Warwick, the commander of Parliament's navy, reported that the royalists had 250 ships. Ohlmeyer has shown that in the 1640s privateering communities sprang up in Waterford and Wexford, with a total of fifty to sixty frigates.[85] The Irish and royalist privateers were most common in the Channel and the western approaches, in early 1644 it was reported that they were interrupting all trade with France, but privateers were active off all coasts around Britain, even entering the mouth of the Thames. Parliament's authorities at first left the northern and Scottish coasts unguarded, and they paid the price for their neglect. By April 1644 the committee for both kingdoms was receiving reports that vessels were frequently being lost in these waters.[86]

As the war continued the privateering problem escalated. In late 1644 and early 1645 Walter Strickland, Parliament's envoy to the Netherlands, reported that royalist privateers were operating off the Dutch coast taking London shipping, and that this was seriously disrupting trade.[87] In January 1645 the Common Council of the City of London was petitioned about the impact of privateering on the East Anglian coastal trade.[88] In May 1645 the

---

[81]   W. Foster (ed.), *The English Factories in India, 1642–45* (Oxford, 1913), 95; *CCMEIC*, 1640–43, 320.

[82]   *The Kingdomes Weekly Intelligencer*, 6, 31 January–7 February 1643, 47.

[83]   *A Perfect Diurnall*, 40, 13–20 March 1643, unpaginated; *The Kingdomes Weekly Intelligencer*, 13, 21–28 March 1643, 102.

[84]   *Certaine Informations*, 16, 1–8 May 1643, 123–124; *A Perfect Diurnall*, 48, 8–15 May 1643, unpaginated.

[85]   Coate, *Cornwall in the Great Civil War*, 38; Powell, *Navy in the English Civil War*, 27–8, 37–8, 43, 51, 62; BL Add. MS. 72437, George Weckerlin's Journal, ff. 80v, 81; *Powell & Timings*, 85; Ohlmeyer, 'Irish Privateers', 123.

[86]   *Certaine Informations*, 56, 8–15 February 1644, 437; Bodl. Rawlinson MS. A221, Journal of the Committee for the Navy, 1643–44, f. 138; *CSPD*, 1644, 111.

[87]   BL Add. MS. 72435, ff. 45, 47v, 53.

[88]   CLRO Jour. 40, f. 120.

London newsbooks were full of complaints about the privateers. One lamented, 'From Sea we have worse newes then by land: for the divelish *Dunkerkers* doe much spoyle by their nimble running Frigots'.[89] A further report stated that, 'The Dunkirkes and others have taken 22. small ships...within these 15 daies'.[90]

Londoners complained that the navy was not deployed effectively to protect trade. At the end of April one London newsbook reported that 'Those that come along our cost say, that our Seas are full of Dutch and other Strangers, and of his Majesties party, but he saith, he met with no ships of the Parliaments untill he came into the Downes'.[91] This led to further agitation in the Common Council about privateering in the summer of 1645, and on 7 June they approved a petition to Parliament calling for the navy to be re-organized to provide constant convoys for merchant shipping. They argued that trade was depressed because of the lack of escorts. Later in the same month the Common Council received a petition in the name of ship owners and seamen stating that many merchants were facing ruin unless sufficient convoys were provided.[92] The correspondence of London merchants shows that these complaints expressed the concerns of the merchant community. In January 1646 Richard Best, writing from London to his colleague John Turner, a merchant resident in Tenerife, said that it was 'gods mercy' that Turner's ship had arrived safely in London 'our men of warr being very Faulty for lokeing out to Cleare the Co[a]st'. He had heard of two ships from Oporto that had been attacked only four days previously.[93]

In late 1645 and early 1646 the royalist privateering bases in the West Country fell to the victorious New Model Army.[94] But the complaints in the newsbooks continued. In late October 1645 it was reported in the London press that 'Severall Merchants ships have been lately taken by the Dunkirks, and his Majesty of Englands Royall pyrates, coming from Spaine, and other parts. If we suffer this, it will cause a great decay of trading'.[95] In June 1646 Parliament's navy commissioners claimed that the King had only six men of war left however, in the previous month it had been reported that between six and eight privateering frigates were based at Jersey alone and the complaints about privateering continued. Many Cornish privateers had simply moved their base of operations to the Channel Islands where there was a substantial

---

[89]   *The Scottish Dove*, 82, 9–16 May 1645, 646.
[90]   *The True Informer*, 4, week ending 17 May 1645, 27.
[91]   *The Moderate Intelligencer*, 9, 24 April–1 May 1645, 69.
[92]   CLRO Jour. 40, ff. 131v, 135–v.
[93]   PRO C110/151/2, Richard Best to John Turner, 10 January 1646.
[94]   Powell, *Navy in the English Civil War*, 122.
[95]   *Mercurius Civicus*, 127, 23–30 Oct. 1645, 1115.

increase in privateering activity in 1645 and 1646.[96] The privateers also operated from bases in the Isle of Man and had access to many continental ports. Moreover the Irish privateers were strengthened in late 1646 when the fall of Dunkirk to French forces encouraged privateers from the Spanish Netherlands to move to Waterford and Wexford. Consequently in late 1646 Parliament's admiralty committee received many complaints about the privateers and was frequently petitioned to provide escorts for merchant shipping.[97]

In the early part of 1647 there were numerous complaints about the attacks on the south coast as the Prince of Wales busily issued letters of marque in Jersey to newly recruited royalist privateers.[98] However in May the French, responding to diplomatic pressure from Parliament, issued an edict forbidding all privateers from entering French ports and proceedings were begun to return captured English ships in France to their owners. Moreover the French authorities pressurized the Prince of Wales into revoking the letters of marque he had issued, which halted the activities of the Channel Island privateers. This respite proved short lived as the Prince was again authorizing privateering in August, and the French edict was not properly enforced, indeed the royalists were allowed to establish an admiralty to administer prizes in French-held Dunkirk at around this time.[99]

Royalist privateering was at its height in the last two years of the 1640s. In February 1648 the new commander of Parliament's navy, Thomas Rainsborough, complained that the number of Irish privateers was increasing. Ships from Parliament's Irish squadron had to be sent to south Wales to help put down a royalist rising, forcing the parliamentarians to abandon their blockade of the Irish privateering bases. Worse was to follow as mutiny in Parliament's fleet in May 1648 meant that ships had to be drawn away from protecting merchant shipping.[100]

In the course of 1648 there were frequent complaints about the damage done by the privateers.[101] At the end of the year the press reported that a

---

[96] *The Moderate Intelligencer*, 59, 16–23 April 1646, 397; *The Answer of the Commissioners of the Navie* (1646), 19; *The Scottish Dove*, 134, 13–20 May 1646, 663; Powell, *Navy in the English Civil War*, 121; Appleby, 'Neutrality, Trade and Privateering', 102.

[97] Ohlmeyer, 'Irish Privateers', 123; Powell, *Navy in the English Civil War*, 129; *A Perfect Diurnall*, 169, 19–26 October 1646, 1355–6; PRO ADM7/673, ff. 13, 24, 33, 67.

[98] *A Perfect Diurnall*, 190, 15–22 March 1647, 1520–1; PRO HCA13/61, ff. 291v, 342v; BL Add. MS. 4200, Giles Grene Correspondence, 1645–61, f. 37.

[99] Powell, *Navy in the English Civil War*, 136, 137, 143–4; Groenveld, 'English Civil Wars', 558; Appleby, 'Neutrality, Trade and Privateering', 102; BL Add. MS. 4155, Thurloe Papers, ff. 242, 266–8; BL Add. MS. 4200, f. 42.

[100] *Powell & Timings*, 301, 314.

[101] *CSPD*, 1648–49, 284–5, 288, 324, 359, 360; *HMC Thirteenth Report, Portland MSS*, I, 499.

squadron of eleven Irish frigates 'lies hovering up and down the narrow Seas, seizing on divers Marchants ships'.[102] The complaints increased in 1649, in July there were fifteen English merchant ships in the Sound, carrying desperately needed grain for the home market, which could not return because the Irish warships were lying in wait for them. In August eight merchant ships were captured near Flamborough Head, and the secretary of the admiralty committee described the coast of Flanders as worse than Algiers.[103] In September the Council of State was informed from Rotterdam 'if spiedie care be not taken, by layinge of ships before Dunckerk and Ostind, they [the privateers] will growe potent, and wholly spoylle all trade to these partes, and allso the fishinge trade…and allso all trade alonge the cost from Newcastel to the Downes'.[104]

The letters of London merchants from the late 1640s reveal that they feared that the privateers were doing real damage to the trade of London.[105] In March 1648 Best wrote to Turner that 'thos Rebelyous Ierish with other Roagues are abroad in frigotts and have taken many small ships'.[106] In the autumn of 1648 a petition from the 'well-affected Masters and Commanders of Ships' to the House of Commons stated that 'their Trade is wholly destroyed, some Merchants not daring, and others absolutely refusing, to ship their goods with them'. They called on the Commons to appoint constant convoys between the Thames and the Netherlands and France.[107]

Parliament was already taking steps to defeat the privateers. After the Civil War they began to expand the navy. New frigates were particularly important for combating the privateers and in 1646 and 1647 at least nine were launched. The shipbuilding programme was massively increased during the Commonwealth, doubling the navy by the end of 1651. In November 1650 the Rump was able to establish a constant force of thirty seven warships to provide escorts for merchant shipping. The expansion of the navy deterred foreigners from providing privateers for the royalists. The Dunkirk privateers withdrew their support for Charles II in 1650 when they realized how large Parliament's intended summer fleet would be.[108]

---

[102] *A Message Sent From His Highnesse the Prince of Wales, to the Citizens of London* (1648), 2.

[103] Carte, *Collection of Original Letters and Papers*, I, 248; *CSPD*, 1649–50, 200, 222–3; *HMC Leyborne Popham MSS*, 34, 35; Capp, *Cromwell's Navy*, 61–2.

[104] T. Birch (ed.), *Thurloe State Papers*, 7 vols (1742), I, 117.

[105] Steckley, *Letters of John Paige*, 1, 2, 10, 25.

[106] PRO C110/151/2, Richard Best to John Turner, 13 March 1648.

[107] Rushworth *Collections*, VII, 1258–9.

[108] Capp, *Cromwell's Navy*, 52, 66; A.W. Johns, 'The Constant Warwick', *MM* 18 (1932), 254; J.S. Corbett, *England in the Mediterranean. A Study of the Rise and Influence of British Power within the Straits, 1603–1713*, 2 vols (1904), I, 183–4, 194–5.

The advance of Cromwell's army in Ireland deprived the privateers of their bases. On 12 October 1649 Wexford, 'the Dunkirk of Ireland' fell and in November 1649 one of the most notorious of the privateers, Captain Plunket, was captured when he sailed into Cork, unaware that it had fallen to Cromwell. In March 1651 Waterford was taken, followed by the last significant Irish port, Galway, in April 1652. In 1651 the other major privateering bases were captured. The Scilly Isles, which had been recaptured by the royalists in 1648, fell in June. On 17 October an expeditionary force set sail to take the Channel Islands, and in that autumn the Isle of Man also fell to the forces of the new regime. The privateering threat to London's trade was effectively brought to an end by the growing military and naval might of the Commonwealth.[109]

The constant agitation over privateering in London in the 1640s shows the damage they were doing to trade. The losses were so serious that London merchants even went as far as sending representatives to the Southern Netherlands to attempt to buy back their own ships and goods from the privateers.[110] However privateering did not affect all trade equally, the coastal trades and those with England's closest neighbours suffered the most. These trades used smaller ships, which were considered most vulnerable to the privateers. In August 1649 *The Moderate Intelligencer* reported that the Irish frigates dared not encounter merchant ships which went well manned and armed, but instead attacked colliers, and those engaged in the coastal trade or which traded with Holland, France and Denmark. This is confirmed by a list of vessels brought by privateers to Ostend, from 1648 to 1650, the majority of the ships taken tended to be small vessels carrying cereal crops, coal and similar commodities, and were probably engaged in the coastal trades.[111]

Long distance trades did suffer losses; in December 1643 royalist privateers took the *George* of London, returning from a voyage to the West Indies with a cargo valued at £4,000 or more.[112] Consequently privateering affected all areas of London's merchant community. In 1645 ships carrying goods belonging to the Guinea Company and members of the Merchant Adventurers were lost to privateers based in the southern Netherlands. The *Mary and Dorothy*, taken a year before, was in the service of a consortium that included the former custom farmer Sir Paul Pindar, one of the most prominent London merchants of the first half of the seventeenth century. The ship was returning from Amsterdam towards London, but this was the last leg of a

---

[109] R.C. Anderson, 'The Royalists at Sea in 1649', *MM* 14 (1928), 327; Ohlmeyer, 'Irish Privateers', 130; Birch, *Thurloe State Papers*, I, 142; Capp, *Cromwell's Navy*, 64–71; R.C. Anderson, 'The Royalists at Sea in 1650', *MM* 17 (1931), 143, 157; J.R. Powell, 'Blake's Reduction of Jersey in 1651', *MM* 18 (1932), 65.

[110] PRO C24/699/31; PRO C24/701/43.

[111] *The Moderate Intelligencer*, 233, 30 August–6 September 1649, 2239; Steckley, *Letters of John Paige*, 2, 10; PRO SP18/9, ff. 223–5.

[112] PRO HCA13/59, f. 244.

trading voyage, which had taken her to the Mediterranean. Although a parliamentarian warship quickly recaptured the *Mary and Dorothy*, Pindar and his colleagues had to pay a salvage fee before their own goods were returned to them, demonstrating that privateering could be costly even when it was unsuccessful.[113]

London merchants and seamen made strenuous efforts to avoid falling prey to the privateers, but even when successful, this added to their costs and consequently to the economic impact of privateering. The commanders of Parliament's warships often demanded payment for convoying merchant ships. Parliament tried to stop this in 1644 but further orders to this effect in 1649 and 1650 show it continued.[114] Moreover escorts could entail further additional costs for merchants such as hiring extra pilots for the warships.[115] Without an escort even the crews of the heavily armed ships of the East India Company preferred not to sail alone. On 16 August 1644 the crew of the *Dolphin*, returning to England, learnt from another ship that 'the Kings forces of shipping on the West Part of England, dayly to encrease' and 'that [the King's] protection was withdrawn from his Subjects & they thereby left as a spoile & pray to our owne & other Nations and the West Parts of England in generall infected with rovers, both English Dunkerkirs & others; that little safety for a single ship, (but even by accident) could be expected'. It was concluded that, as the *Dolphin* had lost contact with its companion the *Discovery*, it would be safer for them to return to India.[116] This decision undoubtedly had a financial cost for the company and its investors. Incidents such as these demonstrate that the damage inflicted by the privateers on the London economy was greater than the value of the ships and goods they captured.

The revolt of the fleet

The mutiny of Parliament's navy at its main anchorage on the Downs in May 1648 has often been discussed, but the focus is usually upon the protagonists. Although the impact on trade is generally acknowledged, it has never been explored.[117] On 26 May Parliament's seamen mutinied taking control of Rainsborough's flagship, the *Constant Reformation*, and five other warships. More ships subsequently joined the mutiny and on 10 or 11 June the rebel

---

[113] PRO C24/701/43; *CSPD*, 1644–5, 433; PRO HCA13/59, ff. 256–8, 300v, 304; *CJ* III, 568.

[114] *CJ* III, 503; *CJ* VI, 310; *CSPD*, 1650, 379.

[115] PRO ADM7/673, ff. 13, 18.

[116] BL IOL/E/3/19, East India Company, Original Correspondence, 1644–48, f. 42.

[117] Capp, *Cromwell's Navy*, chapter 2; R.C. Anderson, 'The Royalists at Sea in 1648', *MM* 9 (1923); Powell, *Navy in the English Civil War*, chapters 10–12; D.E. Kennedy, 'The English Naval Revolt of 1648', *EHR* 77 (1962).

ships left the Downs for Helvoetsluys in Holland. A month later the Prince of Wales arrived to take command.[118]

On 13 June the mutiny was described as 'a terror to this Citty'.[119] For the first time the royalists possessed a fleet of major fighting ships, which gave them the chance to contest Parliament's naval supremacy. With a fleet the royalists could hope to blockade the port of London. Whereas previously the threat to merchant shipping was principally to the smaller ships and the local trades, now the royalists were in a position to threaten the largest and most heavily armed merchant vessels. The importance of the fleet to the City was clear to all; one royalist remarked 'this Citty must goe with the fleet, and neither can nor dare doe other'.[120]

In June 1648 the Court of the East India Company debated whether to send the *William* around the north of Scotland to avoid the Channel, although this was rejected. In early July the Levant Company was unsure whether it was safe for the *Sampson* to set sail for Istanbul. Though the ship was dispatched many merchants decided it was too risky to send their goods in her, some of which was still on their hands in October.[121] In a petition to Parliament, the City argued that unless the situation was resolved:

> Navigation will be destroyed, Seamen desert us, the Merchants inforced to leave off Trading, Cloathing and other Manufactures of this Kingdom fall to the Ground, Wool (which is the Staple Commodity of the Land) remain unsold, the Mint stand still, Customs and other Profits by Merchandizing will be very much abated, if not utterly destroyed, Corn, Salt, Coal, Fish, Butter, Cheese, and all other Provisions brought by Sea to this City and Kingdom stopped; the innumerable Number of the poorer Sort, depending only upon the Manufactures, wanting Work and Bread (as is greatly feared), will in a very short Time become tumultuous in all Parts of the Kingdom, and many inforced to remove themselves and Families into Foreign Parts, and there to settle the Manufacture of this Kingdom, never to be regained.[122]

On 17 July the royalist fleet left Helvoetsluys and returned to the Downs. The royalists initially intended only to seize merchant ships to supply their fleet but by the 28th they were intercepting all English vessels they could find, which they continued to do until 29 August. On 12 July Parliament prohibited merchant ships from leaving London, partly to enable Warwick to recruit mariners but also for fear that the ships would join the royalists. At the same

---

[118] Capp, *Cromwell's Navy*, 20–23; Anderson, 'Royalists at Sea in 1648', 34–36.

[119] S.R. Gardiner (ed.), *The Hamilton Papers, 1638–50*, Camden Society, new series, 27 (1880), 212.

[120] Ibid., 221.

[121] *CCMEIC*, 1644–49, 274; PRO SP105/150, ff. 188–v, 200v.

[122] *LJ* X 427.

time they ordered small boats to be stationed in the western part of the Channel to warn incoming ships of the dangers ahead so that they could take refuge in the ports of the West Country. The latter measure was ineffective and the former led to a stream of complaints, for example two London merchants claimed they were losing £20 a day, consequently they and several others were given special permission to sail.[123]

The royalists were able to capture a large number of London merchant ships, amongst which were two ships belonging to the Guinea Company returning from Africa, the *Cormitant* and the *Star*, which carried £12,000 in gold.[124] Also taken were a ship from New England and the *Love*, returning from the Adriatic, both with valuable cargoes.[125] On 24 July the Merchant Adventurers obtained permission to dispatch their cloth ship, the *Damsel*, and two smaller vessels, all of which were taken. Royalist sources valued the cloth at £40,000, and she also carried forty five barrels of indigo, worth £2,500, belonging to the radical merchant Richard Shute.[126] The royalists seized at least five other vessels: the *Chapman* of London, the *Elizabeth and Susan*, the *Thomas and Margaret*, the *Goodspeed* of Hull, and the *Concord*, which was bound for New England. Therefore at least eleven vessels were taken.[127] One royalist source claimed that the fleet took prizes worth £100,000–120,000, however the blockade may not have been completely effective, another royalist claimed that shipping worth £50,000 evaded the fleet.[128]

On 29 July the Prince wrote to the City of London demanding a 'loan' of £20,000 to support his fleet, in return for which he promised to release the ships he had taken. At the same time contact also seems to have been established with the Merchant Adventurers. The Commons promptly prohibited all contact with the Prince, and on 4 August the Common Council dissolved the committee that had been set up to consider the letter from the Prince. On 5 August the Prince addressed himself to Parliament proposing to release all seized shipping in return for money for his fleet, but unsurprisingly this was rejected.[129]

The ships and goods taken by the royalists were too important to their London owners to be simply abandoned. The merchants therefore ignored

---

[123] *HMC Pepys MSS*, 210, 219; *LJ* X, 379, 393, 440, 443, 449; *HMC Seventh Report, House of Lords MSS*, 45.

[124] PRO HCA24/110/74.

[125] Capp, *Cromwell's Navy*, 23; PRO HCA13/61, ff. 225–231v; *CSPD*, 1648–49, 262.

[126] *LJ* X 393, 417; *HMC Pepys MSS*, 219; *Powell & Timings*, 378; Clarendon, *History of the Rebellion*, IV, 362; PRO HCA13/61, ff. 275v, 345v, 363v–4, 425, 458v–9; PRO HCA24/109/89, 182, 216.

[127] PRO HCA13/61, ff. 345, 375, 376, 505v, *HMC Pepys MSS*, 285.

[128] *Powell & Timings*, 376, 379.

[129] Ogle, *Calendar of Clarendon State Papers*, I, 432; *CJ* V, 660, 662; CLRO Jour. 40, ff. 291v, 292v, 293; *LJ* X, 426.

Parliament's prohibition and sent representatives to negotiate the release of their ships. The owners of the *Love* employed one of their number, Captain William Ryder, for this purpose, while the Guinea Company and other merchants used Lawrence Lowe, a London surgeon. Negotiations between the Merchant Adventurers and the Prince of Wales also continued.[130] In order to obtain the release of their ships the merchants agreed to pay large sums of money to the royalists. On 10 August the Earl of Lauderdale wrote from the Prince's flagship on the Downs: 'Heer are ships taken to a great value, for which London is treating to send money abroad'.[131] Merchants may also have paid money to forestall seizure. The Levant Company, expecting the imminent arrival of four ships from the Mediterranean, sent a representative to Dover to try to procure a free passage for their ships to either London or Holland, it is difficult to see why the royalists should have agreed to this without some financial inducement. Consequently the royalists may have extracted money from a much wider cross section of the London merchant community than the list of ships captured suggests.[132]

The fact that the London merchants were able to ransom their ships mitigated the impact of the mutiny on London's trade, but this benefit was bought at considerable cost. One royalist source stated that £30,000 was received for the release of the ships. Other evidence substantiates this figure. A letter from a London royalist printed in *Perfect Occurrences* says that the City paid £20,000. In September another newsbook reported that £2,000 had been paid for the release of the ship from New England, and when Nicholas Trence, master of the *Chapman*, tried to get his ship and cargo released, £2,000 was proposed, on the grounds that they were worth £7,000.[133]

The royalists also extracted money from the Merchant Adventurers in Rotterdam. They initially demanded a loan of £50,000. However separately Sir John Berkeley requested a loan of £1,000 a month for the maintenance of the Duke of York. In response to the latter request the company paid 12,000 guilders, probably hoping to thereby avoid paying more, and they took the opportunity to petition for the release of their ship. The royalists kept hold of the *Damsel* in hopes of obtaining more money but on 30 August Berkeley reported that the Rotterdam merchants were refusing to pay any more money until the cloth ship came to harbour. The *Damsel* was eventually returned to its

---

[130] *LJ* X, 417; PRO HCA13/61, ff. 230v, 279v–280; *CSPD*, 1648–9, 234.

[131] Gardiner, *Hamilton Papers*, 238.

[132] PRO SP105/150, ff. 381–4.

[133] Capp, *Cromwell's Navy*, 33; *Powell & Timings*, 376; *Perfect Occurrences*, 86, 18–25 August 1648; *The Moderate Intelligencer*, 183, 14–21 September 1648, 1544; PRO HCA13/61, f. 345. On 28 November 1648 Prince Charles promised to repay three Londoners £1,500, which he had presumably received in return for release of a ship. *HMC Pepys MSS*, 285.

owners, according to Clarendon in return for £12,000. This was substantially less than the royalists had hoped for but it left the company heavily in debt.[134]

Moreover the merchants had to wait some weeks before they could obtain the release of their ships, even when they were willing to pay. Walter Strickland, Parliament's representative in the Netherlands, reported on 26 October that 'Divers of the merchants, whose ships were taken in the Downs, have compounded for them'. The owners of the *Chapman* appear to have paid for the release of their ship by the 10 October, but others do not seem to have paid until late November. This indicates that many merchants did not get their ships back until after the return of the fleet to Holland. This delay would have added to the merchants' costs.[135]

Not all the goods and ships taken by the royalists were returned to their owners. Of the forty five barrels of indigo taken in the *Damsell*, twelve were not recovered and the recovery of the other thirty three barrels cost Richard Shute 8055 guilders, plus between £200–250 expenses.[136] In September goods taken from some of the ships seized by the Prince's fleet were sold, including the gold in the *Star*. In December the owners of sugar on board the *Elizabeth and Susan* were promised payment of £2,300, presumably because their goods had been sold.[137] The Guinea Company recovered the *Star*, in return for a 'loan' of £500 to the Prince of Wales, but was unable to get any restitution for the gold she had carried. The *Cormatine*, worth between £6,000–£10,000, and the *Love* were added to the royalist fleet, although the *Love* was recaptured in November.[138]

On 29 August the royalist fleet sailed for the Thames, but, after a stand off with the parliamentary fleet, it then returned to Holland, arriving at Helvoetsluys on 1 September. On 19th of that month Warwick sailed in with Parliament's navy, and blockaded the royalist fleet until 21 November. He then returned to England with his entire fleet, leaving the royalists to resume their attacks on English merchant shipping.[139] In January 1649 the royalists sent out six vessels to capture prizes to raise funds. Among those taken was a ship from Hamburg bound for London, which was said to be worth £40,000, and one

[134] *HMC Pepys MSS*, 215–16, 219, 222, 225; Ogle, *Calendar of Clarendon State Papers*, I, 435; Clarendon, *History of the Rebellion,* IV, 363; H. Cary (ed.), *Memorials of the Great Civil War in England from 1642 to 1652,* 2 vols (1842), II, 206.

[135] Cary, *Memorials of the Great Civil War,* II, 44; *HMC Pepys MSS*, 285, 286.

[136] PRO HCA13/61, ff. 345v, 458v–9; PRO HCA24/109/182, 216; Ogle, *Calendar of Clarendon State Papers*, I, 441.

[137] *HMC Pepys MSS,* 284, 291; *The Moderate Intelligencer* 183, 14–21 September 1648, 1544.

[138] PRO HCA24/109/33; PRO HCA24/110/74; R. Spalding (ed.), *The Diary of Bulstrode Whitelocke, 1605–1675* (Oxford, 1990), 220 & n; Anderson, 'Royalists at Sea in 1648', 45; *HMC Pepys MSS,* 283.

[139] Capp, *Cromwell's Navy,* 40; Powell, *Navy in the English Civil War,* 184, 186–7.

royalist claimed she contained silver for the use of the East India Company.[140] A further ship was lost by the already straitened Rotterdam Merchant Adventurers, who were said to be willing to pay £2,000 had the royalists been willing to return her.[141] Strickland wrote despairingly: 'thus prince's men bring in our merchants like slaves and captives'. He wrote that English merchants were reduced to beggary.[142] Nevertheless Warwick had successfully contained the mutiny. The royalist fleet, commanded by Prince Rupert, would remain at large until 1653, and continued to capture London merchant ships, but it would never again be able to blockade the Thames, and was chased by the increasingly effective Commonwealth fleet further and further away from English home waters.[143]

In the summer of 1648 London's maritime trade was virtually brought to a halt by the combined efforts of the royalists and parliamentarians. The period when the royalists were on the Downs was less than a month and a half, and most of the ships and goods taken were returned to their owners, albeit at a price. However even for those merchants who chose not to trade during the blockade the delay caused considerable disruption. For those merchants like the members of the Levant Company who delayed exporting their cloth in the Sampson, for fear the royalists would capture the ship, the delay meant a longer turnaround on their capital. Their goods would have lain longer, unproductively, in their hands, which in turn delayed the time when they could be sold and re-invested in imports. At a time when merchants aimed for a speedy turnover of their capital this was a major disruption.[144] Moreover much of London's trade were seasonal, any delay could mean missing the right time of year to dispatch shipping.

Conclusion

Economic warfare caused considerable damage to London's trade networks. Nevertheless London's commerce was very diverse, and at no stage were all parts of the network affected at once. Also trade was usually diminished rather than cut off completely, and the effects were short lived. Internal trade was intensely disrupted during the first Civil War, but the worst period was probably only from the summer of 1643 to the summer of 1644, and some

---

[140] Anderson, 'Royalists at Sea in 1649', 321; Carte, *Collection of Original Letters and Papers*, I, 205.

[141] Carte, *Collection of Original Letters and Papers*, I, 208.

[142] *Powell & Timings*, 405.

[143] Capp, *Cromwell's Navy*, 63–5; Anderson, 'Royalist at Sea in 1649', 320–38; Idem, 'Royalists at Sea in 1650', 134–68; Idem, 'The Royalists at Sea in 1651–1653', *MM* 21 (1935), 61–90.

[144] Supple, *Commercial Crisis*, 10.

aspects of internal trade were entirely unaffected because they were within parts of the country under the control of Parliament.

The actions of foreign governments had a major impact on particular branches of overseas trade, but their activities were too uncoordinated to have a general effect on the economy. In the second half of the 1640s London's trade came under increasing attack at sea, first from the privateers and subsequently as a result of the mutiny in the navy and the undeclared war with France, until by the end of the decade London's maritime trade was at crisis point. However by this time the disruption of internal trade was already over. Moreover Parliament had access to far more maritime resources than the Irish and royalists, while the French were distracted by their own political troubles and their war with Spain. The Commonwealth was therefore able to build up her fleet and defeat her maritime enemies, which salvaged London's overseas trade.

Although the war did not bring trade completely to a halt two distinct periods of disruption in London's trade can be identified, 1643–44 and 1648–49. The first of which was primarily a crisis in internal trade, while the second affected London's overseas trade. Trade adapted to deal with these threats, routes were changed and escorts provided, but this had costs and consequently diminished economic efficiency. The Civil War, therefore, struck at the heart of London's ability to function within the national economy both as the principal port of England, and as the centre for the distribution of goods around the nation.

Chapter 6

Domestic Trade and Consumer Spending

Domestic trade was directly affected by the war as a result of the economic blockades established by both the royalists and the parliamentarians in 1643. Consequently the pattern of disruption reflected the division of the country between the two warring parties. The royalist controlled areas tended to be further away from London so the long distance trades were the most affected: especially trade in cloth, cattle and coal. Trade links with areas closer to London generally remained open throughout the war, and goods received predominantly from those parts, most importantly grain, never seem to have been in short supply.

Domestic trade was also affected by the diminished demand that arose from the high wartime taxes and plunder and the general reluctance of consumers to spend in the midst of a civil war. This affected all parts of domestic trade, including demand within London itself. Indeed it is difficult to distinguish clearly between demand for goods from London in the provinces, and demand in London itself, partly because many London tradesmen were active in both retailing and wholesaling, and partly because much of the goods bought by provincial customers were sold in London. The gentry took the opportunity of visits to London to catch up on their shopping, and metropolitan tradesmen sold their goods to provincial shopkeepers through their London establishments and provincial fairs.[1]

It is therefore difficult to distinguish between London demand and provincial demand. However this raises the problem, to what extent did the decline in demand originate outside the metropolis, as a result of the blockading of internal trade and the devastation brought about by the war? Or did it originate within London, as a result of the massive increase in taxation and other economic difficulties?

---

[1] L. Stone, *The Crisis of the Aristocracy, 1558–1641* (Oxford, 1965), 387–9; PRO C2/CHASI/N3/41.

The cloth trade

The first significant signs of disruption of the cloth trade can be detected in November 1642. In the aftermath of the battle of Edgehill the royalists attacked carriers bringing cloth to London. Clothiers were soon too afraid to send their cloth to the capital. For example John Ashe, reputedly the richest clothier in the country, sent weekly consignments of cloth from Somerset to London up until the end of October but sent nothing in November.[2] This quickly led to a shortage of cloth in London. On 29 November 1642 the Hamburg factor of one London Merchant Adventurer wrote to his principal: 'I take notice allsoe what you write of the stopping of Cloth from London by reason of the Kings Armie Lieing theare abouts'.[3] Ashe resumed deliveries in December, following the King's free trade proclamation. From then on he sent fewer but larger consignments. Before November he had dispatched an average of fourteen cloths a week, in December he sent one consignment of fifty cloths and in the following month he sent a single delivery of forty eight cloths. He probably thought that it was safer to send his goods in large convoys but it meant that when a consignment was intercepted, as in March 1643, his losses were all the greater.[4]

The disruption of the cloth trade was intensified by the royalist blockade of London in July 1643.[5] On 25 November the Levant Company, which generally exported West Country cloth, informed their treasurer at Istanbul that they were sending 'little store of Cloth & that at deare rates, & yet hereafter likely to be still dearer. We could not get any vests of such Cloth & colours as you desire, the kingdom & this City especially being in such disturbance'.[6] In March 1644 the East India Company informed their representatives in India that, because of the Civil War 'broad Cloathes & other Wollen Manufactures' were very difficult to obtain in London.[7] The following August the Levant Company decided to send the *Hercules* to Turkey with eight hundred cloths, but they had only managed to load four hundred by May 1645.[8]

The impact of the royalist blockade on the cloth trade can be quantified using the receipts of the 'hallage' toll from the cloth market at Blackwell Hall recorded in the accounts of Christ's Hospital. Annual totals, published by Jones in 1972, show that receipts fell only slightly in the first year of the war. In the year to August 1643 £1,062 was received compared with an average of £1,381

---

[2]   See above p. 110; J. Wroughton, *A Community at War: The Civil War in Bath and North Somerset, 1642–1650* (Bath 1992), 158–9.

[3]   PRO SP46/84, f. 301.

[4]   Wroughton, *A Community at War*, 158–60; *Royalist Newsbooks*, I, 161.

[5]   See above p. 112.

[6]   PRO SP105/111, f. 148v. See also ibid., f. 149v.

[7]   BL IOL/G/40/12, East India Company, Factory Miscellaneous, f. 64v.

[8]   A.C. Wood, *A History of the Levant Company* (Oxford, 1935), 54.

for the five years to August 1642. The major decline came after the King prohibited trade with London in the summer of 1643. Receipts fell to £627 in 1643–44, less than half the pre-war level. The 'hallage' receipts need to be treated cautiously as they do not represent the entire London cloth trade. Textiles manufactured in Norfolk were exempt from the toll. East Anglia remained under parliamentary control throughout the Civil War giving the Norfolk textile manufacturers uninterrupted access to London. These figures therefore almost certainly exaggerate the extent of the disruption of the cloth trade. Nevertheless Blackwell Hall was by far the most important market for the sale of English cloth in the kingdom, and, with the exception of Norfolk textiles, the toll had to be paid on all cloth brought to London. Consequently the 'hallage' toll receipts are the best source available for quantifying the fluctuations of the cloth trade.[9]

The cloth trade can be examined more closely through the monthly receipts recorded in the hospital's accounts. This shows disruption before the imposition of the blockade that is masked by the annual totals. As early as 11 January 1643, the treasurer of Christ's complained to the Court that the revenue from the toll was declining.[10] Figure 6.1 compares the monthly receipts for the year to the 15 July 1643, just prior to the initiation of the blockade, with average receipts for the previous five years.[11] This shows that in the early months of the war, to the beginning of November 1642, the cloth trade followed its usual course; receipts were over ninety per cent of the pre-war average. However this changed dramatically in November, in the four weeks to the 3 December receipts were only forty seven per cent of normal. After the King's free trade proclamation receipts began to recover, reaching ninety three per cent of average by February, but they again fell in March to fifty three per cent. This coincides with renewed complaints about royalist attacks on carriers. Then the receipts again rose but remained significantly below the average. Receipts whole year were seventy nine per cent of average. The receipts confirm the picture derived from the qualitative sources in showing that the cloth trade was disrupted before the embargo, particularly in November 1642 and March 1643, but that the disruption remained limited.

---

[9]   D.W. Jones, 'The "Hallage" Receipts of the London Cloth Markets, 1562–1720', *EcHR* 2nd Series, 25 (1972), 569, 576.

[10]   GL MS. 12806/4, Christ's Hospital, Court Minutes, 1632–49, f. 381.

[11]   GL MS. 12819/6, Christ's Hospital, Treasurers' Accounts, 1632–44. The accounts for each year are separately foliated. It should be noted that the receipts are recorded in fiscal months of 28 days. This means that the fiscal months do not correspond with calendar months, and they fall behind the calendar month by one and a half days every year. However this is sufficiently gradual not to invalidate short-term comparisons.

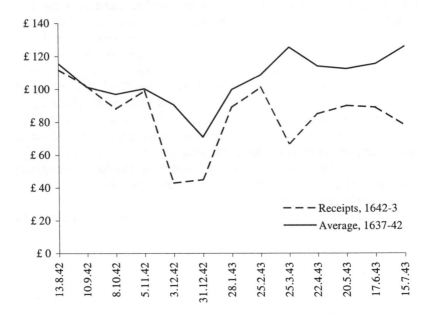

Figure 6.1
'Hallage' receipts, 1642–43

Source: GL MS. 12819/6, Christ's Hospital, Treasurers' Accounts, 1632–44.

The monthly receipts also provide a more accurate picture of the impact of the royalist blockade, showing that the disruption was greater than the annual figures suggest, but that the impact of the blockade was short lived. Figure 6.2 compares the receipts of the cloth trade for the year to 13 July 1644 with the average pre-war receipts for the same period as in Figure 6.1. In the year as a whole receipts were forty four per cent of the pre-war average. In the first month after the beginning of the blockade receipts were forty nine per cent of the average. Thereafter they were not above forty per cent until April 1644, the nadir was the four weeks to the 3 February 1644 when the receipts were only twenty two per cent of average. This indicates that, at its most effective, the royalist blockade reduced the cloth trade by more than three-quarters. By June the royalists were beginning to loosen their blockade and, consequently, in the month to 13 July 1644 receipts were eighty seven per cent of the pre-war level.

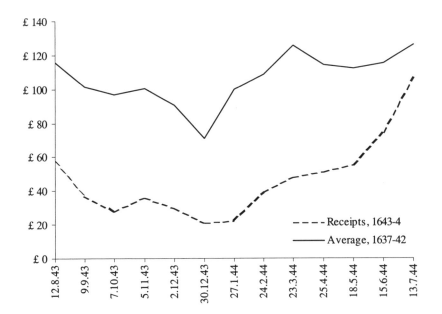

Figure 6.2
'Hallage' receipts, 1643–44

Source: GL MS. 12819/6, Christ's Hospital, Treasurers' Accounts, 1632–44.

The disruption caused by the blockade probably continued after it had been abandoned, as London merchants' stocks of cloth would have remained low for some period. The impression given by the rapid recovery in the monthly receipts from the middle of 1644 may therefore be misleading. A thirteen month moving average derived from the monthly receipts enables us to track the amount of cloth passing through the market over the previous year, smoothing over seasonal fluctuations and, consequently, giving a more accurate picture of the underlying trend in the cloth trade. It is notable that this average, having reached its nadir in the four weeks to 15 June 1644, does not return to the pre-war levels until the middle of 1646.[12]

---

[12] See below Figure 6.7 In the early part of this chart the moving average is depressed by the recession which resulted from the 1636–7 plague epidemic.

The coal trade

The disruption of the coal trade caused huge concern to Parliament and the governors of the City.[13] When Parliament prohibited the coal trade with Newcastle in January 1643, the lord mayor certified that there were five months of supplies of coal in London. The Scots gave assurances that sufficient additional supplies could be provided by the Firth of Forth coalmines, but in reality the Scottish mines were never able to produce enough to meet London's needs.[14] Moreover in the early part of the Civil War Newcastle's coal exports fell massively, in the year to Michaelmas 1643 only 53,403 tons of coal left the Tyne, compared to over 450,000 tons a year in the early 1630s. Consequently although Newcastle coal continued to find its way to London in early 1643, either from Newcastle ships captured by the parliamentarians or smuggling, it must only have been a small fraction of the pre-war trade.[15]

The consequence of such a major decline in the coal trade was a massive price increase. Parliament tried to set the price of coal at 23s the chaldron in order to stop speculation, but repeated orders to enforce the set price show that there were considerable difficulties in keeping prices down. On 13 July 1643 the Court of Aldermen was informed that the wharfmongers had bought up all the supplies of coal, and would not sell except at very high prices. Even those colliers who had entered into bonds with the navy committee to sell at the fixed price, were found to be selling their coal well above it.[16] In 1642 Christ's Hospital paid 20s per chaldron for coal and Westminster College paid 22s 4d. In January 1643 the newsbooks stated that coal prices had risen from 22s per chaldron to 34s and by June 46s a chaldron was being quoted in the City. Westminster College paid on average 37s 3d per chaldron in 1643. Christ's Hospital only paid the regulatory 23s per chaldron but that was because they only purchased five chaldrons sent by the lord mayor, which meant accepting a major reduction in supplies. In 1642 the hospital had purchased twenty three chaldrons.[17] These figures may underestimate the wartime increase in prices as one way traders evaded the price restrictions was

---

[13] See above p. 110.

[14] *Powell & Timings*, 58–9; J.U. Nef, *The Rise of the British Coal Industry*, 2 vols (1932), II, 286–8.

[15] Bodl. Rawlinson MS. A221, Journal of the Committee for the Navy, 1643–44, ff. 126, 131, 133, 134, 135–6, 141; C. Thompson (ed.), *Walter Yonge's Diary of Proceedings of the House of Commons, 1642–5, Vol. 1, 1642–1643* (Wivenhoe, 1986), 312; J. Hatcher, *The History of the British Coal Industry, Vol. 1 Before 1700: Towards the Age of Coal* (Oxford, 1993), 489, table 14.1 (a).

[16] *An Order Concerning the Price of Coales* (1643); CLRO Rep. 56, f. 209.

[17] *A Perfect Diurnall*, 34, 30 Jan–6 February 1643, unpag; *A Perfect Diurnall*, 35, 6–13 February 1643, unpaginated; GL MS. 4384/2, St Bartholomew by the Exchange, Vestry Minutes, 1643–76, f. 2; Hatcher, *History of the British Coal Industry*, 582, table B.5; GL MS. 12819/6, accounts for 1642–43 and 1643–44.

by selling short measure, as the Middlesex Justices complained in April 1644.[18] Rising fuel prices damaged manufacturing industry, trades as diverse as brewing, brickmaking and cookery were all affected by rising fuel prices, and the increased costs were inevitably passed on to the consumer. In June 1643 the gunmakers of London petitioned the Commons that they could not continue manufacturing armaments unless they were provided with coal.[19]

The illicit coal trade from Newcastle became much more difficult after the King prohibited all trade with London in July 1643, and by 1644, Parliament's blockade of Newcastle was much more effective. In the year following Michaelmas 1643, 188 ships left Newcastle carrying 2321 tons of coal, and only one ship left between May and November 1644. In comparison over three thousand vessels had left the port in 1641.[20] Consequently prices rose even further in London. In 1644 40–50s per chaldron was quoted by examinants in the High Court of Admiralty while Christ's Hospital paid as much as 49s per chaldron for coal from Scotland. In February and March 1644 Newcastle and Sunderland coal captured by parliamentarian ships was valued at between 40s and 55s. Even in July, when prices were usually lower than in the winter, coal was valued at 55s a chaldron.[21]

On the 18 July 1643 Alderman Thomas Adams told the House of Commons of the 'great and pressing Necessities that lay upon the City in regard of the Necessity of Coals; which will so pinch the Poor, that the Consequences thereof will be full of Horror and Danger', a conclusion which was confirmed by the rising tide of disorder the fuel shortage created.[22] The author of one tract stated that 'the *cold* makes some turne Thieves that never stole before, steale *Posts*, *seats*, *Benches* from *doores*, *Railes*, nay, the very *Stocks* that should punish them'.[23] Wood was stolen from the forests and woods in the vicinity of the capital. When the woodward of Enfield Chase, John Butcher, together with the high constable and petty constable tried to search Winchmore Hill hamlet, on the edge of the Chase, for stolen wood on 13 November 1643 they were attacked by the local inhabitants. In the following March a number of men from Edmonton broke into the Chase armed with bills and long clubs, and cut down and carried away trees in front

---

[18] LMA MJ/SBB/46, ff. 21–2.

[19] *Sea-Coale, Char-Coale, and Small-Coale* (1643), 5–6; *CJ* III, 141. Evelyn argued that most of the coal consumed in London was for industrial uses. J. Evelyn, *Fumifugium, or, The inconveniencie of the aer and smoak of London dissipated* (1661), 6.

[20] Hatcher, *History of the British Coal Industry*, 86, 489, table 14.1 (a).

[21] PRO HCA13/59, ff. 229, 239v (this is from testimony in which the price in London was compared unfavourable with that in France, and consequently may be an underestimate); GL MS. 12819/6, accounts for 1644–45; PRO HCA4/1, appraisements of coal on board the *Seahorse*, *Grace* of London, *Fortune* of Utland, *Margaret* of Milton, *William* of Southwold; Hatcher, *History of the British Coal Industry*, 478.

[22] *CJ* III, 171.

[23] *Artificiall Fire, or Coale for Rich and Poore* (1644).

of the powerless keeper.[24] Also vulnerable were episcopal estates; in May 1643 the committee for sequestration ordered that the Archbishop of Canterbury's woods around the capital be preserved from the 'rude & disorderly people cominge from London & elswhere'.[25] In July 1644 Thomas Taylor of Hornsey was committed to the house of correction by the Middlesex Justices for being 'a common wood stealer', and particularly for stealing wood belonging to the manor of the Bishop of London.[26] It was not only royal and episcopal estates that suffered. In December 1643 the Court of St Thomas' Hospital agreed to sell trees on land they owned in Shoreditch, because they were in danger of being cut down and carried away by the poor. Even the guards around London were suspected, on 26 October 1643 the House of Commons ordered Sir John Hippisley to provide them with fuel to safeguard the woods around London.[27]

In July 1643 a committee of the Court of Aldermen concluded that the existing fuel provisions for London were inadequate.[28] In response Parliament appointed officers to take wood from royal, episcopal or royalist estates within sixty miles of London for the supply of the poor. In so doing they hoped to control the process of plunder, direct it onto the estates of their political enemies rather than their friends, and to make sure it did the least long term damage.[29] However by the summer of 1644 the Venetian ambassador reported that most of the trees round London had been felled.[30] A further ordinance was passed for cutting peat and turf for fuel in July 1644 but Parliament was concerned that timber stocks were being irrevocably damaged. In September 1644 the Commons ordered a committee to consider the ordinance for providing wood for the city and to bring in an ordinance for suspending it, if necessary.[31]

During the course of 1644 the success of Parliament's military forces and their Scottish allies in the northeast meant that the coal trade could be re-opened. On 21 March 1644 trade was resumed with Sunderland, but before the war the Sunderland coal trade had been much smaller than that of Newcastle. In October 1644 it was reported that colliers from Sunderland sent only small quantities of coal to London to keep prices high. Christ's Hospital paid 32s per chaldron for Sunderland coal in 1644, less than it had paid for Scottish coal but still substantially more than it had paid in 1642. The Court of Aldermen continued its efforts to prevent speculation. On 14 November 1644 trade with

---

[24] D. Pam, *The Story of Enfield Chase* (1984), 63–5.

[25] PRO SP20/1, f. 20v.

[26] LMA MJ/SBB/49, f. 30.

[27] LMA H1/ST/A1/5, St Thomas' Hospital, Court of Governors Minute Book, 1619–77, f. 78; *CJ* III, 288.

[28] CLRO Rep. 56, f. 209.

[29] *Firth & Rait*, I, 303–5.

[30] *CSPV* 1643–47, 106.

[31] *CJ* III, 619; *Firth & Rait*, I, 481–2.

Newcastle was finally reopened, but because of damage to the collieries during the war, it took several years for production to recover to pre-war levels.[32] Consequently, the plundering of the woods around London continued. In February 1645 John Browne, Clerk of Parliament, petitioned the House of Lords that his woods in Twickenham were being despoiled and in Enfield prosecutions in the manor court show that wood stealing continued unabated in 1645 and 1646.[33] Nevertheless from 1645 the price of coal was falling in London. Christ's Hospital paid between 22–23s per chaldron in 1645; falling to 17s 3d by 1647.[34]

Despite all the efforts of the City authorities and Parliament, Londoners suffered massive increases in fuel costs during the war years. Alternatives to coal, such as charcoal and timber, may have gone some way to compensate but the high prices paid for what coal did reach London show that the alternatives were inadequate. If the prices paid by Christ's Hospital are an accurate guide then coal prices increased 145 per cent. If demand for fuel was constant, and assuming that the attempts to regulate the price was entirely ineffective, then this suggests that supplies fell to less than half of what they had been before. John Evelyn subsequently said that the reduction in pollution led to a bumper harvest in the orchards and gardens in and around London but this was at the expense of industrial production. A petition approved by the Common Council on 17 December 1644 stated that the high cost of fuel was a major factor in increasing poverty in the City. Jeremy Boulton has estimated that coal represented about eight per cent of Londoners' expenditure on food and fuel. If this is correct then a 145 per cent increase in the price of coal would equal an 11.3 per cent increase in the cost of living.[35]

Foodstuffs, lead and tin

One aspect of domestic trade that was of great concern to the authorities in Parliament and the City was the food supply.[36] However, despite widespread fears that the conflict would lead to a famine, bread prices did not rise during the war.[37] In the seventeenth century the high cost of land transport meant that the grain trade was predominantly local. It was only economic to move grain

---

[32] *Firth & Rait*, I, 397–8, 569–70; *CSPD*, 1644–45, 103, 220; GL MS. 12819/6, accounts for 1644–45; CLRO Rep, 57/1, ff. 227v, 228v–9, 236.

[33] *HMC Sixth Report, House of Lords MSS*, 46; Pam, *Story of Enfield Chase*, 65.

[34] GL MS. 12819/7, Christ's Hospital, Treasurers Accounts, 1645–52, accounts for 1645–46, 1646–47, 1647–48.

[35] Evelyn, *Fumifugium*, 7; CLRO Jour. 40, f. 118; J.P. Boulton, 'Food Prices and the Standard of Living in the "Century of Revolution", 1580–1700', *EcHR* 2nd Series, 53 (2000), 468.

[36] See for example CJ *III*, 359, 363; *CSPD*, 1644, 74.

[37] B. Mitchell, *Abstract of British Historical Statistics* (Cambridge, 1988), 769.

over longer distances by water. Even London's waterborne grain trade was relatively short distance, either along the coast from Kent and East Anglia, or down the Thames and the Lea rivers. Parliament controlled most of the country immediately around the capital throughout the Civil War, consequently the royalists were only able to blockade one part of London's grain supplies, the trade down the Thames. Nevertheless there is some evidence of upward pressures on grain prices, but this only encouraged farmers in those areas that still had access to the London market to increase production. In May 1644 Thomas Knyvett, a Norfolk landowner, wrote to his wife informing her that grain prices were rising in London and he advised 'I think we must plowe & sowe all our ground, for corne is like to be the best commodity & saf'est to be injoy'd'.[38] Moreover the first civil war coincided with a run of good harvests, which probably ensured that landowners like Knyvett could produce enough grain to compensate for the loss of the Thames trade.

In contrast to the grain trade there was a national market for livestock. Cattle for the London market commonly originated from the highland regions of the north of England, Wales and Scotland. The royalists either occupied these areas or were able to obstruct their contact with London. Nevertheless there may well have been a time lag between the disruption of the cattle trade and its impact on the London economy, as cattle was first fattened in the counties around London before sale, consequently there would have been a significant stock of cattle in areas under parliamentary control. As a result it was not until the latter part of the war that there was a shortage of meat in the metropolis. In February 1645 the lord mayor and the Court of Aldermen wrote to the Speaker arguing for powers to restrict slaughtering to conserve stocks. Later in the same month the lord mayor issued a precept to enforce the observance of the fish days to reduce the consumption of meat.[39] A shortage of cattle had potentially significant consequences for the London economy. Beef played a major part in Londoners' diet. It has been suggested that London paupers ate an average of four ounces a day and that this represented about eighteen per cent of their daily expenditure on food and fuel. Moreover cattle provided hides and tallow, vital raw materials for London manufacturing.[40]

London also became cut off from its usual sources of lead and tin. In November 1643 the East India Company informed their representatives in India that they had no hopes of sending them any lead, which had previously been one of their main exports, unless peace was made soon. In March 1644 they informed them that lead was 'not at any reasonable Rate to be procured by

---

[38] B. Schofield (ed.), *The Knyvett Letters, 1620–1644* (1949), 151. See also GH, Court Book, W, 1642–45, f. 43.

[39] Whitelocke, *Memorials*, I, 385; *A Perfect Diurnall*, 80, 3–10 February 1645, 203; CLRO, Minutes of Common Hall, I, f. 240v.

[40] Boulton, 'Food Prices', 464, table 4.

reason of the stopp of that commodity in coming from the Mines in Darbyshire'.[41] The company's representatives in the east were forced to purchase lead from their Dutch rivals.[42] The royalists also stopped the shipment of tin from Cornwall, not only as part of the general blockade, but also so that tin could be diverted to France to pay for the import of munitions. Consequently tin had to be imported from Amsterdam, with a resulting substantial increase in price.[43]

Further evidence of declining trade in the war comes from the fall in the receipts from the tolls at the City beams. All non-freemen had to weigh their goods at one of the beams before selling them in the City, for which a toll was payable. There were two main beams, the great beam at Cornhill, and the iron beam at the Steelyard by the river. The beams were probably mainly used by non-Londoners bringing produce to the capital for sale, although London merchants who were not freemen also used them. It is likely that the main goods traded were those that were specifically mentioned in the table of fees: hops, madder, copperas and lead. In 1681 the great beam was described as the main market for hops in London.[44] As Figure 6.3 shows receipts at both beams fell substantially during the war. Receipts from the great beam fell from £185 for the year to Michaelmas 1642, to £118 for the year to Michaelmas 1643, a fall of more than one-third. This is substantially smaller than the fall in the 'hallage' cloth duty, which was over half. The reason why the fall in receipts from the great beam was smaller than the fall in the receipts for 'hallage' was probably that hops, like grain, generally came from counties close to London. Receipts at the iron beam fell further, from £35 to £16 in the same period, but

---

[41] BL IOL/G/40/12, ff. 54, 64v.

[42] BL IOL/I/3/28, Dutch Translations, Letters from the Indies, 1644–45, DDL.

[43] M. Coate, *Cornwall in the Great Civil War and Interregnum, 1642–60*, 2nd edn (Truro, 1963), 38, 117, 184; I.S., *A Declaration of Sundry Grievances Concerning Tinne and Pewter* (1646).

[44] CLRO 49, f. 209; CLRO Alchin Papers, Box C, No. 4 'Papers & Documents concerning the Beams', I/2, I/8–10. The beams only needed to be used for goods sold by weight.

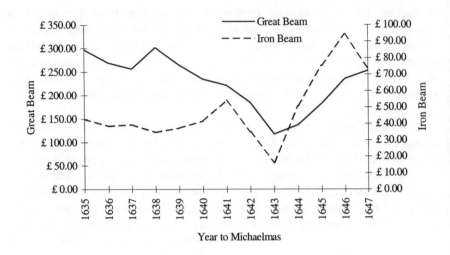

Figure 6.3
Receipts from the great beam and iron beam, 1635–47

Source: Barts HB 1/5, Treasurers' Ledgers, 1629–42, unfoliated; Barts. HB 1/6, Treasurers' Ledgers, 1643–55, unfoliated, receipts for the year to Michaelmas.[45]

the amount of goods traded at this beam was probably substantially smaller than the amount at the great beam.[46]

There was a substantial reduction in trade from the provinces to London in the Civil War. This can be attributed to the impact of the blockades. The royalists tended to control those parts of the country that were furthest away from London, so consequently the decline was greatest in the long distance trades. The cloth and coal trades probably fell by more than half, and the disruption in trade in tin, lead and cattle may have been as great. However the impact on the trade in hops and grain, which came from closer to London, was limited.

Londoners paid higher prices for fuel, and probably for other goods such as meat, which would have reduced demand. Manufacturing industry was

---

[45] Changes in jurisdiction mean that receipts after 1647 are not comparable with those for the earlier period. CLRO Rep. 59, ff. 111–13.

[46] Barts HB 1/5, Treasurers' Ledgers, 1629–42, unfoliated; Barts. HB 1/6, Treasurers' Ledgers, 1643–55, unfoliated; A.M. Everitt, 'The marketing of agricultural produce, 1500–1640', in J. Chartres (ed.), *Chapters from the Agrarian History of England and Wales. 4. Agricultural Markets and Trade. 1500–1700* (Cambridge, 1990), 60. It was reported that the price of hops imported from Flanders fell during the Civil War, which suggests that there was no shortage of this commodity. PRO HCA13/59, f. 470.

affected by the rising fuel prices and diminished supplies of raw materials such as lead and tin. Woollen cloth, London's principal export, became scarce and consequently expensive. However the disruption was short lived. From 1644 Parliament conquered more of the country and the royalists abandoned their blockade and, as consequence, internal trade started to recover before the war was over. Already by the middle of 1644 the cloth trade was beginning to improve. The receipts from beams also began to pick up in 1644 and coal prices were falling by 1645.

London wholesaling

The Civil War did not immediately disrupt the commercial networks of the London wholesalers. In December 1642 it was still possible to send tobacco and spices from London to royalist controlled Stafford apparently unimpeded by the fighting.[47] It was only the advent of the blockades of internal trade in 1643 that prevented London wholesalers from supplying their provincial customers. The booksellers of the Stationers' Company were dependent on the national distribution of certain standard publications and consequently they suffered during the war. The result was a substantial fall in apprenticeship recruitment and admissions of freemen: sixty seven apprentices were bound in 1641 falling to thirty five apprentices in 1642 and only twenty four in 1643. The numbers made free fell from forty nine in 1641 to twenty two in the next year and twenty one in 1643.[48]

The economic problems of the wholesalers led to agitation in London against Parliament's restrictions on trade with the royalists. In January 1644 a group of London shopkeepers complained to the Court of Aldermen that parliamentarian soldiers had seized goods, which they had recently sent to their chapmen in Wickham. The following September a petition was presented to the Common Council calling for the re-opening of trade with royalist controlled parts of the kingdom. Although the aldermen were initially sympathetic they realized that even if Parliament lifted their trade restrictions Londoners would not benefit because the royalists would still deny them access. The danger was that foreign merchants based in London would be able

---

[47] S.A.H. Burne (ed.), 'Chetwynd Papers in the William Salt Library', *Collections for a History of Stafford*shire (1941), 94. A royalist garrison was established at Stafford in autumn 1642 which was not taken by the parliamentarians until May 1643. D.H. Pennington and I.A. Roots (eds), *The Committee at Stafford 1643–45: The Order Book of the Staffordshire County Committee* (Manchester, 1957), lxi-lxiii.

[48] C. Blagden, 'The Stationers Company in the Civil War Period', *The Library* 5th Series, 13 (1958), 16; Idem, *The Stationers Company: A History 1403–1659* (1960), 286 & n.

to take over London's pre-war trade with the provinces because they were not subject to the royalist embargo.[49]

The disruption of the wholesalers' marketing networks led a collapse in demand for imports. One report to the House of Commons refers to the 'extreame deadnes of Trade of late within this Kingdome for ventinge of Merchandizes brought in'.[50] The East India Company found the sales of their goods in August 1643 very disappointing. When the governor of the company told a general meeting of the investors that he did not think they would be able to sell the remainder in England there was a general silence. The company decided to ship the rest of their pepper to Italy and divide the other goods among the investors.[51] The impact of the blockade is illustrated by the fact that in that same month, Lord Herbert of Cherbury was lamenting the high price of pepper in Shrewsbury. Evidently there was still demand for the company's imports, the problem was getting them to where they were wanted.[52] In November 1643 the East India Company complained that 'all trade & commerce in this Kingdome is almost fallen to the ground through our owne unhappie divisions at home', they feared that if they imported large quantities of goods 'wee might lacke sales'.[53] Things were little better in the new year. In March 1644 the company lamented that 'the marketts in all places are much declined & Commodities much fallen in their wonted prize & reputation'.[54]

Consumer spending

In 1645 Nehemiah Wallington, a London turner and shopkeeper, lamented that 'trayding is dead & Costomers hard'.[55] However it could be argued that this is the perennial lament of shopkeepers throughout history. In his recent study of prices and wages in seventeenth-century London Jeremy Boulton found no decline in real wages during the Civil War period and consequently argued that it was not a time of particular hardship. This would suggest that there was little decline in consumer spending in London. However Boulton's price data, drawn from the accounts of a small number of London institutions, probably under represents the impact of the war on prices. Boulton's data shows the price of coal declining every year from 1640 to 1647, although the rising price of coal during the war is otherwise well documented. The blockades and the excise

---

[49]   CLRO Rep. 57/1, f. 44; CLRO Jour. 40, f. 104v.

[50]   Longleat House, Whitelocke Papers, vol. 9, f. 38.

[51]   *CCMEIC* 1640–43, 342, 345, 347–8, 349. For further evidence of lack of demand for imports see PRO SP16/503/87.

[52]   R. Warner (ed.), *Epistolary Curiosities* (1818), 32.

[53]   BL IOL/G/40/12, f. 53v.

[54]   BL IOL/G/40/12, f. 59v.

[55]   BL Sloane MS. 922, Nehemiah Wallington's Letters on Religious Topics, f. 146v.

exerted extra inflationary pressures on the prices of a wide variety of commodities during the war. Moreover these goods included a significant number of the staples of even the poorest London consumers, including, as well as coal, beer, affected by the excise, and beef, affected by both the excise and the blockades.[56]

Wage rates may not be an accurate guide to the earnings of Londoners. Boulton's wage rates are derived from the building industry, but the prevalence of wage labour in this sector was probably not typical of the economy as a whole. Large economic premises were rare and labourers made up less than five per cent of London workers in the seventeenth century. Moreover builders wages may have been untypically high in Civil War London because of the large amount of work created by the building and maintenance of London's massive defences. Merchants formed only a small sector of the population but represented a high proportion of London's wealth and spending. It is likely that during the war their profits were depressed by the reduction in trade.

Demand in the 1640s was also affected by factors other than income fluctuations. The parliamentarian authorities closed the theatres in 1642 and they also mounted vigorous campaigns to enforce Sunday observance and abolish traditional Christmas festivities. Moreover there were widespread fears that war would lead to famine, which lead the livery companies to cancel their feasts and presumably had a similar constraining effect on Londoners' private consumption. More generally Londoners were reluctant to spend what money they had during the Civil War because of their uncertainties about the future.[57]

One area that suffered dramatically during the Civil War was the West End. The royal court, traditionally a major source of demand, was absent from Westminster. Noble and gentry residents suffered a major decline in their income because of the falling rents, and those who chose the royalist side followed the court and had their estates sequestered by the parliamentarians, which made it difficult for their creditors to recover debts. There was also a substantial decline in the business done at the central law courts in Westminster, which would have reduced lawyers' earnings and brought fewer litigants to London.[58]

---

[56] Boulton, 'Food Prices', 474, 475; Boulton's price index for coal shows a steady decline from 1640 to 1646. Ibid., 481–2. For the impact of the excise on the price of beer see above pp. 31, 36.

[57] GL MS. 11588/4, Grocers' Company, Court Minutes, 1640–68, 75; E.M. Symonds (ed.), 'The Diary of John Greene (1635–57). II', *EHR* 43 (1928), 603; W. Lithgow, 'The present Surveigh of London and England's State' (1643), reprinted in *Lord Somers' Tracts*, 16 vols (1748–52), IV, 536.

[58] L. Stone, *Family and Fortune, Studies in Aristocratic Finance in the Sixteenth and Seventeenth Centuries* (Oxford, 1973), 146–52; J. Broad, 'Gentry Finances and the Civil War: The Case of the Buckinghamshire Verneys', *EcHR* 2nd series, 32 (1979), 186–9; D. Hirst, *England in Conflict, 1603–1660: Kingdom, Community, Commonwealth* (London, 1999), 228.

The economy of Civil War Westminster lies outside the scope of this book, nevertheless the decline in West End demand also affected the City. In 1645 the City tailor turned newsbook editor, John Dillingham, estimated the loss to the London economy at nearly £20,000 a year.[59] Another tailor, William Perkins, who before the war had had a large land-owning clientele, suffered a major reverse in fortunes and was imprisoned for debt by April 1647.[60] The impact was probably mostly concentrated on the western side of the City. Perkins and Dillingham both lived near Fleet Street. In a chancery case it was claimed that during the war, the tavern keeper of the 'King's Head', on the corner of Chancery Lane and Fleet Street, sold less French wine in a week than he had previously sold in a day, and the kitchen was not one-quarter as profitable as it had been.[61]

The decline in consumer demand was not confined to the western parts of the City. The 'King's Head' may well have been typical of taverns all over London. Imports of wine fell and there were sharp declines in receipts for quarterage, the enrolment of apprentices, and the admission of freemen in the Vintners' Company, reaching a nadir in 1643–44.[62] Selling to customers in the country was a part of the vintners' trade; consequently they also suffered from declining provincial demand as a result of the blockades. However wholesaling was probably only a minor part of their trade. The economic problems of the vintners suggest that demand for luxuries fell substantially during the war, and this was not just because of the absence of the royal court.

The demand for necessities also declined, this is reflected in the slump in London's weekly markets, such as the Stocks. The Stocks was a fish and meat market first established in the thirteenth century situated in a large stone market house in the centre of the City. From the late sixteenth century the market was let out to a single tenant who sublet the stalls to fishmongers and butchers. In February 1645 a committee of aldermen found that the lessee was losing money because 'the Fish marketts throughout London and especially in the Stockes is much decayed'.[63] However there is no evidence of decline in the brewing industry until 1647. Beer was a major part of the diet of the population, and consequently demand for it was relatively inelastic.[64]

One aspect of consumer spending in London that can be quantified is the size of the St Bartholomew's Day fair. The fair was originally established in the Middle Ages for the sale of cloth and took place annually over three days in

[59] *The Moderate Intelligencer*, 18, 26 June–3 July 1645, 143.
[60] *HMC Ormonde MSS, New Series*, I, 53–4, 112, 114, 115.
[61] PRO C24/697/28.
[62] See Figure 6.4.
[63] I. Archer et al (eds), *Hugh Alley's Caveat: The Markets of London in 1598*, London Topographical Society Publications 137 (1988), 4, 33, 89; CLRO Rep. 57/2, f. 57.
[64] See above pp. 35, 37.

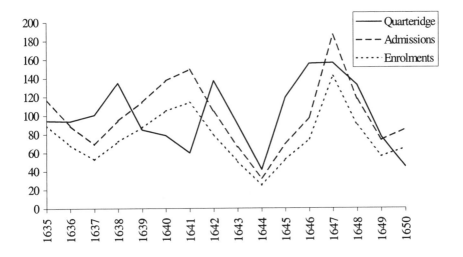

Figure 6.4
The Vintners' Company, 1635–50

Source: GL MS. 15333/4, Vintners' Company, Wardens' Accounts, 1636–58. Receipts for the year to Midsummer. 100=mean 1635–50.

late August in the churchyard of the Priory of St Bartholomew's Smithfield. By 1641 it had expanded to cover four London parishes. The fair, although still important for the sale of cloth, had become a general 'pleasure fair', as depicted by Ben Jonson in 1614, drawing large crowds and providing an opportunity for London craftsmen and shopkeepers to sell a wide range of consumer goods.[65] From 1642 the traditional wrestling and shooting matches, performed before the Lord Mayor and Court of Aldermen, ceased, but otherwise there is no sign of any official interference in the fair, and it was not until 1653 that any attempt was made to reform it.[66] Consequently John Evelyn was able to record that in 1648 he 'went to see the celebrated follies of *Bartholomew* faire'.[67] Many fairgoers were not Londoners, but the majority probably were.

---

[65] J. Stow, *The Survey of London*, A. Munday et al (eds), (1633), 419; H. Morley, *Memoirs of Bartholomew Fair* (London, 1892), 144–8; J. Haynes, *The Social Relations of Jonson's Theater* (Cambridge, 1992), 122.
[66] Stow, *Survey of London*, 651–2; CLRO Rep. 56, f. 1; CLRO Rep. 62, f. 370v.
[67] E.S. De Beer (ed.), *The Diary of John Evelyn*, 6 vols (Oxford, 1955) II, 543.

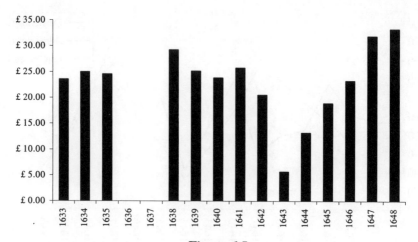

Figure 6.5
Pickage from the St. Bartholomew's Day fair, 1633–48

Source: CLRO Cash Books, vols 1/1–1/6.[68]

Fluctuations in the size of the fair can be followed through the receipts of 'pickage', a toll paid for establishing a stall or booth. Receipts from the first fair of the war, that of 1642, were £20 10s 9d, a fall of about nineteen per cent compared with the average from 1633 to 1641, however by 1643 receipts had fallen by over three-quarters of the pre-war average, to only £5 13s 6d.[69] The decline in receipts can be partly attributed to the crisis in the cloth trade, but the wardens of the Goldsmiths' Company, who traditionally searched the fair for substandard wares, described the 1643 fair as very small, with only one goldsmith's stall in it.[70] This indicates that the retailing side of the fair also declined sharply, suggesting that there was a general slump in consumer spending.

The impact of the war on the shopkeepers of London can also be seen in the receipts of the Founders' Company from the assize of weights. All brass weights sold within three miles of the City had to be stamped with the arms of the Founders' Company before they were sold, and a fee had to be paid to the company. The war led to a major fall in receipts, from £10 13s in the year to October 1642 to £4 10s 11½d in the year to October 1643, a fall of over fifty

---

[68] The 1636 and 1637 fairs were cancelled because of the plague.
[69] CLRO Cash Books, vol. 1/4, ff. 28v, 123; vol. 1/5, f. 31v.
[70] GH, Court Book, W, 1642–45, f. 86.

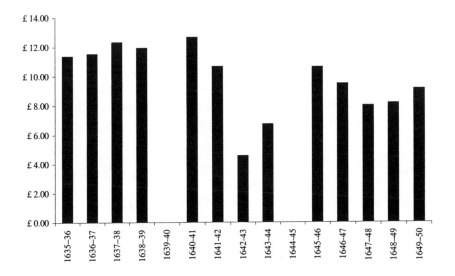

Figure 6.6
Receipts from the assize of brass weights, 1635–50

Source: G. Parsloe (ed.), *Wardens' Accounts of the Worshipful Company of Founders of the City of London 1497–1681* (1964), 303, 305, 306, 308, 312, 315, 318, 321, 327, 330, 333, 335, 338.[71]

per cent. Moreover the 1642-43 receipts were only forty per cent of the 1630s average. The following year, to October 1644, saw some improvement, but receipts still only totalled £6 14s 1½d. This suggests that there was a substantial fall in demand for weights during the war. As most weights were presumably sold to retailers for use in their shops this indicates a major fall in retailing activity.[72]

Consumer spending did decline during the Civil War, but the decline was greatest in demand for luxuries, such as wine in taverns and silverware at the Bartholomew's fair. Demand for necessities seems to have fallen less dramatically, as consumers were apparently willing to pay the extra cost of the excise even on heavily taxed items such as beer. Further evidence that tends to

---

[71] No receipts are recorded for the assize of weights in the accounts for 1639–40 or 1644–45, however the former records an unspecified receipt of £7 7s 7d as part payment from the clerk, and also records that he owed a further £4. The account for 1644–45 records receipt of £9 from the clerk. The clerk usually collected the assize of weights. Parsloe, *Wardens' Accounts of the Worshipful Company of Founders*, 310–11, 323.

[72] G. Parsloe (ed.), *Wardens' Accounts of the Worshipful Company of Founders of the City of London 1497–1681* (1964), xxvi, 218 n., 292–308, 315, 318, 321.

discount the impact of the excise on consumer spending is provided by the pickage receipts, which were lowest in 1643, before the introduction of the excise in September of that year. The fair took place after the introduction of the royalist blockade. It is probable that the principle cause of the decline in consumer spending was the blockade, and the consequent reduction in internal trade, as tradesmen, finding their income reduced cut their expenditure accordingly. The evidence for the vintners substantiates this, as their prosperity began to recover after 1644, when the blockades began to ease.

Post-war

From the middle of 1644 onwards a combination of Parliament's military success and the relaxation of the royalist blockade meant that London's domestic trade began to recover. After the defeat of the northern royalists at Marston Moor, on 2 July 1644, London wholesalers returned to the north in force, and were soon in dispute with the corporation of Hull over the taxation of their warehouses.[73] The defeat of the royalists in the north also enabled lead from Derbyshire and Yorkshire to be sent to Hull for shipment to London again. The demand for munitions meant that 1645 was a boom year for the lead trade, total shipments to London in that year exceeded the average for the previous twenty years by more than one-third.[74] The recovery of internal trade is also reflected in increasing toll receipts at the great beam, which rose from £138 in the year to Michaelmas 1644 to £183 in the year to Michaelmas 1645, not far short of the 1642 total.[75] The recovery in the cloth trade, already detectable in mid 1644, continued in the latter part of the war. In the year to August 1646, the last year of the war, receipts of 'hallage' totalled £1,356, which was ninety eight per cent of the average annual receipts for the five years before the war.[76] There was also a substantial increase in receipts from the assize of brass weights, the money collected by the Founders' Company from this source rose from £6 14s 1½d in the year to October 1644 to £10 12s

---

[73] T.T. Wildridge (ed.), *The Hull Letters Printed from a Collection of Original Documents found Among the Borough Archives in the Town Hall, Hull, 1884, During the Progress of the Work of Indexing* (Hull, 1886), 52, 55–6, 62, 63, 66, 71, 83; L.M. Stanewell (ed.), *City and County of Kingston Upon Hull, Calendar of the Ancient Deeds, Letters, Miscellaneous Old Documents, &c in the Archives of the Corporation* (Hull, 1951), 336.

[74] D. Kiernan, 'Lawrence Oxley's accounts, 1677–81', in J.V. Beckett et al (eds), *A Seventeenth Century Scarsdale Miscellany*, Derbyshire Record Society 20 (1993), 130.

[75] Barts HB 1/5, Treasurers' Ledgers, 1629–42, unfoliated; Barts. HB 1/6, Treasurers' Ledgers, 1643–55, unfoliated.

[76] Jones, '"Hallage" Receipts', 569.

1½d in 1645–46, which suggests that retailing recovered to almost pre-war levels.[77]

A recovery in consumer spending in London turned into a full-scale consumer boom in the immediate post-war years. Increasing pickage receipts indicate that the St Bartholomew's Fair was expanding, receipts for the 1644 fair totalled £13 4s 11d, more than twice the 1643 total. Receipts continued to rise in the post-war period, until by 1647 they were higher than any year since 1633, when the recording of receipts begins. The consumer boom was apparently unaffected by the renewal of fighting in 1648. Receipts for the 1648 fair were actually slightly higher than the previous year.[78] The increase in consumption was partly due to the influx of royalist gentry and their agents into London to negotiate with the parliamentary authorities to release their estates from sequestration. Lady Verney, who was acting for her husband, complained in December 1646 about the cost of living in London, and stated that 'the towne was neavor so full as tis now'.[79]

Although the influx of royalists certainly contributed to the consumer boom it primarily derived from a change of mood among London consumers. With the end of the war some of the previous fears about the immediate future ended and many Londoners wanted to enjoy themselves again. This is reflected in the increasing antisabbatarianism and the revival of Christmas observance in the late 1640s. A further sign of this was the reopening of the theatres. Although theatrical performances were still theoretically banned, by the end of 1648 four of the old theatres were again open for business, only to be closed by the soldiers of the New Model Army.[80]

By late 1647 there is evidence that the recovery in consumer spending was being undermined by renewed economic problems. In October Pedwarden Rumsey, a London wholesaling grocer, claimed he had lost money re-selling goods he had purchased from the East India Company. As a result of this and 'divers other casualties by bad debts in these distracted tymes' he had become insolvent.[81] By the end of the decade even the St Bartholomew's Day Fair was diminished. Pickage receipts are no longer recorded in the Chamberlain's accounts after 1648, but in 1649 the wardens of the Goldsmiths' Company

---

[77] Parsloe, *Wardens' Accounts of the Worshipful Company of Founders*, 321, 327. The improvement may have been greater than these figures suggest as the accounts for 1645–46 specify that the receipts are for only forty eight weeks.

[78] CLRO Cash Books, vol. 1/5, ff. 31v, 135, 237; vol. 1/6, ff. 29, 130.

[79] F.P. Verney, *The Memoirs of the Verney Family*, 4 vols (1970) II, 246. The diarist John Greene recorded that London was very full of gentry in September 1646. E.M. Symonds (ed.), 'The Diary of John Greene (1635–57). III', *EHR* 44 (1929), 107.

[80] R. Ashton, *Counter-Revolution, The Second Civil War and its Origins, 1646–48* (New Haven, 1994), 234–41; Symonds 'The Diary of John Greene (1635–57). III', 108–9; C.V. Wedgwood, *The Trial of Charles I* (1983), 83–4.

[81] BL IOL/B/22, East India Company, Court Book, 1646–50, pp. 161–2.

found 'but 4 goldsmithes within the precinct of the Fayre'. This suggests that the Fair was much smaller in that year than in the previous two years.[82]

The consumer boom was largely confined to London's better off inhabitants. The majority of the population found their income diminished by the impact of a run of bad harvests, which began in 1646. Privateering exacerbated the dearth by disrupting the coastal shipment of foodstuffs. As early as January 1645 it was alleged in a petition to the Common Council that the disruption of trade by the privateers would lead to shortages of fish, butter and cheese in London.[83] The attacks on the Newcastle colliers pushed up the price of coal. Christ's Hospital paid only 17s 3d per chaldron in 1647 but this had risen to as much as 27s per chaldron by 1649.[84] Jeremy Boulton found that the cost of living rose by one-third in the late 1640s, and he argues that this was the highest inflation of the period 1580–1700. Wages failed to keep pace with rising prices and consequently, Boulton argues, the late 1640s saw the greatest fall in the standard of living since the 1590s.[85] The brewing industry began to decline from 1647 as high barley prices pushed up costs. Moreover the authorities tried to restrict beer production as a means of lowering grain prices. Nevertheless although the Founders' Company's receipts from the assize of weights declined in the late 1640s the fall was much more moderate than that during the First Civil War. Receipts declined by only one-quarter between the year to October 1646 and the year to October 1648, and then began to recover, suggesting that the dearth of the late 1640s had a more limited impact on retailing than Civil War.[86]

Because consumers had to spend a higher proportion of their income on food they had to reduce their spending on clothing, which cut short the recovery in the cloth trade.[87] Thanks to surviving excise accounts it is possible to quantify the turnover of the woollen cloth trade for two years, 1645–46 and 1646–47. These show that sales of cloth in London declined from £584,032 to £452,222, a fall of twenty three per cent.[88] The recovery in the 'hallage' receipts peaked in 1646, and then fell steadily until the year to August 1651, by which time they had fallen by one-quarter.[89] The continuous steady decline suggests that the renewal of fighting in 1648 had little impact on the cloth trade. The only significant source of cloth production to be cut off from London was Colchester.

---

[82]   GH, Court Book, Y, 1648–51, f. 80v.

[83]   CLRO Jour. 40, f. 120.

[84]   B. Capp, *Cromwell's Navy, the Fleet and the English Revolution, 1648–1660* (Oxford, 1992), 61; GL MS. 12819/7, accounts for 1647–48 and 1649–50.

[85]   Boulton, 'Food Prices', 468, 475.

[86]   Parsloe, *Wardens' Accounts of the Worshipful Company of Founders*, 327, 333.

[87]   G.D. Ramsay, *The Wiltshire Woollen Industry in the Sixteenth and Seventeenth Centuries* (1945), 112–13; J. Lilburne, *An Impeachment of High Treason* (1649), 37.

[88]   PRO SP46/122B, f. 1.

[89]   Jones, '"Hallage" Receipts', 569.

The decline in the cloth trade was shallower than the crisis of the first Civil War but was longer in duration.

Conclusion

The disruption of London's commercial links with the rest of the country was never complete. Some trade always seeped through the blockades. Moreover Londoners continued to trade freely with the large parts of the country that remained constantly under parliamentary control. This was particularly important because it meant that London's grain supplies were never cut off. Had they been, the impact of the Civil War would have been far worse than it was.

Nevertheless London's domestic trade fell substantially in the first two years of the war, primarily because of the trade embargoes. Neither side's economic blockade was totally watertight, but they had a major impact on the London economy. In particular the fluctuations in the cloth trade follow very closely changing royalist attitudes to trade with London. The blockades also led to a major slump in consumer spending as incomes from domestic trade fell. Increased taxation also had a major impact, especially the excise, but the collapse in consumer spending pre-dated the introduction of the new tax. Moreover demand for beer, on which the excise fell heavily, remained buoyant during the Civil War. The burden of the war on the rest of the country also diminished London's domestic trade. Provincial consumers could not afford to buy so many London goods and the landowners of the West End were forced to cut back their spending because of falling rents. The political turmoil diminished demand within London because it led to the flight of the royal court to Oxford, diminished business at the central law courts, and because it led to a crisis in consumer confidence.

In the long term the war did not harm London's dominance of English internal trade. London wholesalers moved quickly back into the north after it was conquered by Parliament in 1644, and the same was probably true of other regions as Parliament's victories continued. They may even have strengthened their position in the national economy, as the losses suffered by provincial merchants, who experienced the war at first hand, were almost certainly even greater than those suffered by Londoners. In 1651 a conference of northern merchants complained that virtually all the trade in their region was monopolized by Londoners, and demanded that they be excluded from all fairs and markets north of the Trent.[90]

---

[90] F.W. Dendy and J.R. Boyle (eds), *Extracts from the Records of the Merchant Adventurers of Newcastle-upon-Tyne*, Surtees Society Publications, 2 vols, 93 (1895) and 101 (1899), I, 164–7.

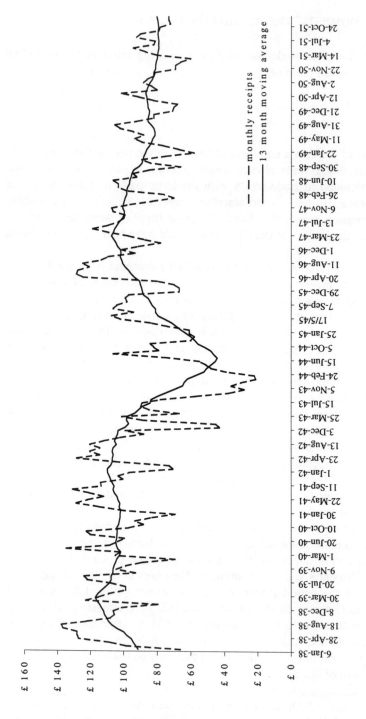

Figure 6.7
Blackwell Hall receipts, 1638–51

Source: GL MS 12819/6, Christ's Hospital, Treasurers' Accounts, 1632–44; GL MS. 12819/7, Christ's Hospital, Treasurers' Accounts, 1645–52.

Chapter 7

International Trade and Shipping

Overseas trade slumped in the 1640s, with two major troughs, in 1643 and 1648. The first trough was the result of the crisis in England's internal trade, detailed in the previous chapter. It was therefore a direct consequence of the war and, in particular, the economic blockades. The second trough was the result of obstructions and competition in overseas trade, but it was only partly the result of the war. As well as the continued conflict, which had a greater direct impact on overseas trade because it was increasingly fought at sea, London merchants faced increased competition from the Dutch because the treaty of Munster, in 1648, brought their eighty-year conflict with Spain to an end. Historians such as Christopher Clay and Brian Dietz have argued that the treaty of Munster was more harmful to overseas trade than the Civil War.[1]

The impact of the Civil War on overseas merchants was mitigated by the greater range of economic options open to them compared to other sectors of London society. They could more readily disengage from the domestic economy because it was relatively easy for them to move their capital out of the country. Importers were able to redirect their shipments to foreign markets. It is possible that cloth exporters compensated for their inability to obtain stocks from royalist controlled regions by establishing alternative sources of supply in the Netherlands.[2] None of these options would have been as profitable as their pre-war trade. Because of the Thirty Years' War, which continued until 1648, the economic situation in much of Europe was probably worse than in England. In 1643 the East India Company lamented to their agents in India that not only was trade bad in England but 'all Europe in little better Condition, but in a turmoyle either forraighne or domestique warr'.[3] In 1644 one London merchant wrote that 'all Christendome is now in Combustion and wars is the Ruyne of all'.[4]

---

[1] C.C. Clay, *Economic Expansion and Social Change: England 1500–1700*, 2 vols (Cambridge, 1984), II, 188; Brian Dietz, 'Overseas trade and metropolitan growth', in A.L. Beier and R. Finlay (eds), *London 1500–1700, the Making of the Metropolis* (London, 1986), 129–30.
[2] BL Stowe MS. 759, Register of Letters of Philip Williams, 1639–47, f. 81; Longleat House, Whitelocke Papers, vol. 9, f. 38; E. Kerridge, *Textile Manufacture in Early Modern England* (Manchester, 1985), 31.
[3] BL IOL/G/40/12, East India Company, Factory Miscellaneous, f. 53v.
[4] BL Add. MS. 11049, Letters of William & Thomas Northey, f. 117.

Imports and exports, 1642–50

Trying to quantify overseas trade in the 1640s is difficult. The use of the customs to this end is hampered by administrative changes that make comparisons between receipts from the Civil War period and those from earlier years of limited value. In his pioneering study of the English economic history Cunningham argued that the rise in customs receipts in the 1640s and 1650s is deceptive. He attributed increased receipts to the ending of customs' farming and more rigorous collection. Despite this warning Maurice Ashley argued the war did not damage overseas trade because the receipts of the customs' commissioners during the 1640s were generally higher than the amounts received by the exchequer from the customs' farmers in the 1630s.[5]

However, as Kepler argued, the comparisons between the two sets of figures are not valid. Before the war the customs' farmers negotiated with the crown to pay a fixed rent to the Exchequer in return for the gross receipts from the customs of tonnage and poundage, whether they were higher or lower than the agreed rent. No accounts of gross receipts of the farmers in the 1630s have survived. Kepler argues that they were probably substantially higher than the rent in the 1630s, possibly £300,000 to £400,000 per annum in the peak years. Farming was abandoned in 1641 and instead commissioners, whose gross receipts are recorded in accounts submitted to the Exchequer, administered the customs. The highest annual total of the war years was £267,000 for the year ending 25 December 1646. Consequently Kepler argued that during the war trade was 'extremely depressed'.[6] Nevertheless, despite Kepler's criticisms, historians have continued to use the customs' receipts to argue that the 1640s and 1650s were years of growth in London's overseas trade and that the impact of the war was limited.[7]

Moreover the ending of customs' farming was not the only administrative change to affect the customs' receipts. There was also a substantial revision in the customs' rates. The tonnage and poundage duties received by the farmers were, by 1640, only a fraction of the customs duties paid by merchants. In addition Charles I levied the impositions; these were surcharges levied over and above tonnage and poundage on a large numbers of goods and were not farmed. In 1640 Charles I received over £500,000 from the

---

[5]   W. Cunningham, *The Growth of English Industry and Commerce in Modern Times, Part 1, The Mercantile System*, 6th edn (Cambridge, 1921), 186; M. Ashley, *Financial and Commercial Policy Under the Cromwellian Protectorate* (1962), 56–60.

[6]   J.S. Kepler, *The Exchange of Christendom, The International entrepôt at Dover 1622–41* (Leicester, 1976), 114, 152, n. 33.

[7]   D.C. Coleman, *The Economy of England, 1450–1750* (Oxford, 1977), 134–5; G.F. Steckley (ed.), *The Letters of John Paige, London Merchant, 1648–58*, London Record Society (1984), ix. See also J.S. Wheeler, *The Making of a World Power: War and the Military Revolution in Seventeenth Century England* (Stroud, 1999), 132, 142.

customs, of which the rent from the customs' farm amounted to only £172,500.[8] Parliament decided to abolish the impositions but to make up for the loss of revenue they had to increase the tonnage and poundage duties. To this end a committee of the House of Commons drew up a new Book of Rates, which was introduced in the summer of 1642.[9]

The new system was not a simple combination of the two previous sets of rates. There was a net increase in the taxation on some duties, and a reduction on others. The major reductions were in the duties on exports. The most important commodities were the various types of woollen cloth, which constituted over ninety per cent of exports. The majority of cloth exports were old draperies. The taxation of these fabrics was unchanged, the previous duty of 6s 8d per shortcloth was retained. Before 1642 exports of new draperies were charged with both tonnage and poundage and impositions. The new Book of Rates taxed one type of new draperies, bays, at a very similar rate to the old tonnage and poundage duty. The other varieties of new drapery were divided into two categories of 'stuffs', which were now taxed according to their weight, whereas previously they had been taxed according to their length. It is difficult to be certain what impact this had, nevertheless the net result was almost certainly a reduction in the taxation of these goods. Giles Grene, the chairman of the committee that produced the 1642 Book of Rates, subsequently said that the new system had eased the burden on cloth exports. The new duties may even have been lower than the old tonnage and poundage rates alone. Most other manufactured goods had not been subject to impositions, and generally the new Book of Rates kept the old tonnage and poundage duty. Export duties on agricultural goods, foodstuffs and minerals were increased over the old tonnage and poundage rates, although in the case of lead the new duties were still less than the combined tonnage and poundage and impositions. However exports other than cloth formed such a small proportion of overseas trade that the changes in these categories can only have had a marginal impact on total receipts. The major increases came in the rates on imports. Parliament increased the import rates on wine, the most valuable import in 1640, and manufactured goods. The rates on other goods, such as currants, were the same as the combined tonnage and poundage and imposition rates. However they reduced the rates on tobacco from English colonies, raw materials and spices. The impositions had fallen particularly heavily on imports and even when rates were reduced they were often still substantially higher than the old tonnage and poundage rates. The new duty on pepper was twice as

---

[8] F.C. Dietz, *English Public Finance, 1485–1641*, 2nd edn, 2 vols (1964), II, 376.
[9] C. Russell, *The Fall of the British Monarchies 1637–1642* (Oxford, 1991), 256–7, 347; *Firth & Rait*, I, 16–20; PRO E122/230/8.

much as the tonnage and poundage rate, and that on currants was four times higher.[10]

If the revised system did compensate for the abolition of the impositions then, for the same volume of trade, receipts from the customs after 1642 should be substantially higher than receipts from the custom farm in the 1630s. Giles Grene even claimed that the new system increased receipts by one-third. If this is taken to imply that the new Book of Rates substantially increased the level of taxation it is almost certainly an exaggeration. Nevertheless it is equally unlikely that the new system significantly reduced taxation levels, an early draft of the Book of Rates was rejected in 1641 because it would have led to a substantial loss of revenue. Parliament allowed a fifteen per cent discount on the new rates until 1650 but the slump in receipts is far greater than this can account for. The income derived from the customs fell from over £500,000 in 1640 to less than £200,000 in 1643; moreover it did not rise above £300,000 until 1653. It is very difficult to account for this decline without a major slump in trade.[11]

Those responsible for administering the customs were convinced that trade was declining in 1642 and 1643. On 6 December 1642 Giles Grene, whose committee had taken over the supervision of the customs, reported to the Commons that 'the comittee hath conferred with the custome howse which from £20,000 per moneth they have not receaved £10,000 per monthe And the reason of this abatement is decay of trade'.[12] In January 1643 Parliament appointed a new group of customs' commissioners, all highly committed to their cause, but when a loan for the navy was sought early in March 1643, the new commissioners replied that they could not advance any money because of the decay of trade. In April Grene privately told Sir Simonds D'Ewes that he thought total customs receipts for that year would be less than £150,000, compared to £400–500,000 per annum before the war.[13] When Parliament again approached the commissioners for a loan in the following August they replied discouragingly 'That Trading in respect of these Troublesome Times did much decay'.[14]

From 1641 frequent changes in the customs' commissioners mean that few of their accounts cover a full year, making analysis of trends difficult, especially as trade in many goods was seasonal. The following table gives the

---

[10] G. Grene, *A Declaration in Vindication of the Honour of the Parliament* (1647), 4–5; *The Rates of Marchandizes* (1635), unpag; *The Rates of Merchandizes* (1642), 7, 42, 62 64, 75, 83.

[11] Grene, *Declaration in Vindication*, 7; Ashley, *Financial and Commercial Policy*, 57; Russell, *Fall of the British Monarchies*, 358–9.

[12] C. Thompson (ed.), *Walter Yonge's Diary of Proceedings in the House of Commons, 1642–1645, Vol. 1, 19th September 1642–7th March 1643* (Wivenhoe, 1986), 164–5.

[13] Ibid., 341; *CJ* II, 901, 927, 1001, 1003, 1004; BL Harl. MS. 164, Parliamentary Journal of Sir Simonds D'Ewes, 1642–43, f. 354.

[14] BL Harl. MS. 165, Parliamentary Journal of Sir Simonds D'Ewes, 1641–43, f. 154v.

average daily receipts from the port of London for each account between May 1641 and June 1650. The first account covers the period between the ending of farming and the introduction of the new Book of Rates. It includes gross receipts from tonnage and poundage and the impositions. The subsequent accounts, from July 1642 onwards, are receipts from the new Book of Rates. To compensate for the fifteen per cent discount the original figures have been increased proportionately.

Table 7.1
Customs' receipts in the port of London, 1641-50

Period	Days	Receipts	Daily Average
25/5/41–1/7/42	402	£323,148.71	£803.85
2/7/42–22/1/43	204	£85,602.57	£419.62
21/1/43–25/12/43	338	£159,722.12	£472.55
25/12/43–24/2/45	427	£212,329.85	£497.26
25/2/45–25/12/45	303	£176,908.13	£583.86
25/12/45–25/12/46	365	£243,910.88	£668.25
25/12/46–25/12/47	365	£226,665.35	£621.00
25/12/47–25/12/48	366	£170,248.91	£465.16
25/12/48–21/7/49	208	£135,580.69	£651.83
22/7/49–24/6/50	337	£253,391.01	£751.90

Source: PRO E122/230/8, f. 4 (1641–42); PRO E122/226/17/4 f. 1 (1642–43); PRO E351/643–50 (1643–50).

These figures show that the customs' receipts slumped dramatically in the early months of the war. The daily average between July 1642 and January 1643 was only slightly over half that for the previous period, and this was the lowest average of the 1640s. However it is likely that this was the result of a temporary panic among importers prompted by the royalist advance on London after the battle of Edgehill. In December 1642 Grene attributed the decline in receipts primarily to importers sending their goods to Holland, instead of bringing them to London. This had an exaggerated impact because customs receipts came predominantly from imports and because the period of this account is so short.[15]

Exports probably fell only slightly during the early months of the war. The accounts suggest that 41,919 taxable shortcloths were exported during this time, on average 205 a day. In comparison receipts for the period 25 June to 25 December 1641 indicate that 41,153 shortcloths were exported, an average of

---

[15] PRO E122/226/17/4, f. 1; Thompson, *Walter Yonge's Diary*, 164–5. Between July 1642 and January 1643 only a third of the customs' receipts came from exports.

226 per day. There was therefore only a nine per cent decline in the export of old draperies between these two periods.[16] This indicates that, although the cloth trade was interrupted in November 1642, the impact on exports was relatively short lived. It is probable that once the King had issued his proclamation guaranteeing free trade on 8 December exporters were able to make up for most of the shortfall in exports of the previous month.[17]

Between July 1642 and January 1643 an average of £65 per day was collected in customs on exports other than shortcloths. In contrast in the second half of 1641 average receipts from tonnage and poundage on these goods were £89 per day.[18] This is a fall of nineteen per cent, much greater than the decline in receipts from old draperies. It is difficult to conceive of a reason why exports in this sector, primarily new draperies, should have fallen so much more than exports of old draperies. A more likely explanation for the fall in receipts is the revision of the rates, indicating, as has been suggested above, that the taxation of the new draperies had been reduced.[19] The early months of the Civil War saw a major decline in imports but only a slight decline in exports.

The customs' accounts for 1643 only give the total receipts from the port of London.[20] The average daily receipts show a slight improvement on the early months of the war but were still only fifty eight per cent of the average between May 1641 and July 1642. However it is likely that underlying the improvement in the gross receipts was a transformation in the way the war affected overseas trade. As shown in the pervious chapter the King's embargo on trade with London, introduced in July 1643, cut the domestic cloth trade by half; which almost certainly led to a slump in exports.[21] Conversely during 1643 imports probably began to recover as fears for the city's immediate safety began to recede.

The slump in exports and recovery in imports are substantiated by customs figures for 1644. These are derived from the accounts of the treasurers of the Plymouth duty, which record receipts from the port of London. The duty was a surcharge on the customs, at first ten per cent and after Michaelmas 1644 twenty per cent. They can therefore be used to extrapolate the total customs' receipts. These accounts are useful because, unlike the accounts of the

---

[16] PRO E122/226/17/4, f. 1; PRO E122/230/6, f. 7. In this chapter in calculating shortcloth exports from customs accounts in the 1640s the duty free wrappers have been ignored, true exports would have been about eleven per cent higher than the figures given here.

[17] For the interruption of the cloth trade in November 1642 see pp. 110, 140 above.

[18] PRO E122/226/17/4, f. 1; PRO E122/230/9.

[19] F.J. Fisher, 'London's Export Trade in the Early Seventeenth Century', in his *London and the English Economy, 1500–1700*, P. Corfield and N. Harte (eds) (1990), 122, table 4.

[20] PRO E351/643.

[21] See above p. 141.

customs' commissioners, these receipts are divided into five categories: imports of wines and currants, other imports by English merchants, other imports by foreign merchants, exports of shortcloths and other exports. The results are tabulated below.[22]

Table 7.2
The overseas trade of London, 1644

Imports of wine and currants	£50,625
Other imports, English merchants	£78,891
Other imports, foreign merchants	£15,707
Exports of old draperies	£15,383
Other exports	£21,318

Source: PRO E122/236/14, ff. 1v–5v.

The receipts from the export of old draperies suggest that the equivalent of 46,148 taxable shortcloths were exported in 1644. In comparison 87,427 had been exported in 1640, and customs accounts suggest that 86,073 were exported in the year to 24 June 1642. Consequently the export of old draperies had declined by about forty six per cent. These are the worst recorded export figures for over a century. Proportionately the fall was greater than during the Cockayne project or the depression of the early 1620s. In the former exports of shortcloths by English merchants had fallen by only about thirty per cent, while in the latter they fell by about one-quarter. The slump was even greater than the annual total indicates. In the first half of 1644 approximately eighty eight shortcloths were exported per day, compared with about 250 per day between 26 December 1641 and 24 June 1642. Exports had fallen by sixty five per cent between these two periods. However in the second half of the year exports rose to about 165 per day, probably because by this period the royalists were relaxing their blockade.[23]

The decline in cloth exports to the Baltic was particularly dramatic. Total English exports through the Sound decreased from 42,000 pieces in 1642 to eight thousand in 1643 and five thousand in 1644. This was in large part due to the disruption of export of northern kersies from Hull as a result of the war in

---

[22] PRO E122/236/14. For the Plymouth duty see above p. 39.

[23] Fisher, 'London's Export Trade', 121, table 1; PRO E122/230/6/7; B. Supple, *Commercial Crisis and Change in England, 1600–42* (Cambridge, 1970), 44; Clay, *Economic Expansion*, II, 121; F.J. Fisher, 'Commercial Trends and Policy in Sixteenth-Century England', in his *London and the English Economy, 1500–1700*, P. Corfield and N. Harte (eds) (1990), 82. The proportion exported by foreigners in 1644 is unknown but given that only 503 were exported by foreigners in 1640 it has been assumed that exports by foreigners were negligible in 1644.

Yorkshire, however it is noticeable that the export of much more expensive broadcloths also fell, from over eight thousand in 1642 to about 1200 in 1644. These were mainly Suffolk cloths exported from London, which would not have been interrupted by the royalist blockade; this decline must have been principally the result of the seizure of ships in the Sound by the King of Denmark in 1643. A further contributory factor was the impact of the Danish-Swedish War of 1643–45. Cloth exports to Germany were also disrupted by the King of Denmark, who seized one of the cloth ships of the Merchant Adventurers on its way to their staple at Hamburg.[24] In July 1644 the Merchant Adventurers claimed that, as a result of this incident, they had lost more than £40,000, and were 'debarred of the better halfe of their Trade to Hamburgh'.[25]

Exports to the eastern Mediterranean, which consisted principally of coloured broadcloths from the West Country, also slumped in 1644. In 1644 the Levant Company collected £528 from its impositions on exports compared with £1,843 in the previous year. Unfortunately the company's accounts are missing between 1636 and 1642; nevertheless in 1635 the company collected £1,532 from impositions on exports.[26] It is likely that exports increased in the intervening period and were not affected by the war until the royalist blockade. In contrast exports to the western Mediterranean, the main market for the new draperies, were probably relatively unaffected by the war. In 1644 £21,318 was collected on exports other than old draperies, an average of £59 per day. This is about ten per cent less than the daily receipts between July 1642 and January 1643, suggesting that exports of new draperies had declined only slightly. The average for the second half of 1644 is almost identical to the average for the early months of the war. This is probably because these fabrics were made predominately in East Anglia, consequently the royalists could not impeded their transit to London.

---

[24] R.W.K. Hinton, *The Eastland Trade and the Common Weal* (Cambridge, 1959), 50–1, 227, 228, appendix D. See Figure 7.1 below.

[25] BL Add. MS. 4191, Petition of the Merchant Adventurers' Company, f. 37.

[26] PRO SP105/158, ff. 86, 195; PRO SP105/159, f. 87. The Levant Company's impositions had to be paid on all goods imported to and exported from its privileges. See A.C. Wood, *A History of the Levant Company* (Oxford, 1935), 209. Cloth accounted for 90–100% of exports to the Ottoman Empire. B. Braude, 'International Competition and Domestic Cloth in the Ottoman Empire, 1550–1650: A Study in Undevelopment', *Review* 2 (1978–9), 444.

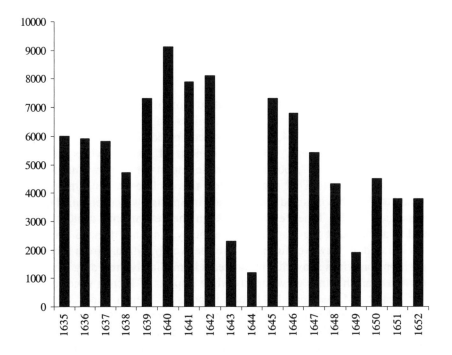

Figure 7.1
Broadcloth exports (pieces) from England to the Baltic, 1635–52

Source: R.W.K. Hinton, *The Eastland Trade and the Common Weal* (Cambridge, 1959), 228–9, appendix D.

The 1644 accounts show that imports had risen substantially since the early months of the war. Receipts for goods other than wines and currants averaged about £217 per day in 1644 compared with only £143 per day between July 1642 and January 1643. However the great number of changes in the valuations of imports in 1642 makes comparisons with receipts for earlier periods of little value. Nevertheless the previous chapter has shown that the royalist blockade prevented London wholesalers from supplying many of their provincial customers and consumer spending in the capital declined in the early years of the war. As a result importers, such as the East India Company, found it difficult to sell their goods. Consequently it is likely that imports were much lower in 1644 than before the war.[27] Imports from the eastern Mediterranean can be quantified from the impositions collected by the Levant Company. In

---

[27] PRO E122/226/17/4, f. 1; see above p. 152 and also *CSPD*, 1644–45, 208.

1643 the company collected only £1,087 from this source. As has been noted the receipts between 1636 and 1642 are missing but in 1635 receipts totalled £2,491. Receipts in 1643 were undoubtedly depressed by the prohibition of imports of currants from Zant and Cepholonia by Parliament in August 1642, however receipts were even lower in 1644, only £760, despite the fact that the prohibition was rescinded in March of that year.[28]

The wine trade can also be quantified from other sources. Millard used the port books to show that at constant prices imports of wines by English merchants totalled only £174,972 in 1644, compared with £307,578 in 1637, a fall of forty three per cent.[29] However imports of Spanish wines grew from £107,200 in 1637 to £137,966 in 1644, while imports of French wines fell from £199,492 to £36,171. This suggests that the decline in wine imports was confined to French wines and that the trade in Spanish wines remained healthy. In his study of the Tenerife wine trade in the seventeenth century George Steckley argued that the war did not seriously diminish demand for Canary wines in London. However further figures derived by Millard from accounts of impositions on wines show that in the years immediately preceding the war the import of Spanish wines grew rapidly while imports of French wines declined. In the year to Michaelmas 1641 total imports of French wines were worth £98,934, while total imports of Spanish wines were worth £211,415. These figures are not directly comparable with those derived from the port books for 1637 and 1644 because they do not differentiate between imports by English merchants and those by foreigners. Nevertheless it is likely that about ninety per cent of imports were by English merchants, suggesting that imports of Spanish wines fell by about twenty seven per cent between 1641 and 1644 while imports of French wines fell by about fifty nine per cent. Consequently the Civil War exacerbated the existing decline in the import of French wines and reversed the previous upward trend in the imports from Spain.[30]

Receipts from the Vintners' Company's tackle-house porters confirm the decline in wine imports. The porters had a monopoly of landing and delivering wine within three miles of London, and the Vintners' Company received a proportion of the fees they collected. Consequently the receipts recorded in the company accounts can be used to establish the trend in imports of wine. As

---

[28]   PRO SP105/158, ff. 147, 187; PRO SP105/159, f. 86; *Firth & Rait*, I, 396–7.

[29]   A.M. Millard, 'The Import Trade of London, 1600–40', 3 vols, unpublished PhD thesis, University of London, 1956, III, appendix 2, table 6, 3.

[30]   G.F. Steckley, 'The Wine Economy of Tenerife in the Seventeenth Century: Anglo-Spanish Partnership in a Luxury Trade', *EcHR* 2nd Series, 33 (1980), 342–3; Millard, 'Import Trade of London', III, appendix 2, table 6, 3; Idem, 'Analysis of Port Books recording Merchandises Imported into the Port of London', PRO Library, Kew, table 27, 6. In 1614 nine per cent of imports were by foreigners. Ibid., table 27, 3.

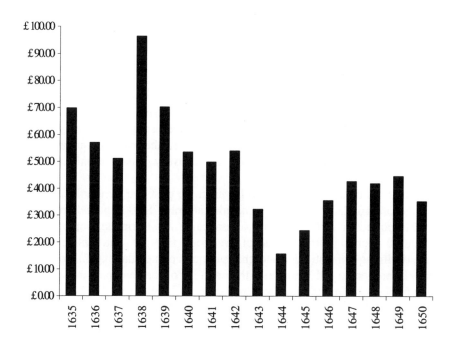

Figure 7.2
Receipts from the Vintners' tackle-house porters, 1635–50

Source: GL MS. 15333/4, Vintners' Company, Wardens' Accounts, 1636–58.

Figure 7.2 shows receipts fell drastically in the early part of the first Civil War, from nearly £54 in 1641–42 to less than £16 in the 1643–44.[31]

As the war began to turn in Parliament's favour trade recovered. By 1646 the average daily customs' receipts from London had risen to £668, an increase of over forty per cent compared with 1643. This is despite the fact that in 1646 trade with the eastern Mediterranean was disrupted by the dispute between the Levant Company and the ambassador in Constantinople, Sir Sackville Crowe. The company's receipts from its impositions, which had recovered substantially in 1645 to total £3,884, fell in 1646 to £1,654, a fall of more than fifty per cent.[32]

---

[31] GL MS. 15333/4, Vintners' Company, Wardens' Accounts, 1636–58, unfoliated; A. Crawford, *A History of the Vintners' Company* (1977), Appendix C, 271–3. The Vintners' accounts run from midsummer to midsummer. The income of the Mercer's tackle-house porters also declined in the Civil War. Mercers' Hall, Acts of Court, 1641–45, f. 120.

[32] PRO SP105/159, ff. 86, 87, 114, 140, 244. See above p 121.

This may in part explain why customs' receipts were still seventeen per cent less in 1646 than they had been before the war. The weakness of the recovery cannot be wholly attributed to the disruption of trade with the eastern Mediterranean. In April 1647 a petition to the Common Council from merchants and others argued that 'there hath beene a generall and greate decay of trade and Comerce by sea to and from this Cittie for these three or foure yeares last past'.[33] Further evidence that the recovery in overseas trade was limited comes from the receipts from the Vintners' tackle-house porters, receipts recovered after 1643–44 but they remained consistently below the pre-war totals. In the five years to midsummer 1642 the average annual receipts were £65, whereas after the Civil War the recovery peaked at only £43 in the year to midsummer 1647.[34]

Imports of tobacco were also lower in the post-war period than they had been before 1642. Kepler has estimated that only 788,000 pounds of tobacco were imported in 1647 from the Chesapeake and Bermuda, compared with 1,463,000 pounds in 1640, a fall of over forty five per cent. Unlike the wine trade declining domestic demand only provides part of the explanation for this drop. Imports also fell because of the collapse of the re-export trade. In 1640 forty per cent of imports had been re-exported, however by 1647 tobacco was carried directly to European markets by the Dutch. Nevertheless London tobacco importers were continuing to re-export tobacco during the 1640s, suggesting that domestic demand for tobacco had fallen.[35]

There was probably also a recovery in cloth exports in latter part of the war. Trade at the Blackwell Hall cloth market increased in this period, although the recovery may have come primarily from the home market. However the recovery in the domestic cloth trade peaked in 1646 and the increase in exports probably also petered out at around this time.[36] In the aftermath of the Civil War there were renewed complaints that the export of wool and poor standards of craftsmanship was stimulating cloth manufacturing abroad in competition to the English industry.[37] In some respect the reappearance of traditional complaints represented a return to normality with the recovery in the cloth trade, but these complaints also reflect the difficulty experienced by the cloth exporters in regaining the markets they had lost as a

---

[33] CLRO Jour. 40, f. 213.

[34] GL MS. 15333/4, unfoliated.

[35] J.S. Kepler, 'Estimates of Direct Shipments of Tobacco and Sugar from the Chief English Plantations to European Markets, 1620–1669', *Journal of European Economic History* 28 (1999), 115, 119, table 1, 124, 130; PRO E122/226/18, f. 107. Re-exports are discussed below.

[36] See above p. 160.

[37] *HMC Thirteenth Report, Portland MSS*, I (1891), 405–6; *To The Honourable House of Now Commons Assembled in Parliament. The Humble Petition of Many Thousands of Clothiers, Weavers, Bay-Makers, Serge-Makers, Say-Makers, Clothworkers, and Worsted-Combers within the Realme of England* (1647).

result of the royalist blockade. In the one area where the cloth trade can be quantified, the Baltic, exports of broadcloths jumped to over seven thousand pieces after the settlement with the King of Denmark in 1645, but they subsequently declined to under two thousand in 1649.[38] In early 1648 Henry Parker, then secretary to the Merchant Adventurers in Hamburg, claimed that the number of ships sent by the company to Germany had fallen from twenty per year, to only six. He argued that a major cause of the decline was 'The late obstructions and calamities of civill war in our Kingdome, concurring with other annoyances done us by the Kings Agents abroad, and millitary Commissions upon the Sea'.[39] What expansion there was in the cloth trade may have been largely in the export of white cloths, rather than the more valuable dyed and dressed cloths. In the late 1640s there were allegations that the Merchant Adventurers were using their control of the administration of the customs to evade regulations that required them to export one cloth in ten fully dressed.[40]

By 1647 the limited recovery that had occurred in overseas trade was coming to an end. The upward trend in the customs' revenues ceased, in that year average receipts fell slightly to £621 per day. In late 1647 the House of Commons spent considerable time discussing overseas trade. In early November there were long debates about ways to improve cloth exports. The committee for foreign affairs was instructed to investigate the causes of the decline in cloth exports and negotiate with foreign states to reduce taxes on English woollens abroad. In January 1648 a new committee of grievances was appointed to investigate means of improving trade. All this is indicative of considerable anxieties about the state of English trade and in particular cloth exports, although the only practical outcome of this flurry of activity was an ordinance prohibiting the export of wool.[41]

Worse was to follow in 1648 as the mutiny of the navy led to a further crisis in overseas trade. A pamphlet published in June of that year complained about: '*The sensible decay of forraigne* Traffick, *which even before the late great alteration in the* Navy, *was shrunk to a third part lesse then formerly it was wont to be, as may be demonstrated by the* Customes; *and (as it is justly feared) will now fall to nothing*'.[42] Weekly customs' accounts from the port of London survive for the period between late July and the end of August when the

---

[38] Hinton, *Eastland Trade*, 228, appendix D. See Figure 6.1 above.

[39] H. Parker, *Of a Free Trade* (1648), 35–6.

[40] See p. 214 below, in contrast before the war the Merchant Adventurers were increasingly reluctant to pay for licences to export white cloths because of the decline in this trade. See G.D. Ramsay, *The English Woollen Industry, 1500–1700* (1982), 62–4; PRO PC2/46, 334–5; *CSPD* 1640, 21, 176.

[41] *CJ* V, 351–2, 353, 417; *Kingdomes Weekly Intellgencer*, 233, 2–9 November 1647, 719; *Perfect Occurances*, 44, 29 October–5 November 1647, 311–12; *An Committee Appointed by the Commons Assembled in Parliament* (1648); *LJ* IX, 667–8.

[42] PRO E351/648; *The Necessity of the Speedy Calling a Common-Hal* (1648), 3.

royalist fleet lay on the Downs intercepting merchant shipping going to and from London. These indicate that trade did not entirely cease in this period. Nevertheless in 1648 average customs' receipts fell to £465 per day, the worse level since the early months of the war, suggesting that the mutiny in the fleet had a greater impact on overseas trade than the royalist blockade of 1643–44. The impact of the mutiny can be studied in greater detail thanks to the survival of the weekly accounts already mentioned. Only five weeks are missing between 3 April 1648 and the 2 April 1649. Moreover the receipts are broken down into subdivisions comparable with those in the 1644 accounts of the Plymouth duty. The results are tabulated in Table 7.3.

Table 7.3
The overseas trade of London, 1648–49

Imports of wines and currants	£48,119
Other imports, native merchants	£59,928
Other imports, foreign merchants	£8,254
Exports of old draperies	£16,783
Other exports	£20,590

Source: PRO E122/215/3, ff. 1–5, 8, 11, 13–14, 17–21, 25–7, 32–66, 73–9, 90–7, 102–34; PRO E122/226/15, ff. 17–25, 29, 31–33, 37–9; PRO E122/226/16, ff. 37–42; PRO SP28/57, ff. 886, 888–9.[42]

These figures show that the imports of goods other than wines and currants were much more affected by the mutiny of 1648 than by the blockade of 1643–44. Imports by English merchants of those commodities were nearly one-quarter lower in 1648 compared with 1644, while imports by foreigners were down by forty seven per cent. The mutiny probably caused importers to divert their cargoes to other European markets. In this context the relatively small decline in imports of wines and currants, only about five per cent may seem surprising, but imports of wines tended to be concentrated around Christmas, two-thirds of these receipts were collected in December and January, by which time the royalist fleet had retreated to Helvoetsluys. Given the uncertainty of these figures the difference between the receipts for wines and currents for 1644 and 1648 may be illusory. The same can also be said of

---

[42]   There are no figures at all for the weeks ending 9 October 1648, 30 October 1648 and 27 November 1648. Figures for exports are also missing for the weeks ending 10 July 1648 and 23 October 1648. Figures for the imports of wines and currants are missing for the weeks ending 10 July 1648 and 18 September 1648. Figures for other imports are missing for the weeks ending 18 September 1648 and 25 December 1648. Figures for the missing weeks have been estimated by taking an average of the next surviving totals for the two weeks before and after the gap.

the receipts for exports other than old draperies, suggesting that the mutiny of the navy, like the royalist blockade, had only a limited impact on exports of new draperies. Receipts from the export of old draperies actually increased by about nine per cent. This may also be an illusion but it probably indicates the extreme extent to which exports of these fabrics were depressed by the royalist blockade in 1644. The impact of the mutiny on exports was probably limited because cloth exports tended to be concentrated in the spring and autumn. Also when the royalists intercepted a ship carrying exports, like the Merchant Adventurers' ship the *Damsell*, the goods on board would already have paid the customs. Exporters may have delayed shipping their goods until after the mutinied ships left the Downs. In this context what is striking is how low the exports of old draperies were, totalling 50,348 taxable shortcloths, only about fifty eight per cent of the totals for 1640 and 1641–42. It is unlikely that this was the result of the mutiny; rather it was probably the consequence of the continued slump in cloth exports which so agitated Parliament in late 1647.[44]

The customs' receipts suggest a rapid recovery in overseas trade during the early years of the Commonwealth. Between 22 July 1649 and 24 June 1650 the average receipts were £752 per day, a sixty per cent increase on the receipts for 1648. These figures have to be treated with some caution, as it was the first year's accounts of new commissioners, who administered the customs much more rigorously than previously. Nevertheless the upward trend in receipts is already evident in the last account of the previous commissioners, suggesting that a real recovery in trade was underway.[45] The customs' accounts enable the receipts for the year to the 24 June 1650 to be broken down into the same five categories as the accounts for 1644 and 1648–49. This enables the recovery to be studied in greater detail. The results are presented in Table 7.4.

Comparing the trade figures for 1649–50 with those for 1644 and 1648, it is evident that the greatest recovery had taken place in imports. Imports by English merchants of goods other than wines and currants had risen by 150 per cent since 1648 and were forty seven per cent higher than in 1644. The recovery in imports of wines and currants since 1648, forty five per cent, is less spectacular than the recovery of other imports because the imports of wines and currants were less affected by the mutiny of the navy. These imports were thirty eight per cent higher in 1649–50 than in 1644. This is a smaller recovery than that of other imports, probably because of the trade war with France. Imports of wine from that country were forbidden in August 1649 as a result of which the Vintners' receipts from their tackle-house porters fell from nearly £45 in the year to midsummer 1649 to only £35 in the year to midsummer

---

[44] For the mutiny of the navy see above p. 132ff.
[45] PRO E351/650; PRO SP105/151, ff. 33, 67v, 72; PRO SP105/144, ff. 15, 32; M. Sellers (ed.), *The Acts and Ordinances of the Eastland Company*, Camden Society (1906), 71–2.

1650.[46] Nevertheless it is unlikely that imports were high by pre-war standards. The run of bad harvests, which had afflicted England since 1646, led a substantial reduction in the standard of living.[47] Moreover in May 1651 the Levant Company, whose members were among the largest importers, complained of the 'deadnes of Trade'.[48] Consequently the growth in imports suggests that in 1644 they had been very low.

Table 6.4

The overseas trade of London, 1649–50

Imports of wines and currants	£69,642
Other imports, native merchants	£150,241
Other imports, foreign merchants	£19,997
Exports of cloth	£16,151
Other exports	£28,238

Source: PRO E351/650; PRO E122/226/15, ff. 82, 87, 90; PRO E122/226/16, ff. 85–7.

Exports other than old draperies were one-third higher than in 1644 and thirty seven per cent higher than in 1648. The average daily receipts from this sector are the highest since the introduction of the 1642 Book of Rates. They are over one-fifth higher than the receipts for the early months of the war and are only slightly less than the receipts from tonnage and poundage for the year to the end of June 1642.[49] If the 1642 rates revisions decreased receipts from this sector then this suggests that these exports, primarily new draperies, were higher in 1649–50 than before the war. However the increase was more than counterbalanced by the continued recession in the export of old draperies. Exports were only five per cent higher than in 1644 and actually slightly lower than in 1648. The receipts suggest that the equivalent of only 48,454 shortcloths were exported in 1649–50, over forty per cent less than before the war.[50]

Contemporaries complained that exports of new draperies were declining in southern Europe, especially in Spain, as a result of competition from the Dutch. However the complaints came from advocates of economic regulation who were using spurious or misleading statistics to bolster their case. It is certainly true that Dutch manufacturers were no longer embargoed by the

---

[46] GL MS. 15333/4, unfoliated, and Figure 6.2 above. For the trade war with France see above, p. 123.

[47] J.P. Boulton, 'Food Prices and the Standard of Living in the "Century of Revolution", 1580–1700', *EcHR* 2nd Series, 53 (2000), 468, 475.

[48] PRO SP105/144, f. 32.

[49] PRO E122/226/17/4, f. 1; PRO E122/230/9.

[50] See note 23 above.

Spanish after 1647, but if, as has been suggested, the customs' accounts indicate that exports of new draperies were healthy in this period this is likely to have been because of strong sales in southern Europe. Although some new draperies had always been sold in north European markets it is unlikely that exports to those regions were expanding. Exports of new draperies declined in the Baltic in the 1640s and the Dutch extended their existing ban on the sale of dyed English cloth to include the new draperies in 1643. Moreover the re-establishment of direct commercial relations between Spain and the United Provinces may not have been a major threat to English new drapery exporters. Before 1647 large quantities of new draperies from the northern and southern Netherlands were exported to the Iberian Peninsula and the western Mediterranean via the Dover entrepôt. It would be a mistake to see the English and Dutch new drapery producers as in direct competition. The Dutch tended to specialize in the production of the coarser fabrics, says and rashes, while the English concentrated on the better quality serges and bays. In the long-term the English industry had the competitive advantage over the Dutch because its costs were lower. Peace with Spain also enabled the Dutch to start exporting large quantities of cloth to the eastern Mediterranean. However the expansion of Dutch exports was mainly at the expense of the Venetian cloth industry. The Venetians had previously been the main suppliers of high quality cloth in the eastern Mediterranean, but their trade declined as a result of the outbreak of war with the Ottoman Empire in 1645, and sales of English cloth in the Ottoman Empire were higher in the 1650s than at any other previous time.[51]

It is probable that the decline in exports occurred mostly in northern markets where, before the war, most of the old draperies were sold. Henry Robinson, who was a Merchant Adventurer, may have had the northern markets particularly in mind when he wrote in 1649 that 'our Trade at present, as touching exportation, is not one fourth part of what it was ten yeares agoe, as will appear by the receipt of Custome'.[52] Before the war the English cloth industry had faced increased competition from manufacturers in the

---

[51] *CSPD*, 1651–52, 88; *A Brief Narration of the present Estate of the Bilbao Trade* (1650[?]), 1–3; Kepler, *Exchange of Christendom*, 105–9; J. de Vries and A. van der Woude, *The First Modern Economy, Success, Failure and Perseverance of the Dutch Economy, 1500–1815* (Cambridge, 1997), 287; J.K. Fedorowicz, *England's Baltic trade in the Early Seventeenth Century: A Study in Anglo-Polish Commercial Diplomacy* (Cambridge, 1980), 93, 96; Wilson, 'Cloth Production', 103; BL Harl. MS. 164, Parliamentary Journal of Sir Simonds D'Ewes, 1642–43, ff. 366–v; BL Add. MS. 34326, Remonstrance and Petition of the Merchant Adventurers' Company, 30 March 1652, ff. 38v–9; J.I. Israel, *Dutch Primacy in World Trade, 1585–1740* (Oxford, 1989), 190–1, 225–6; B. Braude, 'International Competition and Domestic Cloth in the Ottoman Empire, 1550–1650: A Study in Undevelopment', *Review* 2 (1978–9), 441, table II.

[52] H. Robinson, *Briefe Considerations, Concerning the Advancement of Trade and Navigation* (1649), 2. For Robinson's membership of the Merchant Adventurers see Mercers' Hall, Acts of Court, 1637–41, f. 177.

Netherlands, Germany and Poland. The competition was mostly in the production of coarser cloth. During the 1630s the Dutch started producing large quantities of lakens, a high quality cloth made from Spanish wool, imported via England. Manufacturers in the West Country had also started producing cloth with Spanish wool, and exports of these fabrics were rising rapidly on the eve of the war.[53] However during the royalist blockade the West Country producers were cut off from their overseas markets and supplies of Spanish wool. In April 1644 merchants successfully lobbied Parliament to obtain permission to re-export Spanish wool, despite an existing prohibition of wool exports, presumably because of poor demand in England.[54] The lack of demand for Spanish wool in Civil War London is also indicated by a petition to the House of Commons from a group of London tradesmen who had purchased Spanish wool confiscated by the state in July 1644, possibly at a considerable discount, and in June 1645 sought permission to export the wool 'forasmuch as the said Wools are not so vendible here by reason of the deadnes of Trade'.[55] Moreover cloth exports to Germany and the Baltic were particularly disrupted during the war because of the King of Denmark's seizure of English shipping on the Sound and at Gluckstadt. Cloth exports to the Baltic did not recover to their pre-war levels and they declined from 24,000 pieces in 1646 to 11,000 in 1651.[56] Meanwhile the Dutch laken producers were well placed to fill the gap. After the conclusion of peace in the late 1640s the Dutch cloth producers could now obtain wool direct from Spain, and the Dutch came to dominate the Spanish wool trade. The Dutch consolidated their control over the north European markets for high quality cloth while producers in Germany and Poland supplied the cheaper fabrics. As a result sales of English cloth in those regions continued to be low for most of the 1650s.[57]

The trend in imports during the 1640s was one of collapse in late 1642 followed by a limited recovery in 1643 and a fuller recovery from 1645. This was followed by a second collapse in 1648 and a further recovery 1649–50. However it is likely that neither in the recovery after 1645 or that of 1649–50 did imports reach pre-war levels. This is partly because high food prices and continued heavy taxation depressed demand for imports. It is also because of the collapse of the pre-war re-export trade, particularly the re-export of tobacco. London's overseas trade was transformed from a situation of unprecedented strength on the eve of the Civil War to one of barely out

---

[53] Supple, *Commercial Crisis*, 140–1; Clay, *Economic Expansion*, II, 144, 147; Israel, *Dutch Primacy*, 194.

[54] *CJ* III, 459.

[55] *CJ* IV, 170; PRO SP16/502/58.

[56] Hinton, *Eastland Trade*, 228–9, appendix D. See Figure 7.1 above.

[57] T. Birch (ed.), *Thurloe State Papers*, 7 vols (1742), I, 200–1, IV, 86, V, 127; W.S., *The Golden Fleece Wherein is Related the Riches of English Wools in its Manufactures* (1656), 97; Israel, *Dutch Primacy*, 200.

of crisis. In March 1651 the Common Council drew up a petition for abatement of the City's proportion of the monthly assessment, claiming that London had become impoverished: 'By the generall decay of the trade thereof as by many greate losses of Merchants & others & interuption of forreyne trades which within these fewe yeares have bene many'.[58]

The long-term impact of the Civil War on overseas trade can perhaps be established from the statistics published by Ralph Davis for the 1660s. These suggest that exports other than re-exports averaged about £2.04 million per year in that decade and imports averaged about £3.5 million. However these figures cannot simply be compared with the figures produced by Millard and Fisher for exports and imports before the war because of differences in valuations. Unfortunately no set of trade statistics based on constant values has been published for the seventeenth century. The figures from which Davis derived his statistics, include valuations, made probably in 1678, of the goods at London selling prices, aside for adjusting the prices for tobacco, wine and brandy, which were overvalued, Davis used these valuations for his statistics. Fisher and Millard both used the pre-war books of rates. The valuation of the new draperies is much higher in the 1660s than in the 1635 Book of Rates. Singles bays are valued at £2 15s per piece and double bays at £6 per piece in the former compared to £2 for single bays and £4 for double in 1635. Although export of goods other than old draperies appear to have more than doubled between 1640 and the 1660s, rising from £695,000 to over £1.4 million in the 1660s, much of this increase was almost certainly due to the higher valuations. The value of the old draperies exported in the 1660s cannot be directly compared with exports before the Civil War because Fisher does not provide a value for these goods. Fortunately elsewhere Davis has published figures for the export of old draperies in the 1660s converted into notional shortcloths, which suggest that exports fell from about 96,000 in 1640 to about 82,000 in the 1660s. This suggests that, although the exports of old draperies had improved compared with the late 1640s, they did not return to their pre-war levels. In contrast although Davis' figures may exaggerate the improvement in the new draperies it is likely that some improvement did take place. The 1660s figures also demonstrate the success of exporters in the Mediterranean markets despite the Dutch competition after 1647, the majority of the principal new draperies, bays, serges, perpetuannas, and Norwich stuffs, exported in 1662–63 went to the Iberian Peninsula or Italy. Moreover there was a great boom in exports to the Ottoman Empire after 1660, twice as many cloths were exported in the 1660s as in the 1630s. In the late seventeenth century cloth exports to

---

[58] CLRO Jour. 41, f. 46v.

Northern Europe recovered as the result of the expansion of new drapery sales in that area, but there is little sign of that in the 1660s.[59]

Assessing the state of imports in the 1660s is more complicated. Some imports are valued at higher rates in the Davis figures than in the 1604 Book of Rates while others are lower. Currants are valued at £1 10s per hundredweight in 1604 but at £2 4s per hundredweight in the book of tables, while tobacco and sugar are valued at lower rates in the 1660s than before the war. Some important imports were lower in the 1660s than in 1640, imports of wines had fallen from about 19,000 tons in 1640 to less than 14,000 in the 1660s, imports of currants had fallen from 68,681 hundredweight in 1640 to 35,726 hundredweight in the 1660s. However imports seem to have been generally higher in the 1660s than before the War, both for raw materials such as raw silk and manufactured goods such as linen cloth. Trade in colonial goods rose particularly, tobacco imports increased from 1.25 million pounds to over 8 million pounds. Imports of sugar also increased from 26,355 hundredweight to 183,578 hundredweight, however in neither case can these increases be entirely attributed to the growth of the London economy. The increased imports of tobacco were the result of expanded production in the Chesapeake; this expansion seems to have largely occurred between the mid-1640s and the mid-1650s and was the result of increased trade with the Dutch. The increased sugar imports were the result of the introduction of sugar cultivation in Barbados during the 1640s and initially the Dutch dominated the trade. London merchants probably acquired a greater role in the colonial trade after the 1651 Navigation Act but it is likely that a high proportion of the trade remained directly between the colonies and the European mainland. However the 1660 Navigation Act required all colonial goods to be brought to England, unfortunately the figures for the 1660s do not record re-exports, but it would be reasonable to assume that a large proportion of the tobacco and sugar imports were destined for continental markets. Imports were also boosted by the revival of the East India Company after the 1657 charter, over 2 million pounds of pepper was imported in the 1660s, compared with less than half a million in 1640 and there was also a substantial increase in imports of calicos.

---

[59] R. Davis, 'English Foreign Trade, 1660–1700', in W.E. Minchinton (ed.), *The Growth of English Overseas Trade in the Seventeenth and Eighteenth Centuries* (1969), 78–98; BL Add MS. 36785, An Accompt of the exports from, and imports into, the city of London for the two years ending at Michaelmas 1663 and 1669; PRO E122/73/3, [1604 Book of Rates]; *The Rates of Marchandizes* (1635), R. Davis, *English Overseas Trade 1500–1700* (1973), 53, table II; Clay, *Economic Expansion and Social Change*, 147–8. Davis adds eleven per cent to the exports for shortcloths to compensate for the duty free wrappers. For exports to the Ottoman Empire see B. Braude, 'International Competition and Domestic Cloth in the Ottoman Empire, 1550–1650: A Study in Undevelopment', *Review* 2 (1978–9), 441, table II; R. Davis, 'English Imports from the Middle East, 1580–1780', in M.A. Cook (ed.), *Studies in the Economic History of the Middle East* (1970), 195.

Consequently it is likely that much of the improvement in English imports took place after 1650. [60]

In general the Civil War only marked an interruption in the otherwise upward path of London's overseas trade. The one exception to this is the exports of old draperies, which historians have usually assumed were foredoomed to decline as a result of competition from the Dutch lakens. However before the war the English cloth industry was adapting to changing conditions, a process which surely would have continued during the 1640s had it not been for the interruption arising from the royalist blockade of London. It is possible that had it not been for the war the old drapery industry would have been more successful in holding its own.

The East India Company

The East India Company was the largest commercial concern in seventeenth-century London. By 1640 over £3 million had been subscribed in the company's various ventures and additional large sums had been borrowed on bonds. Initially the main focus of the company's trade had been the Spice Islands of what is now Indonesia. However in the early 1620s the Dutch East India Company drove the English out of the Spice Islands. Consequently in the late 1620s the company's attention turned to India, and in particular to importing cotton textiles from Gujarat. However in the 1630s this region was stricken by a major famine, which disrupted textile production. Moreover Sir William Courteen, a wealthy Anglo-Dutch merchant backed by influential courtiers, obtained permission from Charles I to trade with the East Indies and effectively established a rival company.[61]

By 1640 the prospects were beginning to look much better for the East India Company. The famine in India was over. Sir William Courteen's venture had proved unsuccessful, although his son continued it after his death in 1636. The East India Company may well have hoped that its close connections with the court would render it unpopular with Parliament. The East India Company sought confirmation of its charter from Parliament, on which basis it planned to establish a new joint stock to bring in new capital. Initial moves to petition Parliament were blocked by Charles I's personal intervention. However in August 1641 the King agreed to recommend the confirmation of their charter

---

[60] Davis, 'English Foreign Trade', 78–98; BL Add MS. 36785; Millard, 'Analysis of Port Books', table 3, table 27; R.R. Menard, 'The Tobacco Industry in the Chesapeake Colonies, 1617–1730: an Interpretation', *Research in Economic History*, 5 (1980), 132–3. In 1655 eighty per cent of Barbadian exports were shipped directly to European markets. Kepler, 'Estimates of Direct Shipments', 120, table 2.

[61] K.N. Chaudhuri, *The East India Company: The Study of an Early Joint-Stock Company 1600–1640* (1965), 67–4, 209, table VIII.

to Parliament, but by this time the company had come to the conclusion that a temporary expedient would be needed to continue the trade until the necessary legislation had been passed. As a result they launched the first general voyage in the autumn of 1641. Then in February 1642, after the King had left London, the company drew up a new petition of grievances to Parliament. The Commons referred the petition to a committee chaired by the elder Sir Henry Vane, who had presented it on behalf of the company. The committee held hearings concerning the company's dispute with Courteen and it appears to have found in favour of the company. This encouraged the company to believe that Parliament would soon confirm their charter; consequently they launched the fourth joint stock.[62]

With the approach of war investors proved reluctant to adventure their capital in the East India Company. Consequently only £105,000 was subscribed to the fourth joint stock and the company had to borrow heavily to finance their trade, by 1644 the fourth joint stock owed over £120,000. The lack of capital was exacerbated by the company's difficulties in procuring lead or cloth because of the blockade of internal trade, as a result the company could send little in the way of money or goods to their factors in the east. However the impact of this should not be exaggerated, the company's trade was dependent on imports for its profitability. The only purpose to sending a large stock to the Indies would be to increase its purchasing power there, but in any case in 1643 and 1644 demand in England had fallen so much that the company found it difficult to sell the goods that it was able to purchase.[63]

The declining markets for imports reduced the profitability of investment in the East India Company but this is hidden by the way dividends were paid. The first general voyage made 'divisions' amounting to 221 per cent of the original stock by the time it was wound up in 1648. This suggests a profit of 121 per cent over seven years, or an average annual return of slightly over seventeen per cent. This is high by seventeenth century standards, more than double the statutory rate of interest and exceeds the ten to fifteen per cent profit rate, which, Richard Grassby has argued, was usual for experienced merchants in the first half of the century.[64] However these figures are misleading because the first two divisions, in August 1643 and July 1644, were made in goods

[62] *CCMEIC*, 1640–43, xx, 122, 123, 127–8, 130, 180, 185, 187, 193, 232, 233, 242, 251, 265. The total capital of the First General Voyage is uncertain, an account of dividend payments suggests it was £106,037 10s, while in 1648 the total is given in the company minutes as £104,537 10s. BL IOL/H/6, East India Company, Home Miscellaneous, ff. 113–83; *CCMEIC*, 1644–49, 293.

[63] *CCMEIC*, 1640–43, xxvi; BL IOL/H/39, East India Company, Home Miscellaneous, f. 169A; BL IOL/G/140/12, ff. 48v, 52, 53v–4, 59v, 64v.

[64] W.R. Scott, *The Constitution and Finance of English Joint Stock Companies to 1720*, 3 vols (Cambridge, 1910–1912), II, 120; R. Grassby, *The Business Community of Seventeenth Century England* (Cambridge, 1995), 240.

rather than money. Each investor received, at a set valuation, commodities equivalent to his or her stock, but the rate at which the goods were valued was substantially more than they were then worth.[65]

In August 1643 the investors in the first general voyage found that they could only sell a small fraction of their goods in England. They agreed to ship their pepper to Italy and divide the rest between themselves. Each investor was to receive commodities nominally valued at 125 per cent of their stock, fifty per cent in rich indigo, twenty five per cent in Sarkhej indigo, thirty per cent in calicos and twenty per cent in cinnamon.[66] The rich indigo was valued at 6s 8d per pound, and the Sarkhej at 4s 8d, but in their correspondence with their agents in Surat, the company stated that rich indigo fetched no more than 4s 6d at that time, and the Sarkhej only 3s 6d. Therefore the true value of the rich indigo was about two-thirds of its nominal value and the Sarkhej indigo three-quarters. Whereas in theory the investors were to have received indigo equivalent to three-quarters of their investment, in practice they received only slightly more than half.[67]

The calicos were also overvalued; they were 'for lacke of markett given out upon dividends at 2½ upon their prime Coast'.[68] It is difficult to establish the true value of the calicos distributed to the investors because of the sheer diversity of the product. Rowland Wilson received twenty four different kinds in his dividends.[69] Where comparisons can be made between the values at which the calicos were distributed to the investors and prices at company sales the latter are consistently lower. On 6 September 1643 Mr Mead purchased 480 pieces of 'Synda No. 2' at 7s 6d a piece as part of a large purchase of calicos, in addition he received a discount of 15d a piece on his whole purchase so in practice he paid 6s 3d. In contrast the 'Synda No. 2' cloth, received by Rowland Wilson as part of his dividends, was valued at 9s 9d. Equally, comparisons between the values given for various types of 'Merculees' cloths received by Wilson and the prices paid by James Martin for the same types in February 1644 suggest that the cloths were divided at between sixty nine and seventy seven per cent of their true value. Moreover as Mead and Martin were given two years' credit, the prices for immediate payment would have been substantially less. Only the cinnamon was divided among the investors at its market price. If we assume that the calicos were on average valued at seventy per cent of their true value, then this suggests that the total divisions in August 1643 were in reality worth only 93.5 per cent of the investors' stock.[70]

---

[65] *CCMEIC*, 1640–43, 345; *CCMEIC,* 1644–49, 34.

[66] *CCMEIC*, 1640–43, 342–50.

[67] Ibid., 342; BL IOL/G/40/12, f. 48v.

[68] Ibid., f. 49; 'prime cost' presumably means the original price in India.

[69] BL IOL/H/6, f. 117.

[70] Ibid.; BL IOL/B/21, East India Company, Court Book, 1643–46, pp. 42, 127; BL IOL/G/40/12, f. 51v.

In July 1644 the investors in the first general voyage received a further twelve per cent dividends in goods. Indigo was to be distributed at 4s 8d per pound, but again it was overvalued. It was decided that if there was not enough to go round, those who did not receive any indigo were to have money instead, at a rate of 3s 6d per pound, which was probably the indigo's true value. If so, the indigo was worth only three-quarters of the price at which it had been distributed. All subsequent divisions were made in money. Total divisions in the first general voyage were probably more like 186.5 per cent than 221 per cent, and the profit was 86.5 per cent over the seven years of its existence. That is over ten per cent a year. This is more than the maximum rate of interest and within the usual range of profit rates for the period, but the investors only started making significant profits after the first Civil War was over.[71]

In addition to the adverse trading conditions and lack of capital the fourth joint stock suffered the loss of two of its ships, *Discovery* and the *John*. The result was, that, by 1645, the stock possessed net assets of only about £60,000, a depreciation of over forty per cent. The adventurers began to receive divisions in 1647. Divisions of about 180 per cent had been made by the time the stock was wound up in 1663. The profit was about eighty per cent over twenty one years, or less than four per cent per year.[72] In 1648 Sir Peter Ricaut valued his shares in the fourth joint stock at only half of their face value because of its great losses, stating that others had sold their shares for fifty five per cent of their original investment at long credit.[73]

Despite the hopes of the East India Company the report of Sir Henry Vane's committee was not ratified by Parliament and consequently the Courteen association continued to trade with the east, but it proved even less successful than the old company. In December 1642 the Dutch East India Company wondered how the Courteen association survived, as they did not appear to be making any money. Indeed the Dutch contributed to the failure of the Courteen association by continually harassing their ships and agents in the east, possibly believing that the association's ambiguous status meant that there was little danger of reprisal. They captured one of Courteen's ships in the summer of 1643. In that year Courteen went bankrupt and was forced to flee England. His former partners tried to continue to trade in the East Indies but when they sent out a ship in 1645 Courteen's creditors seized its cargo. Not surprisingly the Dutch East India Company did not regard the English as a threat to their commercial hegemony during the Civil War.[74]

---

[71]   *CCMEIC*, 1644–49, 34.

[72]   Scott, *Joint Stock Companies*, II, 119, 120, 127 & n. 9 & 11, 128 & n. 2; *CCMEIC*, 1650–54, 362.

[73]   PRO SP23/204, ff. 322, 354.

[74]   *CCMEIC*, 1644–49, x–xi, 305, n. 1; *CJ* IV, 101; *HMC Seventh Report, House of Lords MSS*, 66; BL IOL/I/3/24, Dutch Translations, Letters from the Indies, 1639–42, CCCCXXXVI, f. 4; PRO HCA13/58 ff. 693–4; PRO HCA13/59, f. 531; PRO HCA13/60,

In the immediate post-war period the prospects for the East India Company seemed to improve. In December 1646 the Commons agreed to confirm the company's charter, but the Lords' blocked it. Initially the company was thrown into despair and they agreed to abandon trading with the Indies, but this reaction was quickly followed by a renewal of optimism. This was probably fuelled by the willingness of the Commons to put pressure on the Lords to reverse their decision and perhaps also by the company's awareness that the Courteen association no longer presented any real threat to their trade. In the event further consideration of the company's ordinance was lost in the political crisis of the summer of 1647 and consequently the company started another general voyage. Robert Brenner has argued that investors who had previously been part of the Courteen association, and were the leaders of his 'new merchants', dominated the second general voyage. But only four of the sixteen members of the committee elected to manage the second general voyage were previously investors in the Courteen association. In contrast ten members of the committee were existing directors of the East India Company, including the governor, deputy governor and treasurer, and the latter was elected treasurer of the second general voyage. The two remaining members of the committee were former directors of the East India Company. The former Courteen investors seem to have had little influence on management of the voyage, they were refused permission to send out ships to obtain restitution for the goods seized by Courteen's creditors in India, and they were unsuccessful in opposing proposals to wind up the voyage in 1648. By 1649 they were again seeking to trade outside the company, this time under the guise of a project to colonize the island of Assada in the Indian Ocean. However the Commons resolved that trade with the East Indies should be continued by a single company with a single joint stock: the Assada adventurers were therefore forced to join the East India Company in the new united joint stock.[75]

The second general voyage was more successful than the fourth joint stock; it made a 48.5 per cent profit in five years, or nearly ten per cent per year. By 1649 the renewed vigour of the East India Company was attracting

---

Examinations of George Gawton, Jerman Honeychurch, John Darell, 20 July 1646; BL IOL/I/3/28, Dutch Translations, Letters from the Indies, 1644–45, DDXLVIII. For criticism of Courteen from planters he had sent to Madagascar see BL IOL/E/3/20, East India Company, Original Correspondence, 1646–48, f. 23.

[75] *CCMEIC*, 1640–43, 262; *CCMEIC*, 1644–49, xii–xvi, viii–xix, xxii, 210, 218, 303, 304–5, 361; *CJ* VI, 353. Two of the six members of the committee of the Second General Voyage whom Brenner identifies as former investors in the Courteen Association, Thomas Andrews and Nathan Wright, were prominent members of the East India Company. There is no evidence that either of them were investors in the Courteen Association. Brenner appears to be confusing the former with his namesake the radical alderman who, although an investor, was not a member of the committee. R. Brenner, *Merchants and Revolution, Commercial Change, Political Conflict and London's Overseas Traders, 1550–1653* (Cambridge, 1993), 178–9, 516–17.

the attention of their Dutch rivals, who considered some of their practices worth emulating. Although the profits were over the maximum interest rate, they were less than the usual mercantile profit rate in the first half of the seventeenth century. Moreover the East India Company argued that the general voyages made relatively high profits, because many of their charges had been borne by the third and fourth joint stocks, and they had not been encumbered with shipping, forts or houses. The profits on the general voyages do not, then, genuinely represent the profitability of the East India trade in this period.[76]

It is undoubtedly true that the troubles of the East India Company in the 1640s were exacerbated by its peculiar political problems and the competition with the interlopers. However in its correspondence with its factors the company placed greater emphasis on the impact of the war, especially the resulting difficulties in raising money, purchasing goods to export and selling their imports.[77] Moreover in some respects the company was probably relatively fortunate because it was able to borrow large sums of money below the legal rate of interest and it was much less vulnerable to privateering, as its ships were large and well defended.[78]

Shipping, re-exports and multilateral trade

The London shipping industry was badly affected by the war as the decline in trade led to surplus capacity. As early as January 1643 a petition from seamen of the eastern suburbs complained that 'most of the Merchants Shipps ride at Anchor in the River, neither now imployed, nor (without sudden redresse of these michiefes) likely to be imployed in merchandize againe'.[79] At the end of the year the Venetian ambassador reported that there was little employment for London shipping other than as privateers. Particularly important was the interruption of the coal trade. In the early seventeenth century it employed over one-quarter of all English shipping and the proportion was probably substantially greater by the eve of the Civil War. As a result of the embargo on

---

[76] Scott, *Joint Stock Companies*, II, p 122; BL IOL/I/3/92, Dutch Translations, Letters from the Seventeen to the Indies, 1633–66, 125; BL IOL/I/3/32, Dutch Translations, Letters from the Indies, 1646–51, DX, 8–9; Grassby, *Business Community*, 240; *CCMEIC*, 1650–54, 359.

[77] BL IOL/G/40/12, ff. 53v–4, 59v, 64v–5.

[78] The only ship lost by the company to the royalists, the *John*, arose from the defection of its captain.

[79] *The Humble Petition of the Mariners and Seafaring Men and Other Inhabitants of Stepney* (1643).

trade with Newcastle many London colliers stood idle for most of the war years.[80]

The value of shipping fell. In July 1644 one Londoner advised a correspondent: 'this is noe time to sell [ships] noe man will give ½ the vallue'.[81] In 1647 the shipbuilder Peter Pett testified in Chancery that the value of ships employed in the Spanish trade had fallen substantially in the Civil War period. Ownership, especially of larger vessels, was commonly subdivided; with as many as twenty one people owning a share of a single ship. Shipping shares were a common investment for the moderately prosperous, as a result ship owning was widely dispersed in London. Consequently the impact of decline in value of ships was widely felt and this probably eroded economic confidence.[82]

The impact of the war on shipping was more far reaching than a short-term lack of employment and resultant drop in value. English shipping expanded rapidly in the early seventeenth century. In the long term this was the result of growth of the long distance trades, especially with the English plantations in America and the West Indies, from which foreign ships were excluded. Moreover in the 1630s England was one of the few neutral European states. In normal circumstances Dutch shipping was substantially cheaper than English in the early seventeenth century. This was because the *fluit*, the mainstay of the Dutch merchant marine, were designed to maximize cargo space, they carried few, if any, guns, and they needed small crews. The English preferred to build 'defensible' ships, they usually carried a number of guns, which reduced the cargo that could be carried and required larger crews. However after the end of the twelve years' truce in 1621 Dutch shipping suffered as a result of Spanish embargoes and privateering. Dutch freight rates and marine insurance rose dramatically on all European routes. The Dutch were effectively excluded from Iberian and Mediterranean ports and as a result, London shipping came to play a dominant role in the carrying trade there.[83]

During the 1640s the attacks on shipping by royalist and Irish privateers and, from 1648, by the French, made English shipping increasing expensive. During the war trade with Virginia and the West Indian plantations was thrown open to foreign shipping. Finally in the summer of 1647, during the course of

---

[80] *CSPV 1642–43*, 220; J. Hatcher, *The History of the British Coal Industry, Vol. 1, Before 1700: Towards the Age of Coal* (Oxford, 1993), 471–2; HCA24/109/355.

[81] BL Add. MS. 11049, Letters of William & Thomas Northey, f. 118.

[82] PRO C24/704/5, f. 4; PRO C2/CHASI/B35/16; K.R. Andrews, *Ships, Money and Politics: Seafaring and Naval Enterprise in the Reign of Charles I* (Cambridge, 1991), 35–8.

[83] Andrews, *Ships, Money and Politics*, 16–18, 22–3; V. Barbour, 'Dutch and English Merchant Shipping in the Seventeenth Century', in E.M. Carus-Wilson (ed.) *Essays in Economic History*, 3 vols (1954–62), I, 227–30, 244; Israel, *Dutch Primacy*, 134–6, 149–56; H. Taylor, 'Trade Neutrality and the "English Road", 1630–1648', *EcHR* 2nd Series, 25 (1972), 255–60.

the negotiations that led to the treaty of Munster, the Spanish ended their embargo of Dutch shipping and their privateering against the Dutch ceased. Even English merchants stopped using native shipping in favour of the cheaper and safer Dutch alternatives. London merchants, especially the Levant and Eastland Companies, became increasingly concerned that they were losing out to competition from imports through the Dutch entrepôt.[84]

The attacks on English shipping led to increased freight rates in the 1640s. The dangers at sea also added to shipping costs through the increased use of marine insurance and higher premiums. Marine insurance was certainly in use in London in the early seventeenth century but it was not often used in peacetime. In the East India Company it did not become common practice until the Civil War, and this may be true in other branches of trade. There was probably some respite in 1647 when, under pressure from the French, royalist privateering was curtailed, but this was short lived and in December James Howell alleged that marine insurance premiums had risen from two per cent to ten per cent.[85]

The correspondence of John Paige, who imported wine from Spain and the Canary Islands, illustrates the impact of privateering in the late 1640s on insurance costs. On 26 December 1648 he wrote to assure a colleague in Tenerife that 'Concerning insurance, I shall follow your order in effecting it at as cheap rates as I can. The times are at present very dangerous for Irish [privateers], which will be a means to make me do it with expedition', but on 8 January 1649 he wrote, that 'The times are so dangerous at present that scarce any man will underwrite a policy, being many ships of late taken by Irish men-of-war and the coasts of France is as dangerous as ours at present'.[86] On 25 May he wrote 'I have the policy ready drawn and they ask no less than 10 per cent from Nantes to Tenerife, which, for ought I see, the profits of your goods will not afford to give such a premium. However, I shall get what possible I can insured, but I think it will be little under abovesaid rate. The times are now very dangerous, and insurers will hardly underwrite upon any ship under 16 or 18 guns. Ten days since there was a ship of London, 14 guns, taken at her coming out of Nantes by one of the Prince's [Rupert's] frigates'.[87] On 22 January 1650 he wrote that he had been unable to insure one ship's return to London, even for a ten per cent premium, because she was small, and news had just arrived that Rupert was in the Channel. On 3 September he wrote: 'I shall

---

[84] Israel, *Dutch Primacy*, 197–8, 204; Clay, *Economic Expansion*, II, 187–8; Hinton, *Eastland Trade*, 84–5, 91.

[85] Hinton, *Eastland Trade*, 85; V. Barbour, 'Marine Risks and Insurance in the Seventeenth Century', *Journal of Economic and Business History* 1 (1928–9), 587; W. Foster, *John Company* (1926), 187; J. Howell, *Epistolæ Ho-Elianæ*, 2nd edn. (1650) III, 26. See above p. 129.

[86] Steckley, *Letters of John Paige*, 1.

[87] Ibid., 2.

now endeavour to insure your adventures homewards, which will cost somewhat dear, being our coast at present is very full of French men-of-war and likewise of Ostend men-of-war.' On 15 November he wrote that 'Insurance is very high upon the news' that Rupert had left Lisbon and had taken a couple of ships from Malaga.[88] Despite Paige's complaints, insurance rates may have been too low; in September 1650 he reported that many insurers had gone bankrupt, suggesting that the insurance market had underestimated the risks to shipping.[89]

Further costs were incurred because of the charges demanded by naval captains for escorting convoys of merchant ships. The repeated attempts by the Long Parliament to stop this practice suggest that it was widespread and that it continued into the early 1650s. In May 1644 the Commons resolved that it was against the law to make charges for escorting English ships. In the following February the Commons again ordered that merchants should receive escorts without charge.[90] On 18 October 1650 the Rump ordered the abolition of convoy money and the act of 31 October, which revoked the fifteen per cent allowance on customs, forbade any captain to charge for escorting convoys. However some charges for providing escorts were officially sanctioned. In October 1646 the admiralty committee ordered the Merchant Adventurers to pay for pilots for the vessels assigned to escort their ships to Hamburg. These charges cut into profit margins and made English shipping less competitive. Consequently English shipping was becoming more expensive at just the time when Dutch shipping was becoming cheaper.[91]

The political impact of the increasing uncompetitiveness of English shipping manifested itself in the pressure that was brought to bear on Parliament to strengthen existing restrictions on the use of foreign shipping. In late 1644 the Greenland Company lobbied Parliament to prohibit the import of the whale oil and fins except directly from the whale fisheries in English ships.[92] In February 1645 a petition was presented to the House of Lords from 'divers Masters and others, Well-wishers to the Increase of Navigation of this Kingdom', complaining that the existing statutes prohibiting the use of foreign shipping were widely ignored. This petition was largely concerned with the Baltic and Scandinavian trades. The impact of the war on English shipping was probably first felt in northern waters because Dutch shipping was least affected

---

[88] Ibid., 10, 25, 28–9.

[89] Ibid., 25. See R. Davis, *The Rise of the English Shipping Industry in the Seventeenth and Eighteenth Centuries* (1962), 318, n. 3.

[90] *CJ* III, 431, 509; *CJ* IV, 56.

[91] *Firth & Rait*, II, 444, 505–8; *CJ* VI, 310, 493, 550; *CSPD*, 1650, 379; PRO ADM7/673, ff. 13, 18.

[92] *CJ* III, 712; *Firth & Rait*, I, 679–80.

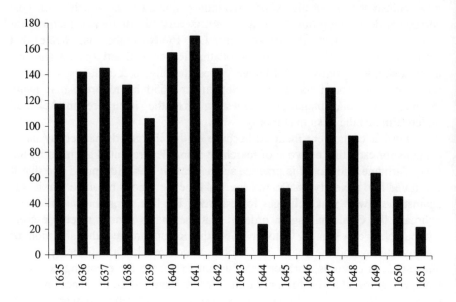

Figure 7.3
English ships passing westward through the Sound, 1635–51

Source: R. W. K. Hinton, *The Eastland Trade and the Common Weal* (Cambridge, 1959), 228–9, appendix D.

by their war with Spain in those waters. Moreover, as Figure 7.3 shows, the seizure of ships from London and other parliamentarian ports by the King of Denmark in 1643 had led to a major drop in the number of English ships passing through the Sound and visiting Hamburg, which probably forced merchants to use Dutch shipping. The numbers of English ships passing through the Sound westward fell from 145 in 1642 to fifty two in 1643, and twenty six in 1644. Nevertheless the war with Spain had increased the cost of Dutch shipping even in northern waters. As a result the number of English ships in the Baltic recovered after a settlement was reached between the representatives of Parliament and the Danish King.[93]

During the Civil War the Dutch made inroads into the trade with England's American and Caribbean colonies. In the 1620s and 1630s the Chesapeake tobacco trade had expanded enormously thanks in large part to

---

[93] *LJ* VII, 185; S.–E. Åström, *From Cloth to Iron. The Anglo-Baltic Trade in the late Seventeenth Century*, 2 vols (Helsinki, 1963–1965), I, 30; Hinton, *Eastland Trade*, 228, appendix D. See above, p. 119 for the seizure of shipping at the Sound and Gluckstadt.

demand from continental Europe. Initially tobacco was taken directly to European markets but in the 1630s government regulation excluded foreign merchants from trading with the colonies and forbade direct trade with European countries other than England. Continental markets were supplied with tobacco via re-exports from London. The Civil War gave the colonies the opportunity to break free from this regulatory straitjacket and consequently in March 1643 the Virginians legalized trade with the Dutch. Initially this had little impact. One Dutchman who was in Virginia in the winter of 1643–44 saw only four Dutch ships compared with thirty English, moreover the Dutch who did trade with Virginia at this date seem to have been only those who had done so illicitly before the war. However in 1644 the Civil War began to disrupt the trade of London merchants with the Chesapeake. Although officially trade remained open, in practice many Londoners were probably deterred by fears that their ships and goods would be confiscated. Moreover the predominantly royalist planters may have preferred to trade with Dutch merchants rather than those the King had declared traitors. Consequently from 1644 there was a major expansion in Dutch trade with Virginia. By 1645–46 it was reported that between twelve and fourteen Dutch ships were trading with Virginia each year. One witness in the High Court of Admiralty argued that, freed from their dependence on the London economy, many planters refused to pay the debts they owed to London merchants. Fears that the London merchants would lose the trade with Virginia entirely proved unfounded, nevertheless in Christmas 1648 it was reported that there were twelve Dutch ships in Virginia, compared with only ten from London.[94]

The Dutch also took over the trade with the English plantations in the West Indies, although, in contrast to the Chesapeake, this take-over was probably more for economic rather than political reasons. Although the planters were also mostly royalist there is no sign of any deliberate attempt to exclude Londoners from trading with the plantations in the Caribbean until 1650. During the 1640s the economy of Barbados, the most important of the Caribbean colonies, was transformed by the introduction of sugar cultivation. However the planters of the island produced mostly muscovado sugar, which needed further refining before it could be sold to the consumer. At this stage

---

[94] Kepler, 'Estimates of Direct Shipments', 115, 122–4; G.L. Beer, *The Origins of the British Colonial System 1578–1660* (Gloucester, Mass., 1959), 197–210, 350, 354, 356; W.W. Hening (ed.), *The Statutes at Large: Being a Collection of All the Laws of Virginia, From the First Session of the Legislature in the Year 1619*, 13 vols (Charlottesville, 1969), I, 258; D.P. de Vries, 'Voyages from Holland to America, 1632–1644', *New York Historical Society Collections* 2nd Series, 3 (1857), 125; PRO HCA13/60, Examinations of Thomas Stagg and Arthur Bayly, 9 July 1646; 'A Perfect Description of Virginia' (1649), reprinted in P. Force (ed.), *Tracts and other Papers*, 4 vols (Washington, 1836–46), II, no. 8, 14. In addition in 1648 there were two ships from Bristol and seven from New England. See above p. 118 for the interruption of London's trade with Virginia in 1644.

sugar refining was still relatively small scale in England, but the Dutch refining industry was well established and probably the largest in Europe. Consequently in the 1640s most Barbados sugar was exported to Holland in the first instance. As a result the Dutch dominated the trade of Barbados to such an extent that by 1646 one London merchant estimated that forty to fifty Dutch ships were trading there annually.[95]

The importance of the royalism of the planters of Virginia and the West Indies in enabling the Dutch to take over the trade with those colonies is suggested by the contrasting example of New England. The rulers of Massachusetts were generally sympathetic to the parliamentarians in the 1640s and consequently trade remained open to London merchants and they were able to establish a new triangular trade. Before the war Newfoundland cod had become a major English export to southern Europe. Initially the West Country ports dominated the fisheries but their trade was disrupted by the hostilities. This enabled the New Englanders to step into the gap. In the 1640s New England merchants did not have the resources to export the fish themselves. Instead London merchants exported manufactured goods to New England, where they purchased fish, which they then took to southern European markets to sell in return for imports for England.[96]

The Civil War led to a major crisis in London's worldwide trade. In 1644 the Dutch, who had good reason to keep a close watch on the activities of their competitors, noticed major reductions in English economic activity in the East Indies and Africa. The representatives of the Dutch East India Company reported that the English were doing little business in India or Indonesia and the Dutch West India Company came to the conclusion that the English had abandoned the Gold Coast. The Dutch were interested in all English competition, whether from the merchant companies or interlopers. Consequently these reports suggest that the non-company merchants were not taking advantage of the weakness of the Guinea and East India Companies to expand their trade during the Civil War. By 1646 London merchants were alarmed that the Dutch were driving them out of all trade in West Africa, the East and West Indies and Virginia.[97]

---

[95] R.S. Dunn, *Sugar and Slaves: The Rise of the Planter Class in the English West Indies, 1624–1713* (Chapel Hill, 1972), 62, 195; Israel, *Dutch Primacy*, 239, 264–5; Kepler, 'Estimates of Direct Shipments', 126; PRO HCA13/60, Examination of Thomas Batson, 20 July 1646.

[96] J.J. McCusker and R.R. Menard, *The Economy of British America, 1607–1789* (Chapel Hill, 1991), 99–100.

[97] BL IOL/I/3/28, DDXXVII, DDXXX, DDL; R. Porter, 'The Crispe Family and the African Trade in the Seventeenth Century', *Journal of African History* 9 (1968), 67–8; PRO HCA13/60, Examinations of George Gawton, John Darnell, George Ireland, Thomas Batson, 20 July 1646, Thomas Stagg, 9 July 1646.

Up until 1647 the exclusion of the Dutch from the Mediterranean masked the impact of the Civil War. During the war the Levant Company was more concerned with the indirect import of Mediterranean goods through Flanders than through Holland. In December 1645 the company was convinced that owners of shipping were making larger profits from freighting their ships in the eastern Mediterranean than merchants were from trade. This suggests that English shipping still dominated the port-to-port trade in the Mediterranean.[98] In the Iberian trades English shipping remained dominant during the Civil War. Between 1641 and 1645 three-quarters of the ships clearing the port of Bilbao were English. This is lower than before the war, when the proportion was eighty six per cent, but the decline was due to the absence of ships from West Country ports; the proportion from London remained the same.[99] English shipping even continued to play a major role in Portuguese trade, one part of southern Europe to which the Dutch did have access before 1647. This might suggest that English shipping could compete with the Dutch on even terms in the Civil War but it is likely that the English were favoured by the Portuguese because of the latter's continued colonial conflicts with the Dutch.[100]

In 1647, when the Spanish embargo was lifted, there was a substantial increase in the number of English ships entering the Baltic and Portuguese ports, possibly due to the reduction in royalist privateering in that year.[101] However the end of the war between the Dutch and the Spanish led to massive reductions in Dutch shipping costs, and a resurgence of Dutch trade in the Mediterranean. This soon had an impact on English trade, as early as January 1648 the Levant Company petitioned the House of Commons complaining about the Dutch threat to their trade.[102] English shipping also lost its grip on Spanish trade. The annual average number of English ships leaving Bilbao fell from 106 in 1641–45 to sixty nine in 1646–50.[103] From 1648 English ship owners in the Iberian trades protested that they faced ruin because of Dutch competition. They demanded that trade with the peninsula be restricted to English ships.[104]

In the Baltic shipping costs were particularly important because the most important Baltic goods, such as timber and grain, were low in value and bulky, consequently transport costs made up a large proportion of the end price.

---

[98] PRO SP105/150, ff. 83, 98v; PRO SP105/143, f. 102v.

[99] Taylor, 'Trade Neutrality, and the "English Road"', 258.

[100] Israel, *Dutch Primacy*, 205; C.R. Boxer, 'English Shipping in the Brazil Trade, 1640–65', *MM* 37 (1951), 199, 229.

[101] Hinton, *Eastland Trade*, appendix D, 228; Israel, *Dutch Primacy*, 205, table 6.3.

[102] PRO SP105/143, f. 105.

[103] Taylor, 'Trade Neutrality, and the "English Road"', 258.

[104] L.A. Harper, *The English Navigation Laws* (New York, 1939), 292; C. Wilson, *Profit and Power, A Study of England and the Dutch Wars* (1956), 43; Taylor, 'Trade Neutrality, and the "English Road"', 259. Although I have been unable to locate the source these authors cite.

Moreover the Dutch had an additional advantage, a treaty concluded in 1649 between the King of Denmark and the United Provinces meant that Dutch shipping was exempted from the Sound tolls in return for an annual lump sum. This meant that Dutch ships could pass quickly into and out of the Baltic, which further reduced their costs. The number of English ships passing westward through the Sound bound for England declined from 130 in 1647 to twenty two in 1651, whereas the number of Dutch ships passing east from England increased from none in 1647 to thirty two in 1650.[105] Consequently the Eastland Company was one of the major advocates on restrictions of the use of foreign shipping in the late 1640s and early 1650s.[106]

By 1648 English merchants were coming to rely on Dutch carriers even in the most local areas of foreign trade. In the autumn of that year a petition to the House of Commons from 'well-affected Masters and Commanders of Ships', concerned primarily with trade with France and the Netherlands, argued that the Dutch had almost achieved a monopoly in the carrying trade.[107] Dutch control over trade in the Channel increased in 1649 when the unofficial trade and maritime war with the French made it too dangerous for English merchants to trade directly with France. Although French wine was officially prohibited in August 1649, large quantities continued to be imported from Holland under the pretence that it came from elsewhere.[108]

Hinton argued that after the peace with Spain the inherently cheaper Dutch shipping would inevitably undercut the English, even without the Civil War. However Steven Pincus has stressed that London merchants attributed their troubles to the attacks of the privateers and the French, rather than competition from the Dutch.[109] The evidence suggests that it was often fears about the safety of English shipping, rather than cost, which led merchants to use Dutch vessels. Those who petitioned the House of Commons in the autumn of 1648 attributed merchants' reluctance to use English shipping to the fact that the Dutch were no longer willing to escort English vessels. In January 1649 John Rookes decided to transport the Spanish wool he had bought for his brother from Bilbao to London on a Dutch vessel via Amsterdam because of the threat from Rupert's ships and the privateers. In 1649 and 1650 the Levant

---

[105] C.R. Hill, *The Danish Sound Dues and the Command of the Baltic: A Study of International Relations* (Durham, North Carolina, 1926), 155; Hinton, *Eastland Trade*, 84, 85. See Figure 7.3 above.

[106] Longleat House, Whitelocke Papers, parcel 7, item 85.

[107] Rushworth *Collections*, VII, 1258–9; *CJ* VI, 18; S.C.A. Pincus, *Protestantism and Patriotism: Ideologies and the Making of English Foreign Policy, 1650–1668* (Cambridge, 1996), 41–3.

[108] P.A. Knachel, *England and the Fronde: The Impact of the English Civil War and Revolution on France* (Ithaca, New York, 1967), 157.

[109] Hinton, *Eastland Trade*, 84–5; Pincus, *Protestantism and Patriotism*, 41, 98.

Company counted it as one of the major advantages of the Dutch in the Mediterranean that the French and royalists did not attack their ships.[110] In a letter to the ambassador in Constantinople they argued that the growth of Dutch trade in the eastern Mediterranean 'is occasioned from our disturbances, which have given them encouragement & advantage over us'.[111] In reality the issues of cost and security cannot be untangled. The Eastland company argued that English shipping could not compete with the Dutch because the English ships needed to carry guns for their defence, which required larger crews and reduced their cargo capacity, whereas the Dutch ships received escorts paid for by the state. Previously the higher running costs of English shipping had been, at least in part, offset by its greater security. In the 1640s the 'defensible' English ships proved no protection against the privateers. In order to compete with the Dutch they would have had to abandon their guns but this would have made them more vulnerable to attack.[112]

The economic advantages that cheaper shipping conferred on the Dutch merchants meant that it was frequently less expensive to import goods indirectly, from Holland, rather than ship them directly from their country of origin. The Eastland and Levant Companies complained repeatedly that Mediterranean and Baltic goods were flooding in from the Dutch entrepôt. Nevertheless these goods were still imported by English merchants, rather than foreigners. It is likely that for many members of the Merchant Adventurers' Company the growth of imports from Holland compensated for the decline of their cloth exports. During the twelve years' truce, before the war between Spain and the Dutch resumed in 1621, the proportion of imports by foreign merchants had risen substantially, totalling forty two per cent of goods other than wines in 1614. In contrast in 1649–50 customs' receipts from imports other than wines by English merchants were 7.5 times higher than receipts from foreigners; the proportion of goods imported by foreigners was probably no higher than in 1640. The Dutch entrepôt exerted much less control over the English economy in the late 1640s than it had between 1609 and 1621.[113]

During the early 1650s the new regime in England began to take steps to protect English trade and shipping. In 1650 an act was passed excluding foreigners from trading with the colonies and in the following year expeditions were sent to Virginia and the West Indies to bring the plantations under the

---

[110] Rushworth *Collections*, VII, 1258–9; PRO C10/17/105; PRO SP105/144, ff. 13v, 30–v.

[111] PRO SP105/112, f. 87.

[112] Longleat House, Whitelocke Papers, parcel 7, item 85; Andrews, *Ships, Money and Politics*, 26–9; G. Pagano De Divitiis, *English Merchants in Seventeenth-Century Italy* (Cambridge, 1997), 45.

[113] Hinton, *Eastland Trade*, 191; PRO SP105/143, f. 105; PRO SP105/144, ff. 13–v, 30–v; Israel, *Dutch Primacy*, 204; Dietz, 'Overseas trade', 126; Millard, 'Analysis of Port Books', table 1; see above Table 7.4.

republic's control.[114] The massively expanded navy was deployed to protect merchant shipping in European waters and from early 1651 regular convoys of merchant ships were escorted to the Mediterranean.

In 1651 Parliament passed the famous Navigation Act, forbidding imports except when directly shipped from the place of origin in vessels of their country of origin or English ships. The origin of the act has been much debated by historians. Recently Pincus has argued that it was passed for purely political reasons, in retaliation against the Dutch for the failure of the negotiations led by Oliver St John for political union in the previous spring.[115] The Act was probably passed for a mixture of political and economic reasons. There were numerous calls for new restrictions on the use of foreign shipping in the late 1640s and when the Commonwealth, in response to pressure from the merchant companies, established the Council of Trade in 1650, this was high on the new body's agenda. The council consulted with Trinity House, the seaman's guild, which proposed a complex system of regulations that took into account the different needs of different sections of English trade. This approach probably found favour with the merchants and seems to have won over the merchant dominated Council of Trade. However the act which finally emerged bore little resemblance to the proposals of Trinity House. It imposed a single formula across the board, apparently with the intention of inflicting maximum damage on the Dutch. It therefore seems likely that St John took up a proposal which was already in the pipeline as a result of lobbying from within the merchant community and adapted it for his own, political, purposes.[116]

A number of provisos and exceptions were written into the act to make it more workable for merchants. These were probably added during the passage of the bill in the House of Commons, presumably as a result of pressure from the merchant community.[117] When the Act was finally passed it led to a storm of complaints from merchants, but these were largely concerned with the lack of time given for compliance rather than its underlying purpose. The complaint of the Eastland Company included a declaration of their support for the purpose of the act, which they had lobbied for.[118]

The impact of the Navigation Act was limited because its enforcement was uneven. The provision requiring imports only to be shipped from their country of origin was enforced, thanks in part to agents employed by the

---

[114] Beer, *Origins of the British Colonial System*, 362–7.

[115] Pincus, *Protestantism and Patriotism*, 40–50.

[116] The best account of the passage of the Act is still Harper, *English Navigation Laws*, 34–50. The proposals of Trinity House are in GL MS. 30045/4, Trinity House Transactions, 1613–61, ff. 64–5.

[117] Harper, *English Navigation Laws*, 48, n. 52.

[118] Pincus, *Protestantism and Patriotism*, 43, 47; Longleat House, Whitelocke Papers, parcel 7, items 45, 85.

merchant companies. However it proved difficult to enforce the restrictions on the use of foreign shipping in the colonies, or to exclude Dutch merchants from trading there. It may be that the greater protection which English merchant shipping received from the navy was far more important in preserving trade, and that it was this, rather than the Navigation Act, which had greater impact. It enabled the shipping industry to cut costs by reducing crews and in the long term it led to a shift to smaller ships. The Civil War made English shipping more efficient because the scale of the crisis which privateering brought about forced the English state to provide efficient protection for the first time, which in turn enabled merchant shipping to be optimized to maximize cargo space rather than for self protection.[119]

Conclusion

The Civil War at first had very little impact on exports. However the royalist blockade of 1643–44 had a devastating effect on exports of old draperies, which before the war made up more than half of all exports, and which never entirely recovered. In contrast other exports, mostly new draperies, were largely unaffected by the war. There was a short sharp decline in imports in 1642 followed by a longer slump in 1643–44. The slump in imports was caused by the royalist blockade, which meant wholesalers could not supply their provincial customers. Also demand was depressed in London and the provinces by plunder, high taxes and uncertainty about the future. There was a further slump in 1648 when the naval mutiny directly obstructed overseas trade. This time the crisis was largely confined to imports, which quickly recovered. However in the second half of the 1640s English shipping came increasingly under attack from royalist, Irish and French warships, which pushed up costs. This coincided with a recovery in Dutch shipping which was becoming cheaper and safer than English. Consequently much of the improvement in imports in 1649–50 accrued to the Dutch as it was either carried in Dutch shipping or imported through Holland.

As Jonathan Israel has argued war did not wipe out all the gains that had been made by London merchants in southern Europe and the Mediterranean since 1621. This is probably because these were largely 'rich trades'. The commodities were generally high in value and low in volume and consequently shipping constituted a low proportion of their final cost. In the late 1640s, before the passing of the Navigation Act, English shipping still made up slightly over half the vessels leaving Bilbao. In early 1652 the Levant

---

[119] Harper, *English Navigation Laws*, 50–2; Pagano De Divitiis, *English Merchants*, 64–5.

Company, supported for the first time by regular convoys to the Mediterranean, went so far as to boast that they had beaten off the Dutch competition. This was written as part of a defence of the company's monopoly and is certainly an exaggeration but as Israel has argued the English and the Dutch had divided the trade of the Mediterranean between them. The Dutch were the main suppliers of high quality cloth, while the English provided the middle quality. The English dominated trade in olive oil and currants while the Dutch had primacy in the trade in spices and raw silk, with the English as the main alternative suppliers.[120]

It was in northern Europe that the Civil War had a long-term impact on London's overseas trade. Cloth exports remained depressed long after the war ended and the number of ships sailing to the Baltic declined rapidly after 1647. Before the war the Merchant Adventurers' Company had advised the Long Parliament against severing trade with the Dutch because England had a favourable balance of trade with the United Provinces. It is doubtful whether this was the case by the end of the decade and the Merchant Adventurers were so dissatisfied with trading conditions in Holland that they were seeking to move their staple to the Spanish Netherlands.[121] The English Civil War had two long-term affects on London's overseas trade. It changed the balance of trade from the north to the south. Trade with the Mediterranean and Southern Europe became relatively more important because of the failure of trade with Northern Europe to recover. Secondly the attacks on merchant shipping by the privateers and others forced Parliament to massively expand the English navy, which enabled merchant shipping to become more economically efficient.

---

[120] Israel, *Dutch Primacy*, 204–5, 226–7; Taylor, 'Trade Neutrality, and the "English Road"', 258; Pincus, *Protestantism and Patriotism*, 98; PRO SP105/144, ff. 44–v.

[121] Longleat House, Whitelocke Papers, volume 8, f. 49; Birch (ed.), *Thurloe State Papers*, I, 129–30, 199, 217–19, 221, 566–9.

Chapter 8

Manufacturing Industry

Manufacturing employed the largest proportion of the London workforce in the seventeenth century; consequently it is vitally important to assessing how the economic impact of the war affected London society. There is evidence of severe economic problems in London industry from the autumn of 1642. In November the hempmen of Bridewell complained that their employees had joined the army, and trading was so dead that they could not sell what they made.[1] The problems of London craftsmen in 1643 are illustrated by the experience of the turner, Nehemiah Wallington. He suffered from falling demand for his goods and his creditors called in their debts. His problems became particularly acute in the second half of the year. In November demand was so low that he was compelled to sell his wares below cost price, although he realized that this would ultimately be self-defeating.[2] As late as 1645 he wrote that 'as for my estate it is something hard with mee. for our ware is deare because workmen are gon and trayding is dead & Costomers hard and taxes greate'. However, he also stated that those who supplied Parliament's armies, which included his brother, were doing well.[3] By this period, large sums of money were going into the London economy from contracts to supply the New Model Army, but not all London craftsmen were able to benefit from this improvement.[4]

With the exception of plumbers' solder and gold and silver plate, it is impossible to obtain statistics for industrial production for seventeenth-century London. However the trends in industrial production can be roughly estimated from apprenticeship enrolments. Industry in early modern London was labour intensive, demand for labour can therefore act as an indicator of levels of production. Moreover it was craft based and, consequently, labour was generally recruited and trained through apprenticeships. Apprenticeship enrolments can therefore be used as a guide to demand for labour. During the

---

[1] GL Bridewell Court Minutes, vol. 9, 1642–58, f. 5.
[2] BL Add. MS. 40883, Nehemiah Wallington's 'The Growth of a Christian', ff. 112–v, 144, 148, 149, 167.
[3] BL Sloane MS. 922, Nehemiah Wallington's Letters on Religious Topics, ff. 146v–7.
[4] See above p. 96.

Civil War apprenticeship enrolments fell by about two-thirds.[5] It is likely that this indicates a substantial fall in industrial production. However many apprentices were enrolled in non-manufacturing trades. Moreover it should not be assumed that the war had the same effect on the output of all sectors of manufacturing. The numbers of apprentices enrolled in different crafts can be examined through the records of the livery companies. This evidence needs to be treated cautiously. There was no requirement for a freeman of the City of London to be a member of his craft's company. In some of the larger companies most members practised a trade other than that of their company. However the manufacturing companies, particularly the smaller ones, remained closer to their trades than others - for example at the end of the seventeenth century ninety per cent of the freemen of the Pewterers' Company were still working pewterers.[6]

Apprenticeship enrolments need to be set against the context of military recruitment. In the early months of the war thousands of London apprentices joined Parliament's armies, it was reported that eight thousand were recruited in July 1642. It has been estimated that there were about twenty thousand apprentices in London at this time, consequently unless the recruits were rapidly replaced this would have substantially reduced the supply of labour in London.[7] Many journeymen also joined the army and declining admissions of new freemen indicates they were not replaced. The resulting labour shortage caused problems in some crafts. In the Cordwainers' Company, where the number of new freemen dropped from forty five in 1641–42 to twenty five in 1642–43, the journeymen took advantage of the shortage of labour to join together to demand higher wages in the autumn of 1642. Similar agitation recurred from 1645 suggesting that demand for labour remained strong in the shoemaking industry.[8]

There is also evidence that shortage of labour was a problem for London's bakers. On 16 September 1644 the Bakers' Company Court decided to petition the Court of Aldermen to allow them to employ foreign journeymen 'to bee continued till theis distracted tymes bee over, that therby the Company may bee in the meane tyme supplyed with servants to doe theyr worke'.[9] However there is little other evidence from the records of the livery companies

---

[5]   See Figure 9.1.

[6]   J. Hatcher and T.C. Barker, *A History of British Pewter* (1974), 116.

[7]   L.C. Nagel, 'The Militia of London, 1641–49', unpublished PhD thesis, University of London, 1982, 64; S.R. Smith, 'The Social and Geographical Origins of the London Apprentices, 1630–1660', *Guildhall Miscellany* 4 (1973), 198.

[8]   GL MS. 7353/1, Cordwainers' Company, Court Minutes, 1622–53, f. 248; GL MS. 7351/2, Cordwainers' Company, Wardens' Accounts, 1636–78, unfoliated. By the late 1640s the company was also seeking permission to employ non-free labour. GL MS. 7353/1, f. 368v.

[9]   GL MS. 5177/4, Bakers' Company, Court Minutes, 1617–48, f. 362.

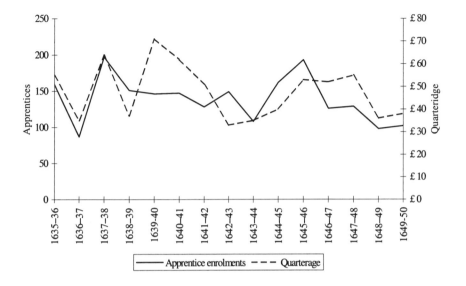

Figure 8.1
The Cordwainers' Company, 1635–50

Source: GL MS. 7351/2, Cordwainers' Company, Wardens' Accounts, 1636–78.

that labour shortages were causing problems during the Civil War. What this suggests is that falling output was matched by falling demand; that London craftsmen failed to recruit new apprentices during the war because they had no work for them to do.[10] The Bakers' and Cordwainers' Companies seem to have been the exceptions which prove the rule. Apprenticeship enrolments remained relatively stable during the war years in these companies, suggesting that where demand for labour remained stable, recruitment did not decline. In the Bakers' Company enrolments were substantially lower in the first half of the 1640s than they had been in the late 1630s but the decline preceded the outbreak of hostilities. The war also had little impact on demand for labour in the brewing industry. Apprenticeship enrolments in the Brewers' Company were already falling before the war began, and actually rose in 1643–44. Enrolments were generally lower in the war years than before but the decline

---

[10] This statement is based on a survey of the records of thirty five livery companies, mostly held at the Guildhall Library. Those omitted are the Drapers, Leathersellers, Salters and Stationers.

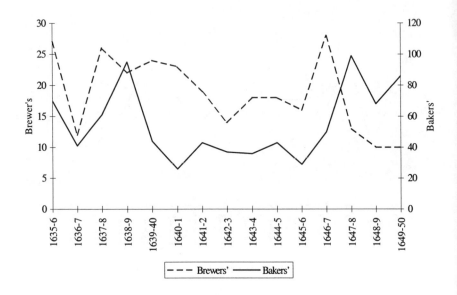

Figure 8.2
Apprenticeship enrolments in the Brewers' and Bakers' Companies, 1635–50

Source: GL MS. 5174/4, Bakers' Company, Wardens' Accounts, 1625–67; Brewers' Company, Wardens' Accounts, 1617–53.

was much smaller than that in other companies, and was not as great as that caused by the plague epidemic of 1637.[11]

The brewers, shoemakers and bakers all produced necessities for the local market. This suggests that demand for, and consequently output of, basic apparel and foodstuffs, remained relatively strong during the war. Additionally brewers and bakers obtained their raw materials from counties close to London; consequently they were relatively immune to the affect of the blockade of internal trade. This does not necessarily mean these trades were unaffected by the war. In 1642–43 the Cordwainers' Company's receipts from quarterage were forty two per cent lower than the average for the previous five years, suggesting that the members' incomes fell during the early years of the war. Moreover the output of clothing other than shoes may have declined substantially. Apprenticeship enrolments in the Merchant Tailors' Company declined from an annual average of 561 in 1637–42 to 203 in the year

---

[11] S.R. Smith, 'The Social and Geographical Origins of the London Apprentices, 1630–1660', *Guildhall Miscellany* 4 (1973), 203; GL MS. 5174/4, Bakers' Company, Wardens' Accounts, 1625–67, ff. 136v–137, 146v, 157, 164v, 177v; GL MS. 5442/6, Brewers' Company, Wardens' Accounts, 1617–53, unfoliated; GL MS. 7351/2, unfoliated.

1643–44, a fall of sixty four per cent. However the Merchant Tailors were one of the largest companies and had many members who were not tailors, including a substantial number of clothworkers. Even those parts of the manufacturing sector that served the local economy felt the impact of the disruption of trade, if only at second or third hand.[12]

From the summer of 1643 those sections of London industry that catered to the national market were cut off from a large part of their consumers because of the royalist blockade of trade with London. Paper was one of the commodities listed by Lord Herbert of Cherbury as unobtainable because of the disruption of trade with London.[13] This also affected the pewterers, who suffered additionally because the trade in tin and lead to London was obstructed, leading to a major increase in prices. The fall in apprenticeship enrolments suggests a major drop in production. In the five years immediately preceding the outbreak of the war on average thirty nine apprentices had been enrolled a year. By 1643–44 this had fallen to sixteen, representing a fall of fifty nine per cent.[14] Also directly affected by the decline in the internal trade of England were the clothworkers, who finished woollen cloth. Between 1637 and 1641 an average of 283 apprentices were enrolled a year in the Clothworkers' Company. By 1643 enrolments had fallen by fifty six per cent, to 124.[15] The decline in trade probably also hit the ship building industry. The reduction in the capital value of shipping during the first Civil War suggests that there was little demand for new ships in the 1640s, which would have depressed shipbuilding and its associated industries in the eastern suburbs. This led to increasing poverty in the eastern suburbs.[16]

Possibly the earliest section of manufacturing to feel the impact of the war was the production of luxury goods. Steven Smith found that the recruitment of apprentices in the Clockmakers' Company was down by about one-fifth in the war years. The war probably also depressed demand for silk textiles: in the Weavers' Company, which in the mid-seventeenth century consisted almost entirely of silkweavers, receipts for quarterage fell from £109 in the year to August 1642, to £52 in the year to August 1643. Quarterage receipts in the first year of the war were only forty six per cent of the average

---

[12]   Ibid., unfoliated; GL, Merchant Tailors' Company, Wardens' Accounts, vol. 17, 1637–41; GL, Merchant Tailors' Company, Wardens' Accounts, vol. 18, 1641–44.

[13]   R. Warner (ed.), *Epistolary Curiosities* (1818), 32.

[14]   GL MS. 7086/3 Pewterers' Company, Wardens' Accounts, 1572–1663, ff. 466v–90, 498–v; I.S., *A Declaration of Sundry Grievances Concerning Tinne and Pewter* (1646); Hatcher and Barker, *History of British Pewter*, 115, 262.

[15]   CH, Apprentices Binding Books, 1606–40; CH, Apprentices Binding Books, 1641–62.

[16]   LMA MJ/SBB/58, ff. 20–1; MJ/SBB/60, f. 22; MJ/SBB/66, ff. 13–14. For the decrease in the capital value of shipping, see above p. 189.

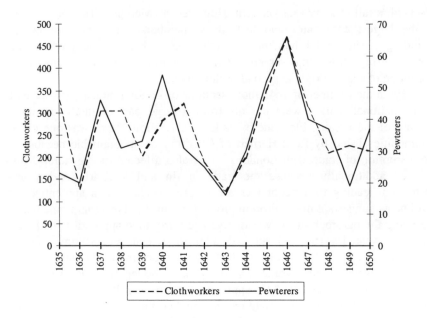

Figure 8.3
Apprenticeship enrolments in the Clothworkers' and Pewterers'
Companies, 1635–50

Source: GL MS. 7086/3 Pewterers' Company, Wardens' Accounts, 1572–1663, ff. 458v–518v;
CH, Apprentices Binding Books, 1606–40; CH, Apprentices Binding Books, 1641–62.

for the previous five years. This suggests that the silkweavers suffered a major
drop in income. Receipts from other sources, including apprenticeship
bindings, the admissions of freemen and fines, also declined substantially,
although unfortunately the company's accounts only give aggregate totals for
all these sources of revenue. In contrast to other sectors of manufacturing, silk
production reached its nadir in the first year of the war. In 1643–44 quarterage
receipts rose again, although they were still only fifty four per cent of the pre-
war average. This suggests that the production of luxury goods fell first in the
war.[17]

---

[17] Smith 'Social and Geographical Origins of the London Apprentices', 203; GL MS.
4646, Weavers' Company, Old Ledger Book, 1489–1741, ff. 79v–83v.

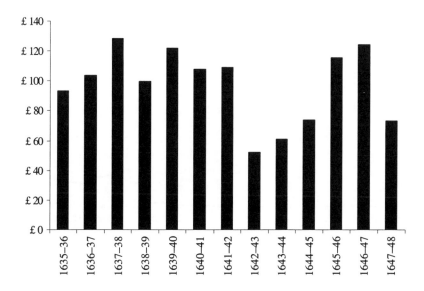

Figure 8.4
Quarterage receipts of the Weavers' Company, 1635–48

Source: GL MS. 4646, Weavers' Company, Old Ledger Book, 1489–1741, ff. 79v–85v.

The gold and silversmiths of London were particularly badly hit by the war; production of plate came to an almost total halt.[18] On 18 January 1643 the beadle of the Goldsmiths' Company petitioned the Court of Assistants complaining that since the war had begun he had been unable to collect the company's quarterage because: 'some are gon for souldiers and many shopps shutt up & the parties will not bee spoken with the hardnes of the times is such & the Goldsmithes trade taken awaye'.[19] The output of London's gold and silversmiths can be gauged from the totals 'touched' at Goldsmiths' Hall. Although this does not include all plate produced in London, as plate made for a private commission was exempted, the totals are probably reasonably representative of total production. It is unlikely that private commissions formed an increasing proportion of production in the 1640s. Plate production was already declining before the war broke out but the outbreak of the war considerably accentuated this trend. Between 16 June and 10 November 1642

---

[18] D. Mitchell, 'Innovation and the Transfer of Skill in the Goldsmiths' Trade in Restoration London', in D. Mitchell (ed.), *Goldsmiths, Silversmiths and Bankers; Innovation and the Transfer of Skill, 1550–1750* (1995), 11.

[19] GH, Court Book, W, 1642–45, f. 39.

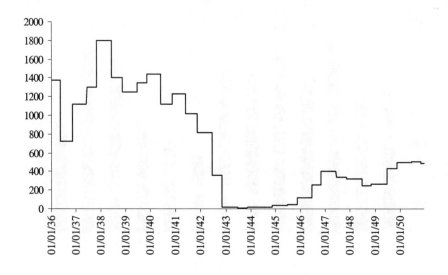

Figure 8.5
Daily averages of plate touched at Goldsmiths' Hall, troy ounces, 1636–50

Source: GH, Court Book, S/2, 1635–37, ff. 400, 449, 532; Ibid., T, 1637–39, ff. 20, 93v, 140, 191v; Ibid., U, 1639–42, ff. 22, 61, 90v, 128v, 150v, 199; Ibid., W, 1642–45, ff. 27v, 70v, 99, 234, 264; Ibid., X, 1645–48, ff. 23, 76v, 101, 151v, 179, 235; Ibid., Y, 1648–51, ff. 1v, 63v, 94, 161v, 194v, 261.

on average only 353 troy ounces of plate was touched a day, compared with 819 between 11 November 1641 and 16 June 1642, a decline of fifty seven per cent. Moreover between 7 June 1637 and 16 June 1642 an average of 1273 ounces a day was touched. Consequently the plate touched between June and November 1642 represented only twenty eight per cent of the average for the five years preceding the war. Between 10 November 1642 and 21 June 1643 the daily average fell to eighteen ounces, a fall of ninety five per cent compared with the first months of the war. This period saw the greatest percentage decline in production but output was at its lowest between 21 June and 8 November 1643 when only 5 troy ounces was touched a day, 0.36 per cent of the 1637–42 average. The experience of the gold and silversmiths, like that of the silkweavers, suggests that the production of luxury goods declined earlier than other sectors of manufacturing.[20]

---

[20]   Mitchell, 'Innovation and the Transfer of Skill in the Goldsmiths' Trade', 11–12; GH, Court Book, T, 1637–39, ff. 20, 93v, 140, 191v; GH, Court Book, U, 1639–42, ff. 22, 61, 90v, 128v, 150v, 199; GH, Court Book, W, 1642–45, ff. 27v, 70v, 99. I am grateful to David Beasley, librarian at Goldsmiths' Hall, for a very helpful discussion of this topic.

Demand for more basic items, including meat and candles, also declined in the early part of the Civil War. The minutes of the Tallowchandlers' Company contain numerous references to the adverse affect of the war on its members. The Butchers' Company accounts suggest that many members found it increasingly difficult to pay their quarterage, in 1643–44 over forty per cent of the yeomanry failed to make any payment at all.[21] Apprenticeship enrolments also fell in the Butchers' and Tallowchandlers' Companies, reaching a nadir in 1643–44. In the Butchers' Company they fell by more than half between 1641–42 and 1643–44, while in the Tallowchandlers' Company they fell by about forty per cent. These industries were dependant on the cattle trade for their raw materials, which was disrupted during the war, however this does not seem to have had much impact on the London economy until 1645. It is more likely that output declined in response to falling sales, possibly because demand for meat and candles was more elastic than demand for bread and beer. This indicates that, despite the apparent resilience of some sections of manufacturing which catered to local markets, there was a significant drop in consumer demand in London, not just of luxuries but also for more general consumer goods, such as candles, which in turn led to falling manufacturing output.[22]

The construction industry also suffered a severe recession during the war and it stayed depressed for longer than other sectors of industry. This was caused by the halt to London's expansion in this period. The building of the forts and lines of communication would have partly compensated for the decline in civilian building but it did not fill the gap. Apprenticeship enrolments in the Masons' Company averaged seventeen a year in the five years before the outbreak of the war; they declined to seven in 1642–43, two in 1643–44 and only one in 1644–45. In the Tylers' and Bricklayers' Company enrolments averaged eighteen a year between 1637 and 1642 but declined to only seventeen per cent of that figure by 1644–45. Moreover between 1637 and 1642 the company received on average more than £16 per year in quarterage from its members. In 1642–43 receipts fell to under £7, and in 1643–44 to £6 1s 10d, a fall of over sixty per cent. In the Carpenters' Company the decline in trade does not seem to have been so great and was over more quickly, possibly reflecting the fact that its members were not tied exclusively to the building industry. Nevertheless by 1643–44 quarterage receipts had fallen to forty five

---

[21] See above p. 148 for the impact of the war on the cattle trade. GL MS. 6153/1, Tallowchandlers' Company, Court Minutes, 1607–48, ff. 213v, 216; GL MS. 6440/2, Butchers' Company, Wardens' Accounts, 1593–1646, part 2, ff. 582–4v.

[22] Ibid., ff. 564–6v, 587v; GL MS. 6152/2 Tallowchandlers' Company, Wardens' Accounts, 1585–1653, ff. 263, 279.

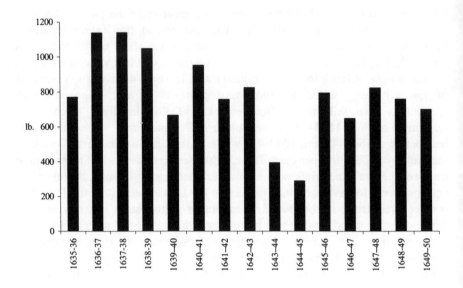

Figure 8.6
Output of plumbers' solder, year to Michaelmas, 1635–50

Source: GL MS. 2210/1, Plumbers' Company, Wardens' Accounts, 1593–1661.

per cent of the average for the five years preceding the outbreak of the war, while apprenticeship enrolments were only twenty nine per cent of the 1637–42 average.[23]

The decline in the building industry is also reflected in the fall in production of solder recorded in the accounts of the Plumbers' Company. This presumably refers to the alloy of lead and tin commonly used by plumbers to connect and mend lead pipes. All solder made or sold within the City of London and within three miles of its borders had to be first assayed by the company, which collected a toll of 4d per pound. Initially there is little sign that the war depressed output of solder, in the year to Michaelmas 1643 it rose by nine per cent. However in the following year output fell by over fifty per cent, from 824 lb. in the year to Michaelmas 1643 to 394 lb. in the year to Michaelmas 1644, moreover in the following year output fell by a further one-quarter, to only 290 lb. It is tempting to attribute the fall in output to the difficulties in obtaining lead and tin during the Civil War, but by 1645 the lead

---

[23] N.G. Brett-James, *The Growth of Stuart London* (1935), 119–120; D. Knoop and G.P. Jones, *The London Mason in the Seventeenth Century* (Manchester, 1935), 92; GL MS. 3054/2, Tylers' and Bricklayers' Company, Wardens' Accounts, 1631–57, unfoliated; GL MS. 4325/8, Carpenters' Company, Wardens' Accounts, 1623–47, unfoliated.

trade with Hull had resumed. Consequently it is more likely to have been the result of the decline in the building industry, and the continued decline into 1645 is further evidence that the building industry continued to decline after other sectors of industry started to recover.[24]

Perhaps surprisingly, the metalworking sector was not initially stimulated by wartime demand for armaments. The pre-war armaments industry has been characterized by Charles Fissel as immature and fragmented. Consequently it was too small to cope with the sudden increase in demand, forcing the authorities to look abroad for a substantial part of their requirements. Moreover even when supplies were purchased at home in the early part of the war contractors had considerable difficulties obtaining payment. Consequently, even in the metalworking sector, increased demand for munitions did not counteract the impact of the general decline in trade. In the Blacksmiths' Company, which included significant numbers of gunmakers among its members, apprenticeship enrolments fell from an average of 109 per annum in the five years to 1642 to only fifty two in 1643–44, a fall of over fifty per cent. The company also found it increasingly difficult to collect quarterage from its members, receipts at courts fell from £19 9s 9d in 1641–42 to £10 9s 1d in 1643–44, although collections at searches did not fall so much, only falling from £14 18s 4d in 1641–42 to £13 12s 3d in 1643–44. This suggests that there was an increased reluctance to pay during the war. Apprenticeship enrolments fell even further in the Founders' Company, from an average of twenty two a year from 1637 to 1642, to five in 1643–44. The records of the Cutlers' and Armourers' Companies are less complete, but in both there were falls in freemen admissions.[25]

During the Civil War increased demand led to a major expansion of the armaments industry until by the middle of the decade Parliament could supply the vast majority of its needs from native producers. Much of this expansion took place in London. The sharp rise in apprenticeship recruitment in the Blacksmiths' Company in 1644–45 probably arose from the increased output of armaments. Newcomers coming into this sector also fuelled the expansion in output. However increased output led to falling prices during the 1640s. The prices of matchlock muskets and snaphance pistols fell by half between 1642

[24] GL MS. 2210/1, Plumbers' Company, Wardens' Accounts, 1593–1661; GL MS. 2205, Plumbers' Company, Copy of the 1611 Charter, ff. 34–5.
[25] See chapter 4 for contracting for the army. M.C. Fissel, *The Bishops' Wars, Charles I's Campaigns against Scotland, 1638–1640* (Cambridge, 1994), 106; G. Parsloe (ed.), *Wardens' Accounts of the Worshipful Company of Founders* (1964); GL MS. 2883/4, Blacksmiths' Company, Wardens' Accounts, 1625–46, ff. 206–266; GL MS. 2884, Blacksmiths' Company, Freedom Admissions, 1599–1694, ff. 58–68; GL MS. 7158/1, Cutlers' Company, Freedom Admissions, 1613–1790; GL MS. 12079/2, Armourers' Company, Freedom Admissions and Apprentices Bindings, 1603–61.

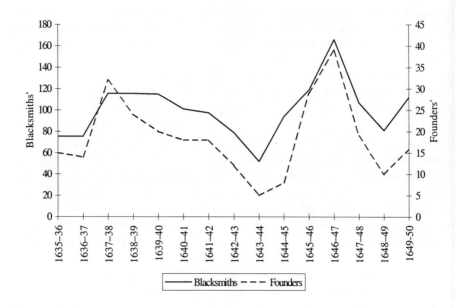

Figure 8.7
Apprenticeship enrolments in the Blacksmiths' and Founders' Companies,
1635–50

Source: GL MS. 2883/4, Blacksmiths' Company, Wardens' Accounts, 1625–46, ff. 119–304; GL MS. 2883/5, Blacksmiths' Company, Wardens' Accounts, 1646–80, ff. 2–44; G. Parsloe (ed.), *Wardens' Accounts of the Worshipful Company of Founders* (1964), 303–337.[26]

and 1645, while there were also falls in the prices of pikes and swords. As a result individual producers probably found their profit margins squeezed. This led to hostility among the existing armament producers against the newcomers. Little could be done against freemen, who were legally entitled to practice any trade they liked within the City, but those who were not free, or who employed non-freemen could be prosecuted. In 1643 workmen armourers in the Armourers' Company several times complained that members were employing non-freemen; they also initiated prosecutions against non-freemen practising their craft. In 1644 workmen gunsmiths in the Blacksmiths', Armourers', and Gunsmiths' Companies agitated against non-freemen practising their trade and those who employed them. Their attacks were particularly focused on Edward Baker, who supplied arms to the army of the Eastern Association. He had not served an apprenticeship in the craft

---

[26] Up until 1639 the Blacksmiths' Company recorded their accounts in two year periods, 1635–37 and 1637–39, enrolments for these four years are therefore half those in their respective accounting period.

and he employed non-freemen, but the Court of Assistants of the Armourers was reluctant to prosecute while Parliament needed arms. In April 1644 the Cutlers' Company agreed to petition Parliament against ironmongers and other craftsmen who were undercutting them by assembling swords from components purchased from others. In the following month they resolved to prosecute ironmongers who were encroaching on their trade.[27] As late as October 1645 the minutes of the Blacksmiths' Company could still refer to 'the troubles of the times & deadnesse of trade'.[28]

The armaments industry was not the only part of London's manufacturing to expand during the 1640s. Cyprian Blagden has argued that the printers prospered in the 1640s. In the 1630s the number of printing presses had been limited by the Court of Star Chamber, however this fell into abeyance with the abolition of that court in 1641. This freed printers to set up new printing presses and the result was a significant expansion in the industry. When controls were re-imposed by Parliament in 1649 nearly twice as many presses were allowed compared to the late 1630s. However the heavy pre-war restrictions on printing were not typical of London manufacturing.[29]

In the middle years of the decade there are signs of recovery across a wide cross section of London's industrial sector. London industry at last began to benefit from contracts for Parliament's armed forces, the first year of the existence of the New Model Army saw very substantial expenditure on equipment and munitions in London, and at last the financial re-organization ensured that bills for supplies were paid promptly. However the recovery went much wider than those trades connected with supplying the army, and gathered pace after the war, when the volume of military contracting declined. This suggests that the upturn in manufacturing was largely the result of the recovery of London's trade.[30]

Ralph Davis argued that the ship building industry boomed after the end of the first Civil War.[31] In the Clothworkers, Pewterers, Blacksmiths, Tyler and Bricklayers, Carpenters and Founders apprenticeship enrolments rose substantially. In all six companies they exceeded the average for the five years to 1642 by over 150 per cent by 1646–47, in the Carpenters enrolments

---

[27] P. Edwards, *Dealing in Death: The Arms Trade and British Civil Wars, 1638–52* (Stroud, 2000), 72, 211, 238; GL MS. 12072, Armourers' Company, Rough Court Minutes, part 2, ff. 1v, 2, 2v; GL MS. 12071/3, Armourers' Company, Court Minutes, 1621–75, ff. 139, 141, 144–v; GL MS. 2881/5, Blacksmiths' Company, Minute Book, 1639–48, f. 159; GL MS. 1751/1, Cutlers' Company, Court Minutes, 1602–70, ff. 346v, 347v.

[28] GL MS. 2881/5, f. 197.

[29] C. Blagden, 'The Stationers' Company in the Civil War Period', *The Library* 5th Series, 13 (1958), 16.

[30] See above p. 96.

[31] R. Davis, *The Rise of the English Shipping Industry* (1962), 11.

exceeded the pre-war average by 206 per cent.[32] To a certain extent the growth in apprenticeship enrolments only made up for the loss of apprentices to the army, and the failure to recruit in the Civil War, but in the Clothworkers' Company some masters were recruiting more apprentices than the company regulations allowed. On 12 May 1647 twenty one masters were brought before the Court of Assistants for keeping too many apprentices. Despite appearances, this does not indicate an economic boom, in most of the cases the master was accused of keeping three apprentices but no journeymen. This suggests that although the masters had work, their profit margins were too narrow for them to employ journeymen. However the Clothworkers' economic problems may well have been specific to their industry. There were allegations that the senior members of the Merchant Adventurers who administered the customs from 1645 to 1649 were allowing members of their company to evade the Elizabethan statute, which stated that at least one cloth in ten should be exported dressed. This reduced the employment available to the Clothworkers and in 1646, under pressure from their yeomanry, the company agreed to initiate legal proceedings against the Merchant Adventurers to enforce this statute.[33]

Further evidence for the recovery in manufacturing industry comes from the increasing receipts for quarterage found in the accounts of the livery companies. Receipts sometimes rose to above pre-war levels, probably because improving prosperity was enabling the companies to collect the arrears that had accumulated during the war. In the Blacksmiths' Company receipts increased sixty three per cent between 1643–44 and 1645–46. By the latter year, the last of the war, they were nine per cent higher than the average for 1637–42. Moreover the proportion collected at the company's courts increased from forty three per cent of the total in 1643–44 to sixty three per cent in 1645–46, suggesting that the members were more willing to pay their quarterage, another indication of increased prosperity. The Blacksmiths' quarterage receipts declined slightly in 1646–47 but as Figure 8.4 shows the receipts of the Weavers' Company continued to grow. In 1645–46 they were already 122 per cent higher than in 1642–43 and were about the same as the average between 1637 and 1642. Moreover in the following year, 1646–47, receipts rose by a further eight per cent. In the Cordwainers' Company, where collections had not fallen as far during the war, Figure 8.1 shows receipts for quarterage rose by

---

[32]   CH, Apprentices Binding Books, 1606–40; CH, Apprentices Binding Books, 1641–62; GL 7086/3, ff. 466–90, 507v–8v; GL MS. 2883/4, 163–228; GL MS. 2883/5, Blacksmiths' Company, Wardens' Accounts, 1646–80, f. 2; GL MS. 3054/2, unfoliated; GL MS. 4325/8, unfoliated; Parsloe, *Wardens' Accounts*, 306–29. For the Clothworkers' and Pewterers' see Figure 8.3, for the Blacksmiths' and Founders' see Figure 8.7.

[33]   CH, Orders of Court, 1639–49, ff. 141–141v, 143v, 163, 163v–4v; J. Lilburne, *An Impeachment of High Treason* (1649), 38. For the Merchant Adventurers and the customs see p. 77 above.

fifty eight per cent between 1642–43 and 1645–46. The construction industry also showed signs of renewed prosperity. By 1645–46 the quarterage receipts of the Tylers' and Brickmakers' Company had risen four fold compared with 1643–44, moreover they were about fifty per cent higher than the 1637–42 average. Receipts declined in the following year but were still substantially above the pre-war average.[34] The one part of London manufacturing industry that did not see a recovery to pre-war prosperity was the production of gold and silver plate. Although output rose to 401 ounces per day by early 1647 this was still only one-third of the output between 1637 and 1642, when the daily average had been 1273 ounces a day.[35]

In the last years of the 1640s the recovery in manufacturing came to an end. Nehemiah Wallington wrote that 'then my trading in my shop failed me very much', and that 'whereas I did take the first half year in 1647 three hundred and twenty-three pounds, fourteen shillings, the next half year, 1648, I did take but three hundred and twenty pounds, but the third half year I did take but two hundred and five pounds and that was very small gain'.[36] The renewed economic difficulties of the late 1640s affected virtually every sector of manufacturing industry, even those parts of the economy which had fared comparatively well during the Civil War. Figure 8.2 illustrates the impact on the brewing industry. The enrolment of apprentices fell from twenty eight in 1646–47 to ten in 1648–49, a fall of sixty four per cent. Figure 8.1 shows that apprenticeship enrolments and quarterage receipts declined in the Cordwainers' Company.[37] The building industry also declined. In the Tylers' and Bricklayers' Company receipts from quarterage fell by sixty three per cent between 1646–47 and 1648–49, while the enrolment of apprentices fell by seventy eight per cent. At the same time the quarterage receipts of the Carpenters' Company fell by seventy six per cent and apprenticeship enrolments fell by eighty per cent. As Figure 8.6 illustrates the output of plumbers' solder recovered strongly in 1645–46, when it rose by over 170 per cent. In the rest of the decade output fluctuated between 649 lb. and 822 lb., which suggests that the decline in the building industry may not have been as great as the records of the Carpenters and Tylers and Bricklayers suggest. However output of plumbers' soldier in the second half of the 1640s never exceeded the average for the five years preceding the outbreak of the Civil

---

[34] GL MS. 2883/4 f. 304; GL MS. 4646, ff. 84, 84v, 85; GL MS. 7351/2, unfoliated; GL MS. 3054/2, unfoliated.

[35] GH, Court Book, X, 1645–48, 151v. See Figure 8.5.

[36] Quoted in P. Seaver, *Wallington's World: A Puritan Artisan in Seventeenth-Century London* (Stanford, Ca., 1985), 121.

[37] GL MS. 5442/6, Brewers' Company, Wardens' Accounts, 1617–53, unfoliated; GL MS. 7351/2, unfoliated. The increase in apprenticeship recruitment in the Bakers' Company in the late 1640s shown in Figure 8.2 was probably due to the amalgamation with the Brown Bakers in 1646.

War, indicating that a return to pre-war levels of prosperity eluded the construction industry.[38] Output of metal goods also fell; apprenticeship enrolments in the Blacksmiths' Company fell by fifty one per cent between 1646–47 and 1648–49. The output of brass and pewter wares declined even further. Apprenticeship enrolments in the Founders' Company fell by seventy four per cent between 1646–47 and 1648–49. In the Pewterers' Company the enrolment of apprentices fell by seventy one per cent between 1646–47 and 1649–50. The decline in the cloth trade in the late 1640s is reflected in the apprenticeship enrolments in the Clothworkers' Company, which fell by fifty five per cent between 1646 and 1648.[39]

The silkweavers suffered a major decline in demand for their goods. In order to drum up extra trade they took to going round the inns of the capital trying to sell their wares, but in so doing they fell foul of the municipality's crack down on hawking. The silkweavers won the support of the levellers and, in some cases, won legal redress against the municipality. Nevertheless, as Figure 8.4 shows, the Weavers' Company receipts from quarterage fell by forty one per cent between 1646–47 and 1647–48, indicating that the silkweavers suffered a major drop in income.[40] Declining demand for silk goods in the late 1640s led to a bitter dispute between the governors and ordinary members of the Weavers' Company in the late 1640s. The dispute focused on the issue of foreign craftsmen, the critics of the company rulers argued that, during the war, large numbers of foreigners had been allowed into the company to the detriment of the freemen who were consequently unable to find work. In particular the foreigners were accused of monopolizing broad weaving. However these allegations probably had little foundation in fact. Foreign craftsmen had long dominated broad weaving, while the English tended to produce narrow wares such as ribbons. Faced with falling sales for narrow wares in the late 1640s the English weavers were seeking to move into broad weaving by using political pressure to exclude the foreigners.[41]

The economic difficulties of the late 1640s led to widespread agitation against non-freemen. In September 1647 there were complaints in the French

---

[38] GL MS. 3054/2, Tylers' and Bricklayers' Company, Wardens' Accounts, 1631–57; GL MS. 4326/8. unfoliated; GL MS. 4326/9, Carpenters' Company, Wardens' Accounts, 1647–53, unfoliated; GL MS. 2210/1.

[39] GL MS. 2883/5, ff. 2, 29; Parsloe, *Wardens' Accounts*, 329, 337; GL MS. 7086/3, Pewterers' Company, Wardens' Accounts, 1572–1663; CH, Apprentices Binding Books, 1641–62. For the Clothworkers and Pewterers see Figure 8.3, for the Blacksmiths and Founders see Figure 8.7.

[40] GL MS. 4646, Weavers' Company, Old Ledger Book, 1489–1741, f. 85v; Lilburne, *Impeachment of High Treason*, 38; *The Mounfull Cryes of Many Thousand Poore Tradesmen* (1648); CLRO Cash Books, vol. 1/6, ff. 50v, 51, 156, 157–v; vol. 1/7, f. 147.

[41] Plummer, *London Weavers' Company*, 51, 152, 181–2; E. Kerridge, *Textile Manufacturers in Early Modern England* (Manchester, 1985), 24; *The Case of the Commonality of the Corporation of Weavers of London Stated* (1648), 3–5.

church that Huguenot craftsmen were being prosecuted for not having served a seven-year apprenticeship. In April 1648 there were complaints about the employment of non-free sawyers from the Carpenters' Company. In November 1649 jewellers in the Goldsmiths' Company petitioned the Court of Aldermen against non-freemen practising their craft. In the Merchant Tailors' Company, after agitation from the working tailors, a sub-committee was established which conducted a vigorous campaign against foreign workers until the Court of Assistants abolished it in 1654. In practice the attack on non-freemen was probably more a reaction to the economic difficulties experienced by London craftsmen, than to any real increase in non-free participation in the economy.[42]

There is only limited evidence to suggest that the regulation of manufacturing was disrupted during the war years. The search book of the Waxchandlers' Company records no searches for faulty goods between 3 May 1642 and 13 May 1647, although previously the company's officers had searched twice a year. In his study of the London Weavers' Company Alfred Plummer argued that the 1640s saw a decline in economic regulation but the evidence for this derives from accusations made by critics of the company's rulers, which, as we have seen, is unreliable.[43] In other companies searching continued in the war years; in December 1643 the master of the Pewterers' Company reported to his Court of Assistants that the traditional search had been conducted, and the officers had found things in 'reasonable good order'. There is evidence that the Clothworkers' Company continued to search and the records of the Bakers' and Saddlers' Companies show a continued stream of fines for faulty workmanship and other economic offences. Thus overall, with a few exceptions, there is little evidence of a breakdown in economic regulation.[44]

Conclusion

The Civil War caused a recession in most sections of London's manufacturing industry. However this recession was not universal, those who produced necessities for which demand was relatively inelastic, such as bakers and

---

[42] CLRO Rep. 59, ff. 198v 414v; CLRO Rep. 60, f. 15v; M. James, *Social Problems and Policy in the Puritan Revolution* (1930), 205–6; A.D. Chamier (ed.), *Les Actes des Colloques des Eglises Francaises, 1581–1654*, Publications of the Huguenot Society 2 (1890), 106.

[43] A. Plummer, *The London Weavers Company 1600–1970* (1972), 50–1, 152; GL MS. 9493, Waxchandlers' Company, Search Book, ff. 153v–153.

[44] GL MS. 7090/4, Pewterers' Company, Court Minutes, 1611–43, f. 355; GL, Merchant Tailors' Company, Court Minutes, vol. 9, 1636–54, f. 207v; GL MS. 5385, Saddlers' Company, Court Minutes, 1606–65, ff. 227v, 229v, 231, etc.; GL MS. 5174/4, Bakers' Company, Wardens' Accounts, 1625–67, ff. 163, 176v, 177v.

brewers, seem to have suffered little, while the armaments and the printing industries appear to have expanded in the 1640s. The recession was initially largely confined to the production of luxury goods. In the first year of the war, production of gold and silver plate collapsed and there was a major crisis in the silk industry. It was not until the second year of the war, 1643–43, that the crisis affected the majority of manufacturing industry, indeed at least one section of manufacturing, the production of plumbers' solder, seems to have been unaffected by the war until this period. This chronology coincides with the impact of the war on domestic trade, which slumped after the inauguration of the royalist blockade in the summer of 1643. This suggests it was the disruption of London's trade networks, rather than the high taxes or labour shortages arising from the recruitment of the armies, which was the primary cause of the manufacturing recession. Moreover if the impact of taxation had been the primary reason for the economic problems of London's manufacturing, then one might expect the brewing industry to have suffered the most, given the high excise rates imposed on beer and ale, but brewing seems to have been one of the least affected sections of industry. Only those sections of manufacturing that were not adversely affected by the war seem to have experienced labour shortages. There is evidence of a strong recovery in the middle years of the decade but this turned into a renewed recession in the late 1640s, which included even those sectors that had previously not been affected by the war. This, however, was probably not primarily the result of the renewal of fighting in 1648; many sections of manufacturing were already beginning to decline in 1647. It is therefore more likely that it was the consequence of the run of bad harvests that started in 1646. These led to rising food prices, which left consumers less money to spend on manufactured goods. The 1640s therefore saw two major slumps in London manufacturing, the first in 1643–44 resulting from war, and the second, from 1647 onwards, resulting from dearth.

Chapter 9

Economic Fluctuations 1642–50

The previous three chapters have shown that the war had a major impact on most of London's trade and manufacturing, but the impact was not uniform, some sections suffered more than others, and different sectors were affected at different times. What therefore was the impact of the war on the London economy as a whole? The purpose of this chapter is to pull together the various aspects so far discussed, to assess the impact of the war on the London economy in the 1640s. It is possible to trace the approximate course of the trends in the London economy using qualitative sources and general measures of economic health, such as rents and apprenticeship enrolments.

By late 1642 the war was clearly having an adverse effect on the economy of London. On 20 October the yeomanry wardens of the Tallowchandlers' Company complained of 'the hardnesse of the times deadnesse of trade and the urgent affaires of the Kingdome dayly drawing money from them'.[1] In November one newsbook commented that 'Trading and imployment [is] ceasing in *London*'.[2] In December the Plumbers' Company complained of 'the decay of trading'.[3] In the same month one London correspondent reported 'all tradinge decayed, and yet our charge by intollerable taxations soe encreasing that we hourely expect some insurrection'.[4]

Fears concerning the cessation of trade featured prominently in the petitions advanced in London in the winter of 1642–43 advocating a compromise peace. The petition of 22 December argued that 'Commerce and Trade (the only Support of this City) [is] exceedingly impaired, whereof none can be equally sensible with us; those with whom we deal, in most Parts of this and of the Kingdom of *Ireland*, are much disabled and impoverished, by the Violence and Rapine of Soldiers; some of them totally dispoiled, others in a fearful Expectation of the like Measure; the Multitude of poor People in and about this City (who by reason of the Cessation of Trade, want Employment, and consequently Bread) infinitely abound'.[5] The petition of apprentices stated

---

[1] GL MS. 6153/1, Tallowchandlers' Company, Court Minutes, 1607–48, f. 213v.

[2] *England's Memorable Accidents*, 7–14 November 1642, 75.

[3] GL MS. 2208/1, Plumbers' Company, Court Minutes, 1621–47, unfoliated, 13 December 1642.

[4] W. Phillips (ed.), *Ottley Papers Relating to the Civil War*, Shropshire Archæological Society Transactions 2nd Series, 6 (1894), 53.

[5] *LJ* V, 511–12.

that they were 'foreseeing the Face of our own Ruin in our Masters present Condition'. If the declining economic conditions did not create the peace party, it certainly created plenty of material for its propaganda.[6]

In 1643 parliamentary taxation began to bite in London, but it is noticeable that contemporaries continued to attribute their economic difficulties primarily to the dislocation of trade. In February a London apprentice informed his parents that 'I doe thincke that theere will Be noe Tradinge in a littell while'.[7] In March the vestry of the extra mural parish of St Botolph Bishopsgate blamed problems in collecting local rates on 'the great povertie of many of the present inhabitants of this parish because of the deadnes in, and lacke of tradeing and also for that divers of the said parishoners have listed themselves for soldiers'.[8] A pro-parliamentary tract published in the same month, stated that 'trading is much decayed by the trouble of the Kingdom', and that this was leading to increased poverty in London. The author argued that the health of the economy of London was inextricably interconnected with that of the rest of the country: 'there is no part of the Kingdome suffers, but *London* suffers, *London* is plundered every day, in all the Kingdome over'.[9] This is illustrated by the example of John Gearing. He appears to have been a London wholesaler who sold goods purchased from the East India Company to customers in Reading, Newbury and Cirencester. However by the beginning of July 1643 his losses as the result of plundering of those towns had made him insolvent, and he was seeking to compound with his creditors. This suggests that even before the royalist embargo the disruption of trade with the provinces was having an impact on the London economy.[10]

The economy was also disrupted by uncertainties in the legal system. Charles I ordered the Westminster courts to adjourn to Oxford, but this was countermanded by Parliament with the result that rival versions of the central common law courts sat in both places during the Civil War. Moreover Chancery was unable to sit in London from May 1642, when Lord Keeper Littleton sent the Great Seal to the King, until Parliament created a new Great Seal in December 1643. This made Londoners reluctant to go to law to resolve their commercial difficulties. For example in 1643 Joseph Bynns, a London surgeon, tried to remit money to Joseph Colston, then in Italy, by purchasing a bill of exchange from one Whittacker. The bill had not been honoured in Italy but Bynns reported that he could not receive adequate compensation from

---

[6]   Ibid., 525. For the peace movement see K. Lindley, *Popular Politics and Religion in Civil War London* (Aldershot, 1997), 336–45.

[7]   W. Phillips (ed.), *Ottley Papers Relating to the Civil War*, Shropshire Archæological Society Transactions 2nd Series, 7 (1895), 261.

[8]   GL MS. 4526/1, St Botolph Bishopsgate, Vestry Minutes, 1616–90, f. 60v.

[9]   *A High Way to Peace* (1643), unpaginated.

[10]   *CCMEIC*, 1640–43, 308, 315, 331, 370.

Whittacker, arguing that with legal system in such confusion 'as the times are we must make the beste of an ill bargaine'.[11]

The depression was at its deepest in the latter half of 1643 as the general effects of the war on business was exacerbated by the King's prohibition on trade with London. Confidence was very low and there was a flight of both capital and people. On 19 August the committee for the navy was informed that large sums of money were being shipped overseas.[12] The Commons became so alarmed about the numbers seeking to leave England that it revoked all orders allowing passage abroad on 10 August. An exception was made for the stranger communities, in September the Commons established a committee to receive certificates from the Dutch and French churches of 'such poor Strangers that are not able to continue here without begging by reason of the Decay of Trade' so that the Speaker might grant them warrant to leave the country.[13]

The adverse economic climate penetrated into the wealthy central city parishes. In St Bartholomew by the Exchange, when the vestry ordered that a special rate should be levied to raise money for the relief of maimed soldiers in November 1643, it was found that only about half the money assessed could be levied because 'there was soe many houses in the parish shut up: & soe many shops that paid nothing'.[14] In the same month William Gibbs, a City Alderman, told the Commons that 'Our rich Men are gone, because the City is a place of Taxes and Burdens; Trade is decayed, and our Shops shut up in a great measure: Our poor do much increase'.[15] In the following February the vestry of St Stephen's Coleman Street complained that the poor were 'in extreme want and misery', but receipts from the poor rate were declining because 'many houses being empty and many parishioners disabled to pay as heretofore'.[16]

It was in the autumn of 1643 that Gerrard Winstanley, a London draper and the future Digger leader, went bankrupt.[17] On 12 December one London merchant wrote 'heere is a most miserable time of tradeing & noe mony to be had from any man allmost that oweth me mony'.[18] Towards the end of that month two partners in the mercery trade drew up a joint account which included over £5,900 of debts which 'allbeit they accompted the same to be

---

[11]   BL Sloane MS. 118, f. 82.
[12]   Bodl. Rawlinson MS. A221, Journal of the Committee for the Navy, 1643–44, f. 219.
[13]   *CJ* III, 201, 238.
[14]   GL MS. 4384/2, St Bartholomew by the Exchange, Vestry Minutes, 1643–76, f. 17.
[15]   *CJ* III, 316.
[16]   GL MS. 4458/1, St Stephen Colemanstreet, Vestry Minutes, 1622–1728, part 1, f. 128.
[17]   J. Alsop, 'Ethics in the Market Place: Gerrard Winstanley's London Bankruptcy, 1643', *JBS* 28 (1989), 104, 113.
[18]   Bodl. Tanner MS. 62, Samuel Crispe to Sir George Strode, 12 December 1643, f. 438.

good, Yet they conceived that the same might not be paid in convenient time by the reason of the distractions of the times'.[19] In March 1644 the Haberdashers' Company agreed to give £20 immediately, and £30 at a later date, to a former member of their Court of Assistants 'for his present relief in theis hard times'.[20] In the following September Humphrey Slaney, whom Robert Brenner describes as 'one of the most adventurous London merchants of his day', was seeking to compound with his creditors.[21]

Londoners withdrew their investments from the provincial economy. Although this began in the summer of 1642 as London tradesmen called in their debts from their provincial customers it probably reached its peak in late 1643. At about that time Henry Bradshaw, a London scrivener, went to Yorkshire to try to withdraw what he could of his estate. Before the war he had invested his own money and funds entrusted to him by clients in loans to the Yorkshire gentry but he was now convinced that those sums were no longer safe. He also owned a share of a ship, plus one-quarter of its cargo of coal, which was stuck in Sunderland from February 1643 until the parliamentarians captured the town in 1644.[22]

The falling receipts for apprenticeship enrolments in the City illustrate the impact of the war, as Figure 9.1 demonstrates. In the year to Michaelmas 1641 £384 was received by the City Chamberlain for apprenticeship enrolments, but in the following year this fell to £286, a fall of about one-quarter. The period from Michaelmas 1642 to Michaelmas 1644 is complicated by the appointment of a new Chamberlain in June 1643. As a result the 1642–43 account stopped in midsummer, after only three-quarters of a year, and the following account covers a year and one-quarter from Midsummer 1643 to Michaelmas 1644.[23] It is nevertheless evident that receipts from enrolments fell sharply in this period. For the three-quarters of a year to midsummer 1643 the Chamber only received £117, and for the year and one-quarter from midsummer 1643 to Michaelmas 1644 only £142. This would suggest that the annual average receipts for this period were about £129, and that during the Civil War the enrolment of apprentices in the City of London fell by nearly two-thirds. The quarterly average receipts were substantially lower in the 1643–44 account than in the 1642–43 account; just over £28 compared with nearly £39, which suggests that it was in 1643–44 that enrolments reached their nadir.[24]

---

[19]   CLRO Rep. 57/2, f. 107.

[20]   GL MS. 15842/1, Haberdashers' Company, Court Minutes, 1583–1652, f. 327.

[21]   Ibid.; R. Brenner, *Merchants and Revolution, Commercial Change, Political Conflict and London's Overseas Traders, 1550–1653* (Cambridge, 1993), 122.

[22]   PRO HCA13/59, ff. 385v-6v. See above p. 110.

[23]   CLRO Cash Books, vol. 1/4, ff. 27v, 121v, 197v.

[24]   CLRO Cash Books, vol. 1/5, f. 19v.

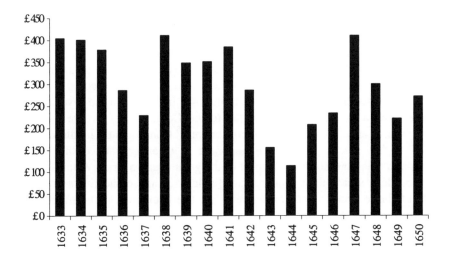

Figure 9.1
Receipts from the enrolment of apprentices, 1633–50

Source: CLRO Cash Books, vols 1/1–1/7. Year to Michaelmas. The receipts for 1642–43 have been increased by one-quarter, those for 1643–44 have been decreased by one-fifth.

The fall in apprenticeship enrolments took place when many existing apprentices were joining the army, so the total number of apprentices in the London economy must have fallen very substantially. It is possible that the failure to recruit new apprentices was the result of the obstruction of communications during the Civil War. Smith found that the geographical area from which London apprentices were recruited became much more restricted during the 1640s. Those apprentices who were enrolled tended to be drawn from the metropolis, or from the counties in its immediate vicinity. An argument against this is that the belligerents were concerned with stopping trade rather than the movement of people. The fall in recruitment may also reflect the reluctance of families to send their sons to London during the early part of the war, when many probably thought that London would be sacked by the royalists, but as has been noted in the previous chapter, in those trades where there was continued demand for labour, apprenticeship enrolments did not decline. This suggests that apprentices were available where there was demand for them, and, conversely, that the general decline in enrolments was the result of falling demand for labour in London.[25]

In the early part of the war landlords had increasing problems in receiving their rents. Joseph Bynns found it very difficult to collect the rents from Joseph Colston's London property, and by April 1643 one tenant had not paid anything since the previous June. There were a number of complaints that property was standing empty in the City in 1643. In July 1644 the royalist press reported that a list had been presented to the Commons of twelve thousand empty houses and shops in and around London.[26] Consequently landlords were forced to lower their rents. One deponent in Chancery stated that in the metropolis many landlords 'in respect of the great decay of trade & taxations & other burdens which their tennants are liable to in these sad times do much abate of theire accustomed former rents'.[27] The decline in rents affected the wealthy central City parishes. The tenant of a cellar in Budge Row requested an abatement of his rent of £10 a year, which was agreed 'in regard of the badnesse of the tymes and decay of trading'.[28]

The fall in rents may particularly have affected the western parts of the City. Robert Meade, collector of the assessment in St Dunstan in the West in 1644, stated that 'the landlords in & about London espeatially in Fleetestreete … doe & have abated the third parte or almost halfe the rent of theire howses in respect of the generall decay of trade & other greate burdens that tenants in this sad tyme are lyable unto'.[29] The rent of the Mitre tavern in Fleet Street was reduced from £120 per annum before the war, to first £60 and later £50 per annum.[30] The rents of the largest houses seem to have dropped the most. In September 1645, Alderman Atkin, wrote to the committee for advance of money concerning the renting of the house formerly occupied by Sir Henry Garway: 'if yow will please to Lett it, as howses are now to be had, I wilbe yowr tennant, the Lady Swinertons house is now lett for £50 per Anno, which would not have bene formerly lett for £150 per Anno also many great howses [are] empty at present'.[31]

The livery companies were partly sheltered from the decline of rents because they often let their property below their market value to tenants, who then sublet them. As a consequence it was mostly their tenants who felt the cost of the fall in rents. In January 1645 William Winders, who rented

---

[25] L.C. Nagel, 'The Militia of London, 1641–49', unpublished PhD thesis, University of London, 1982, 64; S.R. Smith, 'The Social and Geographical Origins of the London Apprentices, 1630–1660', *Guildhall Miscellany* 4 (1973), 203.

[26] BL Sloane MS. 118, f. 78; *Royalist Newsbooks*, III, 178.

[27] PRO C24/697/25..

[28] PRO C24/698/26.

[29] PRO C24/697/25.

[30] PRO C24/700/71.

[31] PRO SP19/82, f. 31.

tenements in Horseshoe Alley in Bankside Southwark from the Cordwainers' Company, petitioned the company complaining that 'by reason of the troubles in this kingdom and the pooreness of the tenants in Horshoe alley he hath byn at great losse of rent of this company's tenements there, in his holding and the likeness of them both to continue'.[32] However this does not mean that the livery companies did not suffer. The Cordwainers' Company received £67 for their tenements in Horseshoe Alley in 1643–44 compared to £77 in 1641–42. Christ's Hospital's arrears of rent rose from £306 in 1642 to £413 in 1643. Rent arrears became a serious problem for the Drapers' Company from 1642 and their tenants petitioned the company for abatements because of the economic problems.[33] In January 1643 the Merchant Tailors had granted a lease on a house in Little Britain to a stationer called Samuel Cartwright, for a £110 fine to be paid in several instalments, but in March of the following year he petitioned the company's Court of Assistants claiming 'That by reason of the presente distractions, his losses & decay of Trade', he could not pay the fine as originally agreed, and the company was obliged to consent to a rescheduling of the payments.[34] In June 1643 the Haberdashers' Company was forced to accept the surrender of the lease of one of its houses in Ludgate Hill because the tenant could no longer afford to pay the rent 'in regard of the hardness of the times and decay of trade'.[35] In September of the following year it was reported that the house was still empty and in great decay.[36]

In the autumn of 1644 one writer described the economic situation as one of almost universal calamity: 'trading and commerce is utterly decaid in the City, and in all Boroughs and Market Townes of the Kingdome, most of the Countrey people are plundered of their moneys, goods and cattell, the Gentlemen have their grounds cast up upon their hands, although they pay all charges and abate halfe their rent'.[37] Thereafter there is evidence that the economy began to improve. In the year to Michaelmas 1645 £207 was received for apprenticeship enrolments, which suggests that recruitment had risen by over eighty per cent on the previous year.[38] The burden of direct taxation fell substantially after 1644, and the economy benefited from the improvements in Parliament's finances in 1645, but the evidence suggests that Londoners

---

[32] GL MS. 7353/1, Cordwainers' Company, Court Minutes, 1622–53, f. 278.

[33] GL MS. 7351/2, Cordwainers' Company, Wardens' Accounts, 1636–78, unfoliated; GL MS. 12819/6, Christ's Hospital, Treasurer's Accounts, 1632–44, unfoliated; A.H. Johnson, *The History of the Worshipful Company of Drapers of London*, 5 vols (Oxford, 1914–22) III, 175–6.

[34] GL, Merchant Tailors' Company, Court Minutes, vol. 9, 1636–54, f. 192.

[35] GL MS. 15842/1, Haberdashers' Company, Court Minutes, 1583–1652, f. 316.

[36] Ibid., f. 327.

[37] D.P.P., *The Six Secondary Causes of the Spinning Out of This Unnaturall Warre* (1644), 50.

[38] CLRO Cash Books, vol. 1/5, f. 29v.

remained reluctant to invest in parliamentary loans, and the stimulatory effect of supplying the New Model Army was short lived. The principal reason for the recovery was the improvement in internal trade as the royalist blockade declined and Parliament's victorious armies controlled more of the country. The improvements in receipts for customs suggest that the recovery of domestic trade fed through into the international sector. Nevertheless there were continued complaints of economic difficulties, in August 1645 it was reported that one of the Assistants of the Clothworkers' Company 'hath had many great losses in the west by reason of these unnatural warrs, whereby all or most part of his estate is in danger to be lost'.[39] In the following December the bachelors' wardens of the Drapers' Company complained 'times are hard, trade decayed, and monies hard to be come by'.[40] Moreover there was growing concern about increasing poverty throughout the metropolis in 1645 and 1646.[41] Receipts for apprenticeship enrolments rose again the year to Michaelmas 1646, to a total of £233, however in the five years to Michaelmas 1642 receipts averaged £356 per annum. Consequently in the last year of the war apprenticeship enrolments were still one-third less than the average for the five years preceding the war.[42]

The recovery began to pick up speed in the immediate post-war period. Demand for labour increased, as a result tradesmen felt the need to replace the apprentices they had lost to the army. In October 1646 a member of the Barber Surgeons called before his company's court justified his employment of a foreigner by alleging that his servants had enrolled as soldiers.[43] This led to an enormous growth in the enrolment of apprentices in the City. In the year to Michaelmas 1647 the Chamber of the City of London received £410 for the enrolment of apprentices, an increase of seventy five per cent compared to the previous year and the highest figure since 1638, and livery companies showed a renewed concern to enforce the limits on numbers of apprentices their members could keep.[44] Immediately after the war rents also began to recover. In 1647 John Houghton of St Andrew Holborn testified in Chancery that 'haveinge bene Imployed in the disposeinge and lettinge of diverse houses in and about this Cittie [he] doeth finde by experience that though the Rents did fall and abate some yeares lately past yett nowe they doe rise againe in value'.[45] The rent receipts of the Cordwainers' Company from their Horseshoe Alley tenements confirm this. In 1646–47 they received £76 from this source,

---

[39]   CH, Orders of Court, 1639–49, f. 120v.

[40]   Quoted in Johnson, *History of the Worshipful Company of Drapers*, III, 173–4.

[41]   L. Lee, *A Remonstrance Humbly Presented to the High and Honourable Court of Parliament* (1645), 5, 2; LMA MJ/SBB/58, ff. 30–1; MJ/SBB/60 ff. 22, 23.

[42]   CLRO Cash Books, vol. 1/5, f. 133v.

[43]   GL MS. 5257/5, Barber Surgeons' Company, Court Minutes, 1621–51, f. 375.

[44]   CLRO Cash Books, vol. 1/6, f. 27v; GL MS. 5257/5, f. 375; see also p. 20 above.

[45]   PRO C24/702/94.

only slightly less than the total in 1641–42. The rent arrears of Christ's Hospital fell from £413 in 1643 to £380 in 1645.[46]

As the London economy was reconstructed concern grew that outsiders would be able to establish themselves, and traditional privileges become neglected. During the Civil War many people had fled to London but there were few economic opportunities for them. With the revival in economic activity opportunities opened up again, and the freemen of London wanted to ensure that they benefited, not the newcomers. At the same time traditional critics of the privileges of groups such as the Merchant Adventurers renewed their attacks on the company's monopoly as the cloth trade picked up. Also the Levant Company again became concerned about the indirect import of goods from the eastern Mediterranean and ship-owners called for restrictions on the use of foreign shipping.[47]

In the second half of 1647 the recovery came to an end. In July an apprentices' petition to the Common Council said trade was 'now mightilie impaired'.[48] The approach of the New Model Army to London in August led to fears that the City would be sacked. On 4 August, two days before the army entered London, the directors of the East India Company learned that the company's treasurer was refusing to accept money from their customers 'in regard of the dangerousnesse of the tymes'. The company also informed the purchasers of their wares that they would not accept responsibility for any goods left in their hands.[49] Thomas Juxon wrote that after the army occupied the City 'trading did very much abate'.[50] In October the Paintstainers' Company concluded 'the tymes contynue full of distractions which is much prejudiciall to trading'.[51] In February 1648 John Cooke argued that 'There was never more need to make some provision for the poore then this yeare; for there is lesse work for them then ever'.[52] In March 1648 the Waxchandlers' Company minuted that 'trading in theis times is verie dead and lowe by reason of the warres that hath bin and great troubles that doe yet remaine and are like to continue in this Kingdome'.[53]

On 10 December 1647 James Howell, writing from London, summed up the economic situation in the metropolis:

---

[46] GL MS. 7351/2, Cordwainers' Company, Wardens' Accounts, 1636–78, unfoliated; GL MS. 12819/7, Christ's Hospital, Treasurer's Accounts, 1645–52, unfoliated.

[47] See p. 74 above; PRO SP105/143, f. 102v; *LJ* VII, 185; CLRO Jour. 40, ff. 146, 149v, 176, 189v–90.

[48] CLRO Jour. 40, f. 239v.

[49] BL IOL/B/22, East India Company, Court Book, 1646–50, p. 134.

[50] K. Lindley and D. Scott (eds), *The Journal of Thomas Juxon, 1644–1647*, Camden Society, Fifth Series, 13 (1999), 169.

[51] GL MS. 5667/1, Paintstainers' Company, Court Minutes, 1622–48, f. 220.

[52] J. Cooke, *Unum Necessarium* (1648), 5.

[53] GL MS. 9485/1, Waxchandlers' Company, Court Minutes, 1584–1689, f. 252v.

a Famine, doth insensibly creep upon us, and the Mint is starv'd for want of Bullion; *Trade* which was ever the sinew of this Island doth visibly decay, and the *Insurance* of Ships is risen from two to ten in the hundred; Our gold is ingrossed in privat hands, or gon beyond Sea to travell without Licence, and much I beleeve of it is return'd to the earth (whence it first came) to be buried where our late Nephews may chance to find it a thousand yeers hence if the world lasts so long, so that the exchanging of white earth into red, I mean silver into gold is now above six in the hundred; and all these with many more are the dismall effects and concomitants of a civil War.[54]

In January 1648 William Clarke told Lieutenant Colonel Reede that 'all the myseryes of the Cittie, decay of Trade, skarcyty, & dearnes of provysion, not bringinge in of Bullion, and all other causes of povertie are imputed to the Army'.[55] In reality the causes of the crisis were much more diverse. The dearth, although variously attributed in London to the after effects of the Civil War, the proximity of the army to London and the excise, is far more likely to have been the result of bad weather than the political situation. Hence although the political problems of the late 1640s probably did contribute to the economic slump, it is likely that these years would have been difficult ones even had a political settlement been reached at the end of the first Civil War.[56]

The price of meat, fish, leather and wool rose at this time. In 1646 Christ's Hospital paid their shoemaker £1 16s over and above the agreed price for shoes because of the rising cost of leather and in the following year they agreed to pay £1. In February 1647 the Fishmongers' Company called for measures to stop the export of fish, stating that the price of fish had more than doubled. In the same month the Common Council called for measures to prevent the export of leather and in March 1649 they requested the Rump to prohibit the sale of meat on certain days to reduce inflation.[57]

The rising prices also fuelled wage inflation. In September 1649 the Court of Aldermen was petitioned by the master and journeymen carpenters employed by the Bridgehouse for higher wages, in response the Corporation agreed to add an extra 2d a day. It is very unlikely that increasing wages in London kept pace with rising food prices, but many London employers may well have found their profit margins squeezed.[58] John Cooke argued that, because of the rising prices, people were keeping fewer servants than before

---

[54] J. Howell, *Epistolæ Ho-Elianæ*, 2nd edn. (1650) III, 26.

[55] BL Stowe MS. 189, f. 39.

[56] CLRO Rep. 58/2, f. 3; CLRO Jour. 40, ff. 221, 263v; *The Necessity of the Speedy Calling a Common-Hall* (1648), 3.

[57] GL MS. 5570/4, Fishmongers' Company, Court Minutes, 1646–64, f. 8; CLRO Jour. 40, ff. 206, 315v; GL MS. 12819/7, 1646 accounts, f. 44, 1647 accounts, f. 19.

[58] CLRO Rep. 58/ 2, ff. 3–v; CLRO Rep. 59, f. 482.

'and every one projects for himselfe, to spend as little as may be'.[59] The dearth therefore reduced employment and demand.

From 1647 the value of sterling dropped on the international exchanges. In Amsterdam it fell by five per cent in 1647 and continued declining, falling by a further ten per cent by 1649. Sterling fell by twelve per cent in exchanges on Hamburg between 1646 and 1648.[60] Moreover merchants were no longer willing to bring their bullion to the mint to be coined. The average monthly output of the mint from April 1646 to the end of March 1647 was £66,219. From April 1647 to May 1649 it fell to only £6,011.[61]

Like the other economic ills, the financial crisis was widely attributed to the occupation of the City by the Army. One tract from late 1647 accused the army of 'frighting the poor Hicklers of the Custome House as far as *Amsterdam*'.[62] A petition drawn up by the Common Council in November 1647 argued that the continued proximity of the Army to the City had caused foreign merchants to withdraw their goods and capital from London, which had led to the fall in the exchange rate. A further petition drawn up by the Common Council in May 1648 argued that merchants were reluctant to bring bullion to the mint because of the City's loss of control over the Tower. In August 1647 Sir Thomas Fairfax, the commander of the New Model Army, had been appointed Constable of the Tower, replacing Colonel Francis West, who had been the City's nominee.[63]

The output of the mint and the value of sterling had remained strong despite successive political crises since the late 1630s. Why did this crisis have so much more of an impact than previous ones? During the war years New World bullion continued to be shipped to the Spanish Netherlands via Dover to pay the Spanish army. Before the war one-third of silver was sent to the mint to be coined, the proceeds being the remitted to the Spanish Netherlands by bills of exchange. During the war Parliament abandoned the previous practice of providing escorts for shipping between Dover and the Flanders ports. This made direct shipments impossible so all the silver had to be coined in England. This, together with the large quantities of plate contributed on the propositions during the war, which also had to be coined, ensured that the output of the Mint remained high. However the Spanish were worried that the bullion in the mint might be seized by Parliament. Moreover the fall in the value of sterling in 1647 made it no longer profitable

---

[59] Cooke, *Unum Necessarium*, 5.

[60] J.J. McCusker and S. Hart, 'The Rate of Exchange on Amsterdam in London, 1590–1660', in J.J. McCusker, *Essays in the Economic History of the Atlantic World* (1997), 116 table 5.3; J.J. McCusker, *Money and Exchange in Europe and America, 1600–1775, A Handbook* (1978), 70.

[61] C.E. Challis, 'Lord Hastings to the Great Silver Recoinage, 1464–1699', in C.E. Challis (ed.), *A New History of the Royal Mint* (Cambridge, 1992), 313 table 35, 321.

[62] *Observations Upon, and in Answer to his Excellencies Late Letter* (1647), 1.

[63] CLRO Jour. 40, ff. 263v, 273–v.

to transmit the proceeds of the silver shipments by bills of exchange. Peace with the Dutch provided the Spanish with new alternatives for transferring their bullion. Although the treaty of Munster was not concluded until 1648 hostilities ceased in early 1647 and normal commercial relations were re-established in the summer. In July the Spanish made an agreement to re-route their shipments via Zealand. Additionally peace between the Spanish and the Dutch meant that England's status as the neutral go-between had ended. Foreign merchants abandoned London in late 1647 because they now had other places to go. Underlying the fall in the value of sterling was probably a shift in the balance of trade. With the exception of the summer of 1648, when trade was hindered by the naval mutiny, imports recovered much more rapidly after the Civil War than exports, also from 1647 the previous invisible earnings from shipping were lost to the Dutch. As a result it is likely that demand for sterling bills of exchange fell, leading to a fall in the value of the currency, and merchants were bringing home less foreign coins needing to be coined into English money.[64]

The economy was further affected by the renewal of fighting in 1648; overseas trade of London was particularly hit by the mutiny in the fleet. Receipts for the enrolment of apprentices fell from £410 in the year to Michaelmas 1647 to £300 in the year to Michaelmas 1648, a fall of twenty seven per cent. Moreover in the following year enrolments fell by a further twenty six per cent. Rents also declined again, by 1648–49 the receipts of the Cordwainers' from their Horseshoe Alley tenements had fallen to £66 9s 9d, and the arrears of rent owed to Christ's Hospital rose to £783 by 1649.[65] In a petition drawn up by the Common Council in January 1649, the new rulers of the City called on the Rump to take urgent action to combat the crisis in the English economy.[66]

Many economic commentators in the early 1650s, such as Thomas Violet, argued that the civil wars were the root cause of the Commonwealths' economic difficulties. Much of the interest in economic improvement shown by England's new rulers in the Commonwealth period can be attributed to their desire to alleviate the continued problems arising from the Civil War. This can be seen in the Act passed by the Rump in 1651 to reduce the maximum rate of interest from eight per cent to six per cent. This authorized the judges in

---

[64] J.I. Israel, *The Dutch Republic and the Hispanic World, 1606–1661* (Oxford, 1982), 345–6; J.S. Kepler, *The Exchange of Christendom, The International Entrepot at Dover, 1622–1641* (Leicester, 1976), 90; BL Add. MS. 4191, petition of divers merchants trading in Flanders, f. 24; J. Battie, *The Merchants Remonstrance*, 2nd edn (1648), 12. See above p. 177.

[65] CLRO Cash Books, vol. 1/6, ff. 128v, 240; vol. 1/7, ff. 37v, 126; vol. 1/8, f. 33v; GL MS. 7351/2, Cordwainers' Company, Wardens' Accounts, 1636–78, unfoliated; GL MS. 12819/7, unfoliated.

[66] CLRO Jour. 40, f. 313.

Chancery to moderate the interest on debts incurred in the 'late troubles', defined as the period between 1 September 1642 and 1 February 1649.[67]

Obviously the war did not prevent the long-term expansion in the London economy. The recovery observed in the middle years of the 1640s demonstrates the remarkable ability of the metropolitan economy to bounce back after periods of adversity, and there can be little doubt that the middle years of the 1650s saw a similar, if not stronger, resurgence.[68] Moreover some Londoners may have successfully adapted to the disruption of the economy by adopting more flexible business practices. According to William Walwyn, Henry Brandeth prospered during the war by searching the inns of the City early every morning to find out what goods had recently arrived. He bought whatever was available, even though he might never have traded in the goods before, and often without any idea of how he would dispose of his purchases.[69]

The London economy suffered two major depressions in the 1640s. The first, which reached its depths in the second half of 1643 and early 1644, can be attributed almost entirely to the impact of the Civil War. The most important factor was probably the blockade of internal trade initiated by the royalists in the summer of 1643, although the increase in taxation in London and the plundering and taxation of Londoners' provincial customers also played a part. However the second, at the end of the decade had more diverse causes. The run of bad harvests and the treaty of Munster were as important, perhaps more important, than the continued political turbulence.

The two depressions had significantly different characteristics. The first had the greatest impact on the better off. It has been noted that craftsmen producing luxury goods did particularly badly in the first Civil War and the rents of the larger houses fell the most. At the same time, there is evidence of upward pressures of wages in some sections of industry, which was probably not typical of the rest of the economy, but the good harvests kept real wages relatively buoyant. This crisis was primarily a crisis of trade and it therefore had the most immediate impact on the mercantile community. Nevertheless, the economic crisis of the first Civil War was not confined to the wealthy. There is considerable evidence of increasing poverty in Civil War London, and high fuel prices and the excise on beer particularly hit the poor. Moreover the very wealthiest had more options when it came to trying to avoid the worst impact of the war, they could move their capital abroad or invest in parliamentary finance.

---

[67] *Firth & Rait*, II, 402, 548–9; *CSPD*, 1650, 178–9.

[68] D. Hirst, 'Locating the 1650s in England's Seventeenth Century', *History* 81 (1996), 377–381; R. Grassby, *The Business Community of Seventeenth-Century England* (Cambridge, 1995), 395–6.

[69] J.R. McMichael and B. Taft (eds), *The Writings of William Walwyn* (Athens Ga. and London, 1989), 427.

In contrast, the second depression of the late 1640s hit the poor hardest than any other section of the London community, primarily because they were most vulnerable to dearth. Those involved in foreign trade were also suffering because of the attacks on English shipping, and the renewed competition from the Dutch. Other sections of the London economy do not seem to have done so badly. Internal trade was not unduly disrupted by the second Civil War, and it is striking that the St Bartholomew's Day fair seems to have been still very large in August 1648. There was a decline in receipts from Blackwell Hall, but this was nowhere near so dramatic as the decline in the first Civil War. The evidence therefore suggests that the wholesalers and retailers, who made up the vast bulk of the London business community, did not do so badly in the depression of the late 1640s. Although the economic depression of the first Civil War demonstrates that foreign trade was dependant on internal trade and a severe crisis in the latter created a severe crisis in the former, the depression of the latter 1640s shows that the reverse was not true, and a crisis in foreign trade had only a limited affect on the domestic trading sector.

Index

Africa, trade, sequestration 41-2
Aleksei (Tsar of Russia) 122
America, trade 12, 118-19
Antwerp, trade 5
Apothecaries' Company, doubling
    66
apprentices, enrolments 201-2,
    213-14, 222-4, 226, 230
  Bakers' Company 37, 203, 204
  Blacksmiths' Company 211, 212,
    216
  Brewers' Company 37, 203-4,
    215
  Butchers' Company 37, 209
  Carpenters' Company 210, 215
  Clockmakers' Company 205
  Clothworkers' Company 205,
    206, 216
  Cordwainers' Company 203, 215
  Founders' Company 211, 212,
    216
  Masons' Company 209
  Merchant Taylors' Company 204-5
  Pewterers' Company 205, 206,
    216
  Tallowchandlers' Company 209
  Tylers' and Bricklayers'
    Company 209, 215
armaments 213
  craft disputes 105
  Hull 94
  imports 96
  local production 2, 18
  London 92, 96, 100-1
  Parliament 93-6
  supplies
    Eastern Association army 95
    New Model Army 96
    Rowe and Bradley 94, 95

Stephen Estwicke 95
Armourers' Company 212, 213
Assada adventurers 61
Atherton Moor, battle 111

Bakers' Company
  apprentice enrolments 37, 203,
    204
  journeymen 202
Baltic
  cloth exports 169-70, 171, 175,
    180
  shipping 195-6
  trade, London 7-8
banks
  and goldsmiths 85, 86
  origins 53, 85, 86
  scrivener 85-6
Barber Surgeons' Company 43, 226
  borrowings 83
beams, toll receipts 149-50, 158-9
beer, excise tax 31-2, 34-5, 36-7
Bermuda Company, customs'
  commissioners 76
Blacksmiths' Company 211-12,
  213, 214
  apprentice enrolments 211, 212,
    216
Blackwell Hall
  cloth market 21, 140, 141, 174
  receipts 162, 232
blockade, domestic trade 110-17,
  139
Book of Rates, customs tax 11, 38-9,
  165-6, 178, 182
book trade, disruption 151
borrowings
  Barber Surgeons' Company 83
  Carpenters' Company 83

cost 80-2, 84
East India Company 79-80, 81,
    82
Fishmongers' Company 83
Goldsmiths' Company 80, 82, 83
Grocers' Company 83
livery companies 82
Merchant Tailors' Company 83
    see also doubling; loans
Brewers' Company 203-4
apprentice enrolments 37, 203-4,
    215
excise tax 34-5, 36
Brickmakers' Company 215
Bristol, trade 13, 16
business partnerships, and
    sequestration 43
Butchers' Company, apprentice
    enrolments 37, 209
butter, source 17

capital
availability 5, 84
cost 80-1
shortage 82
Caribbean, tobacco trade 12
Carpenters' Company 113, 209,
    215, 217
apprentice enrolments 210, 215
borrowings 83
cereals 17
Chambers, Richard 75
Charles I 76, 110, 112, 115, 117-
    18, 120, 123
execution 122, 124
Charles II 122, 130
Worcester, defeat 68
Chesapeake Bay, colonies, trade
    118, 193
Christian IV (King of Denmark)
    119-20, 121
Civil War
coin hoards 11

economic crisis 20-21
navy, expansion 96-7
overseas trade, impact 180-183,
    199-200
shipping, impact 188-9
taxation, growth 22
Clockmakers' Company, apprentice
    enrolments 205
cloth
customs tax 165
excise tax 31
exports 165, 167-8
    Baltic 169-70, 171, 175, 180
    decline 175
    Germany 170, 175
    Netherlands 6
production 16
    see also cloth trade
cloth trade 4, 6-9, 16, 19, 20, 110
disruption 113, 115-16, 140-3,
    160-161
Dutch competition 180
Levant Company 13, 140, 170
monopoly, Merchant
    Adventurers 74
recovery 158
Spanish 8
    see also cloth
clothing
New Model Army 106
supplies, Stephen Estwicke 93-4
Clothworkers' Company 205, 206,
    214
apprentice enrolments 205, 206,
    216
loans 70
coal trade 57, 110, 111, 160
disruption 144-7, 188-9
Newcastle 144, 145
size 17
Sunderland 146
Cockayne project 5, 8
Cockayne, William 97

Common Council, London 28, 160, 174, 181, 229
Commonwealth
  economic problems 230-231
  loans 64-5, 67
  overseas trade 177
construction industry 209, 215-16
consumer spending
  fall 154
  fluctuations 152-61
  growth 15
  recovery 158-61
convoys, escort charges 191
Cordwainers' Company
  apprentice enrolments 203, 215
  loans 70
  rents 225, 226-7
  shoes 101-6, 202, 203, 204, 214
Courteen association 61, 186
  customs' commissioners 76
credit networks 42-3
Crispe, Nicholas, Sir
  loans 73-4
  sequestration 41-2, 46
Cromwell, Oliver, Irish war 131
Crowe, Sackville, Sir 121-2, 173
customs' commissioners
  Bermuda Company 76
  Courteen association 76
  illicit profits 78
  Levant Company 76
  loans 75-7, 166
  Merchant Adventurers 76, 77, 175, 214
  propositions 75
  salaries 76-7
customs tax 38-40
  administration 39
  Book of Rates 11, 38-9, 165-6, 178, 182
  cloth 165
  farming of 6

pepper 165-6
Plymouth 39
receipts 21, 39-40, 164-6, 177-8
  Port of London 39, 166-8
tobacco 39, 165
wine 165
  see also excise tax
Cutlers' Company 211
  swords 102, 213

debts
  Grocers' Company 71-2
  Gunmakers' Company 94
  and sequestration 42-5
Denmark
  Sweden, war 121, 170
  London, trade 119-21
domestic goods, excise tax 32
doubling
  Apothecaries' Company 66
  defaults 69-70
  Fishmongers' Company 66
  popularity 65-6
  receipts 66, 67
  Rump Parliament 67
  see also borrowings; loans
Dutch East India Company 183, 186
Dutch West India Company 41-2
dyeing industry, London 5

East India Company 12, 61, 76, 133, 227
  borrowings 79-80, 81, 82
  charter 183-4, 187
  economic problems 11, 163, 171, 184-6
  loans 73
  pepper trade 20, 152
  sequestration 41, 42, 45
  voyages 187-8
East Indies trade
  growth 10

London 12
Eastern Association army 212
  armaments supplies 95
  finance 88
Eastland Company
  cloth exports 7-8
  trade 120
Edgehill, battle 110, 140
England
  France, trade rivalry 123-4
  Netherlands
    trade rivalry 7, 14, 192-9
    war 67
  Spain
    peace 7
    trade 13
    war 8
Essex, Earl of, army 93, 95
Estwicke, Stephen, supplier
  armaments 95
  clothing 93-4
  shoes 101
Evelyn, John 155
excise commissioners, salaries
    77-8
excise tax
  administration 34
  beer 31-2, 34-5, 36-7
  Brewers' Company 34-5, 36
  cloth 31
  domestic goods 32
  food 32
  impact 38
  imports 30, 33
  introduction 22, 77
  London 22, 30-38
  meat 32, 35
  opposition to 33-8
  rate 30
  receipts 32-3
  salt 32
  soap 31
  tobacco 30-31

Vintners' Company 31, 34, 36,
    37-8
  wine 31, 34, 36, 37-8
    see also customs tax
exports
  cloth 165, 167-8, 175
    Baltic 169-70, 171, 175
    Dutch competition 180
  fall 167, 179-80
  tobacco 174
    see also imports; trade

financial services, goldsmiths 85
fish trade 13
Fishmongers' Company 228
  borrowings 83
  doubling 66
food
  excise tax 32
  shortage 6
  supplies
    disruption 147-8
    New Model Army 91-2
Founders' Company 216
  apprentice enrolments 211, 212,
    216
  receipts, brass weights 156-7,
    160
France, England, trade rivalry 123-4

Germany, cloth exports 170, 175
Gerrard, Gilbert, Sir 93, 94
goldsmiths
  and banks 85
  financial services 85
Goldsmiths' Company 62, 207, 208
  borrowings 80, 82, 83
grain trade 147-8
Greenland Company 191
Grocers' Company
  borrowings 83
  debts 71-2
Guinea Company 41, 46, 134

loans 73
Gunmakers' Company, debts 94

Haberdashers' Company, militia
    47, 49
Haberdashers' Hall 27
Hallage toll 21
    receipts 141-3, 158, 160
horses, New Model Army 106
Hull
    armaments 94
    trade 17

imports
    excise tax 30, 33
    and Navigation Act (1651) 198-9
    recovery 180
    tobacco 174
    wine 172-4
        see also exports; trade
insurance, marine 190-1
interest rate 81, 82
    fall 80, 83-4
Interregnum 30
Ireland
    trade 118
    war 20
        Cromwell 131
        loans for 62, 63, 64, 65, 72, 75,
            81, 83
        privateering 98
        taxation 23
Ironmongers' Company, militia 48

journeymen
    in army 202
    Bakers' Company 202

Kazimierz, Jan (King of Poland)
    122
Kent
    sequestration 40
    taxation 24

labour, demand for 201-2
land
    sales 69, 78-9
    value 68
lead industry 17
    disruption 148-9
    recovery 158, 210-11
legal system, disruption 220-1
Levant Company 121-2, 124, 133,
        135, 171-2, 173, 195
    cloth trade 13, 140, 170
    customs' commissioners 76
    loans 73
    privileges 74
Limehouse 19
Lithgow, William 81-2
livery companies
    borrowings 82
    loans 70-2, 84
    rents 224-5
loans
    against taxation 59-65
    Clothworkers' Company 70
    Commonwealth 64-5, 67
    Cordwainers' Company 70
    customs' commissioners 75-7,
        166
    East India Company 73
    Guinea Company 73
    Ireland, war 62, 63, 64, 65, 72,
        75, 81, 83
    Levant Company 73
    livery companies 70-2, 84
    London money market 79-86
    Long Parliament 63, 70, 71, 72,
        74, 89
    Merchant Adventurers 62, 72-4,
        118
    for navy 72, 75
    for New Model Army 61
    Nicholas Crispe 73-4
    Pewterers' Company 70
    revenue officers 74-9

Rump Parliament 67, 71
  for Scottish Army 62, 64, 65
    see also borrowings;
    doubling
London (City)
  armaments 92, 96, 100-101
  boundaries, expansion 4
  Common Council 28, 91, 160,
    174, 181, 229
  Cordwainers' Company 101-4
  defences, expenditure 80, 91
  dyeing industry 5
  economy
    expansion 4, 5, 231
    fluctuations 5-6, 219-32
    navy mutiny 133-7
    privateering 97
    size 24
    war materials 107-8
  exports 4-5, 6-14, 169
    America 12
    Antwerp 5
    Baltic 7-8
    cloth 4, 6-9, 13, 19
    Denmark 119-21
    East Indies 12
    expansion 6, 7
    fish 13
    Netherlands 6, 119
    ship requirements 5
  food supplies 17
    for New Model Army 91-2
  imports 5, 9-12, 169
    America 10
    East Indies 10
    excise tax 30-8
    growth 9-10
    silk 10
    source 10
    tobacco 10, 11, 12, 15-16
    West Indies 10
  manufacturing 5, 18-20, 201-18
    growth 18

  silk 18-19
  militia 46-9
  population growth 4
  sequestration 40
  taxation 22, 23-52
  trade
    domestic 15-18
      blockade 110-17
      lead 17
      regions 16
    overseas 4-5, 169, 175-83
    threats to 118-32
London money market, loans 54,
  79-86, 89
London, Port of, customs receipts
  39, 166-8
Long Parliament 191
  loans 63, 70, 71, 72, 74, 89
  see also Parliament
luxury goods, production 206-8

manufacturing, London 5, 18-20,
  201-18
Marston Moor, battle 158
Masons' Company, apprentice
  enrolments 209
meat, excise tax 32, 35
Merchant Adventurers 119, 120,
  122, 135, 170, 191
  cloth trade monopoly 74
  customs' commissioners 76, 77,
    175, 214
  loans 62, 72-4, 118
Merchant Tailors' Company 204-5
  apprentice enrolments 204-5
  borrowings 83
  rents 225
Mercurius Civicus 115
metals, precious, availability 11-12
metalworking industry 211
militia
  complaints 49
  composition 47

cost 47
Haberdashers' Company 47, 49
impact 48-9
Ironmongers' Company 48
London 46-9
payments, arrears 48-9
size 46
Southwark 48
Westminster 49
Munster, Treaty of 163, 230
Muscovy Company 122-3
mutiny, navy 117, 132-7

Navigation Act (1651), and imports 198-9
navy 96-7
loans 72, 75
mutiny 117, 132-7
and privateering 130
see also privateering
Netherlands
cloth trade 6
England
trade rivalry 7, 14, 192-9
war 67
Spain, war 2, 14, 163, 195, 230
sugar trade 194
trade
London 6, 119
Virginia 193
West Indies 193-4
New Model Army 26, 46, 117, 227
armaments supplies 96
clothing 106
creation 61, 95
finance 63, 83, 90
food supplies 91-2
horses 106
saddles 102, 104-5
shoes 101-4, 105-6
size 107
taxation for 25, 26

treasurers 75, 77, 78, 87, 88, 90, 96
Newcastle, coal trade 144, 145
Newcastle, Earl of 110, 111
Newfoundland, fisheries 13
newsbooks 35, 113, 114, 115, 117, 128
Noel, Martin 86, 89
Northampton, shoes 101-2

Ordnance Office 95

Paintstainers' Company 227
Parliament
armaments supplies 93-6
armies 93-6
customs tax 38-40
loans
against taxation 59-65
corporate 70-4
London money market 54, 79-86, 89
for New Model Army 61
revenue officers 74-9
size 87
sources 53, 59, 87-8
unpopularity 62, 64-5, 89
military expenditure 90-1
privateering 90
propositions 54, 55
sequestration 40-6
subscriptions 54-9
receipts 55-8
security 57
as taxation 58
taxation 22
see also Long Parliament;
Rump Parliament
pepper
customs tax 165-6
trade 11, 12, 20, 152
pewter industry 16, 18, 205
Pewterers' Company 202

apprentice enrolments 205, 206,
        216
    loans 70
pickage toll 21, 156
pin making industry 18
Pindar, Paul, Sir 89, 131
Plumbers' Company 210, 219
plumbers' solder, production 210,
        215
Plymouth, customs tax 39
port books, overseas trade 6, 9
poverty, Southwark 19-20
printing industry 213
privateering 90
    and Irish war 98
    and London's economy 97
    and the navy 130
    prizes 99
    risks 99-100
    Royalists 129
    shipping, impact on 190
    ships, cost 97-8
    and trade 98-9, 125-32, 160
    see also navy
production, retailing, separation
        106
propositions
    customs' commissioners 75
    Parliament 54
Protectorate 68

rents
    Cordwainers' Company 225,
        226-7
    fall 68, 224-5
    livery companies 224-5
    Merchant Tailors' Company 225
Restoration 30, 94, 97
retailing, production, separation
        106
revenue officers
    illicit profits 78-9
    loans 74-9

Ricaut, Peter, Sir 41, 42
Roe, Thomas, Sir 14
Rowe and Bradley, armaments 94,
        95
Royalists
    cloth trade blockade 140-41
    privateering 129
    trade disruption 118-25, 205, 221
Rump Parliament 124, 130, 191,
        230
    doubling 67
    loans 71
Russell, William, Sir 80

Saddlers' Company, saddles 102
saddles
    New Model Army 102, 104-5
    Saddlers' Company 102
St Bartholomew's Day fair 232
    decline 159-60
    receipts 21, 154-6, 159
salt, excise tax 32
Scottish Army
    loans for 62, 64, 65
    shoes 103
scrivener banks 85-6
sequestration
    administration 43
    African trade 41-2
    and business partnerships 43
    and debts 42-5
    East India Company 41, 42, 45
    impact 40-1, 42, 45-6
    Kent 40
    London 40
    receipts 40, 42
    Sir Nicholas Crispe 41-2, 46, 73-4
    Smithfield butchers 35
    Suffolk 40
Shadwell, docks 19
ship building industry 5, 96-7, 213
shipping
    Baltic 195-6

Civil War, impact 188-9
Dutch competition 192-4
merchant, hirings 96-7
privateering, impact 190
Sound, passage through 192
tonnage 15, 19
value, fall 189
shoes
    Cordwainers' Company 101-5,
        202, 203, 204, 214
    cost 104
    New Model Army 101-4, 105-6
    Northampton 101-2
    Scottish Army 103
silk
    demand for 216
    industry 18-19
    trade 10, 20
Smithfield market 35
soap, excise tax 31
Southwark
    militia 48
    population 4
    poverty 19-20
    taxation 23, 28
Spain
    England
        peace 7
        trade 13
    Netherlands, war 2, 14, 163, 195,
        230
Spice Islands 183
spice trade 151
Star Chamber, Court of 213
Stationers' Company 151
sterling, value 12, 229-30
Stocks market 154
subscriptions, Parliament 54-9
Suffolk, sequestration 40
sugar
    refining 19, 193-4
    trade, Netherlands 194
Sunderland, coal trade 146

Sweden, Denmark, war 121, 170
swords, Cutlers' Company 102, 213

Tallowchandlers' Company 219
    apprentice enrolments 209
taxation
    collection problems 22, 26-8
    growth 22, 28-9
    impact 29-30, 220
    Kent 24
    London 22, 23-52
    for New Model Army 25, 26
    Parliament's finances 22
    receipts 23, 50-2
    Southwark 23, 28
    subscriptions as 58
    as symptom 22-3
    twentieth part 23, 24, 25, 27, 59,
        60
    Warwickshire 24
    Westminster 23, 29
theatres
    closure 153
    reopening 159
Thirty Years' War 6, 109
    economic impact 2, 8, 163
Thompson, Maurice 97-8, 99
tin industry, disruption 149
tithes 26
tobacco
    consumption 15-16
    customs tax 39, 165
    cutting 19
    excise tax 30-31
    exports 174
    imports 174
    trade 10, 13, 118, 151
        Caribbean 11, 12
        Virginia 11, 12
toll receipts, beams 149-50
trade
    America 12, 118-19
    Bristol 13, 16

Chesapeake Bay 118, 193
disruption, Royalists 118-25,
    205, 221
domestic
    blockade 110-17, 139
    importance 17
    recovery 158
Eastland Company 120
England, France 123-4
Hull 17
Ireland 118
overseas
    Civil War, impact 180-183,
        199-200
    Commonwealth 177
    disruption 117-25, 138
    London 169, 175-83
    port books 6, 9
    pepper 11, 12, 20, 152
    and privateering 98-9, 125-32,
        160
    Virginia 11, 12, 118-19
        see also exports; imports
transport
    improvements 15
    infrastructure, damage 116-17
treasurers, New Model Army 75,
    77, 78, 87, 88, 90, 96
twentieth part, taxation 23, 24, 25,
    27, 59, 60
Tylers' and Bricklayers' Company
    215
    apprentice enrolments 209, 215

Vintners' Company
    economic problems 124, 154, 155

Virginia
    Netherlands, trade 193
    excise tax 31, 34, 36, 37-8
    wine receipts 172-4
    tobacco trade 11, 12
    trade 11, 12, 118-19
Vyner, Thomas 85, 86, 89

wages
    inflation 228
    rates 152, 153, 160
Warwickshire, taxation 24
Waxchandlers' Company 217,
    227
Weavers' Company 205, 207, 214,
    216
West Indies, Netherlands, trade
    193-4
Westminster 2-3
    boundaries, expansion 4
    economy 18, 153-4
    militia 49
    taxation 23, 29
wholesaling, disruption 151-2
wine
    customs tax 165
    excise tax 31, 34, 36, 37-8
    French 172
    imports 172-3
    Spanish 172
    Vintners' Company receipts
        172-4
wool, production 16